THE JOURNAL OF JOHN JOURDAIN
1608-1617

THE JOURNAL OF JOHN JOURDAIN 1608-1617

DESCRIBING HIS EXPERIENCES IN ARABIA, INDIA, AND THE MALAY ARCHIPELAGO

Edited by

WILLIAM FOSTER

MANOHAR

2021

First published 1905
Reprinted 2021

ISBN 978-93-90729-50-0

Published by
Ajay Kumar Jain *for*
Manohar Publishers & Distributors
4753/23 Ansari Road, Daryaganj
New Delhi 110 002

Printed at
Replika Press Pvt. Ltd.

THE JOURNAL

OF

JOHN JOURDAIN,

1608—1617,

DESCRIBING HIS EXPERIENCES IN ARABIA, INDIA, AND THE MALAY ARCHIPELAGO

EDITED BY

WILLIAM FOSTER, B.A.,

Editor of 'The Embassy of Sir Thomas Roe to the Great Mogul,' 'Letters Received by the East India Company, 1615–17,' etc.

CAMBRIDGE:

PRINTED FOR THE HAKLUYT SOCIETY.

MDCCCCV.

CONTENTS.

APPENDICES.

MAPS.

PREFACE.

IN the spring of 1608 John Jourdain sailed for the East in the good ship *Ascension*, and it was not until the summer of 1617 that he once more set foot on English soil. During the nine intervening years he had travelled many thousands of miles, had visited several places previously unknown to his fellow countrymen, and had had many exciting adventures, both by sea and by land, with more than one narrow escape from a violent death. Of these experiences he kept a careful diary, commenced, no doubt, in obedience to the instructions given by the East India Company to all their servants, and afterwards continued for his own satisfaction and as a repository of information that he might find useful on some future occasion; and it is this journal which in the ensuing pages is printed for the first time.

The value of the contribution thus made to geographical literature the reader will assess for himself. But it may be briefly pointed out that, amid much else that is interesting, we have here a record of a hitherto unnoticed visit by a British ship to the Seychelles in 1609; accounts of the first English trading voyage to the Red Sea, and of a pioneer journey through the Yaman from Aden to San'a and thence to Mocha; some fresh details of the proceedings of William Hawkins at Agra and of Sir Henry Middleton at Surat—that eventful first chapter in the history of English intercourse with India; and a lengthy narrative of the voyage of the *Darling* to Amboyna and Ceram in 1613, concerning which little has hitherto been known except from Dutch sources. When to this has been added that Jourdain describes in detail the principal places he visited, enough has perhaps been said to justify the decision of the Council of the Hakluyt Society to give his graphic and characteristic narrative a place in their series.

The manuscript made use of for this purpose is No. 858 of the Sloane collection at the British Museum. It is not the original diary, but a contemporary copy, the first four folios of which are in a different hand from the rest. In neither case does the writing resemble Jourdain's (of which several examples are preserved at the India Office), and the blunders that occur from time to time show that the copy was not even revised by him; it is, however, quite possible that we have here a transcript which was made for him while he was in England in 1617, and that he left it behind for record and took the original volume with him on his return to the Indies. It might have been assumed that the copy was made for the East India Company; but it bears no mark of ever having been among their records, and moreover, had this been the case, so interesting a narrative would scarcely have escaped the notice of the Rev. Samuel Purchas when rummaging their archives for materials for his *Pilgrimes*. Probably Jourdain left the transcript in the hands of some relative or friend, and after his death its value was not recognized. In any case we know nothing of its history except that, at some date which cannot now be determined, it came into the possession of Sir Hans Sloane, and so passed into the national collection. In 1862 the late Mr Noel Sainsbury brought it to notice by giving a brief summary of its contents in his valuable *Calendar of State Papers, East Indies*, 1513—1616; and thirty years later Professor J. K. Laughton, who had made use of it for his article on Jourdain in the *Dictionary of National Biography*, suggested to the Council of the Hakluyt Society the advisability of publishing it. This they were quite willing to do, but an editor was not at that time forthcoming.

The Sloane MS. has been copied, for the purposes of the present work, by Miss Alice J. Mayes, whose transcript was then checked throughout by the editor. All contractions have been written out in full; and it has not been thought necessary to follow the seventeenth century copyist either in his eccentric use of capital letters or in his equally eccentric punctuation. Further, some of Jourdain's entries made at sea, recording merely the course of the vessel, the state of the weather, the direction of the wind, etc., have been omitted, as being of no general interest.

The original transcription was evidently done in rather a careless manner, and (as already mentioned) mistakes—especially in the names of places—are frequent. Where these are of importance, attention has been called to the error, either by inserting the right word within brackets or by adding a footnote; in other cases they have been left unnoted, but the reader is asked to believe that all reasonable care has been exercised and that any obvious blunders he may detect occur in the British Museum manuscript.

It is of course much to be regretted that the original journal is not at our disposal, but no trace of it can be found. If, as has already been suggested, Jourdain took it with him on his second voyage to the East, it is probable that after his death at Patani in 1619 it fell with the rest of his papers into the hands of the Dutch. We know that the bulk of the documents thus captured were sent to Holland; and, on the chance that the diary might still be in that country, the editor addressed an inquiry to Professor J. E. Heeres of Leiden, whose researches into the history of the Dutch Indies are well known. That gentleman was good enough to interest himself in the matter, and a search which was kindly undertaken, at his suggestion, by Mr De Hullu, Assistant Keeper of the Colonial Records at the Hague, resulted in establishing the fact that the diary was not in the archives there. It is to be feared, therefore, that the original has been lost for ever.

The editor has received much other friendly assistance in his researches. In most cases acknowledgments have been made either in the introduction or in the notes to the text; but he must here record his indebtedness to Sir Charles Lyall, K.C.S.I., C.I.E., Mr A. N. Wollaston, C.I.E., Professor Blumhardt, and Sir Clements Markham, K.C.B., for help on various points; also to Mr Basil H. Soulsby, the Secretary of the Society, for the useful bibliography printed at the end of the volume.

INTRODUCTION.

REGARDING the life of John Jourdain prior to his taking service with the East India Company but little is now discoverable. We know, from his father's will and other sources of information, that he was the sixth child and fourth son of John Jourdain, merchant, of Lyme Regis in Dorsetshire, and we may presume that he was born, like his elder brothers and sisters, in that picturesque seaport; but as regards the date of his birth we must content ourselves with an approximation. It may be taken to have occurred later than August, 1572, when the extant record of baptisms in the parish church for that century come to an abrupt conclusion[1], for up to that point, though the baptisms of other members of the family are duly noted, we do not find his name. On the other hand we cannot assign a much later date, for he was doubtless of age in 1595, when he was trading on his own account, and moreover we find him describing himself towards the end of 1613 as 'begininge to growe ould' (p. 313)—a phrase which a man would hardly use about himself unless he were at least forty. On these grounds we are perhaps justified in concluding that he was born in the latter half of 1572 or some time in 1573.

---

[1] This document is in reality only an unfinished transcript from an older register now lost. My thanks are due to the Rev. William Jacob, M.A., Vicar of Lyme Regis, for first giving me information concerning the parish registers and afterwards facilitating my personal examination of them.

The following table, constructed mainly from family wills, gives the names of his immediate relatives :—

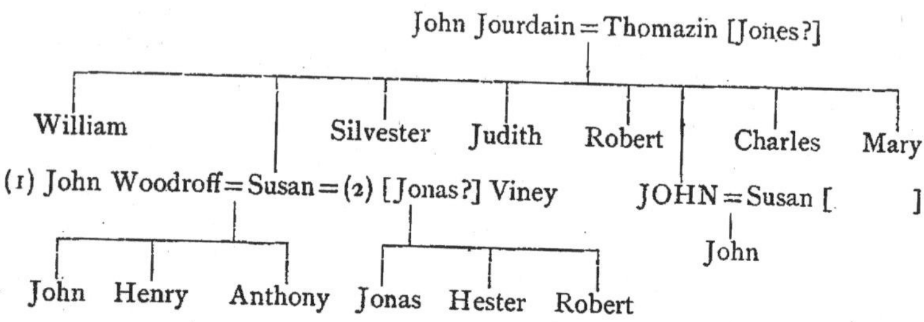

Of these, as we learn from the church registers, William was baptized on March 9, 1561; Susan on December 19, 1562; Silvester on February 14, 1565; Judith on November 20, 1566; and Robert on June 22, 1569. William is not mentioned in his father's will, and we may therefore assume that he predeceased him. There is some reason for thinking that both Silvester and Robert were dead by 1615; and of the whole eight, Susan, Charles and Mary appear to have been the only ones living when their brother John made his will in February, 1618.

Of John's early years we know absolutely nothing. No doubt with other Lyme Regis boys he played about the Cobb or in the narrow streets that cluster round the rushing Lyme. Sundays would see him at the venerable church of St Michael; while on weekdays he would attend the school which was held in the little room over the porch. Many a time he must have gone blackberrying or bird's-nesting in the Ware thickets; and one fancies that he was often on the quay, watching the ships as they entered or quitted the harbour—for Lyme was then a port of considerable trade—and questioning the sailors about the mysterious world that lay below the horizon. Think, too, of the impression the Armada struggle must have made upon the mind of a boy of fifteen, who may perhaps have actually watched from the cliffs at Pinhay the Spanish fleet standing slowly up the Channel, with Howard and Drake hanging on its rear. All this, however, is conjecture, and the first clear fact that emerges is the death of Jourdain's father in the autumn of 1588.

Four years earlier the elder Jourdain had reached the dignity of mayor of his native town (Hutchins' *Dorset*, 3rd edn., ii. 48)[1]; and evidently he was in prosperous circumstances at the time of his death, for he was able to bequeath 400*l.* to his wife, and lands and houses to each of his four surviving sons, besides portions for his two unmarried daughters (Will in P.C.C.: Leicester, 7). John's share was the lease of a house, an orchard hard by, and a fourth part of the residuary estate. The father's own residence was left to the youngest son, Charles, subject to the widow's right to live there rent-free until the intended owner was 25, and for five years longer on paying him a suitable rent. This was no doubt the house in which John was brought up, and he ever held it in affectionate remembrance; for in December, 1615, we find him begging the East India Company 'to paye unto my cossens Ignacios or John Jourdain[2], marchants, dwelling in Exetter, the some of

---

[1] Possibly we may connect with the attainment of this important post the arms borne by our traveller, as shown on the seal of one of his letters now in the India Office (*O.C.* 782), viz. a lion passant guardant: underneath, two bars wavy: above, three bezants or plates. Of these the lion and the two bars constitute the arms of Lyme Regis, and may have been adopted by the new mayor. On the other hand, a lion (rampant) appears in the shields of both Dorsetshire and Devonshire Jourdains of a later date; while the symbol of running water—a punning reference to the river Jordan—was a common device in the arms of foreign branches of the family.

[2] These two cousins merit a passing notice. Ignatius (baptized August 17, 1561) was a prominent citizen of Exeter, whither he had migrated as a youth from Lyme Regis. He was sheriff in 1611, mayor in 1617, and twice represented the city in Parliament, where, as a zealous advocate for Puritan principles, he distinguished himself by his endeavours to get bills passed penalising adultery, Sabbath-breaking and swearing. He died July 15, 1640, in his 79th year (Will in P.C.C.: Coventry, 130). His brother John was sheriff of Exeter in 1623 and died in 1627 or 1628 (Will in P.C.C.: Barrington, 67). To these two brothers the *Dictionary of National Biography* adds a third, whose name will be more familiar to the reader, viz. the Silvester Jourdain who was wrecked on the Bermudas with Somers and Gates in 1609, and wrote an account of the islands which is supposed to have afforded hints to Shakespeare for his 'Tempest.' The

150 *li.* for my use; to whom I have written order to receive it, and is to release a morgaidge of my fathers dwelling house, which otherwise will fall into a strangers hande' (*O.C.* 330). In the same letter, by the way, he remits money 'for the use of a pore brother of myne, which [it] hath pleased God to take his sight from him.' Possibly this was his brother Charles, forced by blindness to mortgage his property.

Our first definite glimpse of the diarist is in 1595, when he was apparently trading on his own account. In November of that year a Council order permitted 'John Jourden of Lime Regis' to proceed in a small ship, of seventy tons or thereabouts, to the Azores, for the purpose of fetching home goods to the value of 3000 crowns which he had left in the hands of certain Portuguese there (Dasent's *Acts of the Privy Council*, vol. xxv.). As we know from a passage on p. 27 that he had been in Portugal, and from references in other parts of his diary that he was well acquainted with Portuguese, we may conclude that his time prior to 1607 was principally spent in trading voyages to that country and its less remote colonies. When we have added that he was married at this time to some one at Lyme Regis with the Christian name of Susan, and had had by her a son named after

---

Dictionary goes on to identify this Silvester with a Jourdain of that name who died unmarried in London in 1650, and whose estate was administered by his brother John (*P.C.C.: Administration Act Book*, 1650, *f.* 83 *b*). Both stories cannot be correct, for (as stated above) the Exeter John had died long before 1650. Moreover, neither Ignatius nor John refers in his will to a brother Silvester, and the omission is strange if the latter were alive at the time. The conjecture is obvious that the Bermudas voyager may really have been our diarist's elder brother (see the genealogical table), who may have been induced to join the expedition by Sir George Somers, as they were both connected with Lyme Regis. It is true that this supposition cannot be reconciled with the statement of General Lefroy (*The Historye of the Bermudaes*, Hakluyt Society, 1882, introduction, p. vii) that at the time of the voyage Silvester Jourdain was page to Sir Thomas Gates, for he would have been much too old for such a post; but after a diligent examination of authorities I can find nothing which bears out the General's assertion, and am inclined to put it down as a guess on his part.

himself, we have recorded all that we have been able to discover concerning the first thirty-five years of his life.

Why Jourdain should have abandoned an independent career for the service of the newly-founded East India Company we cannot tell. The most probable hypothesis is that his business was a failing one, and he was attracted by the opportunities for lucrative private trade enjoyed by the company's factors, both within and without the limits set them by their employers. Another surmise is that his relations with his wife were not satisfactory, and that, as others had done before him, he chose exile in the Indies as a means of escaping from domestic unhappiness. The only basis for this supposition, it must be admitted, is the fact that in his will his wife is markedly excluded from the management of his estate, and benefits only to a limited extent. This will, however, was not made till 1618, and even if our suspicions be just as to their relations at that time, we are perhaps not entitled to draw any inference regarding the state of matters eleven years earlier.

Whatever the reason, towards the end of 1607 we find Jourdain in London seeking a post in the service of the Company. At a court meeting held on November 24 his name was mentioned amongst those 'coñended for men out of which choise might be made of a Generall and cheefe factors'; and on the 7th of the following month he was engaged in the latter capacity at a salary of 3*l.* per month, with 10*l.* allowance for outfit.

The expedition in which Jourdain was now to take part was that known as the Company's Fourth Voyage. The funds, amounting to 33,000*l.*, had been provided by 56 subscribers, each contributing not less than 550*l.*, with liberty to take in others as under-adventurers. From these funds two vessels were purchased, viz. the *Union*, a new ship of 400 tons, which cost 1250*l.*, and the *Ascension*, which had taken part in the First and Second Voyages and was bought from the adventurers in those expeditions for 485*l.* 17*s.* 6*d.* The cost of shipping and victuals is set down as 14,600*l.*; but this amount evidently includes wages, home disbursements, and a host of miscellaneous items. Goods to the value of 3400*l.* were put on board, and a further sum of 15,000*l.* was sent in the form of Spanish pieces of eight rials, the usual currency in Eastern waters[1]. For the 'General' or commander of the expedition it had been first intended to engage Sir Henry Middleton, the successful leader of the Company's Second Voyage; but he declined the post and the choice then fell upon Alexander Sharpeigh[2], who was to hoist his flag in the *Ascension*, while Richard Rowles, the 'Lieutenant-General,' was to command the *Union*. It was at first proposed that Jourdain should be the chief merchant of the latter vessel, in which case we should probably have had no journal to read; but before the voyage commenced there was a change of plans, and he was assigned to the other ship. The important post of master of the *Ascension* was given to Philip Grove or De Grave[3], a Fleming who had been second pilot in the First and master of the *Dragon* in the Second Voyage: an unhappy choice, for he was drunken and headstrong, and the loss of the ship was directly due to his recklessness. The other officers and merchants are sufficiently particularised in the list of authorities and the notes to the text.

The instructions given to the commanders were not to stop at the Cape, but to make first for St Augustine's Bay in Madagascar, there to water and to set up a pinnace, for which they were taking out the materials. If necessary, Zanzibar might next be touched at, but they were warned

---

[1] These figures are taken from a return in the *India Office Records: Home, Miscellaneous*, vol. 39.

[2] Sharpeigh had had no previous experience of the Indies. He had, however, been in Turkey, for he mentions that at Aden he found in the Kādī an old Constantinople acquaintance; see also Brit. Mus. *Lansdowne MSS.* 241, f. 385, which shows that he was in the Levant in August, 1603. A letter in the same volume dated February 20, 1608, mentions that 'Mr. Sharpie is presentlie bonde chefe comander to the East Indies, having put in a stocke with the marchants, and hath great alowance of wagis, besides his charges' (f. 187).

[3] He was possibly a native of Grave, in N. Brabant.

against going to Mozambique or the island of Pemba, which were both in the hands of the Portuguese. Then a course was to be shaped for Socotra, where aloes might be bought and information obtained as to the chances of trade at Aden or Mocha. No attempt was to be made to visit either place if by so doing the monsoon for India would be lost; but it was hoped that this would not be the case, and that it would be possible at these ports to procure lading for one of the vessels, if not for both. Should this be effected, the laden ship or ships were to be despatched direct to England, leaving some merchants behind to establish a regular factory. Failing the provision of cargoes at Aden or Mocha, the vessels were to proceed if possible to Surat; or, should the latter place be deemed upon inquiry unsafe, owing to its nearness to the Portuguese settlements of Diu and Damān, recourse might be had to the port of Lārībandar, at the mouth of the Indus, which had been particularly recommended to the Company's attention by Sir Edward Michelborne. It was hoped, however, that at Surat Sharpeigh would find a factory already established by the ships of the Third Voyage and a safe commerce inaugurated by virtue of the letter from King James which Captain Hawkins had been commissioned to deliver to the Great Mogul. Should no trade be possible at Indian ports, the ships were to go on to Bantam and the Moluccas, and there fill up with pepper and spices. It seems to have been intended that Jourdain and another factor named Glasscock should be sent home overland either from Aden or from India, and for this purpose royal letters of safe conduct made out in their names were provided.

The ships left Woolwich on March 14, 1608, and, after some delays in the Downs and at Plymouth, quitted English waters at the beginning of the following month. A call was made at the Canaries, in order to procure water and a few butts of wine; and a supply of goats was obtained at Maio, one of the Cape Verd Islands. On June 9 they overtook a Portuguese carrack, which the mariners could hardly be restrained from attacking, in spite of her strength; and a month later a Dutch pinnace, bound likewise to the Indies, was spoken. By this time the *Union* was short of water, and many of her crew were down with scurvy. It was resolved therefore, despite the Company's orders, to put in at the Cape, and on July 14 both ships came to an anchor in Table Bay. Of their experiences at this place Jourdain gives an interesting account, and it will be noticed that he, like many other of the old voyagers, was struck by the advantages it offered for the establishment of a colony. Had the English East India Company listened to the advice of its servants on this point, the history of South Africa might have been very different.

In Table Bay the ships remained for more than two months, owing chiefly to the time consumed by the building of their pinnace, which, now that she had to negotiate the stormy waters of the Cape, must be made larger and stouter than had been first intended. At last she was completed and launched, receiving the name of *The Good Hope* in compliment to the neighbouring promontory. On September 19 the fleet put to sea; but the following evening, in a high wind and 'an overgrowne sea,' the *Ascension* lost sight of both her consorts. The pinnace rejoined her at Aden eight months later, the crew having in the meanwhile murdered their master on the coast of Madagascar; but the *Union* she never saw again[1]. Thus

[1] The *Union* proceeded first to St Augustine's Bay and then to Zanzibar, the rendezvous agreed upon in case of separation; but at neither place could she find her consorts. At Zanzibar three of her men were captured by the Portuguese; and not long after, on the ship putting into a bay on the N.W. corner of Madagascar, the captain, two merchants and three attendants were treacherously seized by the natives, who thereupon made two attacks upon the vessel itself, but were beaten off. Thinking it unsafe to remain longer, the master put to sea and attempted to reach Socotra; in vain, however, for he missed the island and found himself on the coast of Arabia. As the monsoon would not serve for Surat he made for Achin, which was reached in safety. There and at other Sumatran ports a cargo, chiefly of pepper, was obtained, and the vessel set sail for England, though with a sadly diminished crew. Sir Henry Middleton, coming out with the ships of

left alone, the *Ascension* stood on a course which was intended to carry her round the east side of Madagascar; but it was too late in the year for that, and, finding nothing but baffling winds, Sharpeigh gave orders to bear up for the Mozambique Channel. On November 25 the ship anchored at the principal island of the Comoro group, where some days were spent in obtaining refreshments and firewood. Zanzibar was the next port aimed at, in the hope of meeting there the *Union* and the pinnace; but the island actually reached, which was taken to be Zanzibar, proved to be Pemba, some distance to the northwards. The natives at first made great professions of friendliness, but after a few days they suddenly attacked the sailors at the watering-place; one man was killed, another wounded, and a third, who had been enticed inland, was made prisoner and handed over to the Portuguese. The voyage was now resumed; but the unlucky vessel escaped one danger only to encounter another, for at midnight she ran full sail on a sandbank, and, but for a lucky puff of wind, which blew her off again without any damage, she might there have ended her voyage. The next day brought an adventure of a different character. Three native vessels, bound from Mombasa to Pemba, were overhauled, and about forty of the principal men were brought on board the *Ascension*. On being told of the attack made by their fellow-countrymen upon the English, they became

---

the Sixth Voyage, found her at St Augustine's Bay in much distress for provisions (Sept. 1610), and relieved her wants as far as he was able. The voyage was then continued in safety until the vessel was almost in the English Channel, when, for want of hands (having only four men on board and those sick) she drifted on to the rocks of Audierne, in Brittany (Feb. 1611). The local fishermen got her into port, but she proved to be quite unserviceable. Part of her cargo was recovered, but much had been embezzled before the arrival of anyone authorised to take charge. The loss of both ships made the Fourth Voyage the most unfortunate venture in the early history of the Company. It is not, however, a fact, as stated by most writers, that the shareholders recovered absolutely nothing. At least one dividend (of 3*s*. 6*d*. in the pound) was declared, and in November, 1613, the stock in the Indies (no doubt left by the *Union*) was valued at 28,000 rials (Court Minute Book, no. 2 A).

alarmed; and when the master attempted to disarm one of their number whom he had invited into his cabin, they suddenly drew their knives and assailed everyone near them. Sharpeigh and his men defended themselves with such weapons as came handy. At the first attack the master, the preacher, and one of the factors were wounded, though not dangerously; but after a short conflict the natives were all killed or driven overboard. Two of the boats were captured and rifled; the third made good its escape. This, as Jourdain notes, was 'the end of three greate dangers passed by us within three daies.'

Now came a time of beating to and fro, endeavouring vainly to make headway against the N.E. monsoon. At last they determined to stretch away to the E.S.E., in hopes of finding more favourable winds in that region; with the result that on January 19, 1609, they came across a cluster of islands which they took to be the Amirantes. It is clear, however, that they were in reality the group now known as the Seychelles; and we have here a hitherto unnoticed British visit to those islands. They were then unpeopled, and the wearied mariners were glad to spend ten days in security and comfort at so delightful a spot, where fresh water, fish, fowl and fruits of every kind abounded. In the enthusiastic words of the boatswain, 'these ilands seemed to us an earthly Paradise[1].'

At the beginning of February, 1609, a fresh start was made; and on March 30—more than a year after the commencement of the voyage—the *Ascension* anchored in a bay on the western side of Socotra. Here they found a ship from Gujarāt bound for the Red Sea, the captain of which, not liking the neighbourhood of a European vessel, slipped away in the night and by dawn was three leagues away. Sharpeigh deemed it important to have, if possible, a guide in the unknown sea they were about

[1] Thus unconsciously forestalling the late General Gordon, who seriously maintained that the Garden of Eden was situated in the Seychelles and that the coco-de-mer was the forbidden fruit.

to traverse; and as moreover there was little wind, and the current rendered it almost impossible to beat along the coast of the island as far as Tamrida (where alone refreshing was to be had), it was unanimously decided to stand after the Gujarāt ship. She was quickly overhauled, and her officers, making a virtue of necessity, agreed with apparent cordiality to the proposal of the English that they should proceed in company. Thus piloted, no difficulty was experienced in making Aden, and on the evening of April 7, 1609, the *Ascension* anchored before that fortress—the first English ship to visit a place that was destined to become an important outpost of the British-Indian Empire.

This 'famous and stronge place,' of which Jourdain gives a striking description, was at that time in the hands of the Turks, who had conquered it some seventy years before. Of old it had been the secure haven where ships from India exchanged their commodities for the European and other goods brought by sea from Suez or by caravans overland. Gradually, however, Mocha—which was equally convenient for the Indian ships and far safer for those that came from Suez, besides being easier of access by land—had risen into favour, and Aden was in consequence declining in importance[1]. Michelborne had told the Company that 'much perill and small hope of trade may be expected at Aden, yt being a garrison towne of souldiers rather then of marchauntes; yett neare to Aden, aboute some ten miles of, there is a towne...called Moccha, governed with marchauntes onelie and a place of spetiall trade' (*First Letter Book*, 247); and the event showed how correct his information was.

The Governor of Aden at this time was a Greek renegade named Rajab, who in the following year, as Governor of Mocha, treacherously seized Sir Henry Middleton and

[1] Since Aden has been under British administration it has more than recovered its position and Mocha has lost practically all its trade.

murdered a number of his companions. To this greedy and unscrupulous individual the appearance of an infidel vessel of no great force and unprotected by the only European flag yet known in those waters must have seemed a heavensent gift, and he at once set to work to draw both ship and goods into his net. Sharpeigh was welcomed with effusion, 'entertayned with tabour and pipe and other heathen musicke,' given a robe of honour and conducted to 'a faire howse' specially provided for his accommodation; he was assured of a ready sale for all his commodities, and his stipulations regarding customs duties were assented to without demur. Soon, however, the iron hand appeared under the velvet glove, for when Sharpeigh intimated his intention of returning to his ship, he found that the Governor could not think of parting with him so quickly. He was told that intelligence of his arrival had been sent to San'a, the residence of the Pasha of the province, and that until an answer was received it was impossible to permit him to leave; while to emphasise the refusal a guard of soldiers was placed at his door. In the interim of waiting, the crafty Governor did all he could to induce the English General to have his vessel brought nearer the shore and her cargo landed. Those in charge, however, were far too shrewd to bring their ship under the guns of the fort; and although a few goods were brought on land, 'the Generall made noe greate haste to unlade; onely, for fashion sake, a little every day in our owne boate, to delaye the time.'

Towards the end of the month the Pasha's reply was received. The Governor told Sharpeigh that it gave him permission to entertain the English, and an order to purchase from them on the Pasha's account a good quantity of cloth and all their lead. The General now made a fresh attempt to get on board, but was told that he must first land the rest of his cargo. However, guile was answered with guile. Under pretext of choosing the cloth for the Pasha, the Governor's principal man and two other Turks were enticed on board and were then held as hostages for the General's return. Thus outmanœuvred, the Governor surrendered his prey, though not without using 'some vile words' to relieve his feelings. Jourdain and another factor named Revett were now sent on shore to settle accounts; and upon their report and a promise of immediate payment the whole of the cloth asked for, together with all the steel in the ship, was delivered to the Governor. In the meantime the latter, anxious to raise the customs payable to as high a figure as possible, informed Sharpeigh that an Indian ship had brought a large quantity of indigo to Mocha, and suggested that a factor should be sent thither to buy a stock and bring it to Aden. Two merchants were thereupon despatched to Mocha in a native boat, and within ten days a letter was received from them confirming the news and urging that the *Ascension* should come round to that port, 'comendinge the place to be farre better then Aden.' Sharpeigh decided to follow this advice, and accordingly sent word to Jourdain to return all the unsold goods and to settle accounts with the Governor, from whom, after deducting the customs agreed upon, about 260*l.* remained due. The latter, however, much disappointed at losing the opportunity of further extortion, claimed double customs on all the goods landed, whether sold or unsold, though he magnanimously offered to accept the 260*l.* in full satisfaction of all demands. If the English General would not agree to this, he added, he should be obliged to send the two factors who were ashore—Jourdain and Glasscock—to the Pasha at San'a to explain matters and settle with him the amount of customs to be paid. Jourdain answered with much spirit that he was quite ready to visit the Pasha, feeling sure that 'soe honorable a person would deale well with stranngers and take nothinge butt what was his due'; and as Sharpeigh was determined not to agree to the Governor's unconscionable demand, the two Englishmen had to resign themselves to a journey into an unknown region, with a lively apprehension of having their throats cut on the road to save further trouble.

On May 26, 1609, the ship set sail for Mocha; and on the evening of the same day Jourdain and Glasscock, with the Governor's secretary and two European renegades who acted as interpreters, set out on the road to San'a. Regarding Jourdain's account of this, the first journey ever made by Englishmen in the interior of the Yaman, nothing need here be said, beyond noting that the hold of the Turks upon the province was evidently quite as unstable then as in the present year of grace. They held little more than the towns and principal roads, and those only at the price of incessant warfare with the hardy mountaineers. At San'a the Pasha received the two merchants with courtesy, and evinced much displeasure at their being brought up to him, declaring that he would at once arrange for their return. It was soon, however, evident that his complaisance did not extend so far as to entertain any demand for the money due, nor would he give permission for the establishment of an English factory at Mocha. The utmost that he would concede was that they should sell there what goods had been brought on the present occasion, but he warned them not to return except with express licence from Constantinople.

Having secured the Pasha's letter to this effect, Jourdain and his companion quitted San'a on June 17, 1609, and reached Mocha in safety on the last day of the month. There they found their countrymen well treated—indeed so confident of the Turks' fair dealing that they had relaxed all precautions against treachery, and went ashore with a carelessness that to Jourdain appeared reprehensible. 'Butt it is a generall rule with the English that if they have but a parcell of faire words given, that there neede noe more feare.' Sharpeigh, however, found little demand for his commodities, though, according to our diarist, he might have sold all his iron had he been more reasonable; and towards the end of July he prepared to depart. The Governor made attempts, first to intimidate and then to cajole him into payment of anchorage dues, in spite of the fact that the Pasha's licence freed the

English from all such claims; but he was afraid to drive matters to extremity, lest Sharpeigh should revenge himself on the Indian ships which were also preparing for departure, and after a little delay all the men and goods were got safely on board.

The *Ascension* and her pinnace quitted Mocha Roads on July 26, and on the 8th of the following month they once again sighted Socotra. In a gale of wind the unlucky pinnace was blown away from the island and forced to continue her course towards India, much to the discomfort of those on board, who were in want of water and fresh provisions. After obtaining a stock of these and purchasing some aloes, the *Ascension* hastened after her consort, and on August 30 reached the Indian coast. Their landfall was near Mahuwa, on the S.E. coast of Kāthiāwār, and there three days were spent in making inquiries and buying provisions. At this place they were fully warned of the dangers that lay ahead of them, and were advised to procure a pilot to take them through the shoals and currents of the Gulf of Cambay; but the proposal was distasteful to the master, who 'stormed very much, that he had brought the shipp soe farre and now must have a pilott to carry him 20 leagues'; and Sharpeigh weakly gave way to his headstrong subordinate.

He was soon to rue this decision. In the afternoon of September 2, 1609, the *Ascension* set sail for Surat, steering a course which was almost certain to set her on the Malacca Banks. Before long she was close to their western edge; but the danger was discovered in time, and going quickly about the ship stood away again into deeper water. Grove next steered due south, and then, having as he thought cleared the shoals, once more turned her head to the eastwards. With criminal recklessness he ran on, in spite of the rapid shoaling of the water, until the vessel struck heavily on a sandbank[1], and with the shock lost her rudder. The sails were at once furled and their only

[1] Apparently the tail of what is now known as the Western Bank.

remaining anchor (which had but one fluke) was put out. With the rising tide the vessel floated off; but as the rudder was gone, and they seemed to be surrounded by shoals, it was judged expedient to remain where they were until some repairs could be effected. They had only two boats, and of these the skiff had been badly crushed against the side of the ship, while the long boat was quite insufficient to carry the whole of the crew; so the carpenters were set to work to mend the one and enlarge the other, in case matters should come to the worst. On the evening of the 3rd their imperfect anchor gave way and the tide drove the vessel once more upon the shoals, with the result that she began to leak badly and all hope of saving her had to be abandoned. Without any serious disorder, those on board were squeezed into the two boats; and in the early morning they pushed off, 'singinge of psalmes to the praise of God, leavinge the shipp as yet standing, with her yards acrosse and the flagg atopp, to our greate griefes.' Jourdain, by the way, in attempting to get into the long boat, was forced into the water and had an extremely narrow escape of being drowned.

They were now by their reckoning fifteen leagues at least from the coast of India, and tightly packed in two crazy boats, with the water coming up to within a few inches of the gunwales. Luckily the weather was fine, the sea smooth, and the wind just strong enough to carry them along at a good rate. Fortune was equally kind to them in other respects. In the first place, they made the mouth of the Ambika river in lieu of the Tāpti, at which they were aiming, but which, unknown to them, was beset by Portuguese frigates; and in the second, they succeeded in entering the river without being discovered by some other frigates which had been sent from Damān to fetch away the English pinnace. This unfortunate vessel, ten days before, had been run ashore there and deserted by her crew, who had made their way in safety overland to Surat.

It is pleasant to note that Sharpeigh and his companions were everywhere treated with great kindness by the natives. They were at once guided up the river to the town of Gandevi, where the Governor received them with the utmost sympathy, gave them such food as he had at his disposal, and after a night's rest set them on their way to Surat. Two days later they reached the environs of that city and were met by William Finch, an English factor resident there. He was unable to procure permission for them to enter the town, as the inhabitants were afraid of reprisals by the Portuguese if they gave any assistance to the English; and they were obliged, therefore, to make themselves as comfortable as they could, first in the neighbourhood of the Gopi tank, and then at a village some distance off, to which they removed at the request of the Governor.

To understand clearly Jourdain's narrative of his stay in India it is necessary to look back for a moment to the commencement of the attempt that was now being made to secure a footing for English trade in the dominions of the Great Mogul. In the spring of 1607—a year before the despatch of the *Ascension* and *Union*—the ships of the East India Company's Third Voyage sailed on what was destined to be an epoch-making expedition. For reasons which need not here be considered, the two previous fleets had made no attempt to touch at any port on the Indian littoral; but the instructions given to William Keeling, the General of the Third Voyage, included the opening-up of trade not only in the Red Sea (if this could be effected without undue delay) but also at Surat; and William Hawkins, the captain of one of the ships[1], was directed,

[1] It has been too generally assumed that because Hawkins was in command of a vessel he was merely a sailor—'a bluff sea-captain,' as a recent writer terms him. As a matter of fact a knowledge of seamanship was only a part of the qualifications required for such a post, as the responsibility of navigating the vessel rested not on the captain but on the master and his mates. The East India Company in 1614 described the ideal 'General' as 'partlie a navigator, partelie a merchaunt (to have knowledge to lade a shipp), and partlie a man of fashion and good respect'; and in the case of Hawkins (who was

in the event of his vessel reaching that port, to land and proceed to the court with presents and a letter from the English king, requesting on behalf of his subjects the grant of 'such libertie of traffique and priviledges as shall be resonable, both for their securitie and proffitt, and that they may for the better handling of their trade settle a factorie there, like as we willdoe to yours yf att any tyme yt shall be requested of us.' In obedience to these orders, Hawkins' ship, the *Hector*, anchored at the Bar of Surat on August 24, 1608, having parted with her consort, the *Dragon*, at the island of Socotra. Hawkins landed and (at once exceeding his instructions) announced himself as an 'ambassador' from the English king. 'At my comming on shore,' he says, 'after their barbarous manner I was kindly received, and multitudes of people following me, all desirous to see a new come people, much nominated but never came in their parts[1].' A number of Portuguese frigates beset the river mouth, and captured a few men; but though they blustered a great deal, they did not venture to attack the vessel itself. With the assent of the Surat officials, a stock of goods was landed; and then, early in October, the *Hector* resumed her voyage for Bantam, leaving behind Hawkins and the William Finch already mentioned, together with two English servants. Placing Finch in charge of the goods, Hawkins set out from Surat at the beginning of February, and reached Agra on April 16, 1609. There he received a warm welcome from the Emperor Jahāngīr, to whom his coming meant an opportunity of hearing from someone other than

'Lieutenant-General' of the voyage) we have no evidence that he was in any sense a naval expert. He had evidently spent a considerable time in Turkey or the Levant, probably as a merchant; and his acquaintance with the Turkish language and with the usages of Muhammadan countries had pointed him out as a suitable person to take a leading part in opening up trade in the Red Sea and on the coast of India.

[1] This and (unless otherwise indicated) all the subsequent quotations relating to Hawkins' experiences in India are from his own account in *Purchas* (see List of Authorities).

the Catholic missionaries of the wonders of the distant West, and—what the novelty-loving monarch prized still more highly—the hope of obtaining by the aid of the new-comer rare and curious presents from Europe. The English 'ambassador' was quite ready to gratify him in both respects, so far as lay in his power, and he quickly found himself in high favour. His knowledge of Turkish enabled him to dispense with that bar to intimate conversation, an interpreter, and for a time, according to his own account, he 'had daily conference with the King. Both night and day his delight was very much to talke with mee, both of the affaires of England and other countries, as also many demands of the West Indies, whereof hee had notice long before, being in doubt if there were any such place till he had spoken with me, who had beene in the countrey.' Jahāngīr was so pleased with his visitor that he pressed him to remain at least until another ambassador should arrive from England; and in order to induce him to stop he not only gave him a *mansab* of 400 horse, with promise of early preferment, but also found him a Christian wife in the person of an Armenian maiden. Nothing loth, Hawkins accepted both wife and salary, and prepared to settle down for a time in India, in the expectation (as he told the Company) that 'after halfe a doozen yeeres your Worships would send another man of sort in my place. In the meane time I should feather my neast, and doe you service.'

This prosperity, however, proved to be ephemeral. The Portuguese were 'like madde dogges' to see an Englishman treated with such favour at court, and their threats of reprisal on the native shipping induced the Gujarātī merchants to petition for his speedy dismissal. The consideration with which he was treated was also an offence to the courtiers, especially the more fanatical among them, for 'it went against their hearts that a Christian should be so great and neere the King.' For a time, however, Jahāngīr showed no signs of withdrawing his patronage. On the news that the *Ascension* was making for the Indian coast, he granted Hawkins a *farmān* 'under his great seale with golden letters...so firmely for our good and so free as heart can wish'; and even when on the heels of the first report came the intelligence that the ship had been wrecked, the Emperor gave him 'another commaundement for their good usage, and meanes to be wrought to save the goods if it were possible.' Still, the disappearance of all hope of a fresh supply of curiosities must have lessened the interest felt by Jahāngīr in his new vassal; while the remonstrances of the Jesuits, letters from the Portuguese Viceroy, the representations both of the Wazīr Abul Hasan (whose enmity Hawkins had unfortunately incurred) and of Mukarrab Khān, who was then in charge of the ports of Gujarāt, all shook his resolution. The arrival at Agra of a number of disorderly sailors from the wrecked vessel, and some faults in Hawkins' own conduct, further wearied the capricious monarch, and after a time the Englishman found himself neglected and his petitions, both on his own behalf and that of his countrymen, put on one side or refused.

Meanwhile Jourdain was living quietly at Surat with Finch. About three weeks after their arrival, the bulk of the *Ascension's* crew started for Agra to join Hawkins, much to the relief of the native officials, whose patience had been sorely tried by the discreditable behaviour of the rougher members. Sharpeigh, whom the men had refused to regard as their leader any longer, accompanied them as far as Burhānpur, where he fell ill. On recovery he resumed his journey and reached the court in safety, though with the loss of all his money and King James's letters, which were stolen from him on the way. The master of the ship, Grove, betook himself to Cambay, where he told Mukarrab Khān that the English at Surat were his servants and their goods his property, and requested him to send for them. This impudent claim was quickly exposed by Jourdain, with the result that Grove lost the Governor's favour. Failing to get a passage from Broach to Achin in a native vessel, he returned to

Surat and thence started overland for Masulipatam; but when within eight stages of his destination, he fell ill and died, making 'a desperate end,' according to our diarist.

In the middle of January, 1610, Finch departed for Agra at the summons of Hawkins, leaving Jourdain to dispose of the small stock remaining. In October came a letter from Hawkins directing him in turn to get rid of the goods at any price and bring the proceeds to Agra. Accordingly on December 15 Jourdain quitted Surat and journeyed up by way of Burhānpur and Māndū to the capital, where he arrived two months later and took up his quarters in the English house. There he found Sharpeigh, and some of the *Ascension's* company. Finch, however, was absent, having been despatched to Lahore to dispose of some indigo he had bought at Biāna. At Agra Jourdain remained about five months and a half. It is unfortunate that his account of the events of this period is so scanty; but we must be grateful for the glimpses he gives us of the imperial city, of the court, and of the Emperor himself, at whose entry into his capital, preparatory to the Nauroz festivities, the little band of Englishmen dutifully attended. Hawkins' favour at court had now almost vanished. The adverse influences had strengthened rather than diminished, and his own indiscretion in disregarding the Emperor's order 'that none of his nobles that came to the court should drinke any stronge drinke before there cominge' (p. 156) provided his enemies with an excuse for excluding him from his favoured position 'within the red rayles, which is a place of honour, where all my time I was placed very neere unto the King; in which place there were but five men in the kingdome before me.'

The prospect appeared now so hopeless that all the Englishmen began to consider their best means of quitting the country. Finch, who was still at Lahore and had fallen out with Hawkins on very reasonable grounds, announced his intention of returning to Europe overland. He invited Jourdain to join him, but luckily the latter refused, or he might have shared his fate, which was to die at Bagdad with most of his companions. Hawkins, on his part, thought it best to 'currie favoure with the Jesuites' whom he had so persistently reviled, and to beg them to procure for him passes from the Portuguese Viceroy to proceed to Lisbon by way of Cambay and Goa; and he too tried to induce our diarist to join him. The latter, however, had no taste for Hawkins' company and no faith in Portuguese promises; and as it was rumoured that a fresh English fleet (Sir Henry Middleton's) had reached the Red Sea and was coming to Surat, he and Sharpeigh decided to return to that port, to await the arrival of those ships, or, failing that, to journey from thence overland to Masulipatam. They accordingly applied for a farewell audience. Introduced by Khwāja Jahān, they presented to the Emperor 'a peece of gould of our Kings quoyne, which he looked earnestlie upon and putt itt in his pockett' (p. 166), and solicited His Majesty to grant them a passport and exemption of their goods from tolls on their way down[1]. 'He awnswered that his passe to travaile was needlesse, because his countrie was a free country for all men; notwithstandinge, wee should have his passe as wee desired.' Furnished with this document, Jourdain and Sharpeigh, with two other Englishmen, quitted the capital on July 28, 1611, and journeyed by way of Ajmer and Jodhpur to Ahmadābād, reaching that city on September 8. They appear to have travelled at a slow rate and by a devious route; apparently because they had with them a quantity of 'private trade,' regarding which Jourdain preserves a tactful silence. From Ahmadābād the latter posted in advance to Cambay, where Sharpeigh joined him

[1] Covert, the steward of the *Ascension*, who had quitted Agra in January, 1610, bound homewards overland, tells us that 'every stranger must present the King with some present, bee it never so small, which hee will not refuse. And I gave him for a present a small whistle of gold, waighing almost an ounce, set with sparks of rubies, which hee tooke *and whistleled therewith almost an houre*. Also I gave him the picture of St. Johns head cut in amber and gold, which hee also received very gratiously. The whistle hee gave to one of his great women, and the picture to Sultan Caroone [Khurram], his yongest sonne.'

again towards the end of the month. At that port Mukarrab Khān, the Governor, gave them the glad news that Middleton had actually reached the Bar of Surat and was inquiring for his countrymen. Evidently the Governor was looking forward to some pickings on his own account, besides the opportunity of securing presents for use at court, for he 'seemed to bee very joyfull of their comeinge' and was profuse in his attentions to Jourdain's party. He gave them a letter to his brother, who was acting as his deputy at Surat, and provided them with guards and *pālkīs* for their journey. Travelling in this comfortable fashion they in a few days arrived at their destination.

It was one thing, however, to get to Surat, and quite another to reach the English ships, although the latter were only a few miles distant. The Portuguese had been warned of the approach of the fleet, and Middleton on his arrival (September 26, 1611) found the mouth of the Tāpti occupied by a squadron of light frigates from Damān and Diu, which effectually prevented him from sending his boats up the river, while the sands and shoals along the coast rendered it impossible for his large ships to anchor near the land. Had there been a strong government on shore, matters would have been on a different footing; but the natives were afraid to interfere, and allowed the Portuguese to occupy the littoral and post their soldiers (of which they had a large number) wherever they pleased. The situation was embarrassing, and as time wore on it grew serious. 'Our water and other provisions fast wasted; our people daily, for want of comfortable refreshing, fell generally into sicknesse; which made our estate doubtfull, not knowing where or by what meanes to get refreshing, we being so garded by these our enemies that none could come to us, neither could we goe from our ships' (Downton). Still Middleton clung doggedly to his position. The cargoes he had brought had been chosen chiefly for the Surat market, and he was unwilling to go elsewhere unless absolutely obliged. Moreover, he had learned from letters smuggled through from Nicholas Bangham, the only

Englishman then at Surat, that Jourdain and his companions were on their way to the coast, and he was determined to rescue them if possible. Some correspondence took place between Middleton and the Portuguese commander; but the latter insisted on his right to prevent our countrymen from trading in Indian waters without the written consent of his King or of the Viceroy of Goa; while as for the Englishmen on shore, he sarcastically offered to transport them to Goa himself. The native authorities professed their inability to help the new-comers in view of the hostility of the Portuguese, and advised Sir Henry to take his fleet to Gogha, where he could anchor close to the shore and trade without hindrance. Middleton, however, had no intention of quitting Surat waters until absolutely convinced that his prospects were hopeless.

One morning in the middle of October, as the English General was standing along the coast in a frigate captured from the Portuguese, the waving of a turban-cloth from behind a sand-hill attracted attention. A boat was despatched to the shore; and as it drew near the sailors saw a European in native costume spring from his hiding-place and wade into the water to meet them. It was Jourdain, who, thus disguised and accompanied by a native broker, had slipped through the Portuguese guards and made his way to the beach. Soon he was on board the *Peppercorn*, narrating to Middleton and Downton all that had happened and explaining the posture of affairs at Surat. One important piece of intelligence he had to give them, namely, that there was a little to the northwards a haven in which the ships could ride securely close to the shore. The information about this place, with 'tokens uppon the land howe to finde itt,' had been imparted to him by Khwāja Nizām, the Governor of Surat, who was evidently desirous of trading with the English. Middleton, however, seems to have doubted its truth, for he took no immediate steps to verify the statement. A careful look-out was kept for further fugitives; and within about a week of Jourdain's arrival four more Englishmen were safely embarked. On October 24 Sharpeigh himself, with a guard of native horsemen to protect the goods he was bringing down, reached the ships; and a little later Middleton had two interviews on shore with the Governor of Surat, who again pressed him to take his fleet to Gogha. This time the General appeared to fall in with the suggestion, and on October 29 his ships put out to sea. But this was merely a blind. Middleton hoped that the Portuguese, seeing him depart, would also withdraw and leave the port open; but, finding that on the contrary they continued to dog him, he soon returned to his former anchorage.

He now determined to test the truth of Jourdain's story of the haven to the northward, and on November 3 Giles Thornton was sent in the pinnace to look for it. He quickly returned, declaring that there was no such place; but fortunately the General persevered, and despatched the master of the *Darling* to renew the search, 'who there found a bard place, whereunto not only all our smaller ships might at high water goe, but also the *Trades Increase*, being a little lightned, might also safely goe over the barr, and there ride within calliver shott of the shore' (p. 179 *n.*). The following day (November 6) the ships entered the newly-discovered haven, which was to be for many a year to come the regular anchorage of the English fleets—the famous 'Swally hole.' Water was soon found close at hand, and under the protection of the ships' guns the natives flocked down to the shore to sell sheep and goats and fruit 'for reliefe of our out-tired weake people[1].'

The plans of the Portuguese were now completely upset. They could no longer prevent the English from

[1] Jourdain's share in this welcome discovery is not referred to by Middleton (at least in the mutilated version of his journal given by Purchas) or by Downton; while Hawkins (who evidently reciprocated Jourdain's dislike) says that the place was 'miraculously found out by Sir Henry Middleton and never knowne to any of the countrey.'

communicating freely with the natives and obtaining all the supplies they required. A policy of ambushes and feints of attacks upon English parties on shore was now adopted; but on one of these occasions an opportune broadside from the ships inflicted some loss upon them, and soon they fell back upon their old plan of cajoling and intimidating the local officials into expelling the intruders. For a time, however, all their attempts came to nothing. On November 24 Mukarrab Khān himself came down in state, and not only had a long interview with Sir Henry on shore, but spent the night on board the *Trade's Increase.* There he bought eagerly 'all such fantasticall toyes that might fit his turne to please the toyish humour of the great King his master,' and begged a 'bever hat,' a 'perfumed jerkin' and a 'spaniell dogge' from Middleton himself; but he eluded all discussion regarding the establishment of an English factory at Surat. Upon his departure Khwāja Nizām and others made some show of dealing with the English for their commodities; but little actual business resulted, and shortly after—doubtless in order to pacify the Portuguese—the country people were restrained by proclamation from supplying provisions to the fleet. On December 8 Mukarrab Khān again appeared, bringing a quantity of calicoes, and on that and the following day some progress was made towards an exchange of goods. The proceedings, however, were dramatically interrupted by a letter from the Great Mogul, acquainting Mukarrab Khān with his dismissal from his post at Cambay, though he was still left in charge of the customs at Surat. 'Hee was very pleasant before he received and perused it,' says Middleton, 'but afterwards became very sad. Hee sate a good pretie while musing, and upon a sudden riseth up and so goeth his way without once looking towards or speaking to me, I being seated hard by him.' Soon, however, he bethought himself and made apology, telling Sir Henry that he must depart at once, but would leave Khwāja Nizām to carry out the contract for the mutual exchange of commodities. Accordingly on the 10th that functionary commenced to weigh up the lead which the English had brought ashore on the strength of the agreement. It was soon discovered that he expected to have it by the 'great maund,' whereas the English price was for the usual maund of Surat; and, finding himself opposed in this, he 'in great rage begann to lade away the goods which he had brought downe for us.' But in this he reckoned without his host; for Middleton, who had been fetched by Jourdain to the scene of the dispute, promptly seized the recalcitrant and carried him on board the *Peppercorn*, where the Shāhbandar, who happened to be visiting her, had already been detained on the first intimation of the quarrel. Khwāja Nizām lay all night on the deck of the ship 'in such a rage thatt wee thought hee would have killed himselfe'; but in the morning he was persuaded to go on board the *Trade's Increase*, where he was pacified and released on giving hostages for the due performance of his bargain. This strong action secured the immediate end Middleton had in view, and possibly increased the respect entertained for the English by the natives in general; but the wisdom of offering such an indignity to an influential official—merely for doing what, according to local custom, he was fully entitled to do—may well be doubted.

While the factors were busy negotiating for further sales of their goods, intelligence arrived that Captain Hawkins had reached Cambay on his way to Goa. For a time his prospects at court had brightened, and it had seemed as though he might after all remain at Agra with advantage. The marriage of the Emperor to Mehr-un-Nisā (who was thereupon given the title of Nūr Mahāl, and later that of Nūr Jahān Begam) had been followed by the promotion of her father to be Wazīr. This not only removed Hawkins' special enemy, Khwāja Abul Hasan, but put in his place one who had always shown himself well-disposed towards the English. Moreover, 'this Vizirs sonne and myselfe,' writes Hawkins, 'were great friends, he having beene often at my house, and was now exalted to high dignities by the King[1].' These changes and the news of the arrival of Middleton's fleet distinctly improved the position of the British representative. Encouraged by the new Wazīr, and provided with a ruby ring as a suitable offering, he repaired to court and once more solicited a *farmān* for the furtherance of his countrymen's trade. His petition was read, and Jahāngīr 'presently granted mee the establishing of our factorie and that the English come and freely trade for Surat, willing the Vizir that with all expedition my commandement be made.' But once again his hopes were dashed to the ground at the very moment when success seemed assured. 'A great nobleman and neerest favourite of the King' intervened and represented to the monarch that 'the granting of this would be the utter overthrow of his sea coasts and people,' and that 'it stood not with His Majesties honour to contradict that which he had granted to his ancient friends the Portugals....Upon the speech of this nobleman my businesse once againe was quite overthrowne and all my time and presents lost; the King answering that, for my nation, hee would not grant trade at the sea ports, for the inconvenience that divers times had beene scanned upon; but for myselfe, if I would remayne in his service he would command that what he had allowed me should be given me to my content; which I denyed, unlesse the English should come unto his ports according to promise; and as for my particular maintenance, my King would not see me want.' Thus rebuffed, Hawkins quitted Agra on November 2, 1611, and reached Cambay towards the end of December. There he received letters from Middleton urging him to abandon his intention of proceeding to Goa and to come to Surat instead. This course, after

[1] He was made Khānsāmān (steward) of the royal household and given the title of Itikād Khān, which was changed two years later for that of Āsaf Khān. Under the latter appellation he is familiar to readers of *The Embassy of Sir Thomas Roe*. For a note on his eager search for novelties to please the King—which was doubtless his main object in cultivating Hawkins' acquaintance—see *Letters Received*, iii. 309.

some hesitation, he decided to adopt; and on January 26, 1612, he reached the ships in safety, bringing with him his Indian wife and a quantity of goods.

A day later Mukarrab Khān told Jourdain, who was then at Surat, 'that our marchandizing was nowe ended, that wee might departe, and the sooner the better.' On being reminded of his promise that the English should be allowed to leave a factory, 'hee annswered we should have none, denieing all his former promises and speeches unto us, bidding and commanding us instantly withowt any delay to avoyd the country and town and nott to come there any more' (p. 188 *n.*). Thus after having long deluded the English with promises, the Mogul authorities finally refused to allow them any footing in the country. The reason is plain enough; and we need not, with Jourdain, put the blame on the shoulders of Captain Hawkins. There is no sign that the native merchants or officials had any objection to the coming of the English ships or the establishment of an English factory; on the contrary, the opening of the port to their commerce meant more customs for the officials and more customers for the merchants. But it was impossible for them to disregard the arguments and threats of the Portuguese. The commerce between Goa and the ports of Gujarāt was a long-standing and a lucrative one; to hazard this for the sake of the new-comers, who might or might not follow up the trade they had begun, may well have seemed unwise. More cogent still was the menace of hostile action on the part of the Portuguese. The Governor of Chaul had already detained a valuable cargo belonging to Mukarrab Khān 'bycawse he gave entertainement and trade to Englishmenn' (p. 187 *n.*); while, according to Downton, 'at the instant of there conference whither fitt for them to permitt us to leave a factorye to vent the rest of our goods brought for that place there or noe, was delivered unto the hands of Muccrob Chaun a letter from Dangee, a Benian in Cambaia, by the instigation of the Jesuits there, advising them that if they gave place to the English in Suratt the

Portugalls would come with force and burne all there sea townes and make spoile of all the ships they should send abroad; the contents whereof was applauded of most, all soone agreing it to be there best course; and thereuppon presently dismist our people as aforesaid.' On learning this decision, Middleton wasted no further time in argument, but at once sent orders to the English at Surat to repair aboard. Accordingly Jourdain and his companions quitted the city and embarked in the fleet (February 6, 1612); and thus ended the first attempt of the East India Company's servants to establish themselves in the dominions of the Great Mogul.

The ships sailed on February 11, and proceeded in the first instance southwards to Dābhol, the chief port of the Bījāpur kingdom. At that place fear of their guns procured them a respectful reception, and a small amount of business resulted. A council was now held to determine their future action. Three courses were put before the assemblage. The first was to sail to the bar of Goa and demand satisfaction from the Viceroy for the wrongs he and his subordinates had done to the English. This was set aside as unlikely to yield any result commensurate with the loss of time it would involve. The second—to proceed in their voyage to Priaman and Bantam—was also ruled out, for various reasons; and finally the third proposal was adopted, namely, to return to the Red Sea and there lie in wait for the Indian ships bound for Mocha—a course the more attractive, in that any injury inflicted on those vessels would fall partly on the port they were bound for, where Middleton had been so cruelly treated fifteen months before. The subjects of the Mogul had refused the English the common right of peaceable trade, after making them lose valuable time by promising to grant it; and they had done this at the instance of another European power which was ostensibly on amicable terms with Great Britain. Middleton was determined to teach them that his countrymen were not to be trifled with, and that they were as well able as the Portuguese to use force in defence of their interests. 'For that they would not deale with us at their owne doores,' he writes (*Purchas*, i. 272), 'wee having come so farre with commodities fitting their countrie, no where else in India [*i.e.*, in the Indies] vendable, I thought wee should doe ourselves some right, and them no wrong, to cause them barter with us, wee to take their indicoes and other goods of theirs, as they were worth, and they to take ours in liew thereof. All mens opinions were for the Red-sea, for divers reasons; as first, the putting off our English goods, and having others in place thereof fitting our countrey; secondly, to take some revenge of the great and unsufferable wrongs and injuries done me by the Turkes there; and the third and last (but not the least), to save that ship [Saris's], men and goods, which (by way of Massulipatan) wee heard was bound for those parts; which we held unpossible to escape betraying.'

Accordingly, on April 4 the *Trade's Increase* anchored between Perim and the Arabian shore, while the *Darling* guarded the wider, but less used, strait between the island and the African coast. Downton, with the *Peppercorn*, had been left off Aden to drive into the net any Indian traders that might be making for that port. During the next three weeks ship after ship fell into Middleton's hands; and on April 24, finding that he had secured as many as he could well manage, he shepherded them into Asab Bay, where he was joined on May 14 by Downton with a further prize. In the meantime complications had arisen owing to the presence in the Red Sea of another English fleet, viz. the three vessels of the Eighth Voyage under John Saris. At the moment when Middleton reached the Straits, Saris was lying off Mocha. The local officials had given him a good reception; and as he was provided with a *farmān* specially obtained from Constantinople, authorising him to trade in 'Yemen, Aden and Moha,' he 'reckoned himselfe sure of trade,' and had 'great hope we might leave a factorye.' The news of Middleton's arrival and of his capture of several Indian ships naturally put a stop to the negotiations, and left Saris no option but to join his countrymen at Babelmandeb. The two Generals met in no cordial mood; for while Saris was annoyed at being disturbed in his trade, Middleton on his part was no less vexed at the prospect of having to share his booty with a rival. On the latter point Saris soon made his intentions clear; he was working on behalf of a distinct group of adventurers, and was determined to lose no chance of making a lucrative voyage. Owing to Middleton's action, he found himself excluded from trade not only at Mocha but also at Surat, and he had made up his mind, therefore, to have his portion of whatever was to be exacted from the Indian ships. Middleton, whose temper had been sorely tried by the ill-success of his voyage, and who was rather disposed to take a high tone with one who had formerly been his subordinate at Bantam, strongly resented this demand. The squabbles that ensued are related at some length in the text, and it is only necessary to record that in the end it was agreed to force the Indians to exchange their commodities for English goods, and to divide the former in the proportion of two-thirds to the ships of the Sixth Voyage and one-third to those of the Eighth. The English merchants thereupon helped themselves to all the calico, indigo, etc. that they wanted, and gave in exchange their own broadcloth, kerseys, lead, iron and tin, the rates fixed for the latter being roughly those at which they were sold at Surat. Then a further dispute arose. Middleton had demanded a large sum from the Mocha officials as further compensation for the wrongs done him the previous year, and had threatened, in case of refusal, to prevent the Indian vessels from proceeding to that port. As the Turkish authorities made no sign of yielding to this demand, he assembled the Indian captains and informed them that he intended to take their ships with him out of the Red Sea, in order to prevent their dealing with his enemies. The captains, who had still the remnants of their cargoes to dispose of, as well as the goods which had been forced upon them, were alarmed at the prospect of losing their monsoon, and reluctantly consented to pay a sum of money in satisfaction of his claims, each ship to be rated in proportion to the value of her cargo[1]. As the payment was nominally made in lieu of compensation due from the Turks to Middleton, the latter thought that he alone had a right to it; but the alert Saris declared that he too must be satisfied or he would take strong measures with the Indians when Sir Henry had finished with them; whereupon the latter, not daring to drive matters to extremity for fear of incurring the displeasure of his employers, agreed, after a fierce explosion of anger, to give Saris one-fourth of the amount received as ransom, leaving the Company to settle whether a larger proportion should be paid. Then came the task of assessing each vessel —'a most troublesome and hart-relenting busines,' says Downton, 'in regard of the outcries of the pore people and the dificultie (according to our hast) for them to gatt the mony; and that which they had from the Turkes was hired at a most excessive ratt.' At last it was ended, the five ships being forced to pay 32,000 rials of eight.

Jourdain did not stay to see the end of these questionable proceedings. Middleton had decided to send the *Darling* ahead of him to Sumatra, 'to provide pepper against his comeinge,' and incidentally to forestall Saris as much as possible; whereupon Jourdain, 'beinge weary to see and heare dailie such controversies betweene the two Generalls,' begged to be allowed to go in charge of that vessel. To this request Sir Henry, though loth to lose Jourdain's services, assented; and on May 19 the *Darling* quitted the fleet and stood away to the eastwards. Saris, determined not to be outdone, four days later despatched the *Thomas* in the same direction.

Tiku, then one of the chief pepper ports of Sumatra, was reached on July 7. Owing to the master having been given wrong directions, the *Darling*, when going in, struck

[1] See Downton's narrative in *Letters Received*, i. 185. It may be noted that this ransom was only extorted from the ships of Surat and Diu (five in all).

a coral reef; but fortunately a strong breeze was blowing, and she lifted over the obstacle without damage. A month was now spent in endeavours to come to terms with the local officials, who thoroughly understood the value of procrastination when a buyer is both eager to purchase and limited in the time he can wait. At last an arrangement was concluded, and a small quantity of pepper procured and stowed upon a little island in the harbour. The probability of getting it to Bantam seemed, however, slight, for their worm-eaten vessel was as leaky as a sieve and most of the crew were sick. Hearing of this, the *Thomas*, which had been refused trade at Tiku and was now endeavouring, with scant success, to purchase pepper at the neighbouring port of Priaman, set sail to join the *Darling*, hoping to induce Jourdain to sell the little stock he had managed to scrape together[1]. But on the very day (October 19) on which she approached the roadstead, Sir Henry Middleton made his appearance from the Red Sea with the *Trade's Increase* and *Peppercorn*—'to our greate comforts,' writes the relieved Jourdain. Middleton, however, made but a short stay. Finding the prospects of trade so poor, he decided to go on at once to Bantam; and with this object in view he changed ships with Downton, leaving him in the *Trade's Increase* to ship the pepper already purchased and procure more if possible, and in the meanwhile to search for a leak which had rendered that ship almost unseaworthy.

In these duties and in patching up the *Darling* a month passed away; and then on the night of the 20th November the two vessels set sail in company for Bantam, Jourdain being now in the *Trade's Increase*. But before they had gone more than three leagues that unlucky ship in the darkness ran on a rock and stuck fast for three hours, with the result that when with much trouble she was got off, she was found to be leaking worse than ever, and was forced to return to Tiku Road. There the greater part of her cargo

[1] Towerson, the captain of the *Hector*, which had also reached Priaman, had already made overtures to the same effect and had been refused.

was landed, and the leak was discovered and stopped. On December 8 they once more put to sea. This time they got safely away from the dangerous coast, and three days before Christmas they anchored at the island of Panjang, in the Bay of Bantam, where they found Middleton busily superintending the repair of the *Peppercorn*. In Bantam Road were Captain Saris's three ships, in one of which, the *Clove*, he was preparing to start on his memorable voyage to Japan; the other two, the *Hector* and the *Thomas*, were lading pepper with a view to an early departure for England, whither was also bound the *Solomon*, another of the Company's ships[1].

Jourdain, too, must have felt tempted to take the opportunity of returning to his native land. But a strong friendship had sprung up between him and Middleton—'Mr. Jurdaine,' wrote Captain Downton a little later (*O.C.* 106), 'in Capt. Sharpeigh his absence is his [Middleton's] greatest help'—and now that all the chief merchants who had come out with the latter were dead, Sir Henry persuaded him to accept the post of head factor at Bantam for the Sixth Voyage. Middleton's own intentions were, after sending Downton home with the *Trade's Increase*, to go himself in the *Peppercorn* to Amboyna, the Bandas, and Borneo, in the hope of procuring sufficient cargo to return to England with some amount of credit. His plans, however, were upset by the discovery that the former vessel was too worm-eaten to be sent to sea without being first careened and sheathed; and he thereupon decided to let Downton take home the *Peppercorn*, which had already been repaired. As it was obvious that his own ship could not be ready in time to save the monsoon for the eastwards, he next resolved to send the little *Darling* in her place, under the command of William Pemberton. But here again his plans seemed to be on the point of frustra-

[1] Captain Hawkins embarked in the *Thomas* with his Indian wife, but only to 'dye on the Irish shoare in his returne homewards' (*Purchas His Pilgrimage*, ed. 1626, p. 521). His widow thereupon married the captain of the *Hector*, Gabriel Towerson.

tion, for the sudden death of Giles Thornton, the master of the *Trade's Increase*, made it imperatively necessary to retain Pemberton at Bantam to superintend the repair of that vessel. In this emergency Jourdain came forward with an offer of his services to command the *Darling* in the proposed expedition—an offer which Middleton, though unwilling to lose his assistance at Bantam, was only too glad to accept; and accordingly in the middle of February, 1613, we find our diarist setting sail from Pulo Panjang, bound for Amboyna.

This voyage opened a new and important chapter in Jourdain's life, for it made him the protagonist on the English side in the struggle that was commencing between the two chief Protestant nations for the trade of the Spice Islands. He had already been a witness of the efforts which the Portuguese were making to exclude all but themselves from commerce in Indian waters; he was now to be brought into contact with a somewhat similar state of things in the Far East, with the difference—an all-important one—that there our opponents were the Dutch, who, having already driven out the Portuguese, were endeavouring to establish an equally exclusive dominion in their place. Their aim, which was being pursued with all the energy and clear-sighted thoroughness of their race, was to establish an absolute monopoly of the trade of the Spice Islands, including not only the Moluccas proper, but also Amboyna, the neighbouring coast of Ceram, and the Bandas—in short, all the regions producing the cloves and nutmegs which were so much in demand in the markets both of Europe and Asia. The war between the United Provinces and their former overlord, the King of Spain and Portugal, had supplied a justification for the despatch of fleets and soldiers and the expulsion of the Portuguese garrisons from most of the islands; and these measures had caused a vast expenditure, for the recoupment of which the desired monopoly appeared to offer the surest and speediest means. The plan of action was a simple one. No attempt was made to conquer the islands or to destroy the native governments. On the contrary, the Dutch posed as the deliverers of the latter from the oppression of the Portuguese. An alliance was concluded with the Sultan of Ternate (whose rival of Tidore was forced in consequence to fall back upon Spanish assistance), and this gave them not only a footing in the Moluccas but a predominant position in the other islands, all of which in a greater or less degree recognised the suzerainty of that monarch. The next step was to negotiate a series of treaties with the local chiefs, by which the Dutch bound themselves to defend the natives against the attacks of the Portuguese or other enemies, and in return were given the sole right of purchasing cloves or nutmegs. These agreements having been concluded, and fortresses and factories established in suitable localities, it may well have seemed that the Dutch domination was practically complete, and that the time was approaching when they would have nothing to do but to receive the spices in due season and despatch them to Europe to a market wholly controlled by themselves and yielding therefore a handsome profit.

We may easily imagine the alarm and indignation with which the English watched the development of their rivals' plans. The first moves, it is true, were regarded with indifference, perhaps with some satisfaction to see the Dutch entangled in hostilities with both the Portuguese and Spaniards (who under the spirited guidance of the Viceroy of the Philippines had come to the assistance of their fellow-subjects) and spending their money in building fortifications and maintaining ships of war. Moreover, there was a certain feeling of security, arising from the intimate relations subsisting in Europe between the two peoples. To Englishmen of that generation it was natural to regard the Dutch as being in a measure dependent upon the British crown; and it took time for them to realise that Holland had stepped definitively into the circle of nations, and that her gratitude for the help doled out so grudgingly by Elizabeth and her successor had its limits. When, however, Captain Keeling in 1609 and David Middleton in the following year were roughly ordered away from the Bandas, it was evident that matters were growing serious. In the autumn of 1611 the Company petitioned the Lord Treasurer for protection against 'these injuryous courses' (*First Letter Book*, p. 429); with the result that King James's ambassador at the Hague was instructed to remonstrate with the States General. This he did, and was assured that representations would be made to the Dutch Company in accordance with his wishes. He doubted, however, whether this intervention would do any good, for that Company was 'a body by themselves, powerful and mighty, and will not acknowledge the authority of the States General more than shall be for their private profit' (*Calendar of State Papers, East Indies*, 1513—1616, p. 234). A little later he mentions a suggestion for a union between the two Companies, 'which is here taken to be the surest course both to live together in good amity and to be master over the Portugal in those islands' (*ibid.*, p. 236); and in March, 1613—at the very time when Jourdain was disputing with the Hollanders at Hitu—three representatives of the Dutch Company, accompanied by the celebrated Grotius, arrived in London to discuss proposals for a settlement of the differences. For nearly a month they debated the matter, but no progress was made. The Dutch stood firmly on the rights given them by their treaties with the natives, and complained of the unreasonableness of the English in expecting to share free of cost in a commerce which had been snatched from the Portuguese by force of arms and at a vast expense, and was being safeguarded by the same means. The English, on the other hand, argued that they had traded with the islanders before the Dutch had appeared in those seas, and that the war between Holland and Spain ought not to be made a pretext for limiting the commerce of another nation; they were entitled by natural right to free and unrestricted trade, and none but a declared enemy could debar them of this. Co-operation, financial or otherwise, in the struggle with Philip they would not hear of, nor would they recognise any obligation to contribute towards the expenditure already incurred with this object. As neither side would give way, the negotiations fell through. It was agreed, however, that they should be renewed later by English representatives to be sent to the Hague for that purpose; and King James accordingly despatched commissioners thither early in 1615. Their efforts, however, were entirely fruitless and they returned in May without having come to an agreement upon any of the points in dispute[1].

Meanwhile in the East the servants of both Companies were zealously bent on doing what they conceived to be best for the interests of their employers—the Dutch to maintain as strict a monopoly as possible, the English to obtain a firm footing in the disputed territories ere it should prove too late. In this endeavour the latter were much hampered by the system of Separate Voyages, which made the commercial success of his particular fleet the paramount concern of each General and thus prevented united action or any continuity of policy. At last, however, the necessity of a change had been recognised, and it is significant that at each of the places he visited—Hitu, Luhu and Kambelo—we find Jourdain pressing the natives for permission to establish a permanent factory. That once effected, it would obviously be impossible for the Dutch to prevent the English from obtaining a supply of spices. Of course, had the islanders stood scrupulously by the contracts made by their chiefs, there would have been no opening for any such trade. But the Dutch policy towards the natives was the reverse of generous. Having constituted themselves the sole market for spices, they sought to beat down the price to the lowest possible figure. The contracts either said nothing at all on this important point, or left it to be determined by the Sultan of Ternate, who

---

[1] See the *Calendar of State Papers, E. Indies*, 1513—1616, pp. 251—2; *Letters Received*, iii. introduction, p. xxxv.; *Hague Transcripts at I.O.*, 1st series, vol. 2, no. 42; *Report of Hist. MSS. Commission* (1899) on Duke of Buccleuch's collection, vol. i. p. 166, and on Mr G. W. Digby's papers, *Tenth Report*, p. 601.

was completely under their influence. As the result, the amount paid to the producers—if the story told to Jourdain at Luhu (p. 264) be accepted—was gradually brought down from 95 to 50 rials of eight the bahar. Further, in order to strengthen their hold on the coming crops, and assist in excluding foreign commerce, the Dutch had established a system of advances (chiefly in cotton cloth) to be deducted later from the payments to be made on the delivery of the spices. Consequently the amount actually received by the cultivators contrasted very unfavourably with what they had obtained in former days; and this unexpected result of the Dutch alliance created a feeling of deep resentment among the natives, which was not lessened by the bitter consciousness that they were practically powerless. It was no wonder, therefore, that Coen denounced the people of Ceram as faithless and treacherous[1]; or that Jourdain found himself welcomed wherever he touched.

The *Darling* reached Hitu, a town on the northern coast of the island of Amboyna, on March 21, 1613. The following day Steven Coteels, the Dutch Resident, came on board and with a show of friendliness begged Jourdain not to attempt to buy any cloves from the natives; he had written, he said, to his superior at Amboyna for permission to sell to the English any quantity they might require for their little vessel and thus obviate any disagreement. To this Jourdain, who had already discovered that the native Captain of Hitu was away on a warlike expedition, replied that he would wait a couple of days for the answer to Coteels' letter. When, however, three days passed without any word from the Dutch merchants, he took advantage of the return of the Captain to demand trade and permission to settle a factory. The latter professed a willingness to negotiate, but deferred the business till he could consult the other chiefs. On March 27 Coteels appeared with the reply of the Governor of Amboyna. It was a peremptory refusal to allow the English any trade in the

[1] *Bouwstoffen*, i. 44.

island, 'advisinge us nott to deale with the countrye people for any cloves; which if wee did the[y] would seeke there uttermost to prevent us, they beeinge protectours of the countrye and people, and [the latter being] bound to them not to sell any cloves to any other nation; alledgeinge farther that they had bene at an extreame charge in buildinge and mainetayneing castles to defend them against their enemyes and wee to come to reape the fruite of their labours.' To this the English captain returned a defiant message. The country, he declared, was one 'free for all men, they not beeinge in any subjection to the Dutch, but onelie as marchannts to trade with them'; he knew of no contracts with the natives, nor, if any such existed, did they concern him; the islanders were not vassals of the Dutch, and if they were willing to sell he saw no reason why he should refrain from buying. Thereupon he renewed his negotiations with the Hitu chiefs; but while they professed their eagerness to deal with him, the threats of the Hollanders 'made them soe fearfull that they durst not give us any enterteynement.' On the last day of March, therefore, Jourdain gave up the attempt in despair and sailed across to Luhu, on the coast of Ceram, the chief of which had twice sent over to invite him to buy the cloves of that district.

The position of the Dutch in Ceram was much less secure than in Amboyna. The latter island is not much larger than the Isle of Man, and the strong castle (Fort Victoria) which Steven van der Haghen had captured from the Portuguese in 1605 was favourably situated for keeping the natives under control. In Ceram, on the other hand, the Dutch had no forts, but merely two factories at Luhu and Kambelo respectively; the people were warlike and the country mountainous and difficult. It was true that the chiefs of the principal clove-producing districts had in 1609 entered into the usual agreement to sell spices to the Dutch alone[1]; but such engagements sat lightly on the

[1] Valentyn's *Oud en Nieuw Oost Indien*, volume 2: *Ambonsche Zaaken*, p. 33.

natives, especially when they considered that the other side was taking an undue advantage of the bargain. Had there been no interference from Amboyna Jourdain would no doubt have procured a lading and established a factory without difficulty; but the Dutch were much too shrewd to leave the natives to themselves, and he was immediately followed by 'our persecutors the Hollanders...who att their arrivall had private conference with the Governor.' The result was seen in a message from the latter 'that hee could not permitt us to settle a factory, because the countrye did belonge to the Kinge of Turnatto, with whom the Dutch had greate league; whoe would not give consent to enterteyne us, threatninge them to build a castle if they did trade with us, and they durst not to displease them without order from the Kinge of Turnatto; but if wee could procure a letter from the Kinge, they would with all their harts give us as kinde enterteynement as might bee.' Some chiefs who boarded the *Darling* assured Jourdain that their people would be only too glad to deal with him were it not for the menaces of the Dutch, and offered that if he would land 'they would speake soe much before their faces.' Accordingly next morning he went on shore, repairing first, by special request, to the Dutch factory. There he found himself face to face with a young man who was afterwards to be the most striking figure in that quarter of the globe—the future Governor-General Jan Pieterszoon Coen. For six years to come these two were to be determined opponents, and we are glad to have this dramatic account of their first meeting. Coen was as downright as Jourdain himself, and at once 'in a chollericke manner' upbraided him for interfering 'in the countries that were under their proteccion, as itt were in dispight of them...affirmeinge that whoe soe ever bought any cloves in these countries without their consent, it was soe much stolne from them; and therefore they would prevent itt, if by any meanes they might.' The Englishman replied in no less aggressive tones, reiterating that 'the countrye was as free for us as for them, if the people of the countrye would deale with us; which they were willinge to doe were it not for the Dutch threatnings.' On Coen denying that the natives were willing to have commerce with the English, Jourdain challenged him to summon the chiefs and put the question: he would abide by their decision and if it were unfavourable would sail the next morning. To this, however, the Dutch, knowing the probable outcome, refused to agree; whereupon Jourdain quitted the factory and proceeded to the place where the natives were assembled. To them he related what had passed; 'in awnswere of which they all with one accord stoode up, sayinge: Our onelie desire is to deale with the English, butt wee are daylie threatned by the Hollanders, as wee have formerlie told, soe that wee dare not almost to speake with you for feare of their forces which are neere.' Growing excited, the assembly insisted on the attendance of the Dutch, who, after making some difficulty, put in an appearance, 'the comander in greate collar.' In their presence the natives solemnly declared their desire to trade with the new-comers, and protested that they were only deterred by the threats of the Hollanders. The latter, however, maintained an obstinate silence, 'awnsweringe neither yea nor naye,' in spite of all appeals; whereupon, says Jourdain, 'I tould the countrye people that I sawe their willingnes and perceived that the Hollanders were the cause that they did not enterteyne us, as they desired. And soe I departed.'

The next day the English interpreter was told by the Governor that he and the other chiefs had decided to write to the Sultan of Ternate for permission to deal with the English; that they hoped the latter would not fail to return next monsoon; and that in the meantime what cloves were available would be sold to them in secret. Accordingly a price was agreed upon, and for some days, with the connivance of one of the leading chiefs, the weighing and purchasing of cloves went on merrily at a spot 'out of sight of the Hollenders.' Before long, however, the latter discovered what was happening and sent to

Amboyna for two ships 'to scare us,' at the same time delivering to the English captain a written protest, which he refused to receive on the ground that he could not understand Dutch. Their threatening attitude towards the natives, and particularly towards the chief who had been prominent in assisting the sale, produced more effect, and Jourdain found it useless to hope for any more cloves. On April 12 a fresh protest was sent to him—this time in Portuguese—'to notifie mee to departe the countrie' or take the consequences; and seeing that no further business was likely, the English captain moved to a harbour about a mile off, where he procured wood and water and bought a few more cloves. While there he received a message from Kambelo, on the western coast of the peninsula, inviting him to bring his ship round to that side; and with this intention the *Darling* set sail on April 20, after a farewell interview with some of the Luhu chiefs, 'desiringe us to come the next yeare with more force; then they would pay the Hollanders what they owed them, and there would remayne cloves enoughe to lade two such shipps as ours was, all which we should have if wee brought two shipps to countenance the matter.' An attempt was first made to fetch Hitu, in the hope of getting there a parcel of cloves which had been promised; but the wind falling light, the current frustrated their intention. One of the factors was sent in a boat to the town, but only to be met with excuses and a promise of cloves the next year. The trip was not, however, entirely fruitless, for an English sailor on board a Dutch ship lying in the roads handed over a letter from William Adams which he had brought from Japan (p. 271). On April 24 the ship anchored off Kambelo. Here a few cloves were bought; but Coen and his party had been there before them and had so terrified the chief that he would not grant permission for a factory to be established. Jourdain resolved therefore to postpone further action till the following year; and on May 3 the *Darling* sailed on her return voyage to Bantam.

It was proposed to call at Buton, an island off the S.E. of Celebes, partly to see whether any of their remaining goods could be disposed of at that place, and partly in order to consult Richard Welden, an Englishman there resident, who was well acquainted with the Bandas and the Spice Islands in general. Owing, however, to the stupidity of the pilot, who failed to recognise the entrance to the straits, the ship was allowed to get too far to the westward. Return in the face of the monsoon was impossible; but, animated by Jourdain, the crew managed to work the ship round the north of Kabaena, amidst rocks and shoals that are still but imperfectly known; and the King of Buton, hearing of their difficulties, sent a number of boats to their aid. After a long struggle the northern end of the straits was reached in safety, and on July 3 they had the satisfaction of anchoring off the town of Buton. The King welcomed them with effusion and pressed hard for the establishment of a factory—perhaps as a counterpoise to the Hollanders, who had already got a footing in the island; but to Jourdain's shrewd eye there appeared to be little or no prospect of profitable trade, and so he made the excuse that he could not spare any men for the present, at the same time holding out hopes of a future compliance with the King's wishes. Some interesting information is given regarding the Dutch establishments in the island; and Jourdain also tells the tragic fate of an Italian who, having dosed the King's eldest son with fatal results, atoned with his life for the ill-success of his medicines.

Macassar was the next port reached by the *Darling* (July 11). There a convenient site for a permanent factory was obtained from the King and a start made with the erection of a suitable building. George Cokayne was left in charge, with three or four others to help him; and then on August 3 the ship resumed her voyage, accompanied by a junk which a couple of Englishmen had brought over from Patani with a cargo of goods belonging to the Seventh Voyage.

Jourdain had intended to call at Sukadana, on the

western side of Borneo; but his pilot again proved incompetent and it was discovered, when too late, that they had got too far to the westward to be able to make that port. The only course now open to them was to go straight on, and without further incident they reached Bantam on August 18, just about six months after they had quitted it.

A fishing-boat which they met while going in gave them the sad intelligence that Sir Henry Middleton was dead. His was indeed a melancholy ending. Three years before, he had sailed from home in command of the largest and finest merchant ship that had ever been turned out of an English dockyard, and King James himself had given her a name which it was hoped would prove prophetic of a rich and successful voyage. Instead of that, disappointment and disaster had awaited him everywhere. Imprisoned and ill-treated at Mocha, repulsed at Surat, his hopes of cargo frustrated at Tiku, he had reached Bantam with his ships half-laden and almost unseaworthy. Although he had managed to send home the *Peppercorn*, she had started in such a state that it was doubtful whether she would ever see the English coast; while all hope of taking back his own vessel had gradually vanished. The mortality amongst his men was frightful, and the natives and Chinese hired to repair the vessel died faster still. With much trouble she was moved from Pulo Panjang to Bantam Roads; and there at length the task was abandoned as hopeless and the vessel was left to rot in the mud. Her commander, worn out by privations and fatigue, and struck to the heart by the failure of his voyage, sank into the grave towards the end of May, 1613, his last hours, it would seem, being troubled by the intrigues of the resident factors to oust the absent Jourdain from the post to which Middleton had appointed him.

Jourdain gives a dramatic description of his arrival at Bantam. The first object that met his gaze was the unfortunate *Trade's Increase*, lying aground in the harbour. No sign of life could be perceived on board of her, nor were the English colours flying from any of the buildings on shore. The flag on the Dutch factory was hoisted and struck twice; and Jourdain, thinking this to be a friendly warning of some treachery intended by the natives, cast loose his ordnance and called the crew to arms. At length a boat crept out from shore, and four Englishmen, 'all of them like ghostes or men fraighted,' climbed feebly on board. They had a sorrowful tale to tell: 'I could not name any man of noate but was dead, to the number of 140 persons; and the rest which were remayneinge, as well aland and aboard the *Trade*, weare all sicke, these four persons beinge the strongest of them, whoe were scarce able to goe on their leggs.' Sickness, however, had not tamed the rancour of faction. The two sets of merchants—those of the Sixth and those of the Eighth Voyage—were at open enmity; and Jourdain, on going ashore, unwittingly gave great offence to the 'upper house' by visiting the 'lower house' on his way. By virtue of Middleton's appointment, he was entitled to resume his place as head of the factory of the Sixth Voyage; but Robert Larkin, who had succeeded temporarily to that post, flatly refused to give way, and was supported in this by the other merchants. Jourdain made a protest and then withdrew to his ship to await developments; with the result that two days later overtures were made for a reconciliation. Larkin and his associates, 'with greate protestacions of love and freindshipp,' requested his advice as to the disposal of the *Darling*, 'for they cared not whether [whither], nor what they gave mee, soe I would not staie in Bantam to trouble them.' Jourdain was equally willing to be gone, and at once suggested that he should take the ship to Masulipatam, to sell the cloves which were already on board, together with a stock of Chinese goods from the Bantam warehouse. To this proposal a ready assent was given; the ship was provisioned, the remainder of her cargo was hurried on board, and on September 20 Jourdain put once more to sea.

A month was spent in beating up the coast of Sumatra, and at last on October 22 the *Darling* was forced by want of water to put into Tiku Roads. There she found Thomas Best, the General of the Tenth Voyage, who had re-established the English factories at Surat and Achin, and was now on his way to Bantam with his two ships, the *Dragon* and the *Hosiander*. On learning their plans, he strongly urged the merchants of the *Darling* to abandon their voyage and return to Bantam in his company. As the main reason he adduced, viz. that it was the wrong season to go to Masulipatam, was proved to be incorrect, it is possible that his real motive was (as our diarist insinuates) to get the cloves the *Darling* was carrying transferred to his own Voyage at a valuation. This did not at all suit Jourdain's designs, and he did his best to prevent the change of plan. However, upon a general consultation being called, the point was carried against him, and he had no alternative but to submit.

Accordingly, on November 11 the *Dragon* and *Darling* anchored in Bantam Roads. A few days later a consultation of all the English merchants was held. Best had ample powers as General, and he was determined to put an end to the scandal of having the factors of different Voyages working against one another in the same place. Until the system of separate voyages was abolished (as was done shortly after) it was necessary to keep the accounts apart; but this need not prevent all the merchants being placed under one strong and capable Agent, who would do his best impartially for the benefit of the various sections, with a careful eye to the good of the Company as a whole. To this course, strangely enough, no opposition was raised by the merchants chiefly concerned; though possibly this was due rather to a consciousness that resistance would be useless than to any real desire for such an alteration. The next question was who should fill this important post; and the unanimous choice of the assembly fell upon Jourdain. In vain he represented his desire to resume his voyage to Masulipatam, and then to return to England: that his term of service was nearly out and that he himself was growing old. No other man was so acceptable to the majority of the factors; and being pressed by the General he unwillingly consented to accept the post until the arrival of a suitable successor.

This was on November 14, 1613. A month later Best departed for England in the *Dragon*; and on the day following Newport arrived from England with the *Expedition*. With Jourdain's aid the ship was quickly filled with pepper and despatched homewards again. As she went out of the Roads Captain Saris came in, returning from his memorable voyage to Japan. At first he showed some annoyance at finding Jourdain in the post of Agent; but he was soon mollified and acquiesced in the arrangement. Jourdain assisted him in procuring a cargo of pepper, and in February, 1614, the *Clove* too spread her sails for England.

From this point till Jourdain's own departure in December, 1616, the journal is extremely scanty, containing in fact little more than an enumeration of the various wrongs done by the Dutch to the English during this period, and the disputes that arose in consequence. Of these only a brief sketch can here be given, the reader being referred for details to the introductions to the *Letters Received by the East India Company*, vols. ii.—vi. The main cause of quarrel was the persistent endeavour of the English to obtain a footing in the Spice Islands, an object which Jourdain kept steadily in view. He was hampered by many difficulties, especially by restricted authority and utterly inadequate means; and the weak and halting policy of the English at this time must not be laid to his charge. The monsoon of 1614 passed away without any attempt being made at Bantam to redeem the promises given to the people of Amboyna and Ceram. Jourdain laments the omission (*O.C.* 128) without assigning any cause; but apparently it was due in part to General Best's unwillingness to go so far afield and postpone his departure for England. At the end of February, it is true, Cokayne at Macassar despatched a junk to the Bandas, the inhabitants of which were appealing to the English for aid in maintaining their independence against the Hollanders;

but the monsoon changed at an earlier date than usual, and the vessel got no further than Buton. At last, however, in January, 1615, the *Concord*, accompanied by a small pinnace named the *Speedwell*, sailed under Ball and Cokayne for the Bandas and Ceram. In spite of the angry protests and threats of the Dutch, a few men were left with the pinnace at Pulo Ai, while the *Concord*, passing on to Amboyna, visited in turn Hitu, Luhu, and Kambelo. At the second of these places she was joined by another English ship, the *Thomasin*, which had been despatched from Bantam to her assistance. The natives of Ceram welcomed them eagerly, and offered sites for factories both at Luhu and Kambelo; but the English were too weak to effect anything, and although they actually exchanged shots with the Dutch at the latter place, they were forced to withdraw their men and return to Bantam, leaving the unfortunate natives to settle accounts with the Hollanders as best they might. The arrival, in June, 1615, of General Downton's fleet, bringing Thomas Elkington to be the Agent at Bantam, set Jourdain free, and he determined to lead the next expedition in person; but early in August the death of Downton placed Elkington in command of the fleet, and Jourdain found himself obliged to resume his former post (*Letters Received*, iii. 171, 272). George Ball was thereupon put in charge of a small squadron, consisting of the *Thomas*, *Concord* and *Speedwell*. Just as they were about to start, however, two fresh ships, the *Clove* and *Defence*, arrived from England under the command of Samuel Castleton, the erstwhile interloper whom Jourdain had met at Priaman in 1612 (p. 233). He seems to have been sent by the Company for the express purpose of making a voyage to the Spice Islands, and it was deemed necessary, therefore, to place under his orders the vessels already prepared. The fleet thus formed sailed early in the new year, its first destination being Pulo Ai, in the Banda group. That island was reached at the beginning of March; but before anything could be effected, Castleton found himself confronted by a strong Dutch fleet of ten ships, with a large force of soldiers, sent to renew the attack on Pulo Ai which had failed the preceding year. At first the English were disposed to give battle, in spite of the disparity of numbers; but soon they recognised that their position was hopeless, and negotiations were opened with the Dutch commander. On Castleton making a declaration that he had in no way assisted the natives, the Dutch undertook, should they conquer the island, to permit the English merchants to withdraw unmolested with their goods. Thereupon Castleton departed with his ships, and the Dutch landed their forces. The unhappy islanders in desperation hoisted the British flag and formally made over their country and the neighbouring island of Pulo Run to King James, Richard Hunt, the factor left behind by Castleton, acting for the nonce as English representative. This expedient, however, availed them nothing. The Hollanders shot down the English colours, and forced the inhabitants either to make their submission or escape to Pulo Run. Hunt fled also to that island, and from thence after many adventures managed to get back to Bantam, to report the loss of Pulo Ai and urge that an attempt should be made to secure Pulo Run before it shared the same fate. Jourdain and his colleagues at once saw that no time should be lost in getting a footing in the Bandas, especially as the surrender of the island to the British crown would render a Dutch attack upon it difficult to justify in Europe. Only two ships were now available, the *Swan* and the *Defence*, but these were despatched at the end of October, 1616, under Nathaniel Courthope, with instructions to obtain a confirmation of the former surrenders and then to hoist the British flag on Pulo Run, resisting if necessary by force of arms any attempt of the Hollanders to take possession of the island.

Before Courthope had reached the spot which his defence was to make famous, Jourdain was on his way to England. In the latter part of September General Keeling had reached Bantam with the fleet which had carried to India Sir Thomas Roe. It had been the Company's intention that the General should remain in the East for five years in absolute control (subject to the advice of a council) of their ships and factories. But, as in the case of Best, Keeling's sole anxiety was to get back to England as speedily as possible, and he had subsequently wrung from his employers a reluctant assent to his return. On October 8, 1616, a consultation was held at Bantam, in which it was decided that he should take home the *Dragon* as soon as her lading could be completed: that Jourdain, who was also anxious to be released, should follow in the *Clove*: and that George Berkeley, the chief factor of the fleet, should succeed him as Agent at Bantam (Peyton's journal, *Brit. Mus. Addl. MSS.* 19276, p. 75).

In accordance with these arrangements, on December 16, 1616, Jourdain had at last the satisfaction of setting sail for his native country. The voyage, as detailed in the diary, was uneventful. After obtaining an interesting glimpse of the Keeling Islands, nothing noteworthy happened until February 19, 1617, when they sighted the coast of Africa. Six days later they anchored in Table Bay. Since Jourdain's previous visit in the autumn of 1608, the natives had made sufficient advance in civilisation to cook their meat instead of eating it raw, and had got over their dread of European firearms. Their progress in other directions, and especially in their knowledge of the exchange value of their cattle, by no means pleased him; but he still adhered to his opinion regarding the advisability of making a settlement at the Cape, as 'a good refuge for all shippinge that travell the East Indias, beinge a fruitfull and healthfull countrye.' After spending nearly three weeks at this spot, the voyage was resumed. On the last day of March St Helena was reached, and there they stayed five days, hunting goats and filling their water casks. Quitting the island on April 5, they passed the Azores two months later, saw the Lizard on June 17, and on the 19th anchored in Dover Road.

At this point the journal comes to an end, and so perhaps should this introduction. But the reader will probably desire to hear the rest of the story, which is both brief and tragic. The Court Minutes of the East India Company between November, 1615, and September, 1617, are unfortunately missing, and we are consequently without information as to the events immediately following the arrival of the *Clove*. When they commence again, we quickly hear news of Jourdain (who may possibly have spent part of the intervening period in visiting his family at Lyme Regis). On September 25 we find a special Committee sitting, presided over by the Governor, Sir Thomas Smythe, at which

> 'A direccion was red of Mr Jourdaines drawne by him as his opinion concerninge the contynueinge and prosecutinge of trade in the Indies and dissolvinge some unnecessarye and unprofitable factoryes, which beeinge conceyved to have bene perfourmed with good judgment and experyence, it was thought fitt to be further considered of hereafter, and were of opinion that hee himselfe were a fitt person to undertake and prosecute thatt place which was intended for Captaine Keelinge, to remayne at Bantam to comand the factours thether, to examine, establishe and dissolve factoryes, as occasion shalbee, with the advise and councell of two more to bee joyned with him; and did nowe appointe Tuesdaie next in the afternoone to proceede in further consideracion of these thinges.'

Accordingly on the 30th Jourdain himself attended the Committee, when the situation in the East and the measures necessary to secure the Company's interests against the encroachments of the Dutch were fully debated. 'All concurd to have a sufficyent force to saufeguard their buysines at Bantam and attempt trade att Banda and the Molluccaes,' and it was proposed to prepare for this purpose a fleet of six ships for the following season. The idea that any serious hostilities would result was scouted by Jourdain, who gave it as his opinion that 'the Flemings either dare not or will not sett upon the English'; and although some of the assembly suggested that it would be safer to come to some agreement with the Dutch Company, the majority were evidently in favour of standing stoutly on their rights. The next few meetings were largely occupied by discussions as to the person to whom should be entrusted the command of the fleet. The impression made upon the Committee by Jourdain's frank and sturdy bearing is shown in a suggestion that he should be appointed to that post, 'in reguard he is of a good couradge, one whoe advised to the buysines, and that the marryners will subject themselves unto'; but the nomination was at once set aside on the ground that 'hee is unexperyenct in maryne causes, and for sea fights upon occasion, which is an espetiall thinge to be reguarded.' Other candidates proposed were Sir Richard Hawkins, Capt. Parker and Sir Thomas Dale (of Virginia fame); but in the end the Committee could find no one so suitable as Thomas Best, albeit he was pronounced to be 'ungratefull, covetous and prowde'; and it was decided to sound him on the subject.

Meanwhile Jourdain had some personal business to settle with the Company. On the minutes for October 21, 1617, we find the following entry:

'Captaine Jourdaine desiringe to have his wages and an end of his buysines, it was awnswerd by the auditours that nothinge can bee done as yett for his 1500 rials of eight which he delivered unto the Companie[1], butt the bookes stand open and he remaynes creditor for them to the accompts untill they shall heare from thence. It was remembred that noe excepcions have come against him, nor any goods brought home upon his accompt in private trade; and haveinge an entent to employe him againe, they were of opinion that it is fitt to give encouradgment unto the good, as they will endevour to punnishe the yll, and therefore to consider him with some gratificacion, haveinge bene longe employed in the Companies service. In reguard whereof, as alsoe for nott puttinge into the West Countrye[2], they bestowed upon him the some of one hundred pounds as a gratificacion, and ordered to have itt paid unto him, desiringe Mr. Governor and Mr. Deputy to conferre with him upon a newe enterteynement.'

A fortnight later (November 6),

'Captaine Jourdaine delivered up a note of certaine demandes for wages, as by the particuler appereth, whereof there were 17 months and 18 daies upon the accompt of the Fourth Voyage, amountinge to 52*li.* 16*s.* But awnswere was made thatt that voyage beinge a voyage of losse, he must share with the rest and suffer as all other the adventurers did. And perticularizinge the rest of his time, from the 7th of

---

[1] Evidently he had paid this sum into the Company's treasury at Bantam.

[2] The Company were very sensitive about their ships putting into Falmouth or Plymouth, as that was made an excuse for landing private trade at those ports or even embezzling part of the cargo.

September 1609 to the 18th of June 1617, there appeared to be due unto him upon one accompt 72*li.* 16*s.*; and expected an enlargment of sallarie, accordinge to Sir Henry Middletons promise, as well for his service for the Sixth Voyage as the hazard he ranne into to give him intelligence of the Portugall, with the danger of his life passinge amongst the Portugalls in Mogolls habitt, swymminge over a river, to advise him of the porte of Swalley, and for many other services sett downe in perticuler. They therefore, approveinge his care and good service, did bestowe upon him for the same the some of one hundred poundes, besides the 72*li.* 16*s.* due as before. Butt he desiringe to have all made up the full some of 200*li.*, in reguard of his former losses, and promises made unto him by Sir Henry, they were contented to grannte him the same as a full conclusion for all forepassed services; and ordered to have the said 200*li.* paid unto him upon the accompte of the Sixth Voyage, which (as was said) would afford meanes out of the remaynder.'

The remuneration due for Jourdain's past services having thus been settled to the satisfaction of both sides, the re-engagement already foreshadowed was taken in hand. It may seem strange that, having now (as we know from his will) sufficient means to live comfortably in England, he should have been willing to face once more the hazards and hardships of the Far East; but he was still a comparatively young man, the post offered was an honourable one, and its acceptance may well have appeared to him in the light of a patriotic duty. On November 5, 1617, he signed an agreement to serve for a fresh period of five years, to date from his departure, at a salary of 350*l.* per annum, of which 50*l.* was to be paid yearly in England to his assignees, and the rest to himself on his return; while, should he die, his salary to the date of death was to be paid to his representatives. He was to leave in the hands of the Company a sum of 800*l.*[1], on the understanding that on his return after completing his full term of office, they would pay him three times the amount; while in the event of his death during the five years they would at the end of that time make over 1200*l.* to his assignees. Finally, he agreed to enter into a bond 'to forbeare all private trade'

[1] This amount—or at least the greater part of it—probably represents the 1500 rials of eight which (as already noted) Jourdain had paid into the Bantam treasury before his departure. It seems to have been usual to allow about 10*s.* the rial of eight for money thus received (*Calendar of State Papers, East Indies*, 1622–24, no. 285).

and to follow implicitly any instructions he might receive from the Company. It seems also to have been arranged that two of his nephews should accompany him to the East. One of these, John Jourdain, junior, was made a factor; the other, Jonas Viney (a son of Jourdain's sister Susan), went out apparently as a personal attendant upon his uncle without salary from the Company.

Trouble now arose with Best, who, though at first inclined to accept the proferred command, after a while made some trumpery stipulations which displeased the Company and induced them to abandon all thought of employing him. On November 28, 1617, it was decided that Sir Thomas Dale should be the commander of the fleet, with Captain Parker as his vice-admiral, 'and Captaine Jourdaine to goe as principall agent, to give direccions to whatt places the shipps shall be employed, and soe to comand and direct as principall agent for marchandizing; and himselfe to goe in person cheife marchant to the Mulluccaes, and Sir Thomas Dale and Captaine Parker to have the comand of the shipps and men.' Jourdain was thus in effect made the first English President at Bantam, with authority over all the Company's factories in the East except those at Surat and its dependencies, the control of which had been specially entrusted to Sir Thomas Roe, the ambassador at the court of the Great Mogul. Nor should we fail to notice the significant change by which the Company's ships were placed under the control of the President and his council instead of being, as heretofore, at the disposal of the commander of the fleet (*Calendar of State Papers, East Indies*, 1617–21, No. 644 I.).

The preparation of the squadron was now pushed forward in all haste. On December 30, 1617, we find a sum of 100*l.* given to Jourdain towards his outfit; and ten days later a special Committee was appointed to draw up his instructions. On the 20th of the following month the commissions were read, and we learn that the leaders of the expedition were specially charged 'to seeke trade at the Moluccars, and their to endevour it by all meanes possible, and not to be put by with the threats or attempts of the Dutch.' It had been intended that the fleet should sail about the middle of January; but Dale's absence in Holland and other causes retarded their departure, and it was late in February before the ships actually got away.

The outward voyage was not wanting in incidents, mostly of an unfortunate character. At the Cape both Dale and Jourdain had a narrow escape from drowning, owing to the upsetting of a boat; a little later a Portuguese carrack was overtaken and forced to pay a large sum as part compensation for losses caused to the Company by the attacks on English shipping at Surat; in September Capt. Parker, the old and corpulent vice-admiral, died; and on November 15 the *Sun*, Dale's flag-ship and the finest in the fleet, was wrecked on the island of Engano with great loss of life. The remaining vessels reached Bantam four days later, in bad condition and with their crews decimated by sickness. There news of the most serious kind awaited them. In the Bandas the Dutch and English were openly at war; Courthope's two ships were in the hands of the enemy and he himself was blockaded in Pulo Run. An attempt had been made to relieve him in March, 1618, but the two vessels sent on this errand had been attacked and captured when within sight of their goal. English prisoners had been treated with savage cruelty; their country's flag had been insulted; a pinnace had been fired on in Bantam harbour, and Englishmen had been assaulted in the streets. These outrages the factors had hitherto been forced to endure as best they could, for want of means to resent them; but now with Pring's fleet, which was in the roads when Dale arrived, the English were for the moment in a much stronger position than the Hollanders, the bulk of whose forces were far to the eastwards. At a consultation held on November 28, 1618, it was 'with one consent resolved to lay hold upon all occasions to redeeme the disgraces and losses done to our Kinge and countrie' (*Hague Transcripts* (*translations*), series i., vol. iii., no. civ.); and in pursuance of this determination a Dutch ship, the *Black Lion*, which came all unsuspecting into the roads with a cargo which had cost about 14,000*l.*, was seized and held as a hostage for the satisfaction of English losses and wrongs. Coen (now Governor-General) retaliated by burning the English factory at Jakatra, and the war became general. Just before Christmas a fight took place between the two fleets, in which both sides claimed the victory; but the Dutch, finding themselves outnumbered and short of powder, deemed it prudent to retire to Amboyna, leaving the garrison of their fort at Jakatra, under Pieter van den Broecke, to defend themselves as best they could. The English thought it unsafe to follow them and attempt the relief of Pulo Run, especially as a Dutch fleet was expected shortly from Europe, which might take them in the rear. They determined, therefore, to assist the natives in besieging the fort at Jakatra, for which purpose some guns were landed from the ships. The garrison, whose leader with some companions had been enticed outside and there treacherously seized by the Jakatra chief, made overtures for the surrender of the place to the English: and after some negotiations satisfactory terms of capitulation were arranged. At the last moment, however, the Pangaran of Bantam interposed, banished the local chief, carried off Van den Broecke and the other prisoners to Bantam, and demanded that the fort should be placed in no other hands than his. Dale, unable to carry out the terms of capitulation (which included the release of the prisoners), withdrew his men and guns in disgust; whereupon the garrison, thus freed from their only dangerous opponent, kept the Pangaran in play for a time with negotiations, and then defied him. By these means they managed to hold out until Coen relieved them.

In the meantime anxious debates were being held by the English at Bantam as to their future proceedings. The extortions and double-dealing of the Pangaran had reached an unendurable pitch, and the advisability of bringing him to reason by withdrawing, at least temporarily, found strong support. Moreover, it was certain that Coen would soon be back with all the force he could muster, and the English ships, short alike of men, munition and stores, were in no condition to meet him. After much discussion it was decided to dissolve the factory and withdraw to the Coromandel coast, there to refit and concert measures for meeting the ships which would be coming on from Surat. The united forces might then, it was hoped, face the enemy with some prospect of success. Accordingly on May 22, 1619, Dale and Pring with their squadrons departed separately for Masulipatam.

Jourdain did not accompany them. There had been disputes between him and Dale regarding their respective powers, and there was nothing particular for him to do on the coast of Coromandel. So 'itt was concluded by consultation that the President should with the *Samson* and the *Hounde* goe for to new establish both with men and meanes the allmost decayed factories of Jambee, Potania, Siam, Sackadania, etc.' (*O. C.* 826); and on April 24, 1619, he set sail to the northwards on this errand. Jambi was reached on the 4th of the following month, and seventeen days were spent in putting the affairs of that factory in order. On June 2 Jourdain anchored off Patani, a place of considerable trade on the eastern side of the Malay Peninsula, at which an English factory had been established seven years before. Here he found matters in great disorder—in fact in so bad a state that he sent the chief merchant on board the ship as a prisoner and appointed another in his place. The factory having been reorganised, and the Queen visited and propitiated with a handsome present, Jourdain prepared to resume his voyage. One of his assistants was told off to take the *Hound* to Achin, and another to go to Siam in a small Portuguese vessel they had captured on their way. Just, however, as they were about to set sail (July 16), three large ships were seen in the offing, wearing Dutch colours. The implacable Coen had come sweeping back from the eastwards with all the forces he could collect, had relieved Jakatra and had then pressed on to Bantam, only to find that his prey had escaped him. He did not judge it wise to follow Dale to Masulipatam; but learning that Jourdain had gone to the northwards with a weak force, he at once despatched a squadron in pursuit under Hendrik Janszoon, who, as the former commander of the *Black Lion*, was only too eager to avenge himself on the English President. It was his ships, well-armed and full of men, that were now in sight. The English were in no condition to withstand them with any chance of success, and the sailors begged Jourdain to set sail and make a running fight of it. But his answer was that 'it should never be reported that he would runn away from a Fleming'; and so the English looked on quietly while their enemies took up their stations, two by the *Sampson* and one alongside the *Hound*. At daylight the next morning (July 17, 1619) the battle began. Jourdain had 'animated the shipps companye in the defence of our countryes honnor, with the shipp and goods,' and they responded nobly to his call. Though at a great disadvantage—for not more than five of the *Sampson's* guns could be brought to bear—they fought, as the Dutch acknowledged, with stubborn bravery, and the President himself behaved 'with as much resolution as ever did any commander'; but after the combat had lasted two hours and a half even he was convinced of the futility of further resistance. A flag of truce was hung out, and the master of the *Sampson* was sent on board the Dutch admiral to negotiate for surrender. What followed is diversely narrated (see Appendix F). The English story is that Jourdain, relying on the white flag that was fluttering above him, stepped out on the deck and was parleying with Janszoon, when 'the Flemmings, espying him, most treacherously and cruelly shot at him with a musket, and shot him into the bodie neere the heart, of which wound hee dyed within halfe an houre after.' The Hollanders on the other hand declared that he was killed by a volley aimed at the *Sampson* by one of the other Dutch ships in ignorance of the negotiations that were going on. It must be confessed that the evidence available seems to support the English version, and there is little doubt that the deed was the deliberate act of some sharpshooter. Jourdain was looked upon by the Dutch as the person chiefly responsible for their troubles, and their hatred of him was intense. In the rough code of the time, such an action would be regarded as a venial one; and even Coen himself seems to have applauded the murder, for if the statement on p. 374 be correct he gave a hundred pieces of eight to the man who had fired the fatal shot.

Jourdain was no doubt buried on shore at Patani, with his two nephews as chief mourners; and we learn from a chance reference in the Court Minutes (March 6, 1622) that his funeral 'was done with greate charge and solemnitie.' It is needless to pronounce an elaborate oration over his grave. His journal is his monument; and in its candid pages we may easily discern the sterling nature of the man. Fearlessness and energy were perhaps his most striking characteristics: while behind them lay a shrewd judgment and a cool resourcefulness in moments of danger that won him alike the confidence of his superiors and the respect and affection of his subordinates. Some perchance, reading the story of his death, may blame his rashness in trying conclusions with Janszoon's much superior force; but, as his successor wrote, his action 'deserves a favorable censure.' Patani was not, as now, a place of slight importance, but a busy trading centre, its waters frequented by ships of all the countries of Southern and Eastern Asia, from Gujarāt to Japan. That these should see or hear of British ships tamely flying before the Hollanders revolted Jourdain's patriotism; and he deliberately chose to risk everything rather than lower the prestige of his country in the eyes of the natives.

It is a melancholy satisfaction to reflect that at least he was spared the mortification of witnessing the utter discomfiture of his fellow-countrymen and the triumph of his Dutch rival. In August the *Star* was captured in the Straits of Sunda, and at the beginning of October four more English ships were surprised at Tiku and their commander, Robert Bonner, mortally wounded. Reckoning the four previously taken in the Bandas, and the *Speedwell* seized off Bantam, the English had now lost twelve ships, to say nothing of the damage done at their various factories. Their only set-off was the capture of the *Black Lion*, as already related, and from her they had derived no benefit, for she had been accidentally set on fire by some sailors rummaging for liquor and all her cargo burnt with her. Dale's ships lingered long on the Coromandel Coast. Their commander himself, after a lengthy illness, died at Masulipatam on August 9, 1619, and Pring then assumed charge of the fleet; but he made no move till December, when he proceeded to Tiku to effect a junction with three ships from Surat under John Bickley. In March, 1620, the united fleet set out for Bantam, with the intention of trying their fortune against the enemy's forces. On April 8, however, they were met in the Straits of Sunda by an English ship with the news that a peace had been concluded at home—had in fact been signed on July 7, 1619, ten days before the fight that had proved fatal to Jourdain—and that in future the two Companies were to share in certain fixed proportions the trade of the Eastern islands and jointly to bear the cost of defending them against the Spaniards and Portuguese. Three days later the two fleets met, not as enemies but as friends (at least in outward show), and on the following day they anchored in Bantam Roads to exchange congratulations and concert measures for united action in the future. Vain hope! As well might fire and water commingle as Englishman and Hollander—the one smarting under defeat, the other deprived (as he thought) by diplomacy of the legitimate fruits of victory—settle down side by side under a system which required mutual forbearance to make it in any degree workable. Whatever might have been the case had the alliance been concluded in 1613, it was hopeless to look for its success after seven years of fighting and intriguing against each other; and the 'Massacre of Amboyna' was only the climax of a long series of quarrels which started almost immediately after the solemn publication of the accord.

A few words must be said in conclusion about the winding up of Jourdain's affairs. By his will (P.C.C.: Soame, 87), signed at Gravesend on February 16, 1618, his sister, Mrs Susan Viney, was left executrix, and a large part of the estate went to her and her children. We have already alluded to his apparent estrangement from his wife, to whom nothing was directly left, though a sum of money was to be invested and the interest paid to her for the maintenance of their son John, until the time of his marriage, when the principal (550*l.*) was to be made over to him. This son died some time in 1618, and a letter conveying the sad news was sent to the father from the Cape (*Hague Transcripts*, series i., vol. iii., no. cix.), though it probably never reached him. The will was proved by Mrs Viney on September 27, 1620, and she seems to have lost no time in applying to the Company for payment of her brother's estate. But accounts were slow in coming from the Indies, and the Committees were suspicious of even their noblest servants. She was put off first with one, and then with a second, hundred pounds, while vague charges were hinted of moneys not accounted for by the deceased. In March, 1622, she petitioned that 'the charge of Capteyne Jurdens funerall...might be borne by the Companie and not brought to the executors accompte; but shee was forced from that demannd as a thinge unnaturall for her to presse, and danngerous,' for the Company might in that case raise inconvenient counterclaims. Not long after, Mrs Viney died, and on November 13, 1622, her son Jonas, who had returned to England immediately after his uncle's death, took out (as her executor) a commission to administer the remainder of John Jourdain's estate. A year later we find him applying to the Company for 1000*l.*, the balance of the 1200*l.* due on account of the 800*l.* deposited by his uncle, as already mentioned. They objected to pay him the money, on the ground that he was under age and that it was doubtful whether he could give a legal discharge; but finally it was agreed that he should receive 400*l.* at once and the rest when he reached his majority. Towards the close of 1624, however, a fresh claimant appeared in the person of Jourdain's widow, who disputed—and apparently with justice—the right of Jonas Viney to act at all in the matter; and the Company readily agreed to retain the estate until the question was decided. The suit was still going on in April, 1627, when at a meeting of the Committees a petition was read from John Geare[1] and John Hazard, ministers, and Peter Hazard, merchant of London, on behalf of Mrs Jourdain, stating that 'she is in very great misery and beggeth from dore to dore' and soliciting the Company to allow her 'some competent yearely meanes proporcionable to her birth and breeding.' In reply the Court hinted that by the time their own claims were satisfied there would probably be nothing left for anyone else, but 'in comiseracion of her extreame poverty' a sum of 10*l.* from 'the poores box' was sent for her use. In August another 10*l.* was doled out to her, and the Company's solicitor was directed to help her in the legal proceedings she had taken against Viney. The latter's commission to administer had been revoked in 1625, but there had been an appeal, and it was not until October 22, 1628, that the widow obtained a fresh commission empowering her to deal with the estate. In the meanwhile the Company had dribbled out 5*l.* and 10*l.* at a time, and by November of that year these advances totalled 100*l.* Early in December a final settlement was made, and the balance (amount not stated) was paid over to her. She appears then to have commenced an action against Jonas Viney for recovery of the money wrongfully received by him; and in July, 1633, the Company's officers were ordered to attend and give evidence on her behalf. With this entry all reference to her and her affairs ceases; and our story comes at last to a conclusion.

---

[1] This was the Rev. John Geare, who had been vicar of Lyme Regis from 1608.

LIST OF THE PRINCIPAL CONTEMPORARY AUTHORITIES.

General.

The Minutes of the Courts of Committees of the East India Company (*India Office Records*).

Vol. 2. 31 December, 1606—26 January, 1610.

Vol. 2 A. 1 March, 1611—4 May, 1620.

This volume relates exclusively to the Fourth Voyage and is mainly occupied with the measures taken to recover the goods lost in the *Union*.

Vol. 3. [ ] December, 1613—10 November, 1615.

Vol. 4. 19 September, 1617—4 April, 1620.

The intermediate volumes are missing. Of the above mentioned, vols. 2, 3 (with the exception of a few entries at the commencement) and 4 have been calendared by Mr Noel Sainsbury in the *Calendars of State Papers: East Indies*, 1513—1616 and 1617—21.

The Register of Letters, etc., of the East India Company, 1600-19 (*India Office Records*).

Printed in 1893 under the title of *The First Letter Book of the East India Company*, edited by Sir George Birdwood, K.C.I.E., C.S.I., assisted by William Foster.

This volume contains the royal commission for the Fourth Voyage, the Company's instructions, royal letters, bonds, correspondence, etc.

Original Correspondence of the East India Company, from 1602 (*India Office Records*).

This series has been calendared down to 1634 by Mr Noel Sainsbury in the *Calendars* described above. The documents it contains have also been printed at full length (to the end of 1617) in *Letters Received by the East India Company from its Servants in the East.* Vol. i. (1602-13), with introduction by F. C. Danvers; vol. ii. (1613-15), with introduction by William Foster; vols. iii. (1615), iv. (1616), v. and vi. (1617), edited by William Foster.

THE OUTWARD VOYAGE.

A journal kept in the Fourth Voyage (*India Office Marine Records*, no. vii.).

As is proved by internal evidence, this journal was kept by William Revett, one of the factors on board the *Ascension*, who died in India in the autumn of 1609 (see p. 134). At the end are copies in Revett's handwriting of 25 letters written by Captain Sharpeigh during his detention ashore at Aden, dated between April 10 and May 1, 1609. One of these letters, it should be mentioned, is really by Jourdain, with a postscript by Sharpeigh. After Revett's death his journal seems to have passed into the hands of Sharpeigh, who added copies of two letters written by him, the first (see Appendix C) to the East India Company, date and place not given, but evidently sent from Agra about January, 1610, and the second to Captain John Saris from Babelmandel, April 5, 1612.

Brief abstracts of Revett's journal and of Sharpeigh's letter to the Company are given in *The Voyages of Sir James Lancaster*, edited by Sir Clements Markham (Hakluyt Society, 1877). The MS. has been freely drawn upon in the notes to the present volume.

The Report of William Nicols, a Mariner in the *Ascention* which travelled from Bramport by land to Masulipatam. Written from his mouth at Bantam by Henry Moris, September 12, 1612 [1610?] (*Purchas His Pilgrimes*, i. 232).

A Relation of the Fourth Voyage, written by Thomas Jones (*Ibid.*, i. 228).

Jones was boatswain of the *Ascension*, and after the loss of that vessel returned to England by way of Goa and Lisbon (see p. 136).

The unhappie Voyage of the Vice-Admirall, the *Union*, outward bound, till shee arrived at Priaman. Reported by a Letter which Master Samuel Bradshaw sent from Priaman by Humphry Bidulphe, the eleventh day of March, 1609 [1610]. Written by...Henry Moris at Bantam, September the fourteenth, 1610 (*Ibid.*, i. 232).

A copy of Bradshaw's letter will be found in *Letters Received*, i. 251. The date is there given as Feb. 10, 1612-13, but this is really the date of the copy.

Two letters and a memorandum regarding the wreck of the *Union* at Audierne (*Ibid.*, i. 234).

A letter from the Secretary of the English Ambassador at Paris, dated March 14, 1611, printed in Winwood's *State Papers*, iii. 266.

A letter to the Earl of Rutland, dated March 10, 1611, describing the loss of the *Union* (Twelfth Report of the Historical MSS. Commission, Appx. IV. p. 429).

The Voyage of François Pyrard of Laval to the East Indies, etc. (edited by Albert Gray, Hakluyt Society, 1888), i. 45 *n.*, ii. 106, 264.

A True and Almost Incredible Report of an Englishman that (being cast away in the good Ship called the *Assention* in Cambaya, the farthest Part of the East Indies) travelled by Land thorow many unknowne Kingdomes and great Cities...with a discovery of a great Emperour called the Great Mogull, a Prince not till now knowne to our English Nation. By Captaine Robert Covert. London, 1612.

Covert was steward on the *Ascension*, and had apparently no right to the title of captain. He started homewards overland from Agra in January, 1610, accompanied by Salbank and three other Englishmen. Travelling by way of Candahar, Ispahan and Bagdad (where Salbank quitted the party) they reached Aleppo in December, and thence got by sea to England, arriving April, 1611. Covert is last heard of on July 18, 1615, when, 'beinge in extreame want and necessitie, readye to starve for wannte of meanes,' the Court of Committees gave him forty shillings in charity.

His narrative has been several times reprinted, besides being translated into Latin, Dutch and German. It is full of mistakes, but contains some interesting details, many of which will be found quoted in the notes to the present volume.

Events in India.

Captaine William Hawkins his Relations of the Occurrents which happened in the time of his residence in India, in the country of the Great Mogoll, and of his departure from thence. Written to the Company (*Purchas His Pilgrimes*, i. 206).

Reprinted in *The Hawkins' Voyages* (Hakluyt Society, 1878), p. 389. In the same volume will be found Hawkins' account of his voyage to Surat. The MS. from which it was taken was purchased by the

British Museum in July, 1869, and is now *Egerton MS.* 2100; but it was evidently at one time the property of the East India Company, as an accompanying transcript is written on paper bearing their watermark and dated 1821.

Observations of William Finch, Merchant (*Ibid.*, i. 414).

William Finch, who according to Covert had previously been 'servant to Master Johnson in Cheapside,' went out in the *Third Voyage* with Captain Hawkins and was left by him in charge of some goods at Surat. His subsequent career is described in the text.

The Voyage of Master Joseph Salbancke through India, Persia, part of Turkie, the Persian Gulfe and Arabia, 1609 [1610]. Written unto Sir Thomas Smith (*Ibid.*, i. 235).

See *supra*, under 'Covert.' Notes on Salbank's adventurous career will be found in *The Embassy of Sir Thomas Roe* (p. 101).

The Memoirs of the Emperor Jahāngīr (*Tūzak-i-Jahāngīrī*).

Extracts are printed in Elliot and Dowson's *History of India as told by its own Historians*, vol. vi. Use has also been made of the complete MS. translation by Mr Alexander Rogers in the Library of the Royal Asiatic Society, and the versions by Major Price and Francis Gladwin.

THE ARRIVAL OF MIDDLETON'S FLEET; EVENTS AT SURAT; THE SECOND VISIT TO THE RED SEA; AND THE VOYAGE TO BANTAM.

Sir Henry Middleton's journal of the Sixth Voyage (*Purchas His Pilgrimes*, i. 247).

The original is lost, and Purchas's version is unfortunately much curtailed.

Nicholas Downton's journal of the Sixth Voyage (*India Office Marine Records*, no. xi.).

The original is missing, but this is a contemporary copy. Full extracts will be found in *Purchas* (i. 274) and also in *The Voyages of Sir James Lancaster* (p. 151). Part of the journal is abstracted in *India Office Marine Records*, no. xvii. Another narrative by Downton of events between April 2 and August 16, 1612, is printed in *Letters Received* (i. 162).

A journal kept in the Sixth Voyage, April, 1610, to January, 1611 (*India Office Marine Records*, no. ix.).

The writer was on board the *Peppercorn*. An abstract is given at p. 145 of *The Voyages of Sir James Lancaster*.

Another journal, kept by Thomas Love, April, 1610, to December, 1611 (*Ibid.*, no. x.).

Love was a master's mate on the *Peppercorn*, but on June 18, 1610, was transferred to the *Trade's Increase*. Downton speaks of him on February 26, 1612, as 'lately dead.' His journal is abstracted in *The Voyages of Sir James Lancaster* (p. 147).

Another journal, kept by Benjamin Green, November, 1610, to December, 1612 (*Ibid.*, no. xii.).

Green was a factor on the *Darling*, but in April, 1612, was transferred to the *Peppercorn*. His death at Bantam is recorded in the present volume (p. 236). A special feature of his journal is the account of Middleton's journey from Mocha to San'a and back, in which Green accompanied him.

A copy of the journal of the Eighth Voyage, kept by Captain Saris, April, 1611, to Nov., 1613 (*Ibid.*, no. xiv.).

Saris's narrative was printed in *Purchas* (i. 334) from a somewhat fuller text. The latter portion, dealing with Saris's voyage to Japan, was published *in extenso* by the Hakluyt Society under the editorship of Sir Ernest Satow in 1900.

EVENTS AT AMBOYNA, ETC.

Extracts from a letter written by Jan Pz. Coen to the Dutch East India Company, dated Bantam, January 1, 1614, printed in P. A. Tiele's *Bouwstoffen voor de Geschiedenis der Nederlanders in den Maleischen Archipel*, Part i. p. 42. See Appendix E.

THE TENTH VOYAGE.

A Jornal of the Tenth Voyage.... Written by me, Thomas Best, cheiffe Comaunder thereof.... (*India Office Marine Records*, no. xv.).

This is either the original MS. or a contemporary copy. Extracts are printed in *Purchas* (i. 456).

Another journal of the voyage, kept by Ralph Cross, ending August 29, 1613 (*Ibid.*, no. xvi.).

Cross was purser of the *Hosiander*. Extracts from this journal are printed in *The Voyages of Sir James Lancaster*, p. 228. Extracts from another journal kept on the *Hosiander* from August 31, 1612, to April 12, 1613, will be found in *Marine Records*, no. xviii.

Certaine Observations written by others employed in the same Voyage, Master Copland, minister, Robert Boner, master, Nicholas Withington, merchant (*Purchas His Pilgrimes*, i. 466).

JOURDAIN'S HOMEWARD VOYAGE.

Journal of John Monden, master's mate of the *Clove*, February 28, 1614, to June 20, 1617 (*India Office Marine Records*, no. xx.).

Monden was mate of the *Hector* in the outward voyage, but was appointed to the *Clove* at Bantam just prior to her departure for England in December, 1616.

Another Journal, kept by John Bardon, master's mate of the *Clove*, April 20, 1615, to June 19, 1617 (*Ibid.*, no. xxii.).

A JOURNALL kept by JOHN JOURDAIN in a voiage for the EAST INDIES sett fourth by the Honourable Companie of Merchants trading the same, in Anno 1607 [1608], in two good shipps, namely the ASSENTION and UNION. Wherein goeth Generall *Alexander Sharpeigh*, and Vice-Admirall Captaine *Richard Rolls*; Maister, *Phillipp Grove*. The which voiag God blesse and prosper. Began att the Downes neere SANDWICH the 23th of March, anno 1607 [1608]. With an addition of all my travails after the casting awaie of the Assention untill Anno 1617 of any worthy the writtinge.

JOHN JOURDAIN.

We departed from the Downes[1].

March 25th, 1608. Wee sett sayle from the Downes with the winde at N.N.W.

March 26. We came to ancor betwixt the Needles and Dover. The winde calme.

March 27, 28. We sette sayle from the Needles with the wind at E. and E.N.E., which contynued untell we came to Plymoth.

March 29. We came into Plymoth Sounde aboute ten of the clocke in the forenoone, where the Generall, captaine, merchants and maister went aland to buy needfull provision

[1] It appears from Revett's journal (see List of Authorities) that the ships set sail from Woolwich on March 14 and reached the Downs four days later. A week was then spent in getting in provisions, etc.

which was wantinge abord the Union, as fyshes for mastes and tymber to make a halfe decke for the Union &c.

March 30. The Generall and myselfe, after we had supped, came abord, the wind beinge fayre. We came late to hasten the rest which were aland; Captaine Roles being gone some six myles out of the towne.

March 31. In the morning the rest of our companie came abord; and the same daye aboute three a clock in the after noone we sett sayle with a fayre wind at N.N.W. I saye N.N.E.

. . . .[1]

Aprill 10. Wee had the sight of one of the ilands called Savages[2], which lyeth about some 28 leagues from the iland of Teneriffe. Our course S. by W.

Aprill 11. Aboute noone we had sight of the Picke of Teneriffe. And the wind this daye fell calme all the night.

Aprill 12. We had the wind at S.W.; soe that we could not fetch the iland of Tenerife, but stood close uppon a tacke for the Grand Canaria. The wind being more westerley, thy[s] daye in the eveninge about nine of the clocke we ancored a good distance of the roade of the Grand Canaria before the towne.

What passed at the Gran Canarias.

Aprill 13. We shott a peece for a boate, and presently came of a messenger from the Governor to knowe what we were, and what we demaunded. Our Generall willed me to tell them that our comminge was for fresh water, and to buy some wine for our money; and to the same effect our Generall, understandinge of English marchants which were leigers[3] on land, wrote to them to acquainte the Governor with soe much; which the Governor under-

---

[1] The daily entries are omitted when they contain nothing but the course, the direction of the wind, and the state of the weather.

[2] The Salvages group of rocky islets, in lat. 30° N., long. 16° W.

[3] Residents.

standing, sent for Mr. Hassard, an Englishman there resident, to knowe what the letter did import which was sent; who answered that we demaunded some eight butts of wine for our money and some water for our provision. The Governor, understanding what we desyred, sent presently the sayd Hassarde abord with a letter from the Governor, which was to this effect, vizt.—that yf yt pleased our Generall to come nearer into the roade, where all shipps (that are in amitie with the King his maister) doth use to ride, that then he would doe us all the kindnes that in him laye; otherwise he could not graunt us any favour att all. In answer thereof the Generall caused me to write a letter to the Governor in his name; the contents vizt.—that our comming thether was not to any evill intent, but only to take a quantety of water and some wyne; wherein yf he would favour us for our money, we should be behoulding unto him; yf not, that he would be pleased to send us word to the contrarye, that we might not make any more delay but follow our voyage &c.

Aprill 14. The sayde Hassard was sent agayne abord to tell the Generall that unlesse he woulde come nearer with our shippinge and send some of our owne company aland, that he could not suffer us to have any thinge from the shore; for that the cuntry people doubted us to be enymyes, seeing we came noe nearer the roade one [nor?] send our owne boate ashore. Havinge had this answere, the Generall takinge councell what was best to be donne, yt was concluded that two factors, of each shipp one, should goe aland, vizt. William Revet out of the Assention and Geffrye Carliell out of the Union[1],

[1] For Revett (and his journal) see the List of Authorities. Carlisle had been appointed a factor for the Third Voyage, but withdrew owing to dissatisfaction with the salary offered him. Later he applied again for employment, and was engaged at 50*s*. per month and 20 nobles for outfit. He was one of the party 'betrayed by the countrey people' in Madagascar.

who went presently in company with Mr. Hassard; our Generall wrytinge a letter to the Inquizidor, which he understood bore more swaye in the country then the Governor, being somthing angrye that our Generall should write to the Governor and not to him. Theffect of the letter was, vizt.—that we understood that they were doubtfull of us to be enymyes to the Kinge his maister, and not subjectes to the Kinges Majestie of England; and for justyfying the truth unto His Honor he had sent two of his merchants aland to be examyned by them; and for his and their better satysfaction, in the morning, God willinge, he pretended[1] to come nearer with his shipps yf wind permitted; which being once full satisfied of our freindshipp with the Kinge their maister, that we doubted not but he would vouchsafe us such provision as we wanted for our money. After the merchannts were gone aland, a captaine of the castell came abord; the Generall being gone abord the Unyon to cause them to goe about to fysh the mast which was cracte, leaving me abord to entertayne the Spanish captaine.

Aprill 15. Our Generall, accordinge to promise, caused our shipps to sett sayle, and came to anker in fourteen fathom water, betwixt the fort and the cyttye; and this day Mr. Revet, one of the merchannts, came abord, and brought word that we should have both wyne and water, or anythinge els that wee wanted; and presently retourned aland[2].

Aprill 16. Mr. Carleill came abord, and brought with him, by order from the Governor, the Sarjeant Major to

[1] Intended.

[2] Revett says that the Governor treated them kindly, but referred them to the Inquisidor. Accordingly on the following morning they repaired to the house of the latter, 'where wee were sworne whether wee were Inglishe men or nott, whether wee were bound, the burthen of our shipps, what store of men wee had, and many other idle questeons; which were aunswered, and presently a lycence graunted and given us for to goe and buy our necessaryes.'

visitt our shipps for the better satysfaction of the people of the countrye, who doubted of us to be Hollanders, who had not longe before sacked their towne. And this daye had from the shore eight pypes of wyne (vizt., four abord the Unyon and four abord the Assention) with a present of our [their?] cuntry fruites to our Generall.

Aprill 17. In the afternoone William Revett and Geffrey Carleill came abord and brought all things that we wanted, with many *besolos manos*[1] to our Generall from the Inquisidor and Governor.

Aprill 18. Aboute six of the clocke in the morninge we sett sayle from the Gran Canaria with the wynde at W.N.W., and wee steared our course at S.W. & by S.

Aprill 19. We were allmost all the daye becalmed untell four of the clocke, at which tyme we had a pretty gale at West and went our course S.W. & by S.

Aprill 20. We had sight of four carvailes[2], which we supposed to be bound for Cape Blanco[3] or a fishinge. When they sawe us they altred their course; and wee stood our course as before at S.W. & by S. And this daye we observed, and were in 26 deg. 40 mi.

. . . .

Aprill 25. ...We demaunded of the maister of the Unyon in what lattitude he founde [himselfe?] and howe the Ile of Sally[4] was of him. He answered that yt bare S.W.Westerly, he beinge in 18 d. odd minitts, and per observacion [we?] were 17 d. 59 m. And this night we tooke in our maynsayle, because we would not overshute the Ile of Boavista, where the Generall determyned to touch, to take in water and other refreshinge for our fyrst spendinge.

---

[1] Salutations, compliments (Sp. *besar las manos*, 'to kiss the hands').

[2] For a picture of a Portuguese caravel see *The First Voyage of Vasco da Gama*, 158.

[3] On the African coast, in 20° 47′ N. lat.

[4] Sal, the northeasternmost of the Cape Verd Islands.

Aprill 26. We had sight of one of the iles of Cape de Vert, which we tooke to be the Ile of Sall; but the maister and captayne of the Unyon, cominge abord, affirmed to our Generall not to be the Ile of Sall, but another iland called Saint Nicholas. Then yt was concluded to stand for the iland of Boavista to take in water, which iland laye by judgment some twelve leagues to the southward, and that the iland of Boavista (*sic*) was to the eastwarde of us. Soe wee brought tackes a board and steared away E.S.E. and E. & by S. with a fresh gale at [*blank*]; and about six in the eveninge we had sight of an iland W.S.W. of us; soe we slacked sayle all night, and steared as formerly. Some made us this iland to be the Ile of Mayo[1]; others sayde naye. Soe that those that will strike a hodgshed in the sea coulde not find a greate iland bigger then a butt.

Aprill 27. We had sight of another iland, which all the doctors made to be the Ile of Boavista untill we came soe neare the shore that we might allmost discerne the salt pitts of Mayo; then they knewe yt to be the same, as soone as they sawe the heapes of salt. Soe about three of the clocke in the afternoone we ankored in [*blank*] fathom water, good ground.

Aprill 28. Our Generall sent our longe boate aland with 20 men, with two marchants to conduct them, with soe many more out of the Unyon. And cominge on land they sawe three or four Negros, and spake to them in Portuges; who tould them that fourteen[2] sayle of Flemyngs had been there some two monthes before, bound for the East Indias. Soe they retourned agayne abord,

---

[1] Maio is 44 m. S.W. of Boavista.

[2] Thirteen, according to Revett. The fleet referred to was that of Pieter Willemsz. Verhoeff. It consisted of nine ships and four pinnaces.

with a company of leane carren goates dryed, but could find noe water.

Aprill 29. The longe boate retorned aland, and the Generall sent me in her to speake with the Negros to knowe of them where the water was; but before our cominge they were gone, and would not come to speake with us any more. Soe we retourned abord with some 30 more of the leane goates; with much trouble to gett agayne into the boate, the sea beinge rysen with a greate suffe neare the shore, verye dangerous for landinge.

Aprill 30. Our Generall called a councell as consern-inge the proseedinge in our voyage without water, havinge suffycient to carry us to the Cape, yf yt please God to send us any resonable passage. The Unyon (who most wanted) had in her some 20 tonnes of water, 20 tonnes of beare, besydes wine and syder in good plentye. In this councell there was a complaint made by the captayne of the Unyon that the maister[1] and some other of his shipp had abused his aucthorytye; which being examyned was found to be of noe great consequence, and therefore putt of untill our meeting the next daye.

May 1. The captayne and the maister of the Unyon, with the marchaunts, retourned againe abord, where they were made freinds[2]. And in this counsell yt was deter-myned to proseede with what water we had towardes the Cape; but first to romage in hould some two or three dayes, to bringe all things in order, and soe in the name of God to departe.

May 2 and 3. We stayed to rumage our shipps, as is formerlye sett downe in court. Of this iland I need not write, because yt is sufficiently knowne to most

---

[1] Griffin Morris or Maurice. He died at Priaman.

[2] 'This day, beinge Sunday, came capten Rowles, marchannts and master, with most part of the pryncepall offycers aboard and hard a sermon and were partakers at the Lords tabell' (Revett).

of our seamen, who hath at large given informacion of this iland.

May 4. In the morninge aboute six of the clocke we sett sayle from the iland of Mayo, and stayed to the offinge for the Unyon untill eleven of the clocke; and then we steared awaye S. & by E., with a fayre gale at N.E.

May 5. We had the wind at N.E., somtymes calme, and wee stood our course att S.S.E. and S. & by E. amonge. At night yt fell calme, with much raine and thunder and much wind by puffs in the showers. This daye we had sight of a great shipp some two leagues to windward of us, which we judge to be some Portugall bound for Brazill. Having observed, wee were in 13 degrees 15 minitts of lattitude.

. . . .

May 20. The wind as formerlye, and wee stoode awaye at S. and S. & by E. This daye by noone we weare somthinge to the southward of the Equin[o]ctiall.

. . . .

May 22. ...This daye came abord the captayne, merchants and maister of the Unyon to dynner, being invited per the Generall.

. . . .

May 26. ...This daye the Generall, merchants and maister were invited abord the Unyon, where we dyned and supped; where shootinge a peece for our welcome, the gonners mate not sponginge the peece after the first shott, and another goinge to charge the peece agayne, tooke fyre of the powder and blewe awaye an arme of him that went to loade the peece, whereof he dyed.

. . . .

June 9. ...This daye aboute eight of the clocke we had sight of a taule shipp to the westwards of us, and shee stoode awaye S.E. And aboute five of the clocke in the afternoone wee came upp with her, and knewe her to be one of the Portingale carricks. And the Unyons skyff being abord of our shipp (the captayne being invited by the Generall this daye), ytt was thought good to send her of to speake with them; in which boate went William Revett and Geffrey Carleill. And cominge abord, or rather by the shipps syde, they demaunded what they weare and whether they are bound. They answered that they came from Lysborne, bound to the East Indias. They tould them that we weare marchants and Englishmen, their freinds, bound lykewyse for those partes. The captain of the carrick, Donn Christian, came to the shipps syde unto them, and craved pardon that he could not receave them into his shipp, havinge order from the Kinge his maister to the contrarie. The marchants being earnest to knowe for what place of the Indies he was bound, answered and sayd he was of Lysborne and bound whether pleased God. They demaunded for what place we were bound, and the merchants answered him in the same manner: whether pleased God. And with this answere they retorned; and all this night we kept neare the carricke upon her weather quarter, with a fresh gale all night E. & by N. This daye att noone we weare [in] latt. 22½ d.

June 10. Captain Rolles with the merchants of the Unyon retourned agayne abord our shippe to conferre concerninge the carricke; where yt was concluded to write a letter with complements to the captain; which the Generall caused me to write in his name and carrye yt to him; which I did accordinglye. And att my cominge abord, the captain of the carricke came to the shipps syde with many courteous complements, and sent his boatson into our boate with wyne, frute and marmylad with other sweete meates. In the meane tyme he wrote an answere to the Generalls letter, which was that he gave him many thankes for his kind message: that he wanted nothinge, neither could hee keepe company with any: but yf the Generall would keepe him companye, he intreated that he would keepe farther of from him by night. For that the last night, most of our company havinge itchinge fyngers, came soe neare them that we were lyke to board them; which was donne onlye to pyke a quarrell with them, to see yf they would shoote att us, that we might have occasion to deale with them; which in my judgment we should have had a crowe to pull to take her, for she had 300 soldiars, besydes saylors and passengers; as they tould me that they had 800 persons in her[1]. Soe after that the Generall had receaved his letter, we gave them three peeces to salute them, and soe stood our course E.S.E.; and the carreck stoode more easterlye. This daye att noone we weare in 23 d. 42 m.

. . . .

June 16. ...This daye in the morninge we had sight of a sayle to windward of us. We supposed that yt was the carreck which we had formerly spooke with (for she went as well as the Unyon), only shee kept a more easterlye course to free themselves of our companye. This daye lattitude 28 d. 12 m.

. . . .

June 27. ...This daye the captain, marchants and maister [of the Unyon?] dyned abord with us....

. . . .

Julye 3. The wind varyable betwixt the S. and the W., styffe gale; soe that the Unyon spronge her mayne topmast, that of force we stayed for her with our mayne sayle and mayne topsayle in all daye, keepinge our course E.

---

[1] Revett states that the carrack was understood to be bound for Malacca and to have left her consorts at the islands of Martin Vaz. Jones says the carrack was named the *Nova Palma*, that she was bound for India, and that she was cast away on the coast of Sofala, within twelve leagues of Mozambique. He adds that her captain came home as a passenger in the same carrack as he (1610).

and by N. This daye we sawe weedes called *tromboes*[1]; and observing weare in 34 d. 20 m.

Julye 4. ...This daye we sawe a sayle to windward of us, who soone came up with us; and having a fresh gale wee halled them, and we understood that yt was a Holland pynnace that was bound with advice to the fleete, beinge three monthes since he came out[2]. In the eveninge, better of sayle then us, he left our companye and stoode his course towardes the Cape. This daye at noone we weare in 34 d. 12 m.

Julye 5. We had the wind as the daye before, and wee stood away E. and E. & by N. amonge, with a styffe gale. This daye at noone we had lattitude 33 d. 50 m. And this daye came abord Captain Rolles, the merchants and maister of the Unyon, and tould the Generall he had many men sicke of the scurvie downe and many others infected; and understandinge that we were not determyned to putt in for the Cape, sayd that yf the Generall putt alonge and touched not att the Cape that they would goe to their cabins and dye, for they knewe that they weare butt dead men. Soe the Generall takeinge informacion howe many men they had sicke, and the necessitie in puttinge in, having caused a counsell to be held, yt was agreed to stoppe there to sett upp our pinnace[3], considering the

[1] 'From these ilandes of Tristan de Cunha to the Cape de bona Speranza, being in this countrie about the eight of June, you shall see driving in the sea certaine weedes called Sargosso and Trombas, like peeces of thicke reedes. Those reedes are short and full of branches, and are not so long as those that are found by the Cape de bona Speranza' (Linschoten, bk. iii. p. 309 of English edn. of 1598). The word appears to be the Port. *tromba*, a 'trumpet,' etc.

[2] This was the *Goede Hoop*, which had been despatched from Holland with news that a twelve years' truce with Spain was on the point of being concluded. On reaching Bantam her officers told the English factors there 'of two ships which they met withall to the north of the Cape Bona Speranza in thirtie two degrees. They made them to bee English ships, but whether they were bound they were not certaine; but the smaller shippe [the *Ascension*] bore the flagge in the maine-top' [as admiral] (Saris's notes in *Purchas*, i. 388).

[3] The materials for which they had brought with them.

necessitie of the sicke men, and Mr. Grove affirminge that yt was a farre better place for refreshinge and to sett upp our pinnace then St. Augustine[1], where we were determyned to stopp. Soe yt was concluded to putt in att Saldana[2]; our companye of the Assention being all lustye and well, God be thanked. At that tyme we accompted ourselves to be short of Saldana about 120 leagues.

. . . .

Julye 11. ...We tooke in our sayle to staye for the Unyon, who [was ?] falne asterne.

Julye 12. Notwithstanding our staying all night for the Unyon, in the morninge she was soe farre asterne as wee could well discrye her uppon the poope. This daye in the afternoone the wind begann to blowe att [*blank*] and we steared awaye E. and E. & by S. This eveninge the Unyon came upp with us with a fresh gale, and then we stood awaye as before. This daye we sawe many *tromboes* or [*blank*]; the maister, judginge us to be neare the land, looking out for yt. This night we had some raine and gusts.

Julye 13. ...Wee had 33 d. 55 m., fyndinge by observacion to be dryven to the northward with a currant about 15 leagues, accomptinge to be 25 leagues of the shore.

Julye 14. We had sight of land E.S.E. of us, by judgment about 15 leagues short of yt. With the wind at West and W. & by S., we steard awaye East and E. & by S. and E.S.E. amonge, untill five in the afternoone, beinge by judgment in the full lattitude of Saldana, we steared in E.N.E. and E. & by N.; and about midnight, havinge perfectlye made the Table and other heigh land with the moone light, wee ankored in the baye of Saldana (God be praysed for yt) in eight fathom water, in companye with the Unyon, who ankored in halfe an hower after.

---

[1] In Madagascar.

[2] Table Bay.

What passed in the tyme of our beinge att Saldana, with a discription of the cuntrye.

Havinge mored our shippe, the next daye, beinge the 15th, our Generall with the merchants and maisters went aland to seeke fresh victualls and a convenyent place to sett upp our pynnace. And cominge aland we found aboute twenty people or more (of the cuntrye) in lyttle symple cottages made with bowes, better to keepe them from the sonne then from the raigne, which this cuntrye doth afford in plentye. To theise people we made signes for cattle and sheepe; which by our signes they understoode us, and makeinge shewe (as wee understoode them) within three dayes; which was effected att the tyme, we showing them iron hoopes, which is the best money which they doe esteeme. In the interim our Generall caused tents to be sett up for the carpenters, and landed the pinnace which was brought out of England, to sett her upp. And vewing over the stones where the shipps that are bound outward or homeward doe use to sett their names[1], where we found the names of Captain Keelling, Captain Hawkens, Captain Myddleton and divers others, beinge passed towards the Indies, vizt. Captain Myddleton in July, 1607, and Captain Keelinge the moneth of December ditto anno[2].

---

[1] The early navigators were in the habit of chiselling on the rocks near the watering-place in Table Bay the dates of arrival and departure of their ships, directions for finding letters, etc. Several stones bearing inscriptions of this nature have been dug up in Cape Town during recent years, and are now to be seen at the South African Museum.

[2] 'We found here ingraven upon stone the hard suckcesse of a longe passadge the *Dragon* and *Hector* had in this your last voyadge, betweene [being?] nine mounethes or thereabouts betwene England and there departure from this place' (Revett). For the voyages of Keeling, Hawkins and David Middleton see *Purchas*, i. 188, 226, *The Hawkins' Voyages*, 364, and *Lancaster's Voyages*, 108, 113. Keeling mentions that at the Cape he 'found ashore these words

The people of the cuntrye seinge us to sett upp our tents, they removed householde and went halfe a myle farther into the woods with their famelye. And yt seemes that they gave notice to the rest of the cuntrye people of our cominge, for that within shorte tyme wee had stoore of sheepe and other cattle brought dayelye to us, which wee bought, vizt. a cowe for a peece of an ould iron hoope of a yard longe, and a sheepe for halfe soe much. And many tymes, havinge sould them to us, yf we looked not the better to them, they would steale them agayne from us and bringe them agayne to sell; which we were fayne with patience to buy agayne of them, without givinge any foule language, for feare least they would bringe us noe more[1]. As lykewyse yf they stole any thinge, yf yt weare of smale valewe, wee would not meddle with them butt suffer them to carry yt awaye; which they tooke verye kindly, in soe much that they brought such plentye downe, more then wee were able to tell what to doe withall. Yett we refused noone, for feare lesse in soe doinge they would bringe noe more.

Now knowinge that our tyme would be somthinge the longer in this place, because that our Generall was determyned to make the pinnace bigger and higher then in her first bulke, for the better passinge the Cape and more servisable for busynes, therefore yt was concluded to land four peeces of ordynance, vizt. two faucons[2] out of the

engraven upon a rocke, viz. The foure and twentieth of July, 1607, Captaine David Middleton in the *Consent*' (*Purchas*, i. 190); and Hawkins has an entry to the same effect.

[1] Herbert says that the natives 'traine their cattell to such obedience as with a call or whistle (impossible to be counterfeited) a great heard will follow them like dogges; and being sold, with a like call will as readily runne after them, to the purchasers costly mirth and admiration; a deceit so long, so unjustly acted, that now (to prevent them) our men upon delivery of each beast either kill it quickly or fasten their hornes with cords to stakes plac'd here of purpose' (ed. 1638, p. 19).

[2] A falcon was a cannon weighing 1100 lbs. and throwing a ball of $2\frac{1}{4}$ lbs. (Smith's *Accidence for Yong Sea-men*).

Assention and two out of the Unyon, the better to prevent myscheife or assault that might be offred by those heathen people; and to that purpose we made a bulwarke with earth, and in everye corner there was placed a falcon, for feare of assaulte by night to burne our pynnace when she should be ended. But we could not perceave that they gave any such attempt, because we gave them as much content as in us lay. For in the interim of the building our pinnace, our Generall sent our boates to an iland called Pe[n]guin Iland[1], lying at the entrance of the bay, to fetch seales, alias seawolves, to give them content, and partly to renew our store of oyle, which wee had leaked out; having on this iland such great quantitie of those fishes, that within lesse then a day a man might lade a good shipp with them. And having brought our boates laden with these seales, we cutt the fatt from them for oyle, and the rest was throwne a good distannce from the tents because of noysomnes; upon which fish the Saldanians fed very hartilie on, after it had lyen in a heape 15 daies, that noe Christian could abide to come within a myle of itt. Notwithstandinge the loathsomnes of the smell, these people would eate of it as if it had bene better meate, and would not take of that which laye upon the topp, which were the sweetest, but would search under for those which were most rotten, and laye it on the coales without any ceremonyes of washinge; and beeinge a little scorched with the fire, would eate it with a good stomacke; in soe much that my opinion is that if without danger they could come to eate mans flesh, they would not make any scruple of it, for that I think the world doth not yeild a more heathenish people and more beastlie.

Off these kinde of people and there behaviour I neede not to write, because it is sufficientlie knowne to many of

[1] Now known by its Dutch name of Robben (Seals') Island.

our countrymen; as alsoe the iland from whence these seales are brought, called Penguin Iland, because there is on that iland a kinde of fowle called by that name, which hath noe feathers, which are soe naturallie simple that you maye drive them as you would doe a flocke of sheepe; in soe much that I sawe some of our men to drive a good quantitye of them into our boate, haveinge laied a board from the boate to the strand; which wee carryed to the mayne to give content to the Saldanians, they much re-joysinge at our comeinge, makinge a greate feast amongst themselves for the penguins. On this iland wee found some 20 sheepe which had bene lefte by the Hollanders, as we perceaved by a writeinge lefte in a tyneinge[1] platter; which sheepe were the fattest that ever I sawe. Wee tooke the sheepe and left at our departure other in leiu of them, with five cowes and a bull to increase[2]. This iland will make the leanest sheepe that wee cann chuse to bee fatt within one monneth, as per experyence of our time of beeinge there wee made profe; putting sheepe on the iland at our first comeinge, and within the time aforesaid weare very fatt; which seemed to mee very strange, seeinge that there was noe good feedinge for them, onlie wild hearbs and longe grasse, and noe fresh water.

Alsoe within a river half a mile distannt from the waterringe place[3] wee tooke much fishe with our saine, att one draught above 300 fishes of 1½ foote longe and more, lyke a breame, very good fish; not any formerlye knowne to bee taken in this river; which fishe att all

---

[1] Perhaps = 'tinnen,' 'made of tin.' Cf. Sylvester's trans. of Du Bartas: 'Thy tinnen chariot shod with burning bosses.'

[2] Revett confirms this account, and adds that 'there was found upon the iland the Flemishe jenneralls name wrytten in tynn in the mounethe of Apryll last; so that wee immagine they had a favorabell and quyck passadge.'

[3] This is the stream known as the Salt River. Mr Sclater informs me that there are no fish in it now.

tymes when our companie were desirous to eate fishe, wee went and tooke within twoe howers as much as both the ships could eate in a daye. And at the rivers mouth at our comeinge away where wee waterred wee took 3,500 mulletts at twoe draughtes, which served us well in our voyage. And in my opinion the reason whie there was much store of fishe at this tyme was because the baye in 15 daies before was full of whales playinge on the water, which the fishe did shunne and came neere the shoare, where the whale could not come at them.

Our time beinge longe at Saldania by reason of settinge upp our pinnace, haveinge little buysines, for recreation my selfe with other of the marchannts would take our walke to the topp of the hill called the Table, which before wee retourned found it to bee a wearysome journey. And beinge on the topp of the Table wee des[c]ryed to the northward as it seemed to us a harbour, and that the sea entred into lande; which the next daye, haveinge leave of the Generall, my selfe with ten persons more, well armed, went by the rivers side untill wee came to the place supposed to be a harbour; but when wee came at it wee soone perceaved yt to bee but a standinge poole of two miles or more aboute, not above a fathome water, beinge fresh water which came from the mountaynes when it raigned, the sea comeinge neere it but entered not, but upon a storme[1]. This water out of this poole or pond runneth into the river where wee take our fish, and from thence takes his issue into the sea; which is the reason that the water of this river is brackish and not salte, notwithstandinge the sea floweth daylie into it, that weare it not for the fresh water which cometh out of the mountaines it would bee as salte as the sea. It is to bee understoode

[1] This 'standing poole' is what is now known as the Riet Vlei, which discharges into Salt River Mouth by a broad, shallow channel running parallel to the coast line.

that this river is a mile from the place where the ships doe water; that beinge very fresh and good, proceeding from divers springes, which cometh from the mountaynes. In this jorney up the river wee sawe many estreges and the footinge of elaphaunts, much fish and fowle &c.

Although I have beene over tedyous aboute this place, which is soe well knowne to dyvers of our nation, yet seeinge it is but my labour to write, and at the readers courtesie to thinke as hee pleases, therefore I will not omitt breiflie to shewe my opinion concerninge this place of Saldania, which I hould to bee very healthfull and comodious for all that trade the East Indyes[1]. As alsoe if it were manured, I am of opinion that it would beare any thinge that should bee sowen or planted in it, as for all kinde of graine, wheate, barlye &c., besides all kinde of fruite, as orenges, lemons, limes and grapes, &c. Beinge planted and sowne in due time, and kept as it ought to bee, if this countrye were inhabited by a civell nation, haveinge a castle or forte for defence against the outrage of those heathenish people and to withstand any forraine force, in shorte time it might bee brought to some civillitie, and within fewe yeares able of it selfe to furnish all shipps refreshinge, for the countrye at present doth abound with fishe and flesh in greate plentie; with [while?] manie kinde of good heaps [of] stonns to build are at hand; onely timber wilbe somewhat tedious in fetchinge, which is aboute three miles of; but if the cattle of the countrye were used to drawe, as in other countryes (which they may easilie bee brought unto), it would not seeme soe tedious. Nowe howe necessarie this place would bee for

[1] Revett says that their sick men were much benefited by their stay on land, except a 'Peguan' they had on board, who died on August 26 of consumption; 'who beinge borne and brought up a heathen untill his beinge in Ingland, yet departed this world a Chrystean and in lyke sorte was burryed by our preacher; his fervencye in prayer was much to the Almighty God for forgivenes of his synnes.'

shippinge to refresh their sicke men, both out and home, I leave it to your better judgments. Though the refreshinge of shipps travailinge the East Indyes bee very comodious, yet there is other hopes to bee expected out of this mayne countrye in future tyme, viz. first, these people beinge brought to civilitie may likewise in tyme bee brought to knowe God, and understand our language, and wee theirs, and by them learne of other trades which maye bee within the countrye; this beinge in the middest of two rich countries, as Ginnee and Moseambique, and noe doubt but here are store of elaphaunts teeth within the land, for that wee sawe the footinge of many. If all this faile, yet lampe oyle and hides will bee had and seales skinns, to free some parte of the charge in the meane time. Thus much concerninge this place of Saldania, where wee weare settinge up our pinnace and refreshinge us from the 14 of Julie to the 16th (*sic*) of September: which haveinge lanched the pinnace, and made John Lufkin master and putt into her three monneths victualls with other necessaries, and named her the Good Hope, wee came aboard, makinge us readye to sett saile.

Sept. 19. Wee sett saile from Saldania Roade in the eveninge. I saie aboute ten in the forenoone turninge out the baye, the winde at N.N.W., and in the eveninge beeinge out of the baye it fell (at night) calme; and haveinge a greate sea sagginge us to the shoare, wee ankored upon a ledge of the shoare, in 15 fathome fowle grownd, and here wee roade untill two in the morninge, our boates taken in.

Sept. 20. In the morninge aboute two after midnight, we wayed with a fresh gale at E.S.E., our cable beinge much galled with the rockes; the pinnace in wayinge brake her anker, and the Union longe in weyinge; the winde increasinge and veeringe to the S.S.E., and wee steered S.W. & by S. Much winde, that wee tooke in our toppsailes and bonnetts; at which tyme the Unyon came up with us and putt out her antient upon the poope, which signe wee knewe not the meaninge, neyther could wee understand what they said, but we suspected that it was some maste crackt. This night there blewe soe much winde with an over growne sea that wee were faine to lye a hull with our mizen. The Union staied with her mayne course and the pinnace hard by us; yet this night wee lost companie of the Union and pinnace.

Sept. 21. Much winde at S.S.E. And aboute eight in the morninge wee sett our fore course and wee ste[ered a]way at S. & by West and S.S.W. Haveinge lost companie of our consortes, wee bare little saile to staie for them, thinkinge that they had bene astarne us. And seeinge them not to come, wee sett more saile, supposinge that they ranne from us of purpose, for that wee kept lightes all the nightes before. And this night the storme beganne againe more then the other night paste, that wee tooke in all saveinge our forecourse. With that wee steered awaie all night S. & by West, the winde at S.E. by S. and S.S.East. Towards the morninge wee had lesse winde and more easterlye.

Sept. 22. The winde variable betwixt the N.E. to the N.N.W., a stiffe gale, and wee stoode our course betwixt the S.E. and S.S.E., makeinge as much haste as the winde would permitt us, haveinge lingred these twoe daies for our consorts.

Sept. 23. The winde at N.W., steeringe our course betwixt the S.E. and E.S.E. at noone, at which time wee made accompt to bee to the east of the Cape Bona Esperanza. All this night our course at East.

. . . .

Sept. 26. ...In the morninge aboute eight wee had sight of land unexpected, supposinge ourselves to bee 40 leagues to the eastward of Cape Dagullas[1]. Then wee

---

[1] C. Das Agulhas.

tacked aboute, and stoode all daye at S.E. and S.E. & by S. A fresh gale, faire weather.

. . . .

October 1. ...Aboute eleven this daye wee had sight of land aboute seven leagues of us, supposinge it to bee Baya Formosa[1]; at which time wee tacked aboute and sounded, butt found noe ground; and then wee steered awaye S. & by West. At six in the eveninge the winde came at E.S.E., a fresh gale, and wee steered away N.E. Raynie weather.

Oct. 2. In the morninge the winde N.E. and N.E. & by E., and wee stoode our course S.E. & by S. and S.E. This daye wee had sight againe of land, which bare of W.N.W. At noone per observation 33 d. 30 minutes.

Oct. 3. The winde at N.W. and N.N.W., a stiffe gale. Wee stoode our course North East and by East amonge. This daye wee finde a corrent to the southward. Haveinge observed, weare in 34 d. 50 m.

Oct. 4. ...This daye at noone wee had againe sight of land, bearinge N. & by East of us. In the afternoone some darke weather and raine. Wee seeinge the land to trend away as wee went N.E. & by E., then wee tacked and stoode S. & by East. Little winde all night.

. . . .

Oct. 7. ...Much winde, that wee shortned our saile and tooke of our bonnetts, beinge very foggie weather and raine, in which the winde came northerlie, unconstant and variable; little winde.

. . . .

Oct. 26. Wee had the winde variable betwixt the West and South; our course E. & by South to double Cape Romania up [upon ?] Saint Lawrence, because our Generall was determined to goe to the southward of itt. This night some raine.

---

[1] Linschoten's 'Baya Fermosa,' apparently Plettenberg Bay.

Oct. 27. The winde at S.S.E. In the morninge wee weare faire by the head land of Saint Lawrence, the Cape Romania beeinge E. & by North of us, by judgment 25 leagues. The winde tooke us shorte that wee could lye but E.N.E. Wee were thwarte of Cape Saint Sebastian[1]. Wee sawe many fires on the mountaines this night, beinge a lowe land by the waterside, and soe risinge highe towards the mountaynes.

. . . .

Oct. 29. Wee had againe sight of Cape St. Sebastian, with the winde at E.S.E.; and wee stoode east untill nine in the morninge, a stiffe gale. Not beinge able to double Cape Romania, the maister perceiveinge impossibilitie in longe time to passe it, hee tould the Generall thereof; and it was resolved not to lye beatinge too and againe, but lett rise our tackes and beare up betwixt Saint Lawrence and the mayne; which was at instant effected, and wee steered away at N.W. & by West. Aboute three in the afternoone wee weare thwarte Cape Santa Maria, which is the southermost head land of the mayne of Saint Lawrence, and lyeth next hand from Cape Sebastian W. & by North and E. & by S. Cape Sebastian riseth with two hummocks, the uttermost higher then the other, with white sand on the topp of it. Cape Romania riseth with two high hills like shugar loaves, which seemeth to be of from the mayne....

Oct. 30. ...This daie wee had sight of land, in latt. 24 d. 40 m. Wee sounded, but noe ground in 70 fathome. The land wee sawe bore east of us.

Oct. 31. ...At noone wee observed, and were in 33[2] d.

---

[1] Linschoten shows 'C. de S. Roman' and 'C. de S. Sebastiano,' the former being apparently the 'Cap Andavaka' and the latter the 'Faux Cap' of modern French maps. Davis (*Purchas*, i. 448) places 'the Cape of S. Sebastian' in lat. 25° 45', and long. 25° from the Cape of Good Hope.

[2] This must be an error for 23. Revett gives the latitude as 23° 30.

35 m., thwarte Cape Saint Augustine, which is heigh land. In the eveninge the land was N.N.W. of us.

. . . .

Nov. 10. The winde in the morninge began to blowe hard betwixt the S. and the S.W., and wee steered E.N.E. Aboute ten in the morninge much thunder, with clowdye weather, little winde; at which time there arose three spoutes within a myle round aboute us, which made us to take in all our sayles, except our fore saile to steere before it, if any of these spouts chanced to come at us; but it pleased God that they came by us very neere butt hurte us not. All this daye after wee had the winde variable, and wee steered as the winde would permitt us. These spouts weare at the breakinge up of the westerley monsonne: for in six months after we had never but easterly winde and faire weather.

. . . .

Nov. 13. The winde North East, and wee steered away E.S.E. In the eveninge wee sounded, supposinge to bee on the head of the shoalds of Saint Lawrence[1], but wee found noe ground. By observacion at noone 16 d. 8 m.

. . . .

Nov. 22. Wee had the winde at S.E. and E.S.E. Aboute ten in the forenoone wee had sight of an iland, which was supposed to be the iland of Comora; but about five in the afternoone wee had sight of annother iland to the northward of us some 12 leagues, verye high land, knowinge it to be Comora by the heigh of itt. The other iland was E.S.E. of us, which wee tooke to bee the iland of Moilla[2]; but it was nott knowne perfectlie to any of us. By observacion at noone weare in 12½ degrees.

Nov. 23. The winde variable betwixt the N.W. and N.E., and againe to the E.S.E., and wee stoode our course

---

[1] The modern Pracel Bank. [2] Mohilla.

towards the N.E. and by E., for soe the iland of Comora bare of us. In the eveninge weare within three leagues of the iland. We sounded and had noe ground in 100 fathome. This daye noone wee observed and weare in 11 d. 38 m.

Nov. 24. Beeinge neere unto the shoare of Comora, our Generall caused the skiffe to be manned (the winde beeinge calme, that wee could not gett in with our shipp), sent her towards the shoare, where there weare many people, which made signes to our men to come on land; butt our men, seeinge canoes a fishinge, went to speake with them, and would have had them come aboard our shipp; which they refused, but told them that there was noe water to bee had on that iland, there drinke beeinge for the most parte the water of coker nutts. The skiffe returned aboute noone, at which time wee had some rayne, with a little gale at south. Wee stood alonge the iland. Wee found a current settinge S.W.

Nov. 25. In the morninge wee weare aboute a myle from a baye betwixt twoe mountaines. The skiffe was sent to sound to see whether there weare anchoringe for our shipp within the baye; whoe shortlie retorned with twoe of the countrye people, which they brought against their wills, whoe enformed us that there was little water or good wood on that iland, and for ankoring there was 30 fathome within muskett shott of the shoare. These twoe men which were brought aboard our Generall entreated kindlie, and gave some toyes of little worth and sufferred them to departe in their canoa, tellinge us that aboute annother pointe there was water to bee had. Soe determyninge to have gone thither, the winde fell calme, soe that wee weare not able to gett aboute the pointe; and, our boate towinge us ahead, wee came to anker within the baye in 20 fathome water, good ground, butt soe neere the shoalds that our shipp had scarcelie scope enough to wend up[1], wee ridinge within a mile of the shoare; and many people upon the shoare makinge signes for us to come aland; which beeinge late we could not effect this night.

Our enterteynement att the Iland of Comora.

Nov. 26. The next daye the Generall sent the skiffe againe on land well mande, wherein went the maister, whoe spake with some of the people by the water side out of the boate, but landed not; but they tould him there was butt little water, but what their countrie did affoard wee should have; and with that awnsweare the pinnace retourned with the maister. And the same daye the two men that went from the shipp the daie before sent some hens aboard, and some of the people of the countrye brought coquer nutts and some goats to sell, which were bought for pintados[2]. And the same daye, being the 26, the Generall determyned to send the long boate and pinnace both aland with a present for the Kinge; which aboute ten in the forenoone it was effected, the maister, my selfe, and Mr. Glascocke goinge in the pinnace, and the longe boate hard by us, manned with small shott upon any occasion, for wee did hardlye trust their faire words. Butt when wee came to the shoare, those which were desirous to have the creditt to carrie the present, seeinge so manie people armed on the land, had noe greate stomacke to goe aland. Soe wee demanded pledges before any of us would land. Amonge those which came neere the boate there was one that could understand Portugues; to whome I desired to bring us pledges to staye in the boate, and twoe of us would land. Hee awnswered that he would first acquainte

---

[1] *I.e.* to turn with the tide.

[2] 'Painted' (Port. *pintado*) cloths, *i.e.* Indian chintzes, of which a supply had doubtless been brought for such emergencies.

the Kinge; which hee had soone effected, and retorned and brought twoe pledges with him into our boate; and I went aland alone with the present. Others which were appointed to goe in that buysines made excuses; whether their harts failed, or seeinge soe many people on the strand, I knowe not; but I was faine to goe with the present to the Kinges pallace, which was halfe a mile from the place wheare wee landed, a most confused waye to goe unto, beeinge narrowe crooked wayes. Butt in fine I was permitted [admitted?] to the Kinges presence, whoe was sittinge on the ground without the gate of his howse, with a companie of antient old men with their beards as white as snowe. The fellowe that spake a little Portugues gave mee to understand that they weare his noble men and counsellars. I approached neare unto him and offred him the present in the Generalls name; which he would not vouchsafe to touch with his hand, but cawsed his men to take it; and therewith offred forth his hand as though he would have mee to kisse it, whereat I bowed my selfe accordinge to the Turkisse manner. And for the present hee gave noe greate thanks, nether would he vouchsafe to looke on it as longe as I was in presence[1]. He caused mee to sitt downe upon the grasse hard by him, and by his interpretour demanded what our desire was; whereto I awnswered that our desire was to have wood and water, with some other refreshinge what his countrye did affoard, for our money. Then he demanded what countrye men wee weare; which when he knewe he bid us welcome into his countrye, and that he was sorrie that there was butt little wood and water neere thereaboute, but such as was wee should make bould with all, or any other thinge whatt-

[1] 'The present was a paire of knives, a shash or turbant, and a lookinge glasse with a combe in it, to the value of some 15 shillings in all; which the King received somewhat scornefully, not scarse looking on it, or at the least thinking it to be but of small value' (Covert).

soever his country did affoard. He demanded of me for the Generall, desiringe to see him. I tould him that the Generall would be glad to see him aboard our shipp, whether if it pleased him to goe I would remayne pledge a shoare for him. He seemed willinge, and went as farre as the waters side, wheare our boats weare; but when he came there his minde was altered by those which weare about him, and entreated to send the boats aboard for the Generall, and he would staie by the waters side with me untill his comeinge; which I excused as well as I could for that time, and wee parted with many complements. Hee had in his companie aboute fifty grave ould men, which weare his nobles, with a good guard besides; their weopons greate knives made with a round edge, like the fishermens choppinge knives which they use to cutt fishe in Portugall, very keene and bright. The Kinge was apparrelled after the Turkish manner, with a tucke[1] upon his heade, and a shorte coate of scarlett cloth. I surmise that the Kinge doth understand Portugues, for that at my first comeinge to him he bid me welcome, sayinge 'Ben vemde, Sor[2]'; but after I could not have one word more from him. He is a man of a middle age of a reasonable stature, and doth stand soe much upon his points after his manner as a greater kinge. At my comeinge aboard I enformed the Generall what passed with the Kinge; and the same daie, not longe after my comeinge aboard, the Kinge sent a fatt cowe to the Generall by his enterpretour, desiringe him to come aland; which he promised to doe the next morninge. Soe giveinge them some toyes, they departed.

And the next daye the Generall, accompanyed with Mr. Rivatt and Mr. Glascocke, went towards the shoare, but

---

[1] Turban; cp. *Purchas*, i. 165: 'The apparell of the better sort is a tucke on their heads....'

[2] *Bemvindo*, *Senhor*: '(You are) welcome, sir.' Probably the King only knew one or two phrases of this kind, picked up from Portuguese visitors.

meanlie guarded to goe amonge such faithlesse people; but haveinge bene at the Kings pallace and spoken with him, he retourned aboard in safetie (God be thanked), comendinge greatlie the good behaviour of the people, which to outward shewe was extraordinarie to other which [are?] almost rude in respect of these; for whether it bee their ordinary behaviour or noe I doe not knowe[1]; but they weare soe full of complements that made mee suspect them the more, knowinge that by their freindship with the Portugalls they had learned it of them, and therefore the more to bee doubted. But in the time of our beeinge there, our people went aland and cutt such wood as the countrye did affoard; butt little or noe water to bee had, for all the people did drinke out of a little well which they had made, which would not yeild a tonne a daie. And the countrie people thought us to bee soe bare of water that the poore would bringe us water to sell in coker shells, notwithstandinge the Kinge gave order that none of the countrie people should not take out any water out of the well but for us; but [when?] wee sawe that it would bee tedious to have water wheareas there was not sufficient for the people of the countrye to drink, wee gave them faire words, intendinge to departe the next daie.

---

[1] Revett gives the natives high praise: 'the humane dysseplyne which is amongst them is worthy memmorye, for that boath others and myselfe, havinge travelled in many forren countreyes, both among Chrystians and heathens, never sawe the lyke, both for curtesye, fydellety and carriadge amongst themselves and converse with straungers.' He notes, by the way, that 'they have three markes burned of their faces whilst they are yonge, to say, one of the each syde of the eye and one upon the forehead betweene the eye browes; which makes them saye the Moores of the iland of Comora have five eyes. It is a great disfiguringe to ther faces, both of men and women beinge personable and well lymmed.' Covert also commends them: 'They seeme to have a very civill government amongst them, for at their meeting in the morning they will shake hands each with other, and speake one to another, which to us seemed to bee their kinde and friendly salutations one to another. They are verie modest, streight, big limmed, and very comely in gesture, both men and women.'

One thinge I sawe amonge these people which I thinke fewe Christians would have done the like; for one of our men straglinge in the woods had left his sword careleslie and had forgott wheare hee laid it; which was found by one of the country people and caried to the Kinge; which when the Kinge sawe, hee thought that the fellowe had stolne it, and therefore apprehended him and sent the sword aboard and demanded whether any of the people had stolne it from us; which if he had, that the partie from whome it was stolne should come aland to see the partie executed before his face. When the Generall had sent word unto him that it was forgotten in the woods, he sett the man at libertie by our entreatie; which justice I much admired to bee amongst such heathen people[1]. Whether it were in pollizie to entrapp us in greater matters, it is some thinge doubtfull; butt howsoever they did us noe hurte, because they could not; but wee quietlie bought such refreshinge as the countrye did yeild, as hens and goats, cokers and plantans. The goats are the fayrest that ever I sawe, and very fatt. Wee acquaynted not the people of the countrye of our departure, but told them that wee weare to staie for our consorte; which wee thinke was the reason they used us soe kindlie, expectinge better opportunitie at their leasure. Soe wee departed without takinge our leave.

Wee sett sayle from Comora.

Nov. 29. Wee sett saile from Comora, haveinge furnished our selves, as is afore said, with wood, oranges, lemons, some hens and goats, coker nutts, &c. With the winde of the shoare we steered our course West and by South untill four in the afternoone; then the winde tooke us shorte, and we steered awaye (as the winde did favour

---

[1] Covert tells the same story.

us) betwixt the N.E. and the N.W., with little winde all night.

. . . .

Dec. 3. ...In the morninge wee had sight of the land[1], which bare S.S.E. of us, aboute 20 leagues of. In the afternoone the winde came up betwixt the N. and the N.N.W., and wee veered [steered?] betwixt the N.E. and E.

Dec. 4. The winde variable betwixt the N.W. and N.E., and we tacked too and againe many times, as the winde veered upon us; and our course towards the east. In the eveninge wee had sight of an little iland called Nattall, aboute [ ] leagues of us N.West[2].

. . . .

Dec. 7. ...This daie wee found a current sett N.N.W. At noone observinge, we weare in 8 d. 15 m.

. . . .

Dec. 9. ...This day in the eveninge it was agreed to bare roome for the iland of Zenzabar[3], and wee steered away all night at N.W. and N.W. & by W.; fresh gale.

Dec. 10. Aboute two after midnight wee were within a mile of the land, beinge lowe land, that our men thought it to bee orizon untill wee came soe neere that wee decerned the trees on the shoare, and then suddenlie wee tacked aboute to the offinge untill day. At which time wee stoode alonge the land with a faire gale, sending our boate a head to sownd to finde an anchoringe place;

---

[1] 'About five of the clocke wee espyed the iland of Comora ageyne' (Revett).

[2] 'In the morninge about five of the clocke...wee had syght of Comora ageyne, and bore S.S.E. the eastermost part....About six of the clock wee espyed a small iland which boore N.W. of us on our larboard syde. It shewed ragged land' (Revett). The identification with the 'I. do Natal' of Linschoten's map (which is possibly meant for Aldabra I.) is evidently wrong.

[3] In order, Revett says, to obtain water and inquire for their consorts, Zanzibar having been named as a rendezvous in case of separation.

which goinge aboute a pointe of the land there was a greate baye with broken ilands to the offinge aboute two miles. Neere to those ilands the pinnace laye; where wee ankored in 14 fathome, good ground, but else where all aboute was nothinge but rocks[1].

Dec. 11. The Generall sent the skiffe towards the mayne iland to see if they could have any speech with the countrye people, to demand for wateringe and other refreshinge. And comeinge to the shoare they spake with some of the countrye, but could nott learne any thinge by them; but returned aboard and tould the Generall that there was a faire river to goe in and 12 fathom water at the entrye, and 4½ and 5 fathome within, and there was one ashore that could understand Portugues but they knewe not what he said. Soe in the afternoone the Generall sent againe the skiffe, sendinge myselfe in her to understand of those which spake Portugues for water and other refreshinge; but att my comeinge aland I found noe bodie to speake with; and beeinge towards night wee retourned aboard without any further veiwe of any thinge to bee had.

Dec. 12. The next daye I retourned againe aland, and went with the pinnace into the river about two miles up, wheare wee sawe some people, which ranne from us; but at length there came out of the woods some eight persons, and wee made them signes to speake with them, and by signes we understood that they would have one of us to come aland, and that one of them would come to speake with us. Soe beeinge deepe ozie ground that we could not land but must bee above the knee in oze, therefore two of the companie carryed me aland, and then they made signes that they would have butt twoe of us to staie aland, which I did accordinglie. And as soone as the

---

[1] Covert gives the latitude of their anchorage as 5° 20′. Revett says 5° 27′.

rest were retorned into the boate, they came downe two of them without weopons. And there first salutacion was that that iland did belonge to the Portugalls: that if wee weare Portugalls wee should be welcome: if not, that they had nothinge to saie to us. Soe I tould them that wee weare Portugalls and their freinds: that wee onlie desired to have water and fresh victualls for our money[1]. But he could not tell us (or would not) of any water, but that first hee would advise the Kinge of our comeinge, and would be with us againe in the morninge and bringe us awnsweare; with which wee departed. And rowinge downe the river, wee made towards some which wee sawe fishinge, which before ranne from us but, seeinge us to talke with the others, stood nowe still untill wee came at them. Soe by signes wee demanded for water; and he tould us that behinde a pointe there was water. Soe I gave drinke, aquavita and some toyes which wee carryed in the boate, and he went with us to shewe us the place, which was aboute two mile from thence, where he brought us to a little springe of fresh water, which came out of a claye ground, not all of the best nor any greate quantitie, but such as it was wee carryed aboard to the Generall to taste it, and tould him that at this place we might fill some two or three tonnes every daie; which they seemed satisfied. Besides I tould the Generall that the partie had tould us that it was the Portugalls iland: that except wee weare Portugalls they had nothinge to saie to us: and that the iland was called Pemba (which untill this time our Generall, maister, and all tooke to bee Zenzabar). With us wee brought the blacke aboard that shewed us the water, to whome the Generall gave some trifles and sent againe aland, and some of our men to

[1] Covert says: 'Master Jordan told them that although our ship were an English ship, yet he was a Portugall merchant and the goods in the ship were Portugals goods.'

make a hole for the water to raine into, for the better fillinge the barricas[1] &c. While our men weare makinge the wateringe place, there came some of the countrie people downe, which seemed of good fashion, and tould our people that further within the woods there was store of water. And they came aboard our shipp to speake with the Generall, leavinge twoe of our men aland as pledges; whoe when they came aboard told the Generall that hee was the Kinges brother[2], and that the Kinge had sent him to furnish us with any thinge that the countrye did affoard; and told him howe the Hollenders had bene at Mozambique[3], and had taken it. Hee staied all the night aboard, and the Generall had much conference with him; in soe much that our Generall and maister weare soe confident of them that the next daie all the marchannts and the cheefe of the shipp were sent ashoare, to accompanie the Kinges brother. It made them soe confident because these men had tould them that the Portugalls weare their enimies and made slaves of them as manie as they could take, and therefore had noe trade with them; which was contrarie to what the poore men which I spake with at first told mee. Soe some six of us went aland with the supposed Kinges brother, haveinge left pledges for them. At our landing they entreated us

---

[1] Port. *barrica*, a water-cask.

[2] 'One of them was the Kings brother, who instantly shewed us a silver ring, whereon was ingraven the number of villages and houses or cottages in the iland, and said he was ruler and governor of all those places' (Covert).

[3] According to Covert the rumour 'that fifteen saile of Hollanders had lately taken Mosembege and put all the Portugals to the sword' was brought from another part of the island by the *Ascension's* pinnace, which had been sent thither for cattle. The reference is to the second siege of Mozambique (July—August, 1608) by the Dutch under Verhoeff. The outer town was sacked and burnt, but the besiegers could make no impression on the fortress itself and were forced to depart without achieving their object. See Mr. Albert Gray's *Pyrard de Laval*, ii. 225–9, and the authorities there quoted.

to goe with them a little further into the woods, where the pledges weare, and they should come with us; besides wee should see if there weare any cattle come downe. And for myne owne parte, although loth to trust to there curtesies, yet I went with the rest, as many goe to church for companie rather then for zeale; yet because I would not bee accompted a coward I said little. But when wee had traveled within the woods halfe a mile wee came to a little cottage where the pledges weare; and at our entringe into the howse, wee must passe betwixt a lane of armed men, some 50 persons with their darts, swords, bowes and arrowes. But seeinge them wee provided our small force if they had offred anye injurie, although to small purpose in the woods amongst soe manie; but wee made noe staie, tooke our pledges and departed without any broyle; which had it not bene that there was one of their companie left aboard our shipp, I thinke that it had bene our last home in this world; but I made slight of it, because that he that feares danger is accompted a coward. Notwithstanding, at my comeinge aboard, I did not omitt to acquainte the Generall therewith, both in publique and private; but awnsweare was made that of certaine they were honest men, with as much confidence as before; in soe much that the same daie our Generall in person accompanyed with my selfe and divers others, went some twoe miles from the shipp with the Moore which was lefte aboarde, to seeke better water. He carryed us some halfe a mile within the woods to seeke it, but could finde none, onlie some hole which the raine had filled. Soe beeinge a troublesome waye to passe, beinge soe thicke of bushes, our Generall would goe noe further. The fellowe telling us that a little further there was water; upon which words I told the Generall that if water weare soe farre from the waters side, that it weare in vayne to seeke it, for that when wee had found it wee could not fetch it, beeinge soe farre within the woods, besides the endangeringe of our men amongst the woods in a countrye of such faithlesse people, with some other speeches; which the Generall harkned unto and returned to the waters side; beinge glad when I came and sawe the boate, for I doubted that whiles he drewe us into the woods, that some might steale away our boats and wee remayne in the woods to have our throats cutt; which was one of the reasons I alledged to the Generall which made him retourne the sooner; but Gods name be praysed, all this fell out well. In this meane while wee weare seekinge water, Mr. Grove, Mr. Rivett, and some other weare makinge merrye aland amongst the countrye people[1]; soe that had they sett upon us both wayes, they had slaine most parte of us; which they pretended[2] to have done if wee had not retorned but followed the fellowe untill he had brought us to the supposed water; but God provided better for us. His name be alwayes blessed. Amen.

Wee retourninge to the wateringe, wee tooke in the maister and Mr. Rivett into the skiffe and retourned aboard, leaveinge the boatswaine with the longe boate to take in the water; at which time the boatswaine went into the woods to the cottage, wheare hee perceived some in Portugall apparrell, with rapyers, and many other strangers which had not bene yet seene, which hidd themselves from them; which he perceiveing made hast to retourn to the boate, and quicklie laded the water and came aboard with this newes to the Generall; whereupon he mistrusted some treason pretended, and that all of us had scaped a scowringe; whereupon hee determined to make an end in the

---

[1] This is not borne out by Revett's narrative. He represents himself as standing on his guard, having suspicion that treachery was meant.

[2] Intended.

morninge to take in what water wee might and a david[1] which was made aland neere the wateringe place, and soe to leave them, if wee could gett noe other refreshinge. And with the longe boate it was concluded to send the skiffe with armed men to attend the longe boate while they weare takinge in the water and david; which was effected the next morninge, being the 19th of December, 1608.

Dec. 19. In the morninge, as is formerlie concluded, the longe boate and skiffe was sent aland to fetch the rest of the water and david which was there made, and to stand upon ther guard, that rather then to endanger any of our men to leave all behinde. The longe boate puttinge of before the skiffe in the meane tyme while shee was makinge readye, at their comeinge aland there came twoe of the cheefest, well knowne to the boatswaine, came to him, demandinge whether our shipp weare to sett saile, because they sawe our saile abroad a dryinge, haveing rayned that night before. Hee tould them the cause as is aforesaid, and that the Generall, marchannts and maister was comeinge in the skiffe, which was then put of from the shipp; wherewith they seemed satisfyed and departed hastelie, as wee suspected to advise the rest thereof to performe their exploite which they pretended. The pinnace our skiffe comeinge to the shoare, the people landed with their armour, and kept by the waters side neare the longe boate, for feare of cuttinge of the boats from them, sendinge one of the saylours[2] who could speake Portugues to the cottage to shewe the Kinges brother that the marchannts were come aland to speake with him, from the Generall. He demanded whie the Generall came not aland and the maister, as they had promised yesternight. He awnswered that he knewe not, but the marchannts could satisfie him.

---

[1] 'Which is a piece of wood or timber wherewith we hale up our ancor' (Covert): in modern parlance, a 'davit.'

[2] Covert gives his name as Nicholas White.

And, because he sawe more armed men then formerlie, standinge in some feare, he told them that the maister was at the waters side. He made there but little staie but came presentlie away and tould us that there were Portugalls or men in Portugall apparrell with their rapiers[1]; and after him came the Kinges brother, entreatinge us to goe up with him to his cottage. But when he sawe not the maister, as the youth had tould, and our men armed in other manner then in former time, he beganne to alter his countenance, and tould us that there weare cattle brought downe for us, if wee would goe up to fetch them. Awnsweare was made that if it pleased them to bringe the cattle or any thinge else they had to sell to the waters side, that wee weare there readye to receyve it and paye for it. Nowe perceiveinge that wee suspected their trecherie he, lieu of blushinge, he turned from the hewe of a Mulata to bee white; and presentlie went his waye without more words, seemeing discontent. Not longe after came downe annother of the gentlemen that had bene aboard, disconte[nte]d that wee would not goe to fetch the cattle that was brought for us: that the partie that brought the cattle was sicke and could not bringe it downe to us; therefore entreated to have one of our men to goe up and see the cattle and bringe downe some orenges and lemons that they had provided to send aboard to the Generall for a present, in recompence of his courtesie done them. Upon his earnest entreatie, and haveing one of the companie[2]

[1] 'Six Portugales, in long branched damaske coats lined with blew taffata, and under the same white callico breeches' (Covert).

[2] 'The young man that went was borne in Greenewich, his name being Edward Churchman, who afterward dyed in Mombasa of a bloudy fluxe, as I was credibly informed of the Portugals. Also, while wee made our abode at Pemba, the Portugals were about to man a Flemmish hulke, which had wintered in Mombasa, to come to take our shippe; but hearing of the force of our shippe they altered their minds. The people of this iland of Pemba be very cowardly people and dare doe nothing of themselves without the inciting of the Portugals' (Jones).

that spake Portugues offringe his service and entreated to goe fetch them, the boatswaine, seeinge his willingnes without feare, bid goe quicklie and make noe tarryinge at any hand, and to have an eye of what he might see by the waye. The gentleman went with him. Hee had not bene wantinge aboute halfe an howre before our men weare sett upon at the watring place, which was aboute a butt shott from the waters side, but soe covered with trees and bushes that at the waters side ther could nothinge bee perceived by those which weare the sentrees; but as soone as they beganne to shoote there arrowes at them, those that weare fillinge there barricos with water came secreetlie thorough the bushes to the water side, stealing one and other, cryinge "Arme, arme, our men are slaine." The doggs, seeinge them to flie from there arrowes, attempted to kill them with their lances, and killed one of our men, beinge first hurte with an arrowe in the head. They gave eleven wounds to annother[1]. The rest of our men came to the waters side without any hurte, God be thanked. As soone as the centrells had the word they lett flye there musketts into the bushes. They fled presentlie. The wounded man was brought aboard; the other which was slaine wee knewe not what was become of him, untill the next daie that wee retorned aland wee found him in the bushes dead with manie wounds, as well arrowes as swords.

The next daie wee weent againe aland with our longe boate and skiffe well armed, with a flagge of trewse for a parley with them aboute a man which they had betrayed the daye before; but none would come to speake with us. They made many bravados out of the woods, not within shott, but would come noe neere to us; but sawe many

---

[1] Covert says that the man killed was named John Harrington, 'the boatswaines man,' and the one wounded Robert Buckler, 'Master Ellanors man.' Jones describes the latter as 'a servant of John Elmors, being one of our masters mates.'

of them which issued out of the woods at many places; which perceiveinge it vayne to loose any more time, wee made a volley of shott into the woods, and went into the wateringe place and brought away the dead man and the david, both lyinge neere together. The man wee burried as wee went aboard, upon one of the ilandes.

This daie in the afternoone aboute three of the clocke wee sett saile, beinge the fourth daie wee had bene in this unluckye place, haveinge had much discontent for a little stinkinge water. Haveing formerlie agreed to meete the Unyon at Zanzebar, which was in sight of us, not above ten leagues from us, yet wee had never the grace to goe thither, butt wee stoode our course, with a stiffe gale at N.E., at N.N.W. along the coaste. And this night aboute midnight wee came aground with our shipp upon a bancke of sand, with all sailes bearinge and a stiffe gale; butt God bee thanked, the shipp flatted of againe[1] without any hurte, haveinge stucke faste aboute halfe an hower, the water very smooth, God providinge for us better then wee deserved. His name bee blessed and praysed for ever. This banke or broken iland wheare wee weare aground lyeth betwixt the iland of Pemba and the mayne land of Muylinde, neere to Mombassa, a towne of the Portugalls. But beinge cleare of this danger wee presentlie sounded and had noe ground in 50 fathome; and wee steered awaye all night E.N.E., sowndinge every twoe glasses, doubtinge to meete with some other sholes before daie; but God provided otherwise for us.

Dec. 21. In the morninge wee weare againe faire by the iland of Pemba standinge our course E. & by N. And aboute nine wee perceived the water to bee very white; wee sownded, and had 19 fathome, beeinge some three

[1] 'At that very instant the wind did lander, so that with the backing of our sayles asterne our ship went off, to our no little comfort' (Jones).

leagues of the shoare; at which time wee tackt aboute and stoode away N.N.West two glasses; at which time wee descried three saile which stoode towards the iland of Pemba. Our Generall cawsed the longe boate and skiffe to bee manned, and sent in each boate one of the maister his mates, willinge them to bringe the maister and some of the principall aboard, if they could fetch them up; which they had soone effected, for as soone as they came within muskett shott of them they strooke their sailes and stayed for them untill the shipp came up with them. At which time wee demanded from whence they weare. They said: Of Pemba. Our Generall willed one of our boats to bringe some of the cheifest aboard and some of our men to staie there untill further order; which they presentlie did effect, and brought aboard our shipp of mullattoes and negros to the number of 40 persons or there aboute, very lustie men, whereof some of them seemed to bee men of accompt[1]. At their comeinge aboard wee demanded from whence they came and whether bound. They awnswered that they came from Mombassa, and bound home to their dwellinge, which was at Pemba, beeinge marchannts that traded from place to place. Further they tould us that in their pengaos or proas[2] they had some quantitye of Indian comodities, wherewith they traded from place to place, which they bought at Mombassa in barter of rice and other provision which they did usuallie carrie from Pemba thether and to other places on the coaste. Our Generall

[1] Covert says that 'sixe or eight were pale and white, much differing from the colour of the Moores; yet being asked what they were, they said they were Moores, and shewed us their backes all written with characters; and when we affirmed them to bee Portugals, they then told us the Portugals were not circumcised.'

[2] Linschoten (p. 10) says: 'These *pangaios* are made of light planks and sowed together with cords, without any nailes.' See also *Lancaster's Voyages*, p. 26, where a 'pangaia' is described as 'a vessell like a barge, with one matsaile of coco nut leaves. The barge is sowed together with the rindes of trees, and pinned with wooden pins.' *Prao* is the Malay *prāū*, 'a boat.'

told them howe treacherouslie their countrye men of Pemba had dealt with us, betrayinge us, and slaine some of our men; whereat they weare much dismaied, and would seeme to denie what they had formerlie tould us, to bee of Pemba. But our hardie maister, with some others which I omitt, made foolish signes unto them, shewinge the yards arme, that they should there bee hanged; which putt them in a desperate feare, although there was noe such matter ment; yet the maister callinge one of the cheefest into his cabin, understandinge that hee had some insight in navigation and understoode the seacard, the fellowe, fearinge that it had bene some other matter, seeinge he had formerlie made such signes unto him, spake to the rest of them that remayned without, as wee conjecture, to provide themselves to dye. Some of the quarter maisters beinge on the decke perceived a knife in his sleeve as he went into the cabin, whoe came and told mee of it, standinge with the Generall talkinge with the rest of the marchannts of Pemba. I advised the Generall and presentlie he sent the boatson to tell the maister thereof, whoe demandinge him for his knife he denyed it. Soe perceiveinge that they knewe that it was in his sleeve, hee made a shewe to draw it and deliver[1] it to them, but suddenlie drewe it and stabd the maister upon the lefte pappe neere the harte, and offerred to doe the like to Mr. Rivett; and therewith he gave a lowde crye, that his fellowes that weare without hearinge him beganne likewise to stabb those that weare neere unto them, as the preacher, Mr. Tindale[2], in the side, and

[1] The MS. has 'delivered.'

[2] Simon Tindall, of Queens' College, Cambridge, graduated B.A. in 1596 and M.A. in 1600 (information kindly furnished by Mr J. W. Clark). He was incorporated at Oxford 11 July, 1606 (Clark's *Reg. Univ. Oxon.*). 'Sir John Tyndall' (probably a relative) and others recommended him to the Company as 'a man of some 30 yeares of adge and well quallified with divers good parts,' and he was thereupon 'thought fitt to be hired to goe in the voyadge' (*Court Minutes*, Jan. 29, 1608). As will be seen later, he died at Burhānpur in the autumn of 1609—the first English clergyman to die in India.

Mr. Glascocke in the necke[1]; which the boye perceyveing cryed out "Kill, kill, my maister is killed." With which word the Generall and the rest tooke such armes as weare next hand and beganne to kill as faste as they could; soe that in very shorte time they weare all overboard, either dead or alive, for manie of them lept overboard, which weare slaine in the water by those that weare in our boats, Soe that I thinke not one of them escaped[2], except a little boye and a mayde of some eight yeares olde; one was taken up in the chaines, and the other out of the pengoa or prowe; which was a girle, which when she sawe her mother drowned, she lept overboard three tymes, that wee had much a doe to save her. This man that first beganne to stabbe the maister three men could not kill him; his owne knife would not enter his flesh; but with much adoe three men cutt his throate with annother knife, where little or noe blud came out; soe they threwe him overboard halfe dead. There weare three of the boats, one of which sett saile with some twoe or three men to carrie newes to Pemba. Had not God the better provided for us they might have slaine the most parte of us, they haveinge all knives aboute them provided for the purpose, and the most parte of our men in the boats and proas, and the rest within board not soe much as a knife aboute him, the maister haveinge a little before given order that none should weare his weopon, seeing that these people came unarmed. I knowe not in what pollicie he did it, but he was the first that was like to paie deere for it; beinge alwayes soe confident in his owne opinion that noe man must contradict him in any thinge; being soe farre in the

[1] In the back, according to Covert. These two, and the master, were the only Englishmen hurt; and they all recovered.

[2] Covert declares that five or six swam to one of their boats and thus escaped to shore. Jones confirms this, and adds that he 'was credibly informed by the Portugals of the great lamentation which was made for these Moores because they were of the cheife gentlemen of all the coast of Melinda, and of the blood royall.'

Generalls bookes that I pray God it end well. This is the end of three greate dangers passed by us within three daies, viz., first at Pemba by treason, secondlie upon the shoales of Mombassa by night, and lastlie by trecherie of these doggs aboard our shipp; all which the Lord by His mercyfull hand hath miraculouslie preserved us from emynent danngers. His name be blessed for ever more, Amen[1].

These pengaoes had in them of Indian comodities aboute 2000 duckatts worth, besides many good thinges which the saylers made pillage of of the best comodities, which did emport more then that was taken for the Companie our employers. Alsoe there was in them some rice and gravances[2] and other provisions, which our Generall

---

1 Revett, in his account of the incident, imputes no blame to the master. He says that the latter called one of the Moors into his cabin 'to shewe him his platt, to see yf hee could gather somethinge from him, my selfe bearinge him company, not mynding the least pretence of evyll ageynst him or them, as they imagined wee dyd. By this fellowes divelyshe pretence, as by his enterpryse hee undertooke, takinge us to bee Flemminges, wee were noe sooner set in the cabbyn but some of our company cam to us and bad us beware of him, for hee had a knyfe, and wyshed us to take it from him to avoyde a further inconvenience; the which omyttinge nott, although not affrayd, began to search for it; the which perceivinge, [he] dessembled the matter, sayenge hee had none, and shewed us with his ryght hand beades, keepinge his knyfe under his lefte arme covered with his gyrdell of checker worke callico; the which hee seeinge wee perceived, drewe it with his ryght hand, wee thinking hee would have given it to us. But the Devell being his master and a quyck helpour, unsuspected gave the master a stab with his knyfe so that by imagination hee had given him his deathes wownd, beinge so nye the harte, although (thanckes bee given to God) it proved otherwyse. Upon which enterpryse, by a watchworde given by this notorious vyllen at his comminge downe with us to the rest of his consortes, they began to fall a stabbing of those our men which stood by them, amongst the rest our preacher, Mr. Tyndall, and Mr. Glascocke, who received severall wowndes, though not mortall, and not so bad to passe as the maysters. Upon this occasyon wee made with them shorte worke, and brought most part of them by sundry wayes to their last home; givinge thanckes to God for this last deliverye, wherein the owld proverbe was verrefyed, that one myscheife comes syldome alone.'

2 Sometimes written 'garvances' (Sp. *garbanzos*), a term employed generally for the peas and beans used for food on board ship. Covert speaks of 'garvances or peason (being their country food).'

was minded to buye of them and let them goe; but they suspected some hard measure, which caused them to procure their owne destruction, and little benefitt to the Honourable Company. The maister beinge soe dangerouslie wounded as is aforesaid, Mr. Mellys[1] was to take charge, our surgeon doubtinge very much of the maisters recovery; which beinge thus ordered, he would not venter to goe betwixt the ilands and the mayne, an unknowne waye full of shoales and dangers, but bare roome the way wee came, to the southward of the iland of Pemba[2].

Dec. 22. The winde at E.N.E. Steeringe alonge the shoare of Pemba, and aboute noone wee weare thwarte the place where wee roode with our shipp....

Dec. 23. The winde at N.E. and wee steered E.S.E. untill five in the afternoone; at which time wee tacked aboute and stoode away N.N.West, and N. & by W., and sometimes at N.; the winde from the E.N.E. to the N.E.

. . . .

Dec. 26. The winde variable as before, and wee tacked too and againe divers times, beeinge neere the easter parte of the iland of Pemba; being a long iland, and the winde hanging contrarie, it was long before we could cleare our selves of it, except wee would goe farre to sea. This day at noone in lattitude 3 d. 55 m.

Dec. 27. The winde variable betwixt the N.E. and the E.S.E., and wee tacked too and againe to cleare our selves

---

[1] 'Captaine [Richard] Mellis of Plymmoth' was engaged by the Company on Feb. 19, 1608, and assigned to the *Ascension* as a master's mate.

[2] Jones gives the following account of their course from this point: 'We put out of the west end of the iland againe, determining to beate up for the iland of Socotora; but the winds hanging betweene the E. and E.S.E., and finding small helpe of the current, did altogether frustrate our determination. Then we determined to stand off to the southward some 200 or 300 leagues, thinking to finde the windes at E.S.E. But heere likewise we were frustrate of our hopes; for in the offing we found the wind to hang at the E.N.E. and at the E.N.E. & by E., that we lay beating in the sea'—till they reached the 'Desolate Ilands.'

of this iland which was neare unto us. At noone per observacion in lattitude 3 d. 45 m.

Dec. 28. The winde variable from the E. to the N.E. We tacked too and againe; sometymes the winde calme; and wee steered towards the east as the winde would permitt us. The dogged iland of Pemba bore of us N.W. At noone lattitude 3 d. 10 m.[1]

Dec. 29. The winde varyable as afore betwixt the N.E. and the E., and wee steered away as neere as the winde would give us leave. These two daies wee have found a current settinge to the [*blank*[2]] with a greate race, with much filth swimming on the water. At noone per observacion 3 d. 00 m.

Dec. 30. The winde at E., and wee steered away N.N.E. Aboute noone wee had sight of the mayne land of the coaste of Amylinde[3], and aboute six in the afternoone wee weare within three leagues of the land; and wee sownded and had 18 fathome water, hard sandye grownd. Here the land trends awaye N.E. & by E., a faire bould coaste. Wee sownded once more, being four leagues of, and had 60 fathome water. This coast is all alonge the strand white sand, and a lowe land per the waters side, and by judgment is neere to a towne of the Portugalls called Patty. At noone per observacion lattitude 2 d. 37 m.[4], and we stered of S.E. and S.E. & by E.

. . . .

Jan. 1 [1609]. Wee had the winde variable betwixt the N.N.E. and the E. Wee tacked too and againe, as the winde would permitt us. At noone by observacion had in lattitude 2 d. 35 minutes[5].

---

[1] Revett says 3° 30′, and the same on the following day.

[2] North-eastwards, according to Revett.

[3] Malindi.

[4] Revett gives 2° 25′. 'Patty' is the present 'Patta,' in 2° 10′ S.

[5] Revett says 3°.

Jan. 2. The winde at E. and S. and [by?] E., and wee stoode away N.N.E. At eleven in the forenoone wee had againe sight of land, the coaste of Melinde, and at eveninge it bore of us N.W. & by N., aboute seven leagues from us. Aboute midnight wee weare neare the land, and wee tacked aboute and steered of S. & by E.

Jan. 3. The winde betwixt the E.N.E. and the N.E. This daye in the morninge, beinge neere the mayne land of Melynde, we sownded and had, some four leagues of the shoare, 60 fathome, faire sand; and we steered away S.E. & by E. and as the winde would permitt us, determyninge to gett farther of the shoare to see if wee could finde a better winde. This daie there was a greate ripplinge of the water, which seemed to bee shold, but we sounded and had 50 fathome.

. . . .

Jan. 19. ...Aboute nine in the morninge wee descryed heigh land, which bare of us E. & by S. At three in the afternoone wee sawe other ilands, which wee made to bee four ilands, and in the eveninge they bare of us N. & by East some five leagues of[1]. And wee stoode with a slacke

---

[1] 'The 19th of January wee fell with many strange [ ] east from Pemba, named on the plott the ilands Do Almirante. In these ilands [ ] of fresh watter and cocker nutts; wher wee stayed in a very good road to refresh our selves [ ] watter untyll the first of February, not finding any people on the ilands' (Jourdain's letter in I. O. Records, *O.C.* 12). 'The 19 day of January wee espied many ilands, which the Portugals call by the name of Almaisant, being to the number of nine ilands, al unpeopled, as the Portugals write and affirme' (Covert). See also Appendix A.

The identification of these islands with the Amirante group was natural enough, if the voyagers' 'plot' was anything like the map given by Linschoten; but there can be no doubt from Jourdain's description that they were really the Seychelles, which lie to the north-east of the Amirantes.

The Seychelles, said to have been discovered by Soares in 1506, are shown in 16th century maps under the names of *Os Sete Irmanos* (The Seven Brothers) or *As Sete Irmanas* (The Seven Sisters). Under the latter title they appear in Linschoten's map, but far to the eastward of the cluster marked 'Do Almirante.' The group was first examined by an expedition despatched in 1742 by Mahé de la

saile all night untill towards the morninge, and then wee stoode in for the land to seeke water and other refreshinge. At noone per observacion 4 d. 20 m.[1]

Jan. 20. In the morninge, beeinge neere the land, wee slacked our saile and tooke out our skiffe to goe sowndinge before the shipp, and to seeke a good place to anker in. Soe they came to a small iland[2], beeing neerest unto us, which lyeth aboute twoe leagues to the north of the heigh iland[3], where they landed in a faire sandy cove, where wee might have ankored very well; butt because our men made noe signe of any water wee ankored not. Soe the boate retourned and brought soe many land tortells as they could well carrie. Soe wee stoode alonge towards the other ilands. The tortells were good meate, as good as fresh beefe, but after two or three meales our men would not eate them, because they did looke soe uglie before they weare boyled; and soe greate that eight of them did almost lade our skiffe. Goinge alonge by the ilands we found ten and twelve fathome within a league of the ilands; and two leagues of wee had twenty and thirty fathome faire shoaldinge. This eveninge we thought to have ankored at an iland which laye E.N.E. of us, which seemed to be a very fruitfull place and likelye of water;

Bourdonnais, then Governor of Mauritius and Bourbon, in whose honour the islands were for a time known as 'Iles de Bourdonnais' and 'Iles Mahé.' . Subsequently the present name was bestowed upon them in commemoration of Moreau de Séchelles, who was Contrôleur-Général des Finances in France in 1754–6 (*Hobson-Jobson*, 2nd ed., p. 815). The French formed a settlement there about 1770, but surrendered it to Commodore Newcome in 1794, and in 1815 the group was formally ceded to England.

The account given in the text is specially interesting, describing as it does the first visit of a British ship. The late Rear-Admiral Sir William Wharton, K.C.B., formerly Hydrographer of the Navy, who was personally acquainted with the Seychelles, was kind enough to examine both Jourdain's and Revett's (see Appendix A) narratives, and to make the identifications of the various islands given in the notes which follow.

[1] According to Revett, 4° 48′.

[2] North Island.

[3] Silhouette Island.

but beinge neere night, and perceyveinge some shoalds and rocks neere the land, and other ilands ahead of us, wee brought our tacks aboard and stoode to the offinge N.E. & by N., hopinge the next daie to finde good ankoringe at the other ilands which wee sawe further to the E.N.E. of us[1]. But in our course there was a small iland[2] which laye aboute two leagues of the shoare, which wee could not double but weare faine to goe betwixt the ilands and it, haveinge faire shoaldinge 15 and 20 fathome. This small iland is noe other then a rocke, alias ilheo. And being passed this rocke, wee stoode upon a tacke untill midnight, and then with a slacke saile wee stoode for the eastermost ilands with a fresh gale. Wee stoode W. & by N. and W.N.W., for soe wee had brought the body of the ilands of us; haveinge seene this daie above thirty ilands, little and greate, faire shoalding round aboute them, I meane to the northward of them. The distance from the southermost of these ilands to the norther of those wee sawe maye bee neere twenty leagues, close one by annother.

Jan. 21. In the morninge wee stoode in for the land, sending the skiffe before the shipp to sound, as alsoe to finde a good place to anker in. Soe aboute nine in the forenoone wee came to anker in 15 fathome water, within halfe a mile of the land. But wee found it full of small rocks; wherefore wee wayed and went further in, where we found cleare grownd and better rideinge; where wee found very good water in dyvers places, but noe signe of any people that ever had bene there[3]. It is a very good roade betwixt twoe ilands, aboute a mile and a halfe

---

1 Praslin and the neighbouring islands.

2 Mamelle.

3 Sir William Wharton concluded that their final anchorage was under St Anne Island, near the present Port Victoria, on the north-east side of Mahé, the principal island of the group.

distant from iland to iland; and there lyeth, betwixt the E.S.E. and S.E. & by E., other three ilands[1] aboute three leagues of from the place where wee ankored; soe that wee weare in a manner land locked, except towards the E.N.E. and E. To knowe the place where wee ankored, there is a small iland[2] which lyeth next hand north from the roade aboute two leagues; and there is a rock or ilheo[3] lyinge betweene the iland where wee ride and the foresaid iland, the roade beinge to the southwards of that. To the W.N.W. there is a very high iland some 10 leagues of, which was the first iland which wee descryed[4]. We ankored in 12 fathome water. The roade is in 4d. 10m to the southward[5].

Jan. 22. Finding a rowlinge to sea to come in out of the E.N.E., wee warped in aboute two cables length farther and anchored in 13 fathome water, very good ground and within a pistoll shott of the shoare; where wee ride as in a pond from the 22th to the 30th ditto; in which time wee watred and wooded at our pleasure with much ease; where wee found many coker nutts[6], both ripe and greene, of all sorts, and much fishe and fowle and tortells (but our men would not eate any of them, but the tortells wee could kill with staves at our pleasure) and manye scates with other fishe. As alsoe aboute the rivers there are many allagartes[7]; our men fishinge for scates tooke

---

[1] Cerf, Long and Mayenne Islands.

[2] Mamelle. [3] The Brisans. [4] Silhouette.

[5] Sharpeigh gives the same latitude. The roadstead indicated above is in 4° 35′ S.

[6] The curious *coco-de-mer*, or double coco-nut, is now found only in the Seychelles.

[7] There are no crocodiles in the group nowadays; but their bones have been found, mixed with those of land-turtles, and that they were common before the advent of colonists is proved by the statement of the Abbé Rochon that 'in 1769, when I spent a month here in order to determine its position with the utmost exactness, Secheyles and the adjacent isles were inhabited only by monstrous crocodiles' (Eng. trans., 1792, p. liii.).

one of them and drewe him aland alive with a rope fastened within his gills. On one of these ilands, within two miles where wee roade, there is as good tymber as ever I sawe of length and bignes, and a very firme timber. You shall have many trees of 60 and 70 feete without sprigge except at the topp, very bigge and straight as an arrowe. It is a very good refreshing place for wood, water, coker nutts, fish and fowle, without any feare or danger, except the allagartes; for you cannot discerne that ever any people had bene there before us[1].

Our travells from the dezert ilanus to Socatra, vizt:—

Februarie 1. This daie, aboute nine in the morninge wee sett saile with the winde at N., and wee steered away E.N.E. untill three in the afternoone; at which time it fell calme, with some raine, and the winde was variable in the showers; soe that wee stoode our course as the winde would give us leave. Wee sounded dyvers tymes, and found 30 fathome and 35 fathome, 10 leagues of. At noone by observacion 3 d. 57 m.

. . . .

Feb. 8. The winde variable with some raine, and calme; and we stoode our course at N. & by W. and N.N.W. This daye in the morninge wee crossed the line by judgment to the norward. At noone per judgment in 10 minutes north lattitude.

. . . .

[1] Jones says they named these 'the Desolate Ilands, because there are not any inhabitants upon them. These ilands are at the least some twelve or thirteene in number, and ought very diligently to be sought of them that shall travaile hereafter, because of the good refreshing that is upon them. Water is there in great abundance, also great store of coco-nuts, great store of fresh fish, and likewise store of turtle-doves, which are so tame that one man may take with his hand twenty dozen in a day; also great store of palmeto-trees. So that these ilands seemed to us an earthly Paradise.'

Feb. 15. The winde at E. Wee steered at N.N.E. At nine wee sawe the mayne land of Melinde, which bare of us N.W. aboute 10 leagues of. Aboute three in the afternoone wee weare within a league of the land. Wee sownded and had ten fathome faire grownd. Then wee tacked and stood awaye S.E. & by S. two glasses, and then sounded againe and had 15 fathome, and after noe grownd in 50 fathome. At ten at night wee tacked again towards the land, and stood N.N.E. untill the morninge. At noone per observacion 4 d. 48 m.

Feb. 16. In the morninge wee weare faire by the land, and with a faire gale wee stoode in N.N.E. The land trendeth N.E. half Easterly. At nine wee ankored in ten fathome water, faire ground, within 1½ mile from the land. The Generall sent aland the skiffe, and sent mee in her to see if wee could speake with any of the countrye people, to understand what the country did affoard. But comeinge aland there wente soe greate a suffe that wee could not land without endangeringe the boate and our selves. Wee sawe people on the shore; therefore I cawsed one of the men of the boate, whoe seemed willinge, to swime aland; and at his comeinge aland there came a man towards him, with sword, bowe and arrowes. We made signes to him to laye downe his weopons; but he seemed rather to provide him to doe the fellowe aland some mischeife then otherwise, making his bowe readye to shute; which the fellowe perceaveinge retourned to the water and came swyminge to the boate. And beinge in the boate wee made signes that if he would leave his weopons that wee would come againe aland; but he would not. Soe seeinge noe good to bee done wee returned aboard, and sownded from within pistoll shott of shore; wheare wee had three fathome, faire grownd, and soe rizinge by degrees to 10 fathome where the shipp roade, faire grownd. At three in the afternoone wee wayed againe and sett saile, and stoode away S. & by E., with the winde E. & by S.

Feb. 17. In the morninge at three wee stoode to the norward, the winde betwixt the E. & by N. and the E.N.E.; but aboute ten in the forenoone, being not above five leagues of the shoare, wee tacked aboute and steered away betwixt the S.E. and S.S.E. By observacion at noone 4 d. 10 m.[1]

. . . .

Feb. 25. ...This day in the morninge we had againe sight of the mayne land, bearinge of us N. & by W., beinge at noone by observacion 5 d. 33 m.

Feb. 26. The winde at E., and wee steered away N.N.E. Aboute six in the morninge wee weare within two leagues of the land, and had 25 fathome water, good ground. Then we tacked againe to the southward, and stood S.S.E. of the land, trendinge awaye N.E. & by E. neerest. At noone per observacion 6 d. 32 m.

. . . .

March 11. The winde at E.N.E. And aboute eight in the morninge, contrarie to our expectacion, we had sight of land. At noone, beinge within three leagues of it, wee sownded; and then findinge 35 fathome. we tacked to the southward, and steered S.E. and S.E. & by S. untill midnight. Then we tacked againe to the northward. This day at noone, when wee tacked aboute, wee weare in lattitude per observacion 5 d. 56 m.

March 12. Havinge stoode to the northward from midnight, at ten in the morninge wee weare againe within two leagues of the shore, in fifteen fathome water, faire grownd, the winde at north. Wee stoode away E.N.E. for six glasses; and then wee steered awaye S.E. and S.E. & by S., the winde shrinking on us, with raine and

[1] According to Revett this should be 5° 17′. They stood south and south-eastward until the 22nd, when finding themselves in latitude 2° 15′ they tacked about and made to the northward again.

gustie weather all night. Per observacion at noone 6 d. 12 m.

March 13. The winde betwixt the E.N.E. and the N.E. & by N. And at four in the morninge wee tacked towards the shore untill five in the eveninge, at which time wee weare within a league of the land, in thirteen fathome water. Then we tacked and stoode of S.E. & by S.; the land trendinge N.E. & by E.

. . . .

March 15. ...Wee steered awaye to the northward as the winde would permitt. At six in the eveninge wee had sight of land aboute ten leagues of by judgment. At noone per observacion 6 d. 20 m.

. . . .

March 26. The winde at E.S.E. Our course N.E. and N.E. & by N. At six in the eveninge wee had againe sight of the land, bearinge of us N.W. & by W. Our observacion 11 d. 00 m.

March 27. The winde at S.E. & by E. and S.E. Wee steered for the land, which bare of us N.N.E.; but the winde beinge variable, wee could not seaze this iland, which was Abdelcura[1], an iland about 20 leagues to the west of Socotora. In the eveninge wee weare aboute six leagues of, and at eight at night wee tooke in our sailes, and tryed all night untill five in the morninge. This iland rizeth like two ilands in twoe partes, by reason of the lowe land, which is a valley, which you cannot perceive until you come neere it. This daye by observation 12 d. 6 m.

March 28. At five in the morninge wee stoode toward the wester parte of the iland; and, comeinge neere the pointe, wee sawe a small rockye iland, which made the maister to take it for Soccatora. The Generall cawsed the skiffe to bee manned to goe betweene the shipp and

---

[1] Abd-el-Kuri.

the shoare, sowndinge, and my selfe in [her?] to see if wee could speake with any people on the shore. But comeinge neere the land, wee perceived it to bee a very barren countrye and noe signe of any inhabitannts on it. Wee had within a quarter of a mile of the shore nine and ten fathome; butt under water, a mile of the shore, there is a rocke, which lyeth a fathome under water. Wee made signes to our shipp to goe farther of, for avoydeinge the danger. Then, perceiveinge [it?] directlie to bee Abdelcura, wee made all the saile wee could, and stoode alongst the shoare a good berth of. The land is aboute seven leagues longe, and all alonge the shore it rizeth in with sharpe rocks and valleys betwixt, with white sand. From the N. to the S. the iland is not aboute [above?] two leagues broad, by judgment. About three in the afternoone wee sawe at the S.E. & by E. very heigh land, and we stoode E.S.E. with the stem. In the eveninge there fell a darke miste on the land, that wee cold not perfectlie make it; and wee weare at night aboute eight leagues of. Our maister judged it to bee Socotora by the course, distannce and latitude....

March 29. In the morninge wee weare faire by the ilands, beinge two small ilands called the Hermanos, or Sisters[1], of a greate height, and one soe well like the other that they may well bee called sisters, beinge both flatt at the topp, and three leagues asunder. But at the sunne rizinge wee had sight of Soccatora. The norther parte bore of us E. & by N., and the souther parte E.S.E., and wee steered towards it, with little winde and that shrinkinge upon us. Wee weare aboute four leagues of the land, and wee tooke in our sailes.

March 30. In the morninge we weare aboute three

[1] Rather the Brothers, which is the present name. Jourdain may, however, be using the older title *Duas Irmanas*, which he would find in Linschoten's map.

leagues of the iland of Soccotora; and the Generall sent of the skiffe, my selfe in her, to see if wee could speake with any of the country people. And descryinge a faire baye wee went in and sounded, and landed, to see if there weare any fresh water or people; but we found neither people nor water, but signe of many goats and people which had bene latelie there. It is a faire baye and good anchoringe, from twenty fathome to five farther [fathome?] within a quarter mile of the shore. Soe that at ten before noone the shipp anchored in seven fathome water. After the shipp was ankered the maister went aland to search for water, but could finde none; but wee sawe twoe men on the topp of a mountayne, but would not come neere us. Soe wee retourned; and aboute six in the eveninge wee sett saile and stoode alonge the shore. This baye is called Golgotha Baye, named soe by Captaine Keelinge[1].

March 31. With little winde wee stoode alonge the shore of Soccotora; but the current settinge to the westward sett us to leeward of the pointe of Golgotha Baye. Aboute ten in the morninge, the winde freshinge at S.S.W., wee made all the saile wee could to gett aboute annother pointe which was ahead of us; and the Generall sent of the longe boate and the skiffe, in which I went, to see if wee could have any speech with the people of the country. At which time wee descryed a saile comeinge from the east plyinge into the farther baye ahead us. Wee, going alonge the shore with our boats, came into the bottome of the baye, where the shipp was ankored, being a Guzarat of Dieu, bound for the Red Sea; but wee would not speake with him, because we had noe order from our Generall, for feare of freighting of them. But wee understoode by some of the countrye people that we spake withall that there [theie?] weare Guzaratts bound

[1] Not recorded in any extant journal of the *Third Voyage*. The bay referred to seems to be that now known as Gubbet Shoab.

for the Red Sea; as alsoe they tould us of Captaine Keelinge and Captaine Hawkins and of settinge up a pinnace; and wee tould them what wee weare and what wee desired. He [They?] tould us that there was not in that place any water, but goats there weare good store, but that they could not sell any untill they had advised the Kinge, which they would doe that night, his towne beeinge aboute a daies jorney from thence; and the next daie he [they?] would retourne with awnsweare. Soe with this advise wee sownded all the baye and retorned to the shipp. Wee found very good sholdinge from four fathome within a quarter of a mile of the shore, to twenty fathoms a league of, faire white sand. Butt before we cold come aboard, our shipp was dryven of with the corrent, haveinge little winde, that they could not have ground in 80 fathome. Wee had little winde all night.

Aprill 1. At sonne rizinge wee sawe a saile to the westwards of us, aboute three leagues of; and haveinge little winde, and our twoe boats towinge, the shipp could gett nothinge ahead, by reason of the current which setteth into the Red Sea; wherefore the Generall called us to councell, to knowe our opinions what was best to bee done, to staie beatinge us [up?] for Soccotora against the current, or els to beate up for the Red Sea (whether wee weare bound) and see whether wee could speake with the saile which was to the westward of us, which wee supposed to bee the Guzaratt which was bound for the Red Sea, got alonge betweene the shore and us by night. And presentlie it was concluded to beare upp for the Red Sea, and see if wee could speak with the saile that was in sight. Then wee made all the saile wee could; soe that at three in the afternoone wee weare within a league of her, and they, seeinge that they could not gett from us, strooke their sailes and staied for us. And the captaine and marchannts came in their boats to us, whoe presentlie tould us that they weare Guzaratts and came from Dieu, and the same shipp that was at anchour in the baye the last night, and for feare of us shee came by night by us betweene the shore and us; alsoe they tould us that aboute six monnethes past there came an English shipp to the barre of Suratt, and was gone for Bantam, but that the captaine of her, with some three marchannts weare lefte at Suratt, and the captaine was gone to the courte of the Greate Mogoll with a present, to a place called Agra, aboute three monnethes journey within the land. Wee tould them that wee weare bound for Aden, and from thence to Suratt. They seemed to bee very joyfull, and desired our companye for Aden, whether they weare bound, laden with cotton wooll and some callicoes of all sorts, beinge a shipp of 150 tonns or thereabouts. Wee entreated them to leave us a pilott to remayne aboard us, to direct us to the port of Aden; which they willinglie agreed unto, and soe departed aboard their shipp. The winde at S.S.E.

Aprill 2. The winde at S.S.E., a pretty gale, and wee steered W.N.W. In the afternoone the Generall, marchannts and maister went aboard the Guzaratt; by whome wee weare at full certified of our countrye mens beeinge at Suratt, and of there enterteinement. And in the eveninge wee retourned aboard; keepinge our course W.N.W. At noone per observacion 13 d. 12 m.

Aprill 3. The winde at S.S.E. Wee stoode our course betweene the West & by North and West & by South. In the afternoone the captaine, marchant and pilott of the Guzaratt shipp came aboard us, to passe the time; and att night retourned. By observacion this daye at noone 12 d. 50 m.

Aprill 4. The winde at E.S.E., a fresh gale; and wee steered awaye N. West, and N.W. & by West. In the eveninge wee had sight of land, on our starrboard side, beinge the coaste of Arabia Felix. All this night wee steered W. & by N., and W.N.W. At noone by observacion 13 d. 20 m.[1]

Aprill 5. The winde at E.S.E. Our course W.N.W. This morninge the pilott which was to direct us for Aden came and staied aboard our shipp, to carry us to the roade of Aden[2]. At night wee stoode W., and W. & by South. At noone per observacion 13 d. 20 m.

Aprill 6. The winde at S., and S. & by West; little wind. Our course W. & by S. and W.S.W. This daie the pilott retorned aboard the shipp, discryinge the land, and knowinge that hee was farther from Aden then he expected, beeinge hazie weather, was deceived of the land which he sawe first.

Aprill 7. The winde at E.S.E. Our course W.S.W. Aboute noone the captaine and marchannts retourned aboard us to passe the time, havinge perfectlie made the land of Aden[3]. Wee beinge then not above two leagues of the shore, sownded, and had grownd in 27 fathome, good ground. This night aboute ten wee anchored in 18 fathome water within two leagues of Aden castell, and the Guzaratts shipp went in within the castell.

Aprill 8. In the morninge wee saluted the castell with five peeces. And aboute ten in the forenoone came off the Guzaratts boate, and brought the Governours Caya[4] and

[1] Revett says 13° 10′, which is probably the more correct.

[2] 'Came ageyne the pylott of the Gooseratt abord of us, and tould us wee should have his brother to carry the shipp into porte; the which was kyndly accepted' (Revett).

[3] 'This foarenoone came the marchannte and pylott abord of us and stayed and heard prayer, the tyme of prayer then presentinge, to which they were very attentive' (Revett).

[4] The 'Caya' was evidently the Governor's factotum. Middleton refers to the 'Cayha' of the Pasha of Sa'na as being 'the lieftenant generall of the kingdome,' but this was rating him too highly. The word is the Turkish *kyāya*, a 'steward,' or 'administrator of affairs,' from the Persian *kat-khudā*, 'headman of a village,' 'head of a house,' etc.

the Sabander[1] of Aden, with the captaine of the Guzaratts shipp and divers others, with many complements of joye from the Caya and Sabander, promising greate matters for the sale of our comodities, as alsoe for our good enter-teynement, with many *besalosmanos*[2] from the Governor, sayinge that for our cotton[3] we should paie five per cent. for whatt wee sould, and what wee could not sell wee should paye nothinge, but retourne our goods againe aboard att our pleasure; with many other faire promises. And beinge entreated by the Caya and Sabendour to land and speake with the Governour, whoe (as he said) was desirous to see the Generall; soe the Generall, beeinge confident of his words, prepared himselfe to goe aland with the Caya and Sabendour, advisinge mee to prepare my selfe and Phillipp Glascocke to goe with him. Soe pre-sentlie wee departed in our owne boate, and they in their boate went before to advise the Governor of our comeinge; soe that at our comeinge aland wee had horses provided by the waters side to carrie us to the Governours howse. When wee came neere his howse wee weare entertayned with tabour and pipe and other heathen musicke, and presentlie carryed to the presence of the Governor, whoe saluted us and confirmed by a writeinge under his hand all that the Caya had promised us, with many more comple-ments; and with the same gave us vests of cloth of gould, and sett us againe on horse backe, to carrye us to a faire howse which he had provided for us, with our former musicke.

---

[1] Persian *Shāhbandar*, 'lord of the haven,' the official who con-trolled the harbour and saw to the payment of the customs dues.

[2] See note on p. 5.

[3] An obvious error. Probably Jourdain wrote 'custom.'

Of whatt passed after our landinge att Aden, in Arabia: as alsoe in Senan and Moccha, untill our cominge from thence.

After our enterteynement at landinge and accompanyed with the Governours cheife officers to the howse which he had prepared for us, hee sent us victualls to eate, in very ample manner. And after dinner the Generall, haveinge conferred with divers of the countrye, sent mee to the Agaa[1] or Governour to knowe whether he would command any service aboard the shipp, for that the Generall would repayre aboard and come againe in the morninge. Whereunto the Governor made awnsweare that hee came but then aland, and he had not as yet taken any pleasure in the countrie, and that it was the order of all captaines that came to the countrye to staie aland two or three daies at least before they returned aboard, to refresh themselves; entreatinge him to have patience, and to send the boate and what people he pleased aboard. Which awnsweare I carried to the Generall, whoe was not a little displeased thereat, but cawsed me to retourne to him againe, to see if hee could have leave; if not, to demand leave for my selfe to goe aboard in the skiffe; which he grannted, and sent a soldiar with me to give order to those which kept the gate to lett mee fourth, havinge first given my word to the Generall to retourne againe in the morninge; hee doubtinge that I would not have returnd, beeinge once aboard. But the 9th in the morninge I retourned in the skiffe aland, havinge setled all thinges in order both for the Generall and my selfe, makinge accompt to make a longe voyage of it aland, doubtinge hard measure, the begininge beeinge distastfull unto us. Soe comeinge aland I found a guard of soldiars at the gate of our howse; which did

---

[1] Of whom see p. 77.

not well like mee, yet I said little. When I came to the Generall, he was well comforted by the Turks which had kept him companie most parte of the night, that this daie he should have leave to goe aboard. Soe wee passed the tyme untill the eveninge; att which time the Generall and my selfe went to the Agaa, shewinge that he had sufficientlie reposed himselfe aland, entreatinge his leave to goe aboard his shipp. To which hee awnswered that he had already sent to advise the Bashaa his maister of our comeinge, and of the Generalls beeinge aland, and before hee had his awnsweare he durst not suffer him to goe aboard; affirminge that within fifteen daies hee hoped to have awnsweare from the Bashaa to his content; with many protestacions of his good meaninge therein, and that hee had wrytten much in his behalfe to the Bashaa. With this awnsweare wee retourned to our lodginge, noe better then prisonners, being guarded with souldiars, which made us abide with heavie harts. Yet wee wanted nothinge, for hee sent us victuals for two or three daies, untill hee beganne to growe wearye and sent us word that wee should provide for our selves; being resolved by the Agaa that wee should not goe aboard untill expresse order from the Bashaa, which would bee twentie dayes.

The Generall, seeinge noe remedye, resolved with patience to abide it, and sent aboard the shipp for such things as was necessarye for victualls and other things; and sent for Robert Covett[1] to bee our cooke. In this tyme wee repayred divers tymes to the Governor, and weare many times invited thether to dinner; the Governor beeing many times very earnest with the Generall to come neere[2] the roade with the shipp and land our goods, as the Guzaratts did, to avoyde suspicion of the countrye people,

[1] Covert, for whom see the List of Authorities.

[2] Here, as elsewhere, 'nearer' is intended.

for some did not lett to saie that wee weare men of warre and not marchannts, because wee would not land our goods, and ride soe farre of with the shipp[1]. To whome the Generall awnswered that for the shipp she could not come soe neere as the juncks, beeinge of a greater draught, and the further shee roade of the more would bee our paine to land our goods, as wee weare purposed to doe if there weare marchannts in the countrye that would buye it. Whereto the Agaa, alias Governor, replyed that hee would procure marchannts to buye all that was in the shipp within eight daies, if it weare once unladen; upon whose words the Generall cawsed a little iron and tynne to bee landed, every daie a little, to keepe stroake with them untill the messenger retorned from the Bashaa. Whatt tynne wee landed was presentlie sold for 340 rialls per baharre, which is 350 li. suttle[2] or thereabouts. Alsoe the Agaa sent some marchannts to buye aboute eight bahars of iron, ready money, at 22 rialls per bahar. This he did in pollicye onelie to animate the Generall to land the rest of our goods; but the Generall made noe greate haste to unlade; onely for fashion sake a little every day in our owne boate, to delaye the time as is aforesaid. Notwithstandinge, wee had landed by little and little aboute ten tuns of iron and eight peeces of broad cloth before the messenger came with awnsweare.

The 28[3] of Aprill the messenger returned from the

---

[1] As mentioned in the List of Authorities, copies of the letters written by Sharpeigh to the ship during his detention ashore are given in *I. O. Marine Records*, no. vii. From these it appears that on April 10 he ordered the ship to be brought a little nearer in, to satisfy the Governor; but three days later he directed her return to her former anchorage. He was inclined to attribute his imprisonment to the instigation of the Gujarātī merchants, and advised those on board, should he be long detained, to sail to the mouth of the Red Sea and seize the Indian ships as hostages for the surrender of him and his goods.

[2] Net.

[3] 24th, according to a letter from Sharpeigh.

Basha; and presentlie the Governor sent for the Generall, and at our comeinge he shewed greate mirth and beganne to read the Bashas awnsweare concerninge us. Whether true or false I knowe nott, but it was interpreted unto us by one which spake very good Portugues, as followeth: That the Governor should give us good enterteynement, and that wee weare welcome into the countrye; and that the Basha would buye of us 500 covedos[1] of broad cloth and all our lead. Whereunto our Generall awnswered that it was at his service at any reasonable price. The Governor made greate signes of feigned joie, protestinge nowe that he had order from the Bashaa and would doe us all the best kindnes that might bee. With these faire words wee flattered our selves for the time, and departed without asking any leave to goe aboard, because they should think that wee doubted nothinge thereof, seeing such good newes from the Bashaa.

The next daie wee returned to the Agaa, because as yet wee perceived that he had not given order for our goinge aboard, to demand of him whether wee might goe aboard: that wee did not demand of him the daie before because wee had thought that upon the receipt of the Bashaas letter that hee had given order for the same. The awnsweare of the Governor was that as yet wee had not landed all our goods: that as soone as it was unladen, that wee might goe and come at our pleasure. The Generall replyed that if himselfe or any marchannt would make price of his goods and buye it, that then hee would presentlie land it: otherwise he sawe noe reason to land goods and carrie it aboard againe, for that if wee could not sell it in Aden wee weare bound for Suratt and other places:

---

[1] Port. *covado*, 'an ell.' It was the usual unit for measurement of cloth in India. At Surat the ordinary 'covet' was about 27 inches, but English cloth was bought by a special 'covet,' equivalent to about a yard.

and that little goods which was landed was not yett sould: and seeinge that wee did owe him onely five per cento of what was sould, accordinge to his owne note, that he would be pleased to suffer him to goe aboard his shipp, and that he would leave me aland to paye all dutyes and for the sale of goods, if any man would buye: and that he neede not feare of his custome, for that there was by much more goods aland then would paye the custome: and that he should assure himselfe that he would not leave his goods and marchannts aland and begone, for that he esteemed one marchannt more then all the goods in the shipp: alledginge alsoe that, seeinge the Bashas letter was come, that if nowe he went not aboard that the marryners would doubt some hard measure and sett saile and begone and leave us all aland. Notwithstandinge all these reasons alledged, he could gett noe other awnsweare of the Agaa but that he must first land all the goods, and then wee might goe and come att our pleasures. With this unreasonable awnsweare wee returned to our howse, alias prizon, the Generall very much discontented, as the Governor well perceived, for presentlie he sent to our howse annother guard of soldiars to keepe us all within the howse and not suffer anie to goe out without a guard with him. And this daie in the eveninge he sent his Caya and his cheife secretarie to our howse, shewinge the Generall that hee ment noe harme towards us, onelie he desired to buye 500 covedos of our cloth for the Bashaa for three altons the covedo (every alton is 3s. 4d.); whereunto the Generall awnswered that he had already 150 covedos in his hands of the choise cloth wee had, which he was content he should have for that price; but for the 500 covedos which he would have more, he should paie three rialls of eight the covedo; whereunto the secretarye seemed well satisfied, and told the Generall that hee might goe aboard in the morninge, willinge him to send for the skiffe to fetch him, for that the

Generall had given order that the boate should not come aland untill he sent for her. Soe that this night he wrote aboard for the boate to come aland in the morninge betimes to fetch him; which was effected. In the morninge the boate came accordinge to order; and upon some occasion of buysines the Generall deferred his goinge untill the afternoone, nothinge doubtinge of any denyall; but before his departure, because he would not bee stopped, he sent his drogoman[1], alias his enterpreter, which was an Italian benegado [renegado], servannt to the Captaine of the Gallyes of Moucha, which was sent from thence by his maister to entreate the Generall to come thither with the shipp[2]. He goinge to the Governor to knowe his pleasure whether he would have any thinge aboard the shipp, he awnswered that before the Generall went aboard he should send aboard for the cloth which he had promised, and that beeinge aland, he should goe aboard, otherwise not; and that he should send his Caya aboard to chuse the cloth and bringe it aland. With which awnsweare the Generall was amased, and retourned awnsweare that he marvelled very much at such dealinge, havinge made him send for his boate, and to detaine him it would cause his companie aboard to bee in a mutinye, seeinge the Agaa in anie thinge did not accomplish his word, and that he feared that they would depart with the shipp and leave us all aland to shifte for ourselves; but if this weare his resolucion, that he might send his men aboard with the Caya and drogaman to chuse the cloth, but that it was alsoe necessarie that he sent mee with them to deliver the cloth, as alsoe to pacifie the companie aboard; which he presentlie graunted. Soe the Caya, the drogaman, and two

[1] Arabic *tarjumān*, corrupted by Levantine traders into *dragoman* and *druggerman*.

[2] Sharpeigh says that this man had been fetched from Mocha to act as interpreter.

Turks more goe aboard, my selfe with them, with order from the Generall to keepe them aboard untill further order from him, doubtinge much his personn aland[1]. Soe att our comeinge aboard it was almost night; soe that it was too late to shewe them anie cloth, butt went to supper, they haveinge brought store of victualls to make merrye. Soe that this night there was shott in healthes above 40 peeces of ordinance, that the people aland wondred at it; butt all was in mirth, they not yet understandinge that wee ment to detayne them. And havinge showed the rest of the marchannts and maister the Generalls order, we determyned to sett saile in the morninge to gett without shott of the castle, and there come to anchor untill wee hard farther from the Generall. Soe in the morninge I shewed them the cloth; and while they were chusinge of itt the shipp sett saile; which they perceiveinge demanded the reason. Soe wee tooke them into the cabbin and told them that seeing the Governor had falsified his promise soe often with the Generall and detayned him aland, doubtinge much his meaneinge towards us, wee ment to keepe them as pledges untill our Generall came aboard; and if it pleased them to send a letter aland to the Governor their maister they might; and wee shewed them 16 chests of rialls of eight, our yrer tynne, steele, and cloth which was aboard, tellinge them wee [were?] not theeves, as some had reported, but marchannts thatt lived by our trade. Soe they went to write to the Governor and to send yt by a fisher boate which was by the ships side. But soe soone as they sawe our shipp at saile from the land, the Governor sent for the Generall, demandinge him whatt wee ment to sett saile. The Generall made awnswere that he knewe nott the cause. The Governor willed him to

[1] This was on April 27 (Sharpeigh's letters).

write aboard and knowe the matter in all hast. Wee seeinge the boate come of, wee stoode againe towards the roade. The boate comeing aboard brought the Generalls letters as is aforesaid. Wee awnswered that the Governor should send our Generall aboard before wee would send his men, for wee would trust to his words noe more, seeinge he had broken it soe often with us; and wee wrote the Generall to thatt effect. Notwithstanding that it was done by his order, wee wrote him soe much, because the Governor should the lesse mistrust that it was done by his consent. But the Governor haveing this awnsweare, he was much vexed against the Generall, and used him with some vile words[1]. But when his chollar was past, he sent againe for the Generall to entreate the Generall to write aboard to send the drogaman aland to declare the cause of our settinge saile and detayneinge his men; which letter beinge receyved, wee sent the drogaman aland, whoe tould the Governor our intent and the cawse of all; in soe much that it was concluded amongst them that the Generall should bee sent aboard the next daie in the morninge in a boate of the towne, and that wee should fetch him in our boate halfe the way and receive the Generall and deliver two of the pledges for him. Soe the next morninge the Generall was sent aboard, and wee received him halfe the way and delivered two of the Turks for him[2].

The next daie wee consulted what was best to be done with the Caya, which yet remayned aboard; whereunto it was agreed that notwithstandinge the Governours order to keepe him aboard untill wee had all things from the shore, that he should bee sent aland, to shewe our selves honest men and not theeves, and our desire to trade with them in

---

[1] From Sharpeigh's letters it appears that the Governor threatened to send him up to San'a to be dealt with by the Pasha.

[2] Apparently this was effected on the 1st or 2nd May. The date is not certain, because Sharpeigh in his letters interpolates a 31st April between the 30th April and the 1st May.

freindlye sorte, and not to detayne there people as they had done ours; that the detayneinge of there men was onelie to have our Generall aboard and not in reguard of our goods, as they might well perceive. Soe the Caya beinge feasted by the Generall this daie, the next morninge was sent aland in our skiffe, my selfe with him. And at our comminge aland, the Governor sittinge in the custome howse and seeing his Caya comeinge, contrarie to his expectacion, seemed very well content, giveinge mee very kinde words, tellinge me that wee might goe and come, buye and sell at our pleasure, with many other complements. Soe in the eveninge I retourned aboard, without any lett or hindrannce. And the next daie I retourned, in companie with William Revett, who had not bene as yet aland; and presentlie went to the Governours howse, whoe gave us kinde words and willed us to send aboard for the cloath which the Generall promysed him, and that he would paie for it accordinge to promise. Soe upon his faire speeches wee wrote to the Generall, whoe sent aland the cloth which the Caya had chosen aboard, and caried to our howse. The Generall being desirous to retourne aland, sent us worde that if the Governor pleased to send his Caya aboard in pledge he would come aland to conferr with him; which the Governor grannted and sent the Caya aboard, and the Generall came aland and made agreement with the Governor for the cloth and for all the steele which was in the shipp. The steele was sent for aboard and sent to the Governours howse by the Generalls order. And after two daies the Generall retourned aboard and the Caya came aland that was there in pledge, the Generall leaveing me aland to end accompts with the Governor; which I effected within two daies after the Generall was gone aboard, verie freindlie and quietlie; which when it was effected I went aboard to advise the Generall thereof, that by his accompt he remayned owinge

1573 altons. The Generall willed me to staie two or three daies before I demanded the money of him, because to give him noe offence; butt at the time appointed I went to him to demand the money. He putt me off untill the next daie. In this meane time there was a greate shipp of Guzaratt come to Moucha, as the said Governor advised the Generall, willinge the Generall to send a marchannt theather to buye there indico, haveinge brought greate store. The Generall was verie glad of this newes, and the more because the Governor himselfe had made the motion to send thither to buye it. Soe that it was concluded to send Mr. Revett and Mr. Glascocke, in a boate which the Governor had provided, to see whatt might bee done in that matter, and to send back present advise; in which boate the Governor sent a chouse[1] of his owne, which was one of his cheife men[2]. This boate retourned from Moucha, with his man and Mr. Glascocke, within tenn daies and brought letters from Mr. Revett, whoe remayned there, by which letters wee understoode that the indico which was there could not be bought for lesse then 80 rials of eight the churle[3], which was too high a rate for us to buye; but for sale of our yron, sword blades and peeces there was some hope of sale at a reasonable rate. This was theffect of his letter concerninge the sale of comodities, perswading the Generall to come thether with the shipp, comendinge the place to be farre better then Aden. Soe that the Generall was determyned to goe downe with the shipp as

---

[1] Turkish *chāush*, an inferior official, such as a sergeant-at-arms or herald.

[2] William Revett's account of his expedition is given in an appendix. He and Glasscock were the first Englishmen to pass through the Straits of Babelmandeb.

[3] An Indian term for the bundle or package by which indigo was bought and sold. Saris was asked at Mocha 'a hundred rials the churle, which is an hundred, seven and twentie pound or rottalas of Moha, and about a hundred and fiftie pound English' (*Purchas*, i. 349). See also a note on p. 270 of *The Embassy of Sir T. Roe*.

soone as hee could end his buysines with the Governor and receive his mony, which untill nowe was putt off from daie to daie with delayes. The Generall wrote unto me to demand the money of the Governour and to send the rest of our comodities aboard, and to enforme the Governor that wee determine to goe for Moucha with the shipp; with all which I acquainted the Governour accordinge to direccion, whoe seemed much discontented that wee would goe for Moucha with the shipp, butt would have us to send for itt, either by land or sea, any thinge that wee had there bought; but if wee would needs goe for Moucha, contrarie to his minde, wee should paie the custome of all our goods, and for every alton a chichin[1] of gold, as well for the entrado as the saiedo[2], which is both in and out, saying that whatt money he owed us was not sufficyent to paye his custome; yet if the Generall would give him what money was in his hands that he would free him of the rest, and might goe whither he pleased, and wee should presentlie send all other goods which was remayninge aboard; which if the Generall denyed to doe, he would send Phillipp Glascocke and my selfe prisonners to the Bashaa for Senan[3], to affirme before the Basha what hee had received of us for the custome, because (as he said) the Bashaa was informed that wee had brought much cloth of gould and cloth of silver and silkes, soe that the Bashaa expected much more custome then he had receyved

---

[1] The Venetian *zecchino*, from *zeccha*, 'a mint,' which is derived from the Arabic *sikka*, 'a coining die.' The latter word, as Sir Henry Yule points out in *Hobson-Jobson*, is the ancestor of the 'sicca' rupee; and as the *zecchino* or sequin also established itself in Indian currency, under the name of chickeen or chick, as the equivalent of four rupees, two words identical in origin were brought together after remarkably divergent careers.

Saris in 1612 valued the 'chicquene' at Mocha at five shillings (*Purchas*, i. 348). Downton (*ibid.* 282) rates it (under the name of *venetiano*) at a rial of eight and a half. Here it seems to be taken as equivalent to two altons, *i.e.*, 6*s.* 8*d.*

[2] Portuguese *entrada*, 'entrance,' and *sahida*, 'egress.'

[3] San'a, the capital of the Yaman.

of us; and bid me thus advise the Generall, and him his awnsweare. I awnswered him that for my owne parte I was very willinge to see the Bashaa, and that I was perswaded that soe honorable a person would deale well with stranngers and take nothinge butt what was his due, which wee weare willinge to paie; notwithstandinge I would, if it pleased him, goe aboard to advise the Generall of whatt he had said. But he would not suffer mee to goe, but to send some other, and write him my minde; the which I forthwith effected, and had present awnswer from him that hee might doe as hee pleased, but he would not consent to give him his demand, for that he was satisfied for his custome with advantage, besides the money which hee ought. Haveinge told the Governor thereof, he bid mee send all our yron and other comodities and our people aboard, except my selfe and Phillipp Glascocke, biddinge us to provide our selves to depart for Senan to the Bashaa within three daies, as horses and all other provision for the journey; which if wee weare not provided by the time lymitted he would send us on foote. I entreated him to provide us two horses, and wee would paie for them as much as they weare worth; because wee weare stranngers, that none dare to sell us horses without his leave. He awnswered that there weare twoe soldiers present that had horses to sell that wee might buye if wee would; biddinge them to sell us twoe horses and to make us paie well for them or not to sell them, as afterwards our drogaman tould us he said to the soldiar that had the horses to sell; and as it appered by his owne words unto us it was trewe, for that he willed us out of hand to buye our horses, for it was in vaine to thinke that wee should hier any in the countrye, and that wee neede not stand upon the price. I awnswered I would give for them what they weare worth, and not willinglie more, entreatinge him to be favorable to us, not to make us paie for them twice as much as they weare worth, for I understood the horses to bee his owne. But he awnswered that the horses weare the soldiars and he might sell them as he liste: he would not be against his profitt; sayinge farther that our goinge to Senan should cost us twice as much as the money which he ought us, before the journey was ended; thinkinge by these threatnings to drawe us to give him the 1573 altons which he owed rather then wee would venture to spend soe much more and in the end goe without it, as at last wee did; for if he could have putt us of from goinge to Senan he would have had it to himselfe, for that the Generall had given him a present for the Bashaa before, besides his custome. But when he sawe that we had bought our horses (which cost us 180 rialls of eight) then he was resolvd that wee determined to goe; and therefore he sent for mee to his howse, demandinge me when wee would bee readie to depart for Senan. I awnswered that, God willing, at the tyme appointed I would be readye, for that I had some yron and lead to be sent aboard, and as soone as it was laden I was readye, which would be the next daie. Soe he paid a little money which rested owinge for his owne accompt, besides the cloth, and withall he tould out the whole some of money which was owinge unto us, and delivered it before us to his secretarie (whoe was to goe with us) to deliver it to the Bashaa, sayinge wee should see that he kept it not to himselfe but would send it with us, and if it pleased the Bashaa to give it to us, it was nothinge to him. It put us in some comfort that the money went alonge with us, for that we doubted nothinge but that the Bashaa would cause it to bee delivered unto us; but it fell out otherwise. I was glad that he sent the money, because, if he should have caused the money to be given unto us, that I should not have annother journey to Aden for it, but goe directlie for Moucha, accordinge to order, where the ship was to meete us.

Thus haveinge laden all the rest of the goods which was aland, and sent all our people and stuffe aboard, and our selves readye, the 26th of Maye wee sett forwards towards Senan, accompanied onely with Phillipp Glascocke, our drogaman, and annother French man[1], a benegado [renegado], but could speake little French; whoe was sent from Senan by the Bashaa, tellinge the Bashaa that he understood both English and French and Italian, whoe had fained an interpretacion of His Majesties letter[2], sent by the Governor to Senan with a present; soe the letter being in the Spanish tongue, he understood some words, and made the Bashaa believe that he understood all; affirminge the letter did entreate of cloth of gold and silver and much silks which was aboard the shipp; which was the cause the Bashaa sent him downe to affirme soe much to the Governor of Aden. This Governour at the first, notwithstanding our detayneinge aland, did use us very kindlie, and offred the Generall that if he would goe or send any to the Bashaa with the Kings letter, that he would give them horses and all other provision fittinge for the journey; tellinge him that it was farre better that he should goe himselfe, or send some other of us, with His Majesties letter; but the Generall would not agree thereunto, although I proferd my service therein, the which could not be permitted; but the letter was sent by a pion[3] or footeman, one of the Governors men; which was much misliked both of the Governor and of our owne people, in soe much that the Governor, perceiveinge in the Generall therein some weaknes, made not soe much reckoninge of him as in former time. Alsoe the Governor gave the Generall a faire gennett and he sent it backe againe, say-

---

[1] Probably we should read 'annother a French man,' as on p. 81.

[2] For this document see *The First Letter Book of the East India Company*, p. 231.

[3] Port. *peão*, 'a footman.'

inge that it was too much charge to keepe a horse for soe little time; butt the Governor well perceived that it was because he would not give him annother in lieu of it, which he tooke very discontenteous. Which if these causes had not bene, and that the Generall had sent some one with His Majesties letter, there had bene greate hope of trade; but wee weare soe sparinge that lost us twice as much, besides contempned of the Turks for our miserablenes.

In the time of our beinge at Aden, the Basha sent the Governor a vest of gold for a favour; which the Governor receyved aboute two miles out of the towne, in greate state, and entreated me to goe with him, and sent me two horses to take my choise, and likewise desired that I would write to the Generall to shute some ordinance out of the shipp when the castell shott; which I performed, and went with him out of the towne, and soe to all the castles aboute the towne after he had received the vest of a gentleman that brought it. Hee rode to the castell with the vest on his backe, and when he came to the castles the ordinance was shott which was in them; soe that in all there were shott above 200 peeces of ordinance within the castles and from the walls, and our shipp shott fourteen peeces, whereat the Governor seemed content; as no doubt he would have bene in all matters, if he had not perceyved such weaknes in our Generall.

Heare followeth a discripcion of the strength of the cittie of Aden in Arabia[1], *lyinge in latitude* 12 *degrees* 9 *minutes*[2]. *Anno* 1609.

This cittie of Aden hath in former time bene a famous and stronge place, but at present is ruinated and destroyed

[1] Cp. Revett's description (in Appendix B).

[2] The latitude is really 12° 47′ N.

by the Turks[1]. There hath bene very faire buildings in it, as by the remainders of the faire howses which are lefte may be seene, falling to the grownd for want of repayringe. There are in this cittie yett remayneinge many Arabs of the poorer sorte, which are but as slaves to the Turke. This cittie is walled round with a stone wall, very stronge, and hath in it three very stronge gates, vizt. one on the north side[2], with yron grates to take up and downe at their pleasure, and within this gate there are twoe other gates, one à prettie distance one within annother; these two gates are of timber, with greate nayles as thicke as they can stand; and the reason why this gate is stronger then the other is because this way is the easiest way for any enemie to assault the cittie, havinge noe other good entrance but over rocks or by the sea. Under their castles on the south side there is annother gate; but this gate is comonlie kept fast, because that way there is noe recourse of people, because it is towards the mountaines, where there is noe travelling. The third gate is toward the sea, which is towards the west, by the castell, which is without the towne, upon the top of the iland[3]. All the gates have a guard kept in them night and daie. The towne is cittuated in a valley envyronned aboute with craggie mountaines, except at the north side, where the three gates are; and on the mountaines there are castells and watch howses round aboute, with ordinance in them, and watch kept in all of them, although with fewe men, for that they are scituated in such stronge places that one

---

[1] The Turks conquered Aden in August, 1538. About twelve years later the townsmen revolted and handed over the city to the Portuguese; but it was recaptured in 1551, and the Turks then held it until their evacuation of the Yaman in 1630.

[2] Probably at what is now known as the Main Pass.

[3] The term 'island' was at one time freely applied to peninsulas (cp. the 'Isle of Portland'). As a matter of fact, at spring tides the Aden isthmus is sometimes all but covered by the sea.

man may keepe out twenty. All these forts are within falcon shott of the towne and doth comand the whole cittie. And for the defence towards the sea there is an iland[1], very high, within muskett shott of the towne, on which there is a very stronge castell, which seemed invincible if they wante not men or victualls, for it is naturallie stronge of itselfe if there weare noe walls aboute it, the mountaine itselfe beeinge as a castell; but ther are stronge walles and plattformes in it, with good store of ordinance. This castell comandeth both the towne and the roade where shipping useth comonlie to ride, but you may ride out of shott of it if you please. In this castle and the rest of the forts of the cittie there are not above 300 soldiars; yett doe they keepe the people in such awe that they dare not looke a Turke in the face. The Arabs are not suffred to carrie any kinde of armes nor suffred to have any weopons in their howses for there owne defence; for at our first comeinge we weare comanded to sell noe kinde of armour[2] to the Arabs, and if any of them should presume to buye any in secrett it would cost him noe lesse then his life; which if the Arabs might buye, our peeces and sword blades would bee a good comoditie in those partes.

In this ruinated citty there is noe fresh water, but some wells which are as brakishe as the sea; whereof the comon people drinke, and being used thereunto it doth them noe hurte. It is an uncomfortable cittie; for within the walls there is not any greene thinge growinge, onelie your delight must bee in the cragged rocks and decayed howses. It doth seldom or never raine in this cittie, which is the reason that there is nothinge that groweth within it. It

---

[1] The island of Sīrah, now connected with the mainland by a stone causeway.

[2] In Jourdain's time this term covered all kinds of military equipment, including weapons.

was reported unto us that in seven yeares they had seene noe raine within the citty.

The Governor of this towne is a younge man called Rajeppo[1] Agaa or Governor. He is a Greeke by nation, benegado [renegado] (as hee himselfe tould mee), and soe are the cheifest of all the Turks of this place, and are slaves to the Bashaa. The cittie walls and forts hath by reporte 200 peeces of brasse in ytt, which the Turks found in yt when they tooke it from the Arabs; for it seemeth to have bene a very greate and famous cittie by the ruines thereof, and in times past it hath bene the staple of Arabia; but nowe there cometh onelie two or three small shipps from India and Muscatt neere Ormus yearlie, for the cheife staple is removed to Giddaa[2] and Moucha within the mouth of the Red Sea. They bringe to this towne onely callicoes and shashes[3] and cotton woll; and retourne gumarabecke, frankencense and mirre, and an herbe which groweth here called fica[4] or ruũa, which they carrie to the Indies to dye red withall; alsoe some rialls of eight and

---

[1] Rajab. It was he who, shortly after, as Governor of Mocha, treacherously seized Sir Henry Middleton and his companions. Downton (*Purchas*, i. 285) says that he was originally 'a servile slave' of the Pasha of San'a, 'and for that he was a beneficiall knave to his master he was preferred to Moha, a better place.' As a result, it would seem, of Middleton's retaliatory measures, Rajab Āghā was dismissed from his post (*ibid.* 341); but while the *Royal Anne*, under Capt. Shilling, was lying at Mocha in 1618, he once more made his appearance as Governor. He then professed great friendliness for the English, and wrote a very amicable letter to Sir Thomas Roe (*O. C.* 681, and *Purchas*, i. 625).

[2] Jiddah.

[3] Turban-cloths. 'Their heads are continually covered with a *shash* or wreath of narrow calico cloth many times wrapt about them (usually for the colour white or red).'—Terry's *Voyage to E. India*, ed. 1777, p. 126.

[4] A copyist's error for 'fua' (cp. p. 95), *i.e.* madder (Arabic *fuwwa*). Varthema sailed to Ethiopia 'together with twenty-five ships laden with madder to dye clothes; for every year they lade as many as twenty-five ships in Aden with it. This madder grows in Arabia Felix' (Badger's transln., p. 85). 'Ruũa' may be meant for 'ruuna,' *i.e.*, *rūnās*, the Persian word for madder.

chickins[1] there are brought by the marchannts which come from Grand Cairo yearlie; but fewe come to Aden, but staie in Gidda or Moucha. The Indian shipps come in November, which is the begininge of the easterlie monson, or in Aprill or Maye, which is the end of the same monsonn; and then at the begininge of the westerly monsonn those which came first departe, and those which came last in Aprill departe in August; and this is their course for their monsonnes continuallie thorough the yeare. But if they chance to be taken shorte with the monsonne, they are faine to gett some place to staie untill the next monsonne, or to retourne backe againe; for the winter in the coast of India beginneth aboute the end of Maye, and lasteth untill September, and then begineth the easterlie monsonne. Aboute the 15th of August departeth all the Indian shipps from Aden, Moucha and Zidda, for that they must have parte of the westerlie monsonn to carrie them home, for feare of beeing taken shorte as is aforesaid; for aboute the end of the monsonns the winde hath noe greate force, but bloweth little winde; otherwise the Indian shipps, although they are great, would hardlie be able to brooke the seas, being laden to the very brime of the shipp and haveing noe decks. Thus much concerninge Aden and the India shipps.

Of the cominge of our pinnace after the murder of John Lufkin, master of her.

In the time of our beeinge in Aden, aboute the 15th of Maye, in the night, arrived our pinnace, which sett up at the Cape, beinge eight monnethes since shee departed from [us?] after our departure from the Cape Bona Esperansa. Beinge aland at Aden, in the night I hard

[1] See note on p. 70.

ordinance out of the roade from our shipp, which made me doubt of some assault to our shipp by the Turks; but it proved to bee at the arryvall of the said pinnace, although noe greate cause to shute for joye, seeinge they had murthered there maister. Yet as the Divell had tempted them to the evill, soe hee brought them to their end; for as soone as they came aboard to the Generall, he demandinge for there maister, they tould him very merilie that hee was dead. Demandinge by whatt meanes, they awnswered that they had slaine him; askinge whoe it was that slewe him, they awnswered: One and all of them; that it was better for one to dye then all. Soe beganne to tell the whole storie; howe that hee had driven them off with delayes a longe time that hee would putt with the land of Saint Lawrence to seeke victualls and had deceived them soe often, thatt they weare almost all famished for wante of water and other refreshinger, and therefore they seeinge him to bee neare the lane in the eveninge and stoode to the offinge againe, although see had promysed that the next daie hee would stand againe with the land to seeke refreshinge, but they not beleevinge any more his promises, as hee was standinge leaneinge over the shipps side, one of them with a mallett strooke his braines out, and had slaine him, and had made one Francis Dryver maister; whoe presentlie went into his cabbin and tooke possession, beinge very sicke, and there dranke carowses one to the other; and Clarke, whoe was the man that killed him, was made his mate[1]. They allegd further that hee had good drinke for himselfe, and would drinke it himselfe and give them none, because it was of his owne provision. The Gennerall, haveinge understood the matter att full, beinge sorrowfull of the losse of soe faire a conditioned man, sent for mee in

[1] Jones says that Clarke had previously been the mate of the pinnace and Driver the gunner.

the morninge to come aboard to conferr aboute the matter; for as yet they had not emprizoned them, beinge councelled by the maister, Phillipp Grove, to winke at it untill they came home, as I perceived by the Generalls letter written mee. Whereunto I wrote him my minde, because this daie haveinge buysines I could not goe aboard; but by letter I advised that if he did winke att such a fowle matter the next boute would bee his, with other inconvenyences which I alledged to him. But the next daie, after my comeinge, the parties were re-examined and their examinations sett downe in writeinge; which beinge examined onelie by one before the Generall, the preacher, the maister, the purser and my selfe, and havinge all of them confessed the matter as at first, there was found accessarie to the fact three of them, and one that ranne from the shipp upon Saint Lawrence the next daie after they had slaine the maister[1]. Soe these three beeinge examined, and confessed the cryme, weare comitted to ward the next morninge; and presentlie there was a jurie of seamen empanelled, and [they] were found guiltie and condempned to dye[2]. Soe the 23th of Maye Francis Dryver and Clarke, the two principall, weare hanged aboard the pinnace, where they had comitted the crime; and the drommer, beeinge younge, was repreeved, haveinge some skill in surgerye; whose name was Andrewe Evens, whoe after dyed of the flixe[3] at Suratt.

---

[1] Covert gives the name of the fugitive as Edward Hilles, and says that he 'was eaten with Caribs or man-eaters.' Jones says 'they left my servant Edward Hilles behind them, who (as they said) going to cut wood, could not bee heard off.'

[2] By the royal commission for the voyage (*First Letter Book of the East India Company*, p. 227) Sharpeigh was authorised to use martial law in cases of 'capitall offences, as for wilfull murther...or muteny...the same being trulie and justlie proved against any of the person or personns aforesaid.'

[3] Or 'flux,' *i.e.*, dysentery.

MAP OF THE YAMAN, SHOWING JOURDAIN'S ROUTES

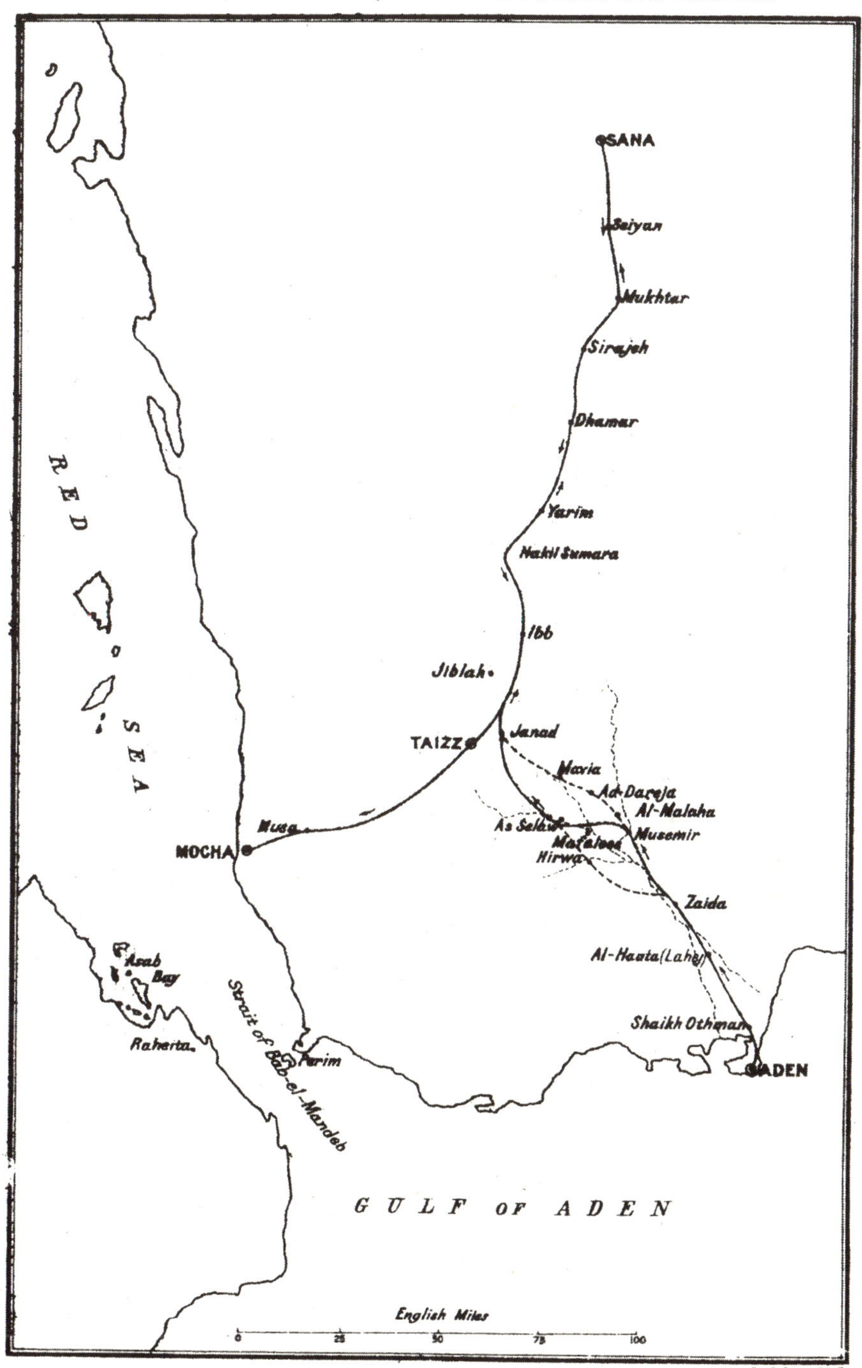

Our journey from Aden to Senan, with the names of the cheife townes wee passed[1].

The 26th of Maye (as is before mentioned) in the eveninge wee sett forth out of Aden towards Senan; and the same daie our shipp sett saile for Moucha. In our companies were twoe renegadoes, our drogamon, one Italian, and annother a Frenchman, with the Governors secretary, whoe had the charge of us to deliver us to the Bashaa. This daie wee travelled untill midnight, at which time wee came neere a walled towne of garrison, called Hatch[2]; butt because wee could not gett into the towne before daie, beinge a towne of garrizon, wee rest upon the plaine untill daie. Soe in the morninge wee came to

---

[1] The latter portion of the route traversed by Jourdain and his companions presents no difficulty. From Yarīm to San'a the road is well-known, and we have as guides (1) Sir Henry Middleton's narrative of his journey in 1610–11 (*Purchas*, i. 254): (2) a MS. account of the same journey by Benjamin Green (*I. O. Records*, *Marine Journals*, xii.) [as this is not available in print it has been quoted freely in the notes which follow]: (3) Pieter van den Broecke's narrative of his visit to San'a in 1616 (Amsterdam, 1648): (4) Niebuhr's *Déscription de l'Arabie* and *Voyage en Arabie*: (5) Mr W. B. Harris's *Journey through the Yemen*: (6) the Rev. S. M. Zwemer's *Arabia: the Cradle of Islam*. The first four give also details of the route from San'a to Mocha by way of Ta'izz. For the first part, however, *i.e.*, from Aden to Janad, but little help can be derived from books. Varthema's account of his travels in this region is short and vague. Mr Harris in 1892 took a more easterly route than Jourdain. Two years later Mr Zwemer proceeded from Aden to Ta'izz by way of Mafalees, but his narrative does not afford much assistance. In these circumstances the editor applied to Col. Robert Scallon, C.B., C.I.E., D.S.O., the acting Resident at Aden, who most kindly interested himself in the matter and forwarded information as to the routes likely to have been followed. In his opinion Jourdain's stages from Al-Hauta were probably: first day, through the Subaihi country to Al-Farsha; second day, to Mafalees; third day, to As-Selaw; fourth day to Janad. There is, however, another way by Hirwa and As-Selaw which may have been taken; and Mr Hamood bin Hasan, headmaster of the Aden Residency Schools, in a memorandum forwarded by Col. Scallon, suggests that our traveller went by way of Musemir, Ad-Dareja and Mawia to Janad. All three routes have been laid down on the map, from a sketch which Col. Scallon has kindly furnished.

[2] Jourdain probably wrote 'Hateh,' *i.e.*, Al-Hauta, the capital of Lāhej. The ancient walled town was about a mile from the present city (information from Colonel Scallon).

the towne, being under the government of the Governor of Aden; where wee staied all daie, the Governor havinge geven such order, to see whether wee would agree to give him the money; which putt us in greate feare, seeinge our ship was gone, that he would secreetlie have putt us to death and soe keepe the money to himselfe, as our drogaman did much feare of it too; but afterward it proved otherwise, for it was to have acquittannce from us that he ought nothinge unto us but the 1573 altons, because he had receyved divers things from us which he had given nothinge for, which was given him for presennts. Soe when wee had signed acquittannce he gave order for us to departe. This cittie hath walles of earth round aboute, made very artificiall, and hath 50 soldiars, Turks horsmen, in itt, which doth governe it under Reejppo, Agaa of Aden. It stands in a very plaine and champion countrie, and very firtill of all fruits and graine, havinge divers rivers of waters in many places to water their corne. Alsoe there is in this place much cotton woll. Soe that I take it to be one of the fruitfull places of Arabia; and is some 18 miles from Aden. This towne doth serve Aden with all kinde of victualls and fruite.

May 28. In the afternoone wee departed out of Hatch, and travelled untill three in the morninge, and then wee rested in the plaine feilds untill three the next daie, neere unto a cohoo howse[1] in the desert; havinge brought victualls with us from Hatch and water, and eight soldiars to conducte us for feare of theeves, being a wildernes where manie are robbed.

May 29. Aboute three in the afternoone wee beganne to travayle all night untill three in the morninge, and then wee rested in the feilds untill daie. This night wee passed

[1] *I.e.*, a travellers' rest-house, where coffee could be procured. Middleton uses both 'coho' and 'coughe' for 'coffee' (Arabic *kahwa*). Roe has 'cohu.'

a high mountaine full of stones and very dangerous for theeves. The next daie aboute ten wee came to a little village, where wee rested all the daie untill night, but could gett noe victualls but what wee brought with us, other then quinces and some peaches. In the eveninge wee sett forwards and travelled all night.

May 31. In the forenoone aboute ten we came to a prettie towne called Salmett[1], which standeth in a plaine countrie and very fertill of all kinde of graine, which doth serve all parts of the barren countrye that wee have passed these two daies. On the topp of a heigh hill neeare the towne is a castle with some ordinance in itt, but of little force. Heare wee stayed all night.

June 1. Two howers before daie wee sett forward out of Salmett, and came to annother prettie towne some 26 miles distannt, called Jenetta[2], this towne alsoe standinge in a fruitfull soile. And betwixt the twoe townes there are manye small villages and very populous and fruitfull, with manie valleyes which yeild all kinde of graine, and very well manured. There are manie howses and little forts on the topp of hills, butt the towne stands in a plaine. Att this towne you might see the great cittie of Tayes[3], which lyeth in the waye from Moucha to Senan.

June 2. Wee came neere the cittie of Hippa[4]; being a walled cittie and a garrison, could not gett in by night, and therefore wee laye aboute five miles short of itt. This daie wee passed many heigh mountaines with paved

---

[1] Col. Scallon thinks this must be As-Selaw, in which case the castle mentioned by Jourdain would be the fort of Ad-Dumlūwah. As-Selaw is in a very fertile district, producing many kinds of grain, fruit and vegetables.

[2] Janad, El-Jenet or Al-Janadiah. Its large and beautiful mosque was a great resort of pilgrims (Kay's *Omarah*, p. 10).

[3] Ta'izz, which has been often described: see *infra*, p. 96; also Varthema (Hakl. Soc. ed.), p. 80; Van den Broecke, p. 32; Niebuhr (*Voyage*), i. 300; Playfair, p. 32; Zwemer, p. 62; etc.

[4] Ibb.

wayes[1] made round about them for men to travaile; otherwise it weare unpossible to goe on horsbacke; and in the middle way of one of the mountaines there is a fountaine of very good water, with a sesterne of lyme and stone to give drinke to beasts that travaile; otherwise the beasts weare not able to contynue travaile, by reason of the greate heate.

June 3. Aboute ten wee came to the cittie of Hippa, where wee laye in the middle of the cittie within the sarraye[2], a howse made of purpose for travellours. Within four miles of this cittie ther is annother cittie, which wee sawe a little out of the waye as wee came, called Gibla[3], which is a greate cittye but not walled; but the cittie of Hippa is walled, and standeth on the topp of a hill, and neere it there is a castle on the topp of annother hill, which doth comand the castle. This cittie standeth very pleasannt, and in a firtill soile, and very populous, and the land round aboute very well manured. In this place they doe sowe their corne all times of the yeare, and doth yeild fruite every three months, as it was crediblie reported to mee, for I have seene some corne sowinge, some reapinge, some ripe, and some greene all at one time[4], which maketh mee beleeve it the sooner. This towne hath not above 50 soldiars to keepe it, and yet very populous.

June 4. The Governour sent mee by his Caia a goate dressed in very good manner, and cawsed his Caia to keepe me companie and eate with mee, because he thought I would feare to eate the meate hee sent mee.

---

[1] These rough pavements are a feature of the Yaman passes.

[2] Pers. *sarāī*, 'a building.' The proper term is *karwānsarāī*, 'a building for the reception of caravans.' A strange perversion of the latter word is to be found in Middleton's narrative, where we read of '*censors*, which are built at the cost of the Gran Signior for the reliefe of travellers.'

[3] Jiblah.

[4] Van den Broecke noticed the same thing (p. 33).

I sent him a sword blade in recompence. Here wee stayed twoe daies, and went to the hott howse to bathe our selves, the Caia keepinge us companie. From Sallamett[1] to Hippa is aboute 30 miles.

June 5. Aboute two in the morninge wee putt off from Hippa in hope to have passed the greate mountaine; but aboute midnight wee tooke up our lodginge halfe the waye and laye in the mountaynes, our camells beeing wearie and our selves little better. This mountaine is called Nasmarde[2], where all the cohoo growes. From this mountaine goeth many rivers of water, that doth water many places in Arabia; and is fruitfull round aboute it of all kinde of graine and fruite. It is paved, that five men may goe abrest all the waye upp. On the topp [of] this mountaine there are two little castells within faulcon shott one of the other, on twoe little hills. There is noe man can passe from Senan but by licence from the Bashaa but he shall be staied at these castells[3]. Neere unto these

---

[1] Probably a slip for 'Jenetta.'

[2] Green and Middleton call it 'Naquelsamarr' and 'Nackhilsamar,' *i.e.*, Nakīl Sumāra, the latter word being the proper name of the mountain, while *nakīl* is a term used in the Yaman for 'a mountain road,' 'a high and difficult pass.'

[3] 'Upon the topp of this hill is a great and stronge castell, which the Turkes have and commandeth that passadge, that noe souldier (yf he be a Turk) may escape withowt the espress commande of the Bashaw; for they live all in such subjecion and feare that they would faine departe the country yf they coulde, being for the most parte runnagadoes and suche as have beene taken, when they weare yong, in the warrs of Armenia and Greece....Heere the Moores and Turkes reporte that St. Allia was invited to a feaste; and comming to the same, seeing the meat stande before him, said: If any ill poyson or elce be in this meat, then lett the meat and dishes be turned into stones; but yf nott, lett them remain as they are. Soe the meat being poysoned, meat and dishes and all turned unto stones, and upon the topp of this hill are to be seene at this day. Moreover, heere is upon the topp of this hill a very fair well or fowntaine, of which the Turkes tould us yf we did drinke, we should retorne thether againe; which half of our companie did, yett (God be thanked) never retornd. Fower dayes jorney from hence is a place called Esscates, where is said to be buried a great sainte, who at certaine tymes of the yeare, when as there commeth many pilgrims thether, is houlden in honnor of that proffett a sollem and great feast, to which commeth

castells there is a little village where there is sould cohoo and fruite. The seeds of this cohoo is a greate marchandize, for it is carried to Grand Cairo and all other places of Turkey, and to the Indias. And, as it is reported, this seede will growe at noe other place but neere this mountaine[1], which is one of the highest mountaines in Arabia. It is 24 howers worke to goe to the topp of it; yet the waye is faire, but steepe that it killeth manie camells and horses before they can gett up with their burthens.

June 6. Havinge with greate paines passed this mountaine of Nasmarde, wee came to a small towne[2], scituated in a barren countrie, where wee lodged in the sarraye, where wee found victualls, because it is not aboute [above?] five mile from the foote of this fruitfull mountayne.

June 7. Wee came to a cittie called Damar[3]. This

many thowsandes of people, soe that all the hills abowt are partly covered; at which tyme the goast of the said saint is said to walke, and telleth them of many strange things, which they houlde and doe beleeve infallible; and with these and the like abominable falshoods is theire develish sect maintained' (Green). This 'Esscates,' it appears from a later entry, was a place on the Ta'izz-Mocha road, twelve miles from the former city; it is described as 'sittuated in the middle of a great hie mountain; yt hath at the nether ende of the towne a great rownd pann full of water, which commeth from owt of the hills.' Middleton, who is made to call it 'Eufras' (probably a misprint) and gives its distance from Ta'izz as 16 miles, says that 'about the fift of January great multitude of people resorteth hither from farre, where they doe some foolish ceremonies to one of their saints and holy men, which lyeth buried there; which being done they goe all in company to Mecca on pilgrimage.'

As regards the story about 'St. Allia,' Sir Charles Lyall thinks that Green (on his interpreter) misunderstood the narrator. The latter probably used the word *auliyā*, 'saints,' and this was taken for a proper name.

[1] This is of course wrong. Coffee grows in many parts of the province.

[2] Most likely Yarīm. Green calls it Erinn; and probably Middleton used the same spelling, which Purchas has misprinted 'Ermin.'

[3] 'We arived at Damar, a confused or despersed cetty in five or six partes, withowt any walls of defence, exept a castle which standeth the south syde therof. This place is distante from Surage 20 miles; sittuated in the middest of a great plain, where is good store of

cittie standeth in a plaine countrie and firtell; and the towne is devided in four parts, like four severall villages. It is very populous and not walled, but very pleasant, full of gardens; yet noe water within the towne, onelie what is in wells without the towne; which water there are men appointed continewallie to drawe with oxen and lett it runne in a gutter every morninge to fill the sesterns which are provided in the cittie for that purpose; and when the sesternes are full, they carrie the water to there corne and gardens, and soe water dailie both there corne and there gardens. In this cittie there are aboute 200 soldiars in garrison, because it is not walled, and a cheape place to laie in. Neere the towne there is a mountaine wher there is found many blud stones, agatts, and catts eyes, and other stones of little value in greate plentie.

June 8. Wee came to a little towne called Mocadar[1], which stands in a desert country betweene the mountaines, where wee laye within a sarraye, havinge this daie passed by a very faire sarraye on the topp of a plaine mountaine, made by the Basha for travellours that come late that waye.

June 9. Aboute ten in the morninge wee came to

---

corne and running streames of water, compassed rownd with hie and asperous mountaines. Heere is good store of all provissions. Also in this place are great store of bloodstones, which the inhabitants cutt and sett in ringes, very curious. The best that are in this country commeth [from?] Amara, which is a place distant from Damar 20 miles or thereabowts. Heere are a great nomber of Bannean gouldsmithes, who inhabitt in this place and make their living by cutting these and the like stones and putting them in rings to sell against the monnson. They have also heere great store of agatts, christall and such like, which the inhabitants make in beades, for the Torks and Moores never goe to churche butt they carry som beades to say their prayers upon, as the Papists doth' (Green).

Dhamār is well described by Harris and Zwemer. See also Van den Broecke's account.

[1] Niebuhr's 'Machdar': the 'Mukhtar' of Playfair's map. The *sarāī* they passed was possibly Sirājeh, called by Niebuhr 'Suradsje,' and by Middleton and Green 'Surage.' According to the last named it was 'a little village...sittuated upon the topp of a little hill in the middest of a plaine.'

a small towne[1] by the side of a barren hill, within a daies journey of Senan; from whence the Governours secretarie sent to Senan to advise the Basha[2] of our comeinge, desiringe to knowe his pleasure.

June 10. Wee proceeded in our waye towards Senan. And aboute eight in the morninge wee mett a messenger sent from the Bashaa, with a letter from the Bashaas secretarie that wee might repayre to the cittie, and there rest our selves two or three daies in a howse that he had provided for us, because the Bashaa was not in the cittie but laie in the countrye aboute six miles off, where hee minded to send for us. Soe that aboute noone wee came into the cittie, and laye at a howse which was provided for us.

June 11. The Governors secretarie that came with us came to our howse and willed us to make our selves readye to goe to the Bashaa, whoe had given order for our comeinge. And aboute ten in the forenoone wee came to the place where the Basha laye with all his trayne, and presentlie wee weare carried to the Basshas secretaryes tent, hee to take charge of us; where wee stayed three howers before wee could have admittance to the Basha, hee beeinge asleepe. Aboute one in the afternoone his secretarie went to him to knowe his pleasure when he would admitt us to his presence, whoe presentlie comanded wee should bee brought before him. And comeinge to his presence passed as followeth, vizt.—

---

[1] Probably the 'Siam' of Middleton and Green. The latter describes it as 'a little towne distante from Zenan 16 miles or thereabowts, sittuated upon the syde of an asperous mountaine, which yeildeth scarce any releefe or sustenance for mann; only the people or inhabitants, being wild and barberous, live upon seedes and rootes, which is their cheefest foode.' It seems to be the Seijān of Niebuhr, and the Seiyan of the Intelligence Department map.

[2] The Pasha of San'a at this time was named Jafar. According to Van den Broecke, who found him still in power in 1616, he was a Hungarian by birth.

The Basha being sate upon a high stoole laid with crimson velvett, in a faire gallerie under his howse, hee sittinge in the middest of the galerie, and his noble men by degrees standinge on each side with their armes crosse. Soe that as soone as I had done my dutye unto him, I was taken by two of his noble men, on each side one, houlding fast both my armes, and soe carried me towards the Bashaa to kisse his vest; which beeing done wee retired backwards a prettye distannce, where they lett me stand in the middle betweene the two rancks of his noblemen. These ceremonies beeinge ended, he demanded me the cause of my comeinge to him. I awnswered that the Agaa of Aden had sent us to His Excellencie; the cause I knewe not, but the partie which brought us could relate to His Excellencye at large the cause, whoe was there in presence. Whereupon the Basha called to him and demanded the cawse of our cominge, seeminge to bee very angrie, which made the poore man in such a feare that he could not in a prettie space make awnsweare; butt after comeing againe to himselfe he made a greate oration to the Basha, his talke tendinge most to the excusinge of the Governour of Aden. Which when the Bashaa had heard, hee awnswered that within three daies wee should retourne; and would have dismissed us presentlie but that I delivered him a letter from our Generall; whoe demanded in what language it was. I awnswered: In the Portugall tongue, and therewith delivered him the letter; whoe willed mee to reade it, and the drogaman should enterprett itt to him. The principall articles vizt.— First was concerninge the setlinge of a factorye in the country; whereunto hee awnswered that it could not bee permitted without expresse order from the Greate Turke his maister; and bringinge his order he would receyve us with all his harte, puttinge it on his head; and his reason was, for that at his beeinge with the Greate Turke at courte there came a Frangay[1], as he tearmed him (which I take to bee an Italian), whoe desired license to come into the Red Sea with one shipp to trade, which could not be grannted unto him because it was neere their holie howse of Mecca; and seeinge that he knewe that his maister would not give leave at that tyme, that nowe he could not permitt any factorie without his order; notwithstandinge, seeinge that he knewe that the English weare freinds to the Greate Turke his maister, and traded in his dominions, therefore we might at present sell such goods as wee had landed and take what wee wanted in that countrie and soe departe for this time; advisinge us to come noe more without order from the Greate Turke. I would have shewed him the coppie of the capitulacions betweene the Turke and us, but he awnswered that hee knewe theffect of them, and therefore needlesse. I tould him that, knowinge this countrie did belonge unto him, as well as Stambull and Aleppo with other places where wee traded, that cawsed us to be bould to come, thinkinge to bee as free as in the other places before mentioned; butt seeinge it could not bee, we craved his license, as hee had promised, to sell our goods and take what wee wanted and soe to departe. He promised that the next daie it should be delivered mee. Alsoe I shewed him of what agreement was made with the Governour of Aden before wee landed any goods, for the custome of it, that wee should paie five per cent onelye upon the goods which wee sould, and the rest to retourne aboard againe without custome, wherewith I shewed him a note of the Governours to that effect; notwithstandinge his promise, he had detayned 1600 altons in his hands more then his custome, demanding nowe ten per cent, not onelie of whatt was sould, but alsoe of what was retorned aboard the shipp;

[1] Arabic *Firanjī*, a Frank or European.

all which is contrarie to his promise and writinge extant. The Basha his awnsweare to this was: Reejypo Agaa the Governour was his slave, and that he could doe nothing without his order. His mullao[1] or preist standinge by spake to him in his eare; whereupon presentlie hee arose, as if hee had bene angrie (as his (*sic*) was) aboute demandinge the money, and spake noe more unto us, but willed his secretarie to carry us to the Caya to decide the matter; and soe he departed.

Presentlie wee weare carryed to the Caya his tent, whoe sate in as greate state as the Basha himselfe; and in the same manner as wee weare carried before the Basha, wee weare presented to the Caya; onelie we had a little more priviledge to kisse his hand, havinge kissed the skirt of the Bashaas gowne. He bid us welcome, and cawsed us to be carried againe to the secretaries tent untill the eveninge and then he would speake with us; where we stayed untill it was almost night. Soe that after that wee had eate with the secretarie, he sent us word that wee should retourne to the cittie, and repaire thether againe the next morninge; and cawsed the Governours man of Aden (whoe was our keeper) to goe with us. Soe wee tooke our leave of the secretarie and departed.

Nowe in the waye, as wee rid towards Senan, the Governours man our keeper had prattica[2] with our drogaman, and told him that the Basha and the rest of his officers, as the Caia and Secretarie, expected greate presennts from mee, which was the cause I was not dispatcht this daie; which although hee had not tould mee, I was minded to carrie a present the next daie, because I had some notice by the Bashas secretarie by signes. Soe that the next daie I carried for the Basha 25 covedos[3]

---

[1] Arabic *maulā*, 'a learned man,' 'a teacher.'

[2] Ital. *pratica*, 'conversation.'

[3] Yards (see p. 63).

of cloth of severall colours for five vests, two barrells of powder, and two faire peeces: to the Caya 12 covedos of severall colours and one peece: to the secretarie 12 covedos of severall colours and one peece. The Basha beinge busie, I could not speake with him, but sent the present before to speake for mee; but hee seemed not satisfied with the present, or not content, although he had formerlie receyved a greater, by the hands of the Governour of Aden, which the Generall sent him; and havinge given the secretarie and the Caya there presents, the Caia was content to give us a little audience. First I showed him what was the cause of our comeinge, beinge sent by Rejppo Agaa, Governor of Aden, his order, and therewithall delivered a certificate from the Caia[1] of Aden, which did testifie all the trueth that did passe at Aden concerninge our buysines; which when he had read, he said to our drogoman that for his life he should not once open his mouth concerninge any money; which if he did he should surelie paye for itt; which made him much dismaide and alter his countenance; which I well perceived, and therefore I would not urge him further to speake of it, seeinge that it was in vaine, and rather a hindrance to our other proceedinges. Therefore I gave over that suite, and entreated to have the Basha his passe which he had promised, to buye and sell what goods was landed and to departe quietlie without payinge any further custome or dutyes; as alsoe to remember the Basha to write awnsweare to His Majesties letter which he had received, which Rejppo Agaa sent him; all which he promised to performe very willinglie, and cawsed me to retourne to Senan without our keeper, and that within two daies without faile it should bee readye. Onelie the awnswere of the Kinges, he said that the Basha durst not write letters to any kinge

[1] A copyist's error for 'Cadie' (*Kādī*, 'a judge'); see Sharpeigh's letter in Appendix C.

without acquaintinge the Greate Turke his maister; which if he should doe otherwise it would cost him his head. Soe upon this promise wee tooke our leaves of him, beinge nowe free men, he havinge discharged our keeper of us and lefte us to our selves. Soe every daie we sent our drogaman thether to remember him; and at the end of the third daie he sent us our passe, very large, signed by the Basha.

The discription of the cittie of Senan, where the Basshaa keepes his courte[1].

This citty of Senan is noe greate cittie, but well seated in a valley, and walled aboute with earth in manner of greate stone squared, very curiouslie made for beeing earth, havinge every fortie paces distannce a watch howse or little tower with battlements. The wall is with battlements round aboute, and twelve foote thicke, and to outward shewe is as faire as a stone wall. The cittie is aboute two miles compasse within the walls, and hath within it a very faire and large castle of stone, with some ordinance, but not much. In which castle there are many greate men, Arabs, kept prisonners, which are delivered as pledges of peace of the citties and townes which are under the subjection of the Turke; and because they shall yearlie paie their tributes, and not rebell, it is an order betweene

---

[1] 'This cettie is in bignes at least two miles in compas; the buildings of stone and lime. They have very good lime, as good as plaister of Parris, in abundance. Yt is walled rownde with mudd walls, and abowte or neere adjoyning to the cetty gates yt is build with stone; and likewise in the insyde, of a manns higthe yt is built with lime and stone rownd abowt. Yt is sittuated in a great plaine. Hether is great resorte of people from all parts, viz. Armenians, Greekes, Persians, Jewes and Indians. Allso they have good plenty of all kinds of victualls, which are brought from farr, for the country neere adjoyning is very barren and mountanous. For wante of wood the[y] burne camells dunge' (Green). See also the descriptions by Middleton, Van den Broecke, Varthema, Niebuhr (with plan), Harris, Zwemer, etc.

them that of every countrye, cittie and towne, there bee one cheife man delivered in pledge as is aforesaid[1]. There are divers places in Arabia which are not under the command of the Turke, but doth hold warre against them. Those when the Turke doth take, doth either putt them to death or keepe them perpetuall prisonners if they bee of accompt. At our beeinge in this cittie, they tooke per composition a noble man of the Arabs which held warre with the Greate Turke twenty yeares, havinge slaine his father because he would have yeilded up the castle to the Turke; and nowe beeinge hardlie beseiged and in want of victualls, yeilded himselfe with all his treasure, which was reported to bee fifteen camells ladeing of gold. His condition was to save his life, and send him to the Greate Turke. Upon which newes there was greate feastinge in the cittie; which was partlie the cause that wee could not have more conference with the Basshaa, hee beeing overjoyed with this prize. The buildinge within the citty is of bricke, and many faire howses and churches with fayre towres and many prettye gardens within the towne, the cittie standinge in a very pleasannt plaine; onelie there is one littell hill neere the towne, upon the topp of which standeth a platforme or bulwarke with some ordinance, and watch kept, because on this mountaine there are found many sorts of stones, as catts eyes, agatts and blud stones

1 'Heere all the cheefe Arabes are kept, some in prison, others owt of prison (upon pledges of theire good behaviour), for feare of rebellion, which questionles would soon tak effecte yf the Arrabes had any heades or leaders, for in this country they are tenn Arrabes to one Turke. We weare innformed that in this country are butt tenn thowsande Turkes souldiers and three thowsande Arrabes on the Turkes syde' (Green). Middleton describes 'a spacious yard, wherein a great number of people, for the most part women and children, are kept prisoners or pledges, to keepe their parents, husbands and allies from rebellion. The boyes while they be little goe loose in the yard; but after they bee come to bignesse they are clapt in irons and carryed to a strong tower, where there bee many more kept in like case. There they remayne during the Bashas pleasure.' Van den Broecke says that the number of hostages was over a thousand.

in greate number, with other stones amongst of better valewe[1].

The trade of this cittye is cheiflie with the Benaianes[2] of Guzaratt, which bringeth yearly all kinde of comodities, as bastaes[3], shasses[4], cotton woll, with other stuffs of their countrye, and lye here as factours for the Banians of Aden, Moucha, Zida[5], to whom they yeild there accompts; for in each of those places before mentioned there is one cheife Banane as Consull or such like, which doth all the buysines in each place. With the Banians marchannts I had some conference concerninge their trade and our countrye comodities, whoe told me that this cittie would vent yearlie aboute 2000 bahars of yron and greate store of tynne, and lead alsoe would sell at a good rate, broad cloth aboute 100 peeces of violett or stamell[6] and Venice redds, with some steele; this cittye yealdinge little comodities for marchandize, onlie some fūa alias Būa[7], which the Banans doe use to carrie much to the Indies to dye red withall, and make greate proffitt thereby. It is a very firtill cittie for all provision of victuall and fruite, and reasonable cheape. A wholesome and pleasant place to dwell in, and a temperate aire, neither too hott nor too cold; but upon the waye in the mornings it is as cold as in England. I never felt soe much cold in any place as by the waye in the mornings before sonne rizinge, with a hoare frost on the grownd. Thus having ended our buysines, wee made our selves redye to take our journie towards Moucha, where wee had notice our shipp was come.

---

[1] This is a hill called Nukomi, from which cornelians and stones like emeralds are still obtained.

[2] Banyans, or Indian traders. Niebuhr found at San'a about 125 'Banians.'

[3] For 'baftas,' a general term for Indian cotton piece-goods.

[4] See p. 77.

[5] Jiddah.

[6] A shade of red not far removed from scarlet.

[7] 'Būa' is probably a slip for 'Rūa'; see p. 77.

Of our travaile from Senan to Moucha, vizt.:—

June 17. Wee departed, and went the same way wee came untill wee came to the cittie of Taies[1], which was the 24th of June; and therefore I neede not write of these seven daies journy, because it is sett downe in my travayles upward.

June 24, 25, 26. Wee came to a greate cittie called Tayes, being as bigg or bigger the[n] Senan, and lyeth on the side of a mountaine, with a very faire castell standing on the topp of the mountaine, with much ordinance in itt, which comandeth the cittie. Here are many Turks soldiars, being one of the best and strongest citties in Arabia, with manie faire buildings of stone in yt, and much trade with the Banians of Guzaratt, this cittie haveinge much of the red stuffe before mentioned, which cost 15 and 16 altons the bahar, and will yeild in Moucha (by their reporte) 20 peeces of eight. Here wee stayed three daies within a faire sarraye, because, as our drogaman said, he could gett noe camells to carrye our provision and stuffe; but I think wee staied rather for his owne pleasure then otherwise, butt here wee wanted noe [*a line omitted*?] came to see us daylie, the howse was full, that wee [were?] faine to keepe our selves within the chamber. The people did soe flocke to see us that once that wee went abroad to see the cittie wee could hardlie retourne for presse of people. Butt within the howse passed the tyme with an old blind Portugall renegado witch[2]. As he said himselfe, his trade was noe other thinge but witchcrafte, and was taken here to bee a saint, and many people would come and kisse his hands in my presence and entreate him to pray for them; which when he retorned from blessinge

---

[1] See p. 83.

[2] 'Witch' (Middle English *wicche*) could then be used of either a man or a woman.

them, he would burst out in laughing to me, sayinge that these foolish infidel people thought him to be a saint, and hee was noe other then a divell, and because he could doe a fewe of the Divells myracles, which he had taught him, that they thought him to bee a saint. This man had licence to begge at the townes end, where he had a little cottage by the side of the waye, and annother howse within, where resorted divers people to knowe many things of him, which hee could tell by aide of the Divell, to whome he had given the blud of his arme, with promise to sacrifice to him every monneth a hen or a kid; which one time being angrie with his maister the Divell, for killinge, as he said, his twoe sonnes and his daughter, he would not doe any more sacrifice to him; but the Divell will have his due, and therefore hee came unto him in the same shape as at first when hee made the agreement with him, to witt in the shape of a younge fawne, but dancinge round aboute him, his heate beeing soe extreame that it putt out his eyes, and is at this howre blind. Soe that he was faine to make an other promise to performe his sacrifice as before; otherwise he saith that he threatned to burne him to coales. Thus with many other tales which he tould me of the Divell, and of his cominge into the countrye and of his marriadge and other histories, wee passed the time these three dayes; which weere too tedious to sett downe, although pleasannt to heare.

June 27. Wee departed from Taies, and came to a towne called Buzeria[1]; which towne standeth on a mountaine, and hath a castle neere belonginge to it, in the which are 200 soldiars of the Turks, which lie in this towne upon all actions.

June 28. Wee departed from this towne and laye in a sarraye which standeth in a plaine feild, where travellours use to lodge.

[1] Not identified.

June 29. Wee departed from the sarraie and came to a towne within five leagues of Moucha, called Musse[1]. This is a greate towne and hath in itt 200 soldiars. In this towne wee rested untill the eveninge, and then wee sett forward, because of the heate.

June 30. Att two in the morninge we came to Moucha to the English house, where wee found William Revett, Gabriell Brooke[2] and William Mellar the purser, with some of the shipps companie; the Generall being gone aboard the daie before.

A discourse of whatt passed at Moucha after my comeinge from Senan.

Assoone as it was daie Mr. Revett and Mr. Glascocke and my selfe went to the Governor of Moucha, and shewed him the Basshaas pattent or passe; who made as though he understoode it not, yet he tould us that hee would performe all things contayned therein; with which awnsweare I went aboard the shipp to advertice the Generall what had passed in our journey to Senan. And the next daie, beinge the first of Julie, the Generall went aland and wee went presentlie to the Governours howse, whoe in outward shewe towards us made semblance to bee very glad that wee had brought a pattent from the Basshaa: that he was readie to obey all things that was contayned therein; and with these complements wee departed.

Nowe ten daies before my comeinge to Moucha our pinnace, beinge leake, was halled aland to be trymd, and most of our men aland at the hallinge up of her, and after for the space of 20 daies not soe little as 20 and 30 men aland; which if the Turks had pretended[3] anie villanie

---

[1] Musa. For a picture of this town see Lord Valentia's *Travels*, ii. 362.

[2] Of whom see note on p. 134.

[3] Intended.

against us, they might at one clapp have taken Generall, marchannts and maister, with the carpenters and the cheifest of all the shipp, which were on land all at halling upp the pinnace; and haveinge taken 50 of the cheifest, it had bene easie to have taken the shipp; which I hould to bee very careleslie done, and without discretion, seeinge howe wee had bene dealt withall att Aden and Pemba, and my selfe att Senan sent prisonner, nott as yett knowinge howe matters would passe with us there. Butt it is a generall rule with the English that if they have but a parcell of faire words given, that there neede noe more feare; which the Turks themselves saye: If thou wilt have anie thinge of an Englishman, give him good words and thou shalt bee sure to wynne him. Butt it pleased God that this danger fell out well; which some in the country did much repent after the pinnace was lanched, as I was secreetlie enformed.

In the interim of all the buysines aboute lanching and endinge the pinnace, wee did our best to sell some of our comodities; which by meanes of a Jewe called David, dwelling in Moucha, whoe brought the Consull or cheife of the Banians and offred us for all the yron 19 rials of eight the bahar, and take it all, which seemed to Mr. Revett and my selfe a reasonable price; notwithstandinge, wee would not make an end of the bargaine before we had advised the Generall thereof. Soe when wee brought the parties before him, thinkinge to have made an end, the Generall burst out in anger, sayinge that they mocked him to offer him soe little; which the marchaunt perceaveinge departed, not sayinge one word, butt after would not buye it at any rate, although it was offred to him for the same price, and some thinge to the Jewe to make the match. Therefore I hould it good to take the first bargaine if it bee with reason; if not, to give good words, for that all men are to buye as cheape as they can.

Nowe the pinnace beinge afloate, and wee seeing little to be done, the Generall and marchannts went to the Governor and shewed him that there were noe marchannts that would buye our comodities, that had lyen aland soe longe: therefore that it would please him to licence us to embarke it abourd our shipp, and leave to departe. Whereto the Governour replyed: To what end, said hee, came yee hither, if you are not minded to buy nor sell? The Generall made awnswere that he was readie to sell any comoditie that was in the shipp, if any marchannts or other would buye them; and as for any comodities that was in the countrie he sawe not any that was for his turne. The Governor, leaveinge his former pratica[1] aboute merchandizing, made a speech to the Generall, saying that the captaines of all the ships that weare in the roade, beeing neere 40 saile, greate and small, had bene with him and said that if hee did suffer us to departe before them, that they stoode in feare to goe home this monsone, fearinge least wee should lye in waite for them and take them; and by way of entreatye desired the Generall that they might departe some four or five daies before us; and then wee might departe in peace.

Soe goeinge homewards discontent wee mett some of the saylars, whoe tould us that they were not permitted to goe aboard, but had their oares taken out of the boate. With this newes, before wee went to our owne howse, wee went to the Captaine of the Gallies, advertisinge him whatt passed; whoe presentlie went to the Governour and gott leave for the boate and the marriners to goe aboard, but the Generall and marchannts must staie aland; wheare wee weare stayed three daies, debatinge of the matter, some times with the Turks and sometimes with the captaines of the shipps, whoe did denie anie matter in

[1] See note on p. 91.

that kinde that they had moved to the Governour, butt esteemed us as their freinds, and therefore they feared not of us; and with these words they all joyned togeather and told the Governor to his face that they feared not of us, and therefore desired him to lett us departe att our pleasure; which if he did staie us perforce, that then they should have cause to feare of us, wee beinge wronged for there cause. Which the Governour perceiveinge, and this beinge required by them of him in a publique audience, the Governor cawsed notice to bee taken of it by the Caia and a scrivano[1] before the Cadee[2] of the towne; which being registred, he gave us leave to departe when wee thought good. Soe that after wee had dined, the Generall and my selfe determined to have gone aboard, leaveinge Mr. Revett aland to send all things aboard the shipp. Soe when wee came to goe into the boate, the guard which was on the key would not suffer mee to goe, but permitted the Generall to departe and staied mee aland. When the Generall was gone aboard, I went to the Captaine of the Gallies, advisinge him thereof; whoe seemed to bee moved at such dealinge, promisinge me to goe instantlie to the Governours, my selfe staieinge at his howse till his retourne; which was not longe before hee brought awnsweare that it was for noe hurte that I was stayed, the cawse was onelie aboute anchorage[3] of the shipp, which the Governor was to have. I awnswered that one marchannt had bene sufficient to have awnswered anie thinge that was due unto him, beeinge freed from all duties by the Bashaas pattent; demanndinge him what the Governor would have. Hee said that he asked 1000 rials of eight, but that he thought that 500 rials would content him, seeinge the Guzaratts shipps paid noe more. I entreated the Captaine

---

[1] Port. *escrivão*, a 'writer,' 'registrar.'

[2] Judge (Arabic *kādī*).

[3] Anchorage dues.

of the Gallies to write unto the Generall the Governours demand, that he might knowe the Generalls minde therein, and if any thinge weare due unto him noe doubt but hee would paie him. The Captaine havinge written his letter, the next daie, being the 21th of Julie, I had leave to cary the letter to the Generall in a small canoe of the shore; in which letter the Captaine wrote to the Generall that hee remayned pledge for the 500 rials due to the Governor for anchorage, intreatinge the Generall to retourne againe ashoare to conferr aboute the matter. But the Generall retourned awnswere that he would neither retourne aland nor give the Governour anie thinge, wondringe that the Captaine would remayne pledge to paie that which was not due, intreatinge the Captaine to shewe the Governor thereof and to send the rest of our people aboard with such stuffe as was remayneinge, otherwise he would gett them and the goods as he might. Whereunto the Captaine retourned awnsweare that they might goe aboard at there pleasure with there goods, not doubting but that the Generall knewe him to be butt a poore man, and that it would be his undoinge to paie 500 rials of eight to the Governor, entreatinge him to consider of itt; butt when he sawe that the Generall would not yeild to any thinge, he entreated for some thinge towards it, as soe much given him for an almes; butt when hee could gett nothinge, hee desired to have some peeces of timber and wood which was left aland; which beinge of little valewe weare given him. Soe they proved all meanes to gett somethinge, first by rigour, next by entreatie, and last by begginge; for these trecherous Turks doe much scorne to begge if they can gett any thinge by rigour or trecherie; and what is freelie given them they thinke it to bee there due, and that it is given them because we stand in feare of them; and if they begge they must not bee denyed, for feare of trecherie, perswadinge them selves that wee are bound to give them all they demand. I would wish all Christians to beware of them, for they are full of trecherie, and never hould their words except it be for their owne profitts.

Havinge had many bickerings aland with Mr. Revett concerninge this ankoradge, at length they permitted him to come aboard with what was remayneinge; more for that they stood in feare of us, because of the Indian shipps that weare in the roade, then for any good they ment us. The 25th of Julie all our people and goods came aboard. And the 20th[1] ditto Phillipp Glascocke, whoe was in companie with mee at Senan, died aboard our shipp of a white flix, which he had taken with the cold comminge downe.

A discripcion of the cittie of Moucha, with the trade and qualities.

This cittie of Moucha standeth hard by the waters side in a plaine sandye feild. It hath in it very faire buildings (after their manner) of lime and stone, and very populous, as well of Arabs as strangers merchants, and espetiallie Bananes of Guzaratt, Dabull, Dieu, Chaule, Bazim[2], Daman, and Sinda[3], as alsoe of Ormus and Muscatt, with all the coast of Melinda. This yeare there is greate reporte [resorte?] of marchannts and ships, because the staple, which was in former time at Zida[4], is at present removed (by reason of the warre which is neere that countrie) to Moucha; soe that this yeare here came from all places aboute 35 saile of ships, greate and small, from the ports before mentioned, bringinge all kinds of comodities made of cotton woll, manye sorts of gums, pretious stones of all

[1] Revett says the 21st or 22nd (see Appendix B).

[2] Bassein.

[3] Lārībandar, the port of Tatta, was also called Diul-Sind to distinguish it from the Diu in Kāthiāwār. The English termed it Sindee, Scindy, and Lowribander.

[4] Jiddah.

sorts, store of indicoe; which yearlie cometh many marchannts from Grand Cairo, who bringe rialls of eight and chickings[1] of gould in greate aboundance to buye these comodities and transporte them by sea and land to Grand Cairo, and from thence to Aleppo and other places in Turkey. Comonlie every yeare there cometh a shipp or twoe from the bottome of the Red Sea, from a port called Swes[2], and doth arrive commonlie aboute the end of Maye or the begininge of June. These ships are very ritch of rialls, gould and silks, and they retourne aboute August with all sorts of Indian comodities. All kinds of comodities are there soe deare that there is noe dealinge for us to buye them for England at the rates which they sell them to the marchannts which comes from Grand Cairo. The Guzaratts and other marchannts of India doe make profitt by their comodities, beinge butt a voyage of 20 daies saileinge from the Indias with the winde in poope and faire weather out and whome. There is one cheife marchant, a Banane, in Moucha which is over all the rest of the marchannts as Consall or Agent; soe that none can buye nor sell without his order nor shewe any comodities. And for their jewells they are soe fearfull to shewe them to any, because if the Turke should knowe them to have any jewell of valewe they must have it by hooke or by crooke for the Basha or Governours. Soe that it is very hard to see any jewell of value before they are readye to departe; and the marchannts which buye these jewells keepe it soe close because, if the Basha should understand of it, he would surelie have it, at his owne price, if he liked it. Alsoe there is brought amber greece, but is kept secrett in the like manner. In this towne there is one Governor, one Cadee or Ovvidor[3], and the Captain of two gallies,

---

[1] See note on p. 70. [2] Suez.

[3] Port. *Ouvidor*, 'a magistrate.'

which lie neere the Captains howse by the waters side; one of them not serviceable, the other hath some six peeces of brasse. I could perceive noe defence in the towne, onelie three brasse peeces mounted at the sea side before the Captaine of the Gallies howse. This towne is unreasonable hotte, by reason that it standeth in sandie grownd and lowe; soe that the people make howses of caves (*sic*) on the tops of their howses to take the aire, otherwise there weare noe bidinge within the howse. There are not in the towne above 40 Turks in all, and yet they keepe the countrie in greate subjection. The countrie people generallie very good and honest; and weare a very pleasant place to bide in, were it not for the Turkes tyrannie. It is very well served with all kinde of victualls, which comes out of the countrye, and cheape. For the water, [it] is some thinge brakish, but not as bad as that at Aden[1].

Our Course from Mocha to Socotora.

July 26. Aboute ten in the morninge wee sett saile from Mocha with a faire gale at N.N.W., and we stood our

---

[1] With this account of Mocha compare Revett's description in Appendix B; also the following, which is extracted from Covert's narrative (p. 22):—'It is a place that is never without shipping, for it is a towne of great trade of merchandise and hath caravans or convoies that come from Seena, from Mecha, from Grand Cairo and Alexandria, and all those places. It is a city of great trading for our commodities, as tynne, iron, lead, cloth, swordblades, and all English commodities. It hath a great bussart [bazaar] or market every day in the weeke. There is great store of fruit, as apricocks, quinces, dates, grapes [in] abundance, peaches, limmons, and plantins great store; which I much marvelled at, in regard the people of the countrey told us they had no raine in seven yeeres before, and yet there was very good corne, and good store, for eighteene pence a bushell. There are oxen, sheepe and goats [in] abundance; as an oxe for three dollars, a goat for halfe a dollar, and a sheepe for halfe a dollar; as much fish for threepence as will suffice ten men to a meale, as dolphines, more-fish, basse, mullets and other good fish. The towne is Arabian, and governed by the Turk; and if an Arabian offend hee is severely punished by their law; for they have gallies and chaines of purpose, which offenders are put into; else were they not able to keepe them in awe and subjection.'

course S.S.E. and S.E. & by S. till the afternoone. Then it fell calme; and in the eveninge a hard gale at S.S.E. And beinge neere the Straicts of Babelmendall, wee lett fall an anchour; but the cable broke in wendinge up the shipp, and for want of a boye was lost; butt presentlie wee lett slipp annother, and rid all night. This night died Mathew Baker, the maister his minion.

July 27. In the morninge we wayed our anchour; and in wayinge our cable brake, and haveing noe buoye wee lost annother anchor. And the winde beeing at S.S.E. wee laye all daie volting too and againe to passe the straits, butt, the current settinge into the gutt against us, could not doe anie good. Wee anchored at night.

July 28. The winde variable till noone, and then it came upp at N.N.W. Wee wayed, thinkeinge to passe the straights, butt beinge in the mid way it fell calme; and, the current against us, were forced to lett fall an anker betwixt the iland and the mayne. This daie wee anchored twice.

July 29. The winde at N.N.W. Wee wayed and passed the Straits of Babelmandell, which is aboute two leagues longe and a league from the iland to the mayne.

July 30. The winde at N.W. We steered our course at E. & by S. and E.S.E. In the eveninge the winde was variable; then it fell calme.

July 31. The winde betweene the S.W. and the S.S.W.; and wee stood away E. & by S. In the eveninge wee had sight of Aden. Then the winde came variable, with a little raine. It grewe calme, and soe contynued all night.

. . . .

August 5. In the morninge the winde at S., and wee had sight of Cape Guardafewe on the coast of Abex[1]. Then wee steered awaie E.S.E. with little winde....

---

[1] Abyssinia. 'Abex' is from the Arabic 'Habash,' through the Portuguese. Middleton uses the form 'Habashe.'

Aug. 6. ...This eveninge wee had sight of Abdelcura, and a small iland which lieth to the norward of itt; and wee went betweene them both, with as much winde as wee could steere under.

. . . .

Aug. 8. ...Very darke and mistye weather, that wee could see noe land, beeinge neere the iland of Soccotora. Soe that with a shorte saile wee laye too and againe untill ten in the forenoone, att which time wee sawe the little iland or rocke which lieth to the norward of Soccotora aboute two leagues; and standing in with it wee sawe the firme iland; standinge towards the shore with soe much winde that hardlie wee could carrie anie saile to seaze the land[1]. Notwithstanding, aboute eight att night, with much adoe wee anchored some two leagues to the westwards of the small towne neere Socotora or Delishaa[2]. But our pinnace, the Good Hope, was not able to seaze the land, with soe much winde that her sailes blew from the maste. In this place wee rid three daies with very much winde att S.S.W., with such flawes of the land thatt it was impossible to waye our anchour; therefore wee rid still, hopinge of faire weather.

Aug. 11. The winde somethinge dullerd, we went aboute to waye our anchour; and in wayinge one of the flucks brake of our shifte anchour, this being the third anchour lost since wee came from Moucha. This daie aboute nine in the eveninge wee ankored againe, some thinge neerer to the town of Delisha.

Aug. 12. Wee had very much winde at S.S.W., thatt wee brooke our ankour; soe that wee weare forced to sett saile, standinge alonge the shore with our forecourse onely, and came to anchour before the towne where the Kinge

---

[1] On the prevalence of strong winds at Socotra at this season see Roe's journal, p. 35.

[2] Delaisha.

dwelt, called Tamarin[1]. And in wending up[2] the shipp our cable brake; soe thatt wee were faine to lett fall annother, and rid by. And havinge not rid aboute [above ?] half an houre before there was a flagge putt out on the shore, and shoote a peece. Wee awnswered them with three peeces; and in the afternoone the winde came some thinge calmer. The Generall sent mee aland in the pinnace, where I found the Kinge by the waters side with 300 armed men, whereof 50 of them had peeces, the rest bowes, arrowes and lances, with three peeces of ordinance planted by the waters side.

Of whatt passed att Socotora with the Kinge.

The Generall sendinge mee aland, I found the Kinge by the waters side, with 300 men armed with peeces and lances, as aforesaid. I had a Jewe in my companie, whome wee brought from Moucha, which could speake good Arab, Portugues and other languages very well[3]; and comeinge to the Kinge wee shewed them [him ?] what wee were and the cause of our cominge. He welcomed us verye kindlie, awnsweringe that any thinge that his country did affoard wee should have; and next hee demandeth whether I knewe Captaine Keelinge and Captaine Hawkins. I shewed him that wee weare all for one companie, where of he seemed to bee joyfull, and told me that I should not wonder to see soe manie armed men by him; that the cause was for that he knewe us not to be English, but feared least wee weare Fleemings that had wrongd him the yeare before, and therefore stoode in doubt of them[4]; but that English-

[1] Tamrida, the chief town of the island. [2] See note on p. 25.

[3] Possibly the Jew mentioned on p. 99.

[4] Revett says that the King stipulated that the English should bring no weapons ashore; 'haveinge had some troubles some 12 monnethes synce with a Flemysh shipp that touched heere, which was the reason hee prohibbited us at this present tyme.'

men should be as welcome to his countrie as to their owne howses; with many other words of complements. Wee departed with a present of five goats, which he sent the Generall.

Aug. 13. The next daie, being the 13th, wee had soe much winde that wee could nott land with our boate untill the afternoone; at which time with much paine we gott the shoare with our longe boate, carryinge a present with mee to the Kinge from our Generall, vizt. a vest of cloth, a peece and a sword blade; which he kindlie received, and carryed mee to his howse, where wee dranke cohoo. His howse is three stories high, and keepeth aboute 50 soldiars att his outer gate and aboute 30 at the inner gate, with their weopons drawne in their hands; and at the entrye of his chamber there are ten armed men for the guard of his personn. The order of the Kings apparell is after the Turkish manner, with a vest of crimson velvett and a shash on his head[1]. He had much conference with mee aboute his [our?] enterteynement at Aden and Moucha; as alsoe aboute our pinnace, which had bene there before they went for Aden; whome he had kindlie used and refreshed with victualls, sheweinge mee a noate of Francis Drivers (which was hanged at Aden), alledginge his kindenesse shewed them, as alsoe to Captaine Keelinge I awnswerd that it was not unknowne to the Generall what kindnes he had shewed to the pinnace, as alsoe to Captaine Keelinge, beeinge att full informed in the Red Sea; which made us the bolder to land without feare. Hee demanded whether wee had any certaine newes of Captaine Hawkins, whoe was bound for Suratt. I tould him whatt newes wee heard by the Guzaratts; wheareat he shooke his head as doubting it to bee true, demandinge me whoe told us the newes. I told him the shrift[2] of

[1] Cp. Roe's journal, p. 31.

[2] Probably 'shroff' (Arabic *sharrāf*, a 'banker' or 'money changer')

Suratt, which was att Moucha, in whose howse the Captaine and marchannts laye at Suratt. Whereunto hee awnswered that it might well bee, but that he was certainelie enformed that four Portugall friggatts had taken the Hectours longe boate, laden with goods, cominge from Suratt to the shipp, and had likewise taken some of the marchannts, amongst whome there was one whose name was Bucke; all which goods and men was carried to Goa[1]; Captaine Hawkins, beeinge aland, presentlie embarked himselfe and went in the shipp to the barre of Goa to ransome his men and goodes, but the Portugalls denyed to ransome any of them; whereupon Captaine Hawkins, meetinge with certaine Fleemish ships, joyned with them and was gone from thence, it was not knowne wheather. This newes he tould us for certaine, as it was reported to him by Guzaratts of good creeditt. Soe after much other conference, wee havinge laden our boate with stones for ballast, and gotten some goats, wee went aboard.

Aug. 14. The next daie we had all the forenoone much winde at S.E.; butt in the afternoone beinge reasonable weather, I retourned aland; and concluded with the Kinge to have of him four goats for a sword blade, and three sword blades for one cowe. Also he tould us that the place where wee rid was not good, wishinge us to goe to Delisha, a league beyond the pointe, where the Dragon and Hectour roade; that there it was a better roade and lesse winde, that we might doe our buysines at pleasure, and there was both water and stones for ballast, and he would send us both goats and cattle thether and all other things which wee wanted, and would send aboard a pylett to carrye us thether; intreatinge us to bee gone the

is meant, the word being used incorrectly for 'merchant.' Hawkins says that at Surat he lodged 'in a merchants house...the captaine of that shippe which Sir Edward Michelborne tooke' (*Purchas*, i. 206).

[1] So far the King's information was correct (see *Purchas*, i. 207, 420); the rest was quite wrong.

sooner, because all the weomen of the towne weare runne awaie for feare of us, and before wee weare gone would not retourne to the towne; therefore he made us make the more haste to bee gone.

Aug. 15. But the next daie, notwithstandinge that the Kinge had sent a pilott aboard to direct us to Delisha, I was willed to retourne aland, and the long boate to fetch water; whereat the Kinge seemed to be very angrie because wee had not sett saile, sayinge that he had sent thether all provision for us, and we trusted him nott. But I excused the matter as well as I might, promisinge that without faile this night wee would bee gone.

Aug. 16. The next daie aboute ten in the morninge wee sett saile; and aboute three the same daie wee anchored beyond the N.E. pointe, where Captaine Hawkins sett up his pinnace. As soone as wee came thether wee landed, where wee mett with the Kinge[s] Caia, a negro Abexim[1], whoe spake a little Portugues; whoe shewed us the place where the water was, which is very good water but is soe farre of that wee could not fetch it without endangeringe our men; which made us suspect some trecherie.

Aug. 17. But the next daie the Generall sent againe aland, to take in ballast and to agree with the Caia for his slaves to bringe downe water and to paie them for their paines, or elce they to leave pledges aboard the shipp while our men did fetch the water. Whereunto he seemed to be verye angrie, and awnswered that neyther one nor the other would he doe. Butt having advised the Kinge, in the eveninge he sent us awnsweare that for 20 rialls of eight his slaves should bring downe water to lade our longe boate; the which was granted to him rather then to adventure up our men.

---

[1] Abyssinian (see p. 106).

Aug. 18. The next daie his slaves beganne to bringe downe water; and we bought of him aboute 14 C[1] of alloes Socatrina, for 20 rialls of eight the 100 waight.

[*Aug.* 19.] And the next daie wee paid for our water, and bought a small parcell of Sanguis Draconis at 30 rialls the 100 waight. And having delivered them a writinge for the Generall for the next shipps[2], wee tooke our leaves and went aboard. Wee made the more hast to begone, because our pinnace was putt of and gone for Suratt, as we supposed, with four dayes victualls; which was a greate greife to us.

Aug. 20. In the morninge wee sett saile. But there was a signe made on the shore; soe wee sent the boate aland to knowe the matter. And at there comeinge aland they delivered a letter left by Captaine Keelinge, which was brought aboard and presentlie retorned againe aland to deliver it to some other shipp that should come after. Theffect of the letter was that they were trecherous people, willinge all men to looke to themselves and stand upon their guard and trust them nott[3]. This daie wee had the winde att S.S.W. Much winde all daie and night.

. . . .

Aug. 28. The winde between the N.W. and the W.N.W. Our course E.N.E. This daie wee sawe many snakes. At noone per observacion 19 d. 12 m.

Aug. 29. The winde betweene the N.N.W. and the West. Our course E.N.E. untill four in the afternoone; at which time the sea began to alter, shewing very browne. Then wee sounded and had 21 fathome water. Then wee steered all night at N. & by West and N.N.W., sowndinge

---

[1] Hundredweight.

[2] On the arrival of Middleton's ships they were told that the *Ascension* had left a letter for them, 'but the Sulltaun of Sacatoria sayd that the letter was loste: that it was guiven to one of his servantes and hee loste it' (*I. O. Marine Records*, no. ix.).

[3] See *Lancaster's Voyages*, p. 118.

every two glasses, and found alwaies from 20 to 22 fathame. At noone per observacion 19 d. 40 m.

Aug. 30. The winde at West. Wee steered N.E. & by N. Aboute seven in the morninge wee sounded and had 17½ fathome; and standinge the same course till noone wee found nine fathome, and sawe noe land. Then wee steered North till three in the afternoone, in the same depth, from nine to ten fathome, at which time wee had sight of land bearing N.N.E. of us. And wee stoode our course towards it, alwaies in nine fathome, the sea beeinge very white and fowle water. Aboute six at night we ankored within a baye neere the land in five fathome water, within the pointe of land, that did shelter us from the force of the winde, a reasonable good roade. Wee sawe many people on the shore, and a faire greene land, and hard by there is a towne called Mūa[1].

To knowe this place, it is a reasonable high land, the highest thereabouts. Upon the pointe of the land where we roade there standeth a little c[h]aple or misquita[2] in a faire greene place, and hard by it twoe small hills or hummocks of earth throwne up in manner of a place of defence or bulwarke; the pointe of the land bearinge west of us, the other pointe E. and by N.

Of whatt passed after wee anchored in Mūa, neere the castelett.

Aug. 31. The next daie the boate was sent aland to have speech with the countrye people and to knowe the place, for that our maister made himselfe to be shorte of Dieu. Presently the people told him the name of the

[1] Mahuwa or Mhowa on the S.E. coast of Kāthiāwār, opposite to the mouth of the Taptī.

[2] A *masjid*, or mosque. Jourdain uses the Portuguese form *mesquita*.

place, and shewed with their hand that Suratt laye of us E.S.E. and Dieu bare of us N.W. neerest. The boate brought some sheepe and goats, which cost $\frac{3}{4}$ riall per peece. In the afternoone we sawe many horsemen.

Sept. 1. The skiffe was sent againe aland with sword blades to buye more sheepe and goats, but the people would have nothing butt money. Soe they gave them money for ten more, and brought them aboard; and alsoe brought with them a Banane of the countrie, beeinge desirous to goe to Suratt in the shipp. He told us that there was newes of a small pinnace which was anchored three leagues farther within the baye, under the castellett, which wee might see from our shipp the place where the castell stoode on a very lowe pointe trending towards the sea. The Generall, thinkinge it to bee our pinnace, would have the Banian to send a man thether with a letter, and if it were a Christian shipp to deliver it and bringe awnsweare; if not, to returne and bringe us word; and to that purpose delivered mony to the Banane. But he retourned the next daie, beinge certified that there was none there; but he brought us certaine newes of Captaine Hawkins beeinge at the Mogolls courte and English-marchannts at Suratt. Alsoe he tould us of the dangers betweene this place and Suratt; wherefore there was a motion made to have from Goga[1] (which was a daies journie from thence) a pilott; whereat our master stormed very much, that he had brought the shipp soe farre and nowe must have a pilott to carry him 20 leagues[2]. Soe it was determyned betweene

[1] Gogha, on the Kāthiāwār side of the Gulf of Cambay, was at this time a place of importance, as the native ships carrying merchandise to or from Cambay mostly laded or unladed at that port, the roadstead at Cambay being shallow and dangerous.

[2] 'One of the countrey people told us that for the value of 20 dollars wee might have a pilot to bring us to the bar of Surot; but our wilfull master refused it and said he would have none' (Covert). Jones confirms this statement, except that he says a pilot might have been had for seven pieces of eight. He, too, blames the

the Generall and the master to sett saile for Suratt, and not to staie three daies longer for a pilott. This was done without councell[1].

Of our settinge sayle from Mūa and of our castinge awaye upon the shoaldes[2].

Sept. 2. The winde beeinge calme, in the morninge our boate was sent aland to buye more sheepe, and the Banane retourned in the boate to goe to Suratt with us. In the afternoone aboute three we sett saile from Mūa, and stoode our course at S. & by East. And havinge sayled two glasses, with a pretty gale, wee sownded and had nine fathome. Then wee stoode three glasses more at E.S.E. and E. & by S., and found six fathome, and within falcon shott to leeward of us wee might descerne the sea to breake on the shoales; and goinge to cast aboute, the shipp would nott staie, soe that wee weare forced to beare up toward the shoaldes, and went soe neere them that wee weare within a butt shott of them; but, God be thanked, with greate danger wee gott cleare this first time; and stood our course N.N.W. towards the land aboute two glasses; at which time wee tacked aboute againe, and stoode away S. aboute two glasses more; and in standinge this course at S. wee had from nine to fifteen fathome. Then the master comanded (without any consideration of the current) to steere awaie S.E. & by E., and presentlie wee found the water to lessen from fifteen to seven fathome, from seven to five fathome, the master bidding lett runne; said he: The

master for the refusal. On the other hand Sharpeigh (in Appendix C) says that they were unable to procure a pilot.

[1] *I.e.*, without assembling the officers and merchants in a consultation, which should have been done before taking a decision of this importance.

[2] Compare Sharpeigh's account of the wreck in Appendix C; also that in Jourdain's letter *O. C.* 12, printed in *Letters Received*, i. 35.

Dragon[1] hath bene in lesse. These words were scarce out of his mouth when we felt the shipp to strike; and the second stroke brake of her ruther. Yett the master would not beleive that shee stroke, till they told him that the ruther was gone. Then he beganne to curse the Companye at home, that had not sought better smithes, and the smithes for puttinge such bad iron on the hooks; but his cursinge could not prevaile. Wee tooke in our sailes as fast as wee could and lett fall the anchour, that had but one flucke; and beinge upon the tide of flood the shipp rid afloate in 3½ fathome, and 4 fathome at full sea. Our shipp wendinge upp[2] with force of the tyde splitt our skiffe by the shipp side; soe that wee weare faine to take her into the shipp to mend her, which with greate travell was effected, for our men weare soe amazed that they knewe not whatt they did. But nowe troubles begin to enter into mens harts, seeinge our ruther gone, our skiffe splitt, wee ridinge in the middest of shoales in 3½ fathome, the shipp sometimes strikinge on the ground, and our long boate not sufficient to save our men, which made us all doubt of our lives. Notwithstanding wee comforted our selves in Gods mercyes; in which wee passed the night untill the morninge.

Sept. 3. The next daie betimes in the morninge, beinge the 3d dicto, our carpenters begann to goe to worke upon the boate which was splitt, being alsoe determyned to make our longe boate a streake[3] higher, the better to save our selves and the monie if need should bee, the money being taken all out of the hold and laide in the steeridge to that purpose. All hands went to worke aboute providinge our boats this daie till the eveninge, but could not end one of them, before our shipp at a low water and turninge of the tide begann to wend aboute; and as wee suppose that in wendinge the anchour, haveing but one flucke, cast the

[1] Which was nearly twice the burden of the *Ascension.*

[2] See p. 25.

[3] A line of planking.

wrong end downwards, soe that our ship did drive with the tide upon the shoaldes; and aboute five at night she begann to strike very hard with the force of the winde and tyde; and presentlie soundinge the pumpe there was 11[1] [foote] water in the hold. Our men went to the pumpe chearfullie, seeinge noe other remedye to save their lyves; yet all in vaine, for the water came in much faster then they weare able to free itt. Notwithstandinge they did what they could, while other[s] went aboute to see if the skiffe could be ended, to save our lives before the turninge of the tide, for feare least the shipp would over throwe with the tyde, as noe doubt shee did. But by night our carpenters made as much haste as they could to mend the skiffe, having noe hope nowe to make the longe boate heigher, neyther to mend the skiffe as she ought to bee, but for hast nayled on boards in the sides of noe force, and chinked it with okom within side in the seames and with a stronge roape wreathed the boate to keepe the sides together, havinge noe time to doe it otherwise, the shipp being alreadye founded, lookinge still when shee would overthrowe with the seeles[2] which she made from one side to the other. We kept contynuall pumpinge and balling of water while the skiffe was providinge, to keepe her from fallinge, beeinge once full of water; but all would not serve turne, for they weare faine to putt the skiffe overboard before shee was fitted, that beeing out they could hardlie keepe her above water; yet the carpenters and seven or eight more of our men (all to the number of thirteen persons) went into her with bucketts and shovells to throwe out the water to keepe her till the morninge that they might see better to mend her.

The skiffe beinge overboard aboute ten at night the

[1] Probably Jourdain wrote 'ii foote.' Covert says '24 inches.'

[2] Rolls.

Generall had advise given him that some who shall goe namelesse had consulted to gett into the longe boate and cutt her of, to save themselves and whome they pleased, doubtinge that the boats not [being ?] able to carrie all our men, that there would be a mutinie (as comonly there is att such times) and by that meanes all lose their lives. The Generall advised me of itt, and told me that he would gett in two chests of money into the longe boate, and goe in with it himselfe, to keepe the boate from cuttinge of. And cawsinge the longe boate to be halled up under the ships starne, brought two chests of money to putt them out of the gallery into the boate; but the marriners, having notice thereof, stoode on the pumpe with half pikes, swereinge that they would kill the first that should sett hand to putt in any chest of monie; which the Generall perceiveinge, lefte all and went into the ladder out of the gallery into the boate, biddinge me to come with him. Soe I followed him; but he beinge in the boate, with the sea and tide she was putt astarne the shipp, leavinge mee hanginge by the hands on the ladder; and before she could come up to take mee in, there were soe many on my backe that they had almost throwne mee into the sea, as in the end they did. The next unto me, I remember well, was Robert Covert, soe laden with mony of the Companies that he could not hardlie goe. Hee, I saye, with all his money was on my backe. I entreated him that he would either goe backe, or suffer mee, for I was not able to abide any longer, I hanginge onelie by the hands and he on my backe; but he awnswered me that nowe there was noe respect of persons, that it was every one for himselfe. Life beeing sweete, with greate paines I hunge by the hands untill the boate came to take mee in. But the sea beeinge highe, and the shipp fetchinge such careers from side to side that the boate dare not to come neare the shipp, for feare of splittinge her; soe that I, seeinge noe remedye, not able to abide any longer,

I gave a springe to gett into the boate. But the gas roape[1] that the boate was made faste withall, stroke me overboard; but I tooke hold of the roape, butt the boate fell againe a starne the shipp. Soe I hanginge by the roape was ducked soe longe under water that my memory[2] began to faile mee. Soe I lett goe the roape, thinkinge to swime to the boate; but the force of the tide and the waight of my cloathes kept mee under water. Butt my memorie not quite gone, I was stirred to shifte for my life; which with all the force I made to gett above water, and beeing cast astarne the shipp with the tide, my head appeared above water at the starne of the longe boate; which the boteson perceived, not thinkinge it had bene my selfe, havinge given mee over for dead, thought it to be some clothes throwne by the board, putt downe his hand and tooke mee by the collar and drewe me in little better then dead; the Lord alwayes bee praised for it. Had not His omnipotent hand saved mee by His miraculous mercye, I had bene drowned; the Lord make mee alwaies thankfull for itt.

Aboute midnight wee were all embarked in the two boats, vizt. in the longe boate 62[3] persons, besides store of luggage, and in the skiffe 13 persons. John Frencham[4] was the last man that came out of the shipp, remayninge behinde to give out the Generalls cabinett and other things

---

[1] Guess-rope or guest-rope, a term of which the etymology is disputed. It is thus explained in *The Seaman's Grammar* (1627): 'The Ghest rope is added to the boat rope when shee is towed at the ships sterne, to keepe her from shearing.'

[2] Or, as we should say, 'senses.' Sir Henry Middleton, describing his capture at Mocha, says that he was stunned by a blow from behind, but the pain caused by his hands being bound 'brought mee to my memorie.'

[3] In *O. C.* 12 Jourdain says 65, and this is borne out by Sharpeigh's statement in Appendix C.

[4] This must be the 'John Frenchman' mentioned by Finch as going from Agra to the Deccan wars in the service of Azam Khān (Jan. 1611). He had left Agra with Covert a year before, but falling ill had been forced to remain behind at Bukkur, whence no doubt he returned to Agra on recovery.

of noe greate valewe, onelie the Kings letters to the Mogoll; soe that by this tyme the water was above the middle decke, the shipp stickinge on the grownd. The most parte of the marryners brought money with them which was the Worshipfull Companyes; for when the Generall sawe that none could bee saved he cawsed some of the chestes to bee broken open, that every man might take whatt he could convenyentlie carrie, which afterward stoode them in good steede to those that did not lewdlie spend it; but by judgment there was brought out of the shipp aboute 10,000 rialls of eight[1]. Soe that our boate was soe laden that there was not above three inches above water astarne, havinge then to goe fifteen or twenty leagues, for the winde would not serve to goe backe to the place from whence wee came, which was not above eight leagues of, but to the other side the neerest place was fifteen leagues.

Sept. 4. Aboute two in the morninge, our men being all embarked, wee fitted our selves to sett saile, stowinge our selves in such sorte as wee would contynue untill it pleased God to send us to land, with a saile round aboute the sides of the boate to keepe out the suffe of the sea, and our men sittinge round aboute the boate side with the edge of the canvas under them, with two men provided to take their turnes to bale out the water that came in over the boats side; the rest all stowed one upon annother. In this manner wee putt of from the shipp, singinge of psalmes to the praise of God, leavinge the shipp as yett standing, with

[1] Covert says the amount brought on deck was about 10,000*l.* sterling, of which the sailors and others took about 3000*l.* The loss to the Company must have been considerable, for the two ships carried out between them 15,000*l.* in money, of which the greater portion was on board the *Ascension.* In their instructions to Saris for the Eighth Voyage, the Court reflected severely on Sharpeigh's remissness in the matter, and directed that in any future disaster of this kind, if it were found impossible to take the money in the boats, it should be buoyed in the sea with a view to subsequent recovery (*First Letter Book*, p. 419).

her yards acrosse and the flagg atopp, to our greate greifes. And after that wee weare putt of from the shipp, whereas before there was much winde and a greate sea, it pleased God to send us a faire leadinge gale, and the sea as smooth as in a river. Some said that the reason of the smoothnes of the sea was because it was then a full sea. Havinge hoisted our saile, wee stoode awaye S.E. untill daie; then wee steered E.S.E., the water very fowle, but wee had noe lead nor line to sound, neyther could any stand to doe itt. Aboute nine the sea was very cleare, wee supposinge as then to be in the channell, and deepe water, and the channell where the shipps did usuallie come in and out from Suratt. This channell was aboute four leagues broad, for wee were three howers passinge of itt, and then wee came into fowle water againe. And aboute two in the afternoone wee sawe high land of Daman, butt could not see the lowe land untill four; att which tyme there fell a shower of raine, with a flawe of winde which broke the thought[1] which stayed the boats maste, blowinge forward the saile on the boats head, that wee weare in greate danger of sinkinge; but noe man durst to move untill the gust was past. And our skyffe, beeinge neere unto us, sawe us in this extremitie, thinkinge wee weare nowe lost men, went further from us, for feare least wee should take hould of theire boate; but, God be thanked, after the gust was paste we righted the saile by little and little as well as wee could; which the skiffe perceiveinge, came towards us. Soe wee held on our course towards the neerest land, S.E., being aboute three leagues of, and yet could scarce discerne the lowe land, onelie the topps of the palmito trees. And approachinge neere the land wee had a greate sea, and the water much troubled, which made us stand in some feare, wee beeinge almost past feare. Beeinge neare the land wee perceived a breach

[1] Thwart.

and within the breach was smooth watter, and betwixt the breach wee perceyved a smooth, towards the which wee steered and sownded with a pole, and had not lesse then twelve foote on the barre; soe that in half an hower wee weare passed within the shoales over the barre, where wee had as smooth water as in a well, to our greate comforts. Although wee knewe not where wee weare, yet wee purposed to land before night to save our lives. But as soone as wee weare over the barre, wee perceyved a boate at saile over the land in a river; to the mouth of which river wee steered. Which when the Banane that came with us [saw, he?] knewe it to be the river of Gandivee[1], aboute four leagues[2] to the southward of Suratt[3]. There came manie of the countrye people to see us, but wee could speake with none[4]. As likewise we sawe a pinnace on drie land, which was our pinnace, that was come thether ten daies before and for feare of the Portugalls had left the pinnace and gone to Suratt; and at this time there weare four friggats come from Daman[5] to fetch the pinnace. All of them sawe us to come into the river; yett it pleased God to alter their counsaile, that they come not to us, some of them sayinge that wee weare boates of the countrye; soe that they fell out with their captaine because he would not see what wee weare, whoe afterward was emprisonned at Daman for the same. Soe saileinge up the river, wee had some speech with some of the countrye, whoe tould us of the pinnace

---

[1] The Ambika River.

[2] Really about thirty miles.

[3] 'But note how the Lord did preserve us. Having, as I said before, delivered us from the danger of the sea, Hee would not now suffer us to fall into the hands of our enemies, I meane the Portugalls; who lay at that time at the Barre of Surat with five sayle of frigats to take our boates at our comming ashore, for they had intelligence of our ships comming before' (Jones).

[4] 'When the country people saw so many men in two boats, they strooke up their drums and were in armes, taking us to be Portugales, and that wee came to take some of their townes' (Covert).

[5] Then, as now, a Portuguese possession.

and the Portugalls, wishinge us to bee gone, for if they knewe of us they would bee soone with us. Soe wee rowed up the river till ten at night and then wee went aland to stretch our leggs, beeinge a faire mooneshine, giveinge God thanks for our delivery; but wee had neither meate nor drinke, onlie the water of the river. Butt as soone as I sett foote on the land the water burst out of my nose like a tappe or fosett[1] for the space of a quarter of an hower. Soe that by channce there was one that had a little alligant[2] in a bottle, which he gave me to drinke; otherwise I thinke I had fainted with the extreame rumbling in my head. But, God be praysed, in shorte time I was well; but had noe victualls till the next daie at night. Before wee went farre into the river, wee sawe a juncke[3] cominge over the barre. Wee sent our skiffe to her with the Banane, who brought us word of our marrchannts beeing at Suratt, and the men which weare gone out of the pinnace; for this juncke was come from the barre of Suratt this daie att noone.

Sept. 5. The next daie in the morninge wee sent the Banane and the Jewe to see if wee could have any speech with the countrye people; but none would come att us untill they had order from the Governour of Gandivee. Notwithstanding, there came a poore man whoe tould us that if wee went not quicklie from that place that the Portugalls would be with us. Wee havinge noe weopons past two or three swords for our defence, kept rowinge up the river against the tide, butt this poore man brought two or three men more, one of the which could speake Portugues. Wee tould him our distresse, desiring him to direct us to the Governour of Gandivee by land, beeinge that it was soe

---

[1] Faucet.

[2] Wine of Alicante, in Spain.

[3] A native vessel. The term is probably derived from the Malay *ajong* or *jong*, and the restriction of it to Chinese ships is comparatively modern.

farre by water; if he pleased not to carrie all of us theather, thatt two or three of us would goe with him to the Governor. He was content to goe with two or three, and soe came into our boate to passe to the other side of the water, from whence he was to take his journey towards Gandivee. Soe Mr. Revett being willinge to goe departed with the man, with one English man more in his companie; and wee remayned with our boats neere the bancks, because it was lowe water and such a stronge tide against us that wee could not rowe aheade. In the meane time that wee were stayinge for the tide there came the Mocadan[1] or constable of that circuite to us, demandinge us what wee weare, havinge with him aboute 20 armed men, amongst the which there was one that could speake Portugues. Wee told him of our mishapp, who seemed to be very sorrowfull of our distresse, and gave us very comfortable words, sayinge that the losse of our goods was nothinge in respect of our lives, which [it had] pleased God to lend us and bringe into a good countrye that wanted nothinge, where wee should finde manie freinds; much wondringe thatt wee had escaped the Portugalls which laie at the barre with the friggatts; counsailinge us to goe further up the river as soone as the tide came, because hee doubted thatt the friggatts, having newes of us, would come in with the tide to take us, which they might well have done without any resistannce of the countrye people or us. We gave him thanks for his counsell; and while wee talked with him there was newes that a Portugall frigatt [was ?] comeing within the barre, which made us make hast to rowe up as farr as wee could, beinge nowe a slacke water. Wee desired this Mocadan to spare us the man thatt could speake Portugues, to direct us the waye up the river, because itt hath manie turninges and creeks which goe to other townes.

---

[1] Headman (Hind. from Arabic *mukaddam*).

But this pilott either knewe not the waye or else was bribed by some, or otherwise to playe the rogue with us, for he would have carryed us in a creeke which went neere unto Daman[1]; but some which stoode on the bancks called to us to goe the other waie, and come to the bancks and drewe our boats with roapes the right waie; whereatt our pilott much stormed, and told us that it was not the right waie that they lead us; soe that wee knewe not which to trust, much doubting some villainie pretended, because they perceyved that wee had money in our boats; but these men caried us the right waie and our pilott proved the knave. These men brought us to a village where there were many juncks drouen upon the land, and manie people came unto us.

At this village the Banane, [which] went over land with Mr. Revett to the Governor, mett us, puttinge us in greate feare when wee sawe not Mr. Revett, and the Banane with a countenance very sad. Wee doubted some hard measure, but haveing noe weopons with us wee weare nowe bound to see it howsoever. This Banane made noe haste to bringe us anie newes, before we called to him to come into the boate to speake with him; whoe presentlie came and told us that Mr. Revett was remayneinge with the Governor, and that the Governor had sent his man to carrie us thether to them. Wee demanded for a letter, wherewith hee drewe out of his turbant a leafe of a table booke, wherein Mr. Revett writte that he was with the Governor, stayinge for us, and that the Governor had sent his man to bringe us thether. Although his letter was not very comfortable, yett it did somethinge lighten our heavye harts, seeinge that he was well, which wee much doubted. But the Governours man came into our boate

[1] Their alarm was needless. Damān was at least twenty miles away, and there was no such creek.

and, the tide beeinge nowe come, wee sett saile, both winde and tide with us, soe that wee weare soone theare, although it be above six leagues from this village. Yet aboute four in the afternoone wee landed att a plaine aboute a mile from the towne of Gandivee[1]. Wee landed all our people and stuffe and went to the towne by land, where wee found Mr. Revett with the Governor, whoe tould us that he had bene very kindlie enterteind by him. The Governor welcomed us in the best manner, entreatinge us to rest our selves while they made ready such victualls as was to bee had, which was rice with butter and fruite, for the Governor is an Abramane[2], whoe doth never eate of any live thinke, and therefore he prayed us to pardon him, that it was against his lawe. But it did serve us very well, for this was the third daye that wee had not eate anie thinke; soe that wee weare very hungrie.

At this Governors howse there laye a fugitive Portugall, whoe made us beleive that we should all bee searched for our money and jewells as soone as wee came to Suratt; animating us to leave all such money as wee had with the

---

[1] Gandevi, 28 miles S.E. of Surat, is the chief town of a patch of Baroda territory to the south of the British sub-division of Jalālpur. 'Gandevee...is a very faire haven, and great store of shipping built there, whereof some are of foure or five hundreth tun. It standeth in a good soile, and is governed by the Gentiles' (Covert).

The date of their arrival at Gandevi is given by Covert as the 4th September; but in *O. C.* 12 Jourdain says that it was the 5th, and this is borne out by the text. Jones makes it the 6th.

[2] Brahman. 'The Governour of this towne of Gandevee is a Bannyan, and one of those kind of people that observe the law of Pythagoras. They hold it a great sinne to eate of any thing that hath life or breath, but live of that which the earth naturally affoordeth of it selfe. They likewise honour the cow and have her in great estimation among them; and also observe the ancient custome of burning of their dead. It hath likewise in old time beene a great custome amongst them for the women, so soone as their husbands were dead, to burne themselves alive with him; but now of late yeares they have learned more wit and doe not use it so commonly. Yet those women that doe it not have their haire cut and ever after are held for no honest women, for that they will not accompany their husbands into the other world, as they say' (Jones).

Governor and him untill wee weare seated at Suratt, and then wee might send for it; all which he did without the Governours knowledge, thinkinge to gett some thinge into his hands. As for the Governor, he used us very kindlie and wold not receyve any thinge of us. Wee presented him with 200 rialls of eight and he would not take it, desiringe us when our shipps came to give him somethinge from our countrye. Notwithstandinge, the next daie when wee departed wee gave him a sword, a dagger, and a ringe, with many other promises which the Generall made him to send from Suratt, but nothinge performed, although the Generall kept the 200 rialls which hee had gathered amongst the companie, to buye some toyes at Suratt and send him in recompence of the courtesie done us, as alsoe to the pinnasses men, whoe had beene there ten daies before in the same case. As soone as wee came to Gandivee, the Generall sent a man of purpose to carrie a letter to the marchannts at Suratt and to bringe us present awnsweare. Havinge well refreshed our selves this night, the Governour provided some horses and some pallankins for us. After he had made us a breakfast with rice, bread, cakes, and fruits of divers sorts and sweete meats wee departed.

Whatt passed after our departure from Gandivee towards Suratt; and att our cominge to Suratt.

Sept. 6. Aboute nine in the morninge we sett forwards towardes Suratt, accompanied with four of the Governours men to conduct us, with six horses and four pallinkins; the rest of the shipps companie, some rid on bullocks[1]

---

[1] This was at one time a common practice: see *Jordanus* (Hakl. Soc. ed., p. 12), the *Travels of Nikitin* in *India in the Fifteenth Century* (p. 10), and Tavernier's *Travels* (Ball's ed., i. 43). Even in the present day it is not entirely extinct.

and some went on foote. This daie wee passed twoe rivers, in passage boats, the rivers beeinge deepe, and came to lodge in a towne called Nassaria[1], a greate towne aboute 15 miles distannt from Gandivee, where wee lodged all night on the topp of an hill in a ruinated castell. Butt wee came soe suddenlie into the castle that the people which were in itt armed themselves against us; butt wee havinge retired our selves, and our guides havinge talked with them, they were presentlie satisfied, and used us with greate kindnes. These twoe townes of Gandivee and Nassaria, espetiallie Nassaria, doe make greate store of baftas, being townes which stand in a very firtill and good countrie. In this towne there are manie of a strange kinde of religion called Parsyes. These people are very tall of stature and white people. There religion is farre different from the Moores or Banians, for they doe adore the fire, and doe contynuallie keepe their fire burninge for devotion, thinkinge that if the fire should goe out, that the world weare at an end; and if the fire of their howses bee out, they must not goe [to?] their neighbours to fetch fire, butt must goe to the holie fire, as they tearme itt. When anie of these people dye, they never burye them, butt sett them upright[2] in a place provided for the purpose, in any open feild; where the fowles of the ayre eate and consume their flesh, but the doggs nor other beasts cannott come at itt, because it is walled round aboute and open above.

Sept. 7. Aboute seven in the morninge wee sett forward from this towne, where the most parte of our companie gott bullocks to ride on. Butt our people

---

[1] Nausāri, in Baroda territory, on the south bank of the Purna, about twelve miles from the sea. As Jourdain notes, it is largely inhabited by Pārsī cotton-weavers, who have a fire temple in the town and Towers of Silence on the river bank.

[2] This is of course a mistake. The Pārsī dead are laid at full length on the gratings of the Tower of Silence.

havinge bene well refreshed with a kinde of drinke of the pamita tree called taddy[1], they beganne to bee unrulie, and espetiallie the steward Covett, whoe told the Generall that hee would noe longer bee comanded by him but would take the horses that weare provided for others to ride on ; giveinge the Generall very unreverent speeches, whoe beeinge moved thereatt strooke him with his fiste and feld him to the grownde ; but all was pacified for that time. This daie wee passed two rivers[2] in boats, beeinge very broad rivers, wherein wee spent a greate time in passinge. But aboute three in the afternoone, beeinge within four miles of Suratt, wee received a letter (by the messenger that was sent from Gandivee) from Mr. Finch[3], cheife factor at Suratt, in which letter hee advised us thatt our pinnace men had bene at Suratt, and that the townes men would not suffer them to come within the towne, butt sent them to a little village aboute two leagues of Suratt, where they remayned ; therefore he doubted the like to bee offred to us, beeinge soe manie of us, promisinge to doe his best. With this could comfort wee went on our journey untill wee came neere the walls of Suratt[4], neere unto a faire tanke or sestron[5], of a mile

[1] The familiar 'toddy,' the fermented juice of the palmyra or other varieties of palms.

[2] The Purna and Mindhola Rivers.

[3] See note in List of Authorities.

[4] According to the *Surat Gazetteer* (p. 308) the (inner) wall of Surat was not built until after Sivājī's attack in 1664. Fryer (1675) saw it in course of erection. The reference in the text is, however, explained by a passage in Finch's account, in which he says that, except near the castle, the city 'is ditched and fenced with thicke hedges, having three gates.' Herbert in 1627 found Surat 'circled with a mud wall.'

[5] Cistern. This is the Gopi talāo, near the Nausāri Gate, described by many of the old travellers (cp. *Roe*, i. 112; *Della Valle*, i. 33; Herbert, Mandelslo, Fryer, Hamilton, etc.). In Fryer's time (1675) it was already dry, and later the stone parapets and steps were removed. Finch says: 'Hard without Nonsary gate is a faire tank sixteene square, inclosed on all sides with stone steppes, three quarters of an English mile in compasse, with a small house in the middest. On

aboute, full of water, with manga trees round aboute it very pleasannt. At this ta[n]ke wee weare stayed. Wee had not bene here longe before Mr. Finch came to us and tould us that the Governour would not suffer us to come within the towne; butt he would demand leave for the Generall and marchannts to goe into the towne, and the rest to remayne untill further order. Butt he could not gett leave for any man to gett into the towne, butt weare faine this night to lye under the greene trees.

Sept. 8. The next morninge Mr. Finch came to us, tellinge us that there was noe lycence to be grannted to come into the towne; and therefore by his order wee removed to the other side of the tanke or sestron, where there was a very faire toombe in a very pleasant place full of trees, where wee laye the next night. And the next daie, beinge the 9th dicto, came manie of the cheife men of the towne to visitt our Generall, and brought presennts of eatinge thinges, as bread, rice, fruite etc. The same daie aboute noone came the Governor of the towne with his guard, with determination to remove us from thence to a village two miles of, for that they stoode in feare of us to lye soe neere the towne; where all things should be brought to us to bee sould. There excuse was that it was not for any ill pretended against us, butt to stopp the Portugalls mouthes, whoe threatned them to take their shipps which were cominge out of the Red Sea if they enterteyned us into the towne, and had friggatts lyinge att the barre to that purpose, which would bee an utter undoinge to a greate manie; as alsoe they had threatned to burne all the villages aboute the townes (*sic*), and take the Kings ship which was to come from Moucha, which would bee a greate reproach unto them. For those cawses

the further side are divers faire tombes, with a goodly paved court pleasant to behold; behind which groweth a small grove of manga trees, whither the citizens goe forth to banquet.'

they entreated us to bee content to goe to the place appointed, which was a very pleasant village, and wee should want nothinge. Butt our unrulie companie beganne to bee in a mutinie amongst themselves; some weare content to goe, but the most parte would stand upon their guard and would not goe to anie other place to have their throats cutt; that they had rather dye wheare they weare then to goe to a worse place. But after their coller was a little laied wee perswaded them to patience, seeinge wee weare in a strannge countrye there was noe resistannce against a multitude and in their owne howses. With much adoe they weare perswaded; and aboute two in the afternoone every man tooke his baggage and departed towards the village, savinge Mr. Revett, my selfe, and the surgeon, whoe had leave to goe into the towne to provide whatt was needfull for our journey towards Agra, where the Generall was determyned to goe with all the men. But when wee came to the gates of Suratt, wee could nott be suffred to goe in untill night; at which time wee weare carried to a contrarie gate, because none should take any notice of our beeinge in the towne[1].

[1] Finch's account of these events is as follows: 'In August I received flying newes of an English pinnasse at Gandove, which departing thence was againe forced thither by three Portugall frigats. I supposed that it might belong to some of our shipping, which, standing for Socatora, might not be able to fetch in, and so be forced to fall on this coast; which proved accordingly, it being the *Ascensions* pinnasse, wanting water, wood and victuall, the master John Elmer, with five men and two boyes. The master and foure of the company came hither on the eight and twentieth, but I had no small adoe with the townsmen of Surat for bringing them into the towne, they taking them from me (pretending we were but allowed trade, indeed fearing the Portugalls) till I should send to the Nobob, foure course off, fearing force; to which evill was added a worse, of the Portugalls comming into the river with five frigats and carrying away the pinnasse, weighing also the two falcons which they had cast by the boord. And yet a woorse report came the fift of September, of the casting away of the *Ascension*, the company, about seventie persons, being saved; which the next day came to Surat, but were forced by the towne to lye without amongst the trees and tombes, I being not able to procure leave for the Generall himselfe (notwithstanding divers letters of recommendation which hee brought from Mocha, besides

Our shipps companie with the Generall beinge at the village weare very well content, beecause it was a very pleasannt place, and wanted nothinge; but our men, with palmita drinke and reason wine[1] made themselves beasts, and soe fell to lewde weomen, which went thether to that purpose, that in shorte time manie fell sicke, and others in their drinke fell to quarrellinge one with annother. And one of our men in his vallour cutt of a calves tayle, which the Banians doth adore. But a greate complainte was made to the Governour, whoe sent word to our howse that if our people did use such prancks they would soone bee cutt off; wherefore Mr. Finch rid thither to pacifie the matter with the Banians, and the fellowe punished before them, untill they entreated for him. And thus the matter was ended for that time[2]. These Bananes in all the India doe give the Kinge of Mogoll a greate some of money because noe cowes nor any bullocke or calfe should bee killed in the countrie; wherefore the Kinge commandeth this lawe to bee most straightlie kept by his officers in all provinces. The Bananes victualls which they eate is milke, butter, rice and fruite, with sweete meates of all sorts.

In the time of their beeinge at the village, every man

---

letters from the King himselfe) into the towne; such is their slavish awe of the Portugalls, two Jesuits threatning fire, faggot and utter desolation if they received any more English thither. That which I could doe was to send them refreshing and carry them to the Tanke, where they were conveniently lodged, yet amongst tombes, till the Governor appointed them a more convenient place at a small *aldea* [village] two course off; and with much adoe got leave for Master Rivet, Master Jordan and the surgion to come hither to provide necessaries for the rest.'

[1] Made by boiling raisins in arrack (see Linschoten, Hakl. Soc. ed., ii. 49).

[2] 'I had other trouble by the disorder and riot committed by some of them, especially one Thomas Tucker, which in drinke had killed a calfe (a slaughter more then murther in India); which made mee glad of their departure, fifteene staying behind sicke, or unwilling to goe for Agra; and some returned againe' (Finch).

provided him selfe with a horse or coatch, as they could convenientlie. But there fell out annother controversie. They would not goe for Agra under the comand of Captaine Sharpeigh the Generall, butt would have Mr. Revett or my selfe, or both, to bee their comander. And the Generall, beinge weary of such an unrulye companie, was content that Mr. Revett should be their comander; Mr. Finch beeinge desirous that I should staie with him att Suratt for the Worshipfull Companies service, havinge none of the Companies servannts, with onelie twoe which weare comon men, namelie, Nicholas Bangham[1], an honest joyner, and Thomas Lucas[2], an unrulie colte; with annother English man, which had travelled longe time amonge the Portugalls, and was come thether, beinge poore, for releife, as hee said, butt there was greate doubt of his honestie[3]; for which causes before alledged I was content to staie at Suratt with Mr. Finch for the Worshipfull Companies service. Thus all things beeinge provided for their journie towards Agra, they departed from the village the 21th of September dicto[4].

---

[1] Left at Surat by the *Hector*. He proved himself so intelligent and trustworthy that on his return to England in 1614 he was made a factor and sent out again. He was in charge of the Burhānpur factory till the spring of 1618, when he went home in the *Bull*. Roe speaks of him as the best linguist in the Company's service in India.

[2] Servant to Finch. He died a short time after these words were written (*O. C.* 13).

[3] Probably the individual referred to by Finch under date Dec. 15, 1608: 'This day came to us R. Carelesse, an Englishman who had long lived amongst the Portugals, from whom hee now fledde for feare of punishment for carrying necessaries to the Dutch at Muselpatan, desiring to bee entertayned, which we did with much circumspection.'

[4] Covert, who was of the company, says that they started Sept. 23, 'with our Generall and 52 men, with 21 coaches of our owne and some others being hired, and 19 horses.' They reached Burhānpur Oct. 7, and remained there till Nov. 11, when Covert, Salbank and Frencham set out for Agra, accompanied by a native guide. They arrived at their destination on Dec. 8, and the next day were presented to the Great Mogul by Captain Hawkins.

A breife discourse of whatt passed in Suratt after the departure of our men from [for] Agra.

After their departure from Suratt towards Agra, every man would comand, and doe whatt they liste, for all their newe captaine; soe that before he was five dayes journey from Suratt he fell sicke with distaste of his newe soldiars, that at the next good towne he staied, with some four or five personns. The rest of them some went one waye and some annother, and some came back againe to Suratt, except some twelve persons whoe kept companie with the Generall untill hee came to Baramporte[1], aboute fifteen daies journey from Suratt, where Captaine Sharpeigh fell sicke; and then they all left him, saveinge the surgeon and annother, every one followinge his owne course as longe as the money lasted. Soe that the preacher and many others died att Baramport and neere thereaboute; Mr. Revett, Gabriell Brooke[2], and as many as staied with him at Daytta[3] died; but it pleased God that Captaine Sharpeigh recovered and went to Agra[4], with divers others of the companie; butt not above two or three kept companie together, for they could not awaye with one an-

---

[1] Burhānpur (see p. 145).

[2] He had been engaged at 20*s*. a month as 'a voluntarie man,' to be employed on any work the Company might see fit to allot. Sir Thomas Lowe, whose wife's kinsman he was, recommended him as 'skilfull in the Spanish and Italian tongues, and hath bene a traveller and verie honest' (*Court Minutes*, Dec. 4, 1607, Feb. 19, 1608).

[3] Dhāita, for which see p. 142.

[4] Cp. Sharpeigh's own account (Appendix C).

The unfinished letter (or copy), dated Oct. 27, 1609, printed in *Letters Received*, i. 40, without name of writer or addressee, is evidently from Jourdain to Sharpeigh. In it he complains that the latter has authorised Finch to take charge of the estates of the deceased men, 'wherin you have donne mee some descourtisye....But it is according to all our proceedinges in this voidge, to have to much trust in those which have nothing to doe with the buyssenes, and those which are apointed for the buissenes to knowe lest.'

nothe[r]s companie. Some which were unwillinge to goe for Agra remayned in Suratt secreetlie for the space of ten or fifteen daies, untill the shipps weare come from Moucha, and then they appeared with the rest which retorned from the companie, to the number of 30 persons. Phillipp Grove, the maister, beinge gone to Cambaia to live by himselfe, had enformed the vizroye Mocrabian[1] that all the goodes which was att Agra with Captaine Hawkins and that att Suratt did belonge unto him, and that we weare all his men; soe Mocrobian willed him to send for us all to Cambaia. Whereupon he wrote a letter to the saillours in generall that if they would repaire to Cambaia, that he would paie for their diett and gett them passage for Achin in a shipp that was bound awaie from Broche. Soe all of them agreed together, except some eight or ten of them which would seeke passage by the waie of Goa, went to Cambaia to Grove, where the Vizroye gave them 100 manuthes[2] towards their charges; and when that was done they retorned againe to Suratt, cursinge Grove, that had made them have a wearie journey to grace him there, makinge his braggs that they weare all his men. The disordered carriage of the most parte of our men at Baramport, Daytta, Cambaia and Suratt, as alsoe by the way as they went, would make a mans eares to tingle to repeate the villanies that was done by

[1] Apparently the copyist has (here and elsewhere) mistaken Jourdain's 'Mocrabcan' for 'Mocrabian.' The person meant is Mukarrab Khān. Hawkins calls him 'Viceroy of Cambaya and Surat,' adding 'but in Surat hee had no command save onely over the Kings customes.' He seems to have been in charge of the customs, etc., at the two ports, the revenues of which were probably retained by the Emperor in his own hands. Mukarrab Khān was thus able to gratify Jahāngīr's passion for curiosities by gifts of European articles obtained from the Portuguese traders. His subsequent career is given in *The Embassy of Sir Thomas Roe.*

[2] *Mahmūdīs.* The *mahmūdī* (so named from Sultān Mahmūd of Gujarāt) was a silver coin extensively current in Western India. Terry calls it 'about twelve pence sterling,' and Peyton says it equalled 30 pice, of which 33½ were equivalent to an English shilling.

them, which for shame and tediousnes I omitt. Those which went for Goa, I had letters from them of there kinde usage by the Jesuite which carried them theather, and that they weare bound home in the carricks, as by a letter received from Thomas Joanes the boateson, whoe write that Mr. Mellys was gone in the Saint Andrewe, and that he and the rest weare to goe in the next shipp, whoe was to departe shortlie[1].

The 29th of October Captaine Hawkins, hearing of the comeinge of the Assention (Mr. Finch havinge advertised him at the arrivall of our pinnace), sent the Greate Mogolls letters pattents to enterteyne us kindlie with our shippinge and goods, as alsoe for the recoveringe of our debts, and to ayde us if neede required against the Portugalls or any other that sought to wronge us; soe thatt with this firmaie[2] and pattent from the Greate Mogoll made us to bee in better esteeme then before[3]. The Kinge grannted this firmae to Captaine Hawkins, hopinge of some strange present in the shipp, his delight beeing all in strange toyes; but as soone as he heard that our shipp was cast awaie, the Portugall preists which laye att the courte sollicited him for annother firmae in contrarye of ours, which with presennts and promises was grannted. Butt as longe as Captaine Hawkins was in favour all men did favour the English; butt after that he grewe in disgrace by his owne folly wee weare not soe well esteemed, as hereafter may appeare. When Captaine

[1] Jones says that at the invitation of a Portuguese priest whose acquaintance they had made at Surat, he, Richard Mellis, John Elmor and Robert Fox left Surat on October 7 and journeyed by way of Damān and Chaul to Goa, where they embarked for Portugal in the fleet which carried also the French traveller François Pyrard (see his narrative, Hakl. Soc. ed., ii. 264 *n.*, 265, 269). Mellis died on the voyage. The rest reached Lisbon in August, 1610, and Jones got back to England on the 17th of the following month.

[2] *Farmān*, 'order.'

[3] See Hawkins' narrative (*Purchas*, i. 211).

Hawkins heard of my beeinge in Suratt to assist Mr. Finch, he presentlie sent downe to have one of us to come for Agra, to ayde him in the Worshipfull Companies buysines. Which letters beeinge receyved, it was determined that Mr. Finch or my selfe should presentlie departe; and Mr. Finch perceiveing that there was not like of any greate affaires att Suratt, hee chose rather to goe then to staie at Suratt with a little lead which was to sell, and that was sould butt easilie. Soe that the 18th of Januarie[1] he sett forward out of Suratt towardes Agra, with Nicholas Bangham, William Hutson[2], and one more Englishman, leavinge mee at Suratt with 300 piggs of lead to sell; all other things, as cloth and money, he carried with him, by order from Captaine Hawkins.

After the departure of Mr. Finch, Phillipp Grove remayneinge in Cambaia, as is aforesaid, affirmed to the Vizroye Mocrobyan that all the leade which was remayneinge at Suratt was belonginge to him, and my selfe one of his servannts, entreatinge the Vizeroye by the aucthoritie of his command to send for me and all the leade to Cambaia; which the Vizroye, thinkinge his wordes to bee true, write to the Governour of Suratt to send all the English with their goods to Cambaia, beeinge soe required by Grove, the owner of the goods. Beeing notyfied by the Governour to prepare to [go to?] Cambaia with all our goods, I awnswered that if there weare any firma from the Kinge I would obey; otherwise I would nott remove, for that I had order from the Kinge to remayne in Suratt to doe our buysines quietlie, by which order they were bound to assist us, and not to molest us, shewing them the Kings pattent

---

[1] Finch gives the same date. In *O. C.* 12 Jourdain says February 16, but this is clearly a mistake.

[2] Hudson got back to Europe by way of Goa (see *Cal. State Papers, E. Indies*, 1513–1616, no. 574). He was probably the husband of the Mrs. Hudson who went to India in 1617 with Mrs. Towerson (see *The Embassy of Sir Thomas Roe*, p. 438 *n.*).

and firmae; which when they had seene they rested satisfied, sayinge that they would advise Mocrabian thereof, willinge mee to write unto him the circumstance of the matter; which I did, certifieinge Mocrobian what Grove was and to whome the goods did appertaine, and that Captaine Hawkins, the directour of theis goodes, was att the Kings courte, as His Excellencye knewe well enough; much marvellinge that he would soe hastelie beleeve such a base drunkard as the pilott, whoe was never maister of a pigge of lead in his life, with many other circumstances of his behaviour. Soe that upon the receipt of my letter, and upon Groves misdemeanour, the Vizeroye told him what hee was, sayinge that I had write him the trueth; soe that after thatt Grove was out of favour I heard noe more of the matter.

When Grove sawe himselfe forsaken of all his men, of whome hee had made his braggs to bee at his comand, and out of favour with the Vizeroye, hee sought meanes to goe for Achin in a juncke which was bound from Broche, as is aforesaid, hee havinge prepared himselfe at the towne of Broche, upon there promises; butt when they were ready to departe they would nott carrye him without order from Hoghanazan[1], Governour of Suratt; soe the shipp departed without him, and two more Englishmen that should have gone with him. Then hee beganne to raile on mee, sayinge that I was the cause of his staie; when God knoweth I would have given money to have rid the countrye of such a crooked apostle. But when he sawe noe remedy, and that he was out of favour with Macrobian, the Vizeroye, he repayred to Suratt. Where the first night he was like to bee slaine by one of the Assentions companie called Clasboocke, whoe gave him a stabb with a knife neere the

[1] One of the principal merchants of Surat, who for a time held the post of Governor. Hawkins calls him 'Hogio Nazam,' which may be either Khwāja Nizām or Khwāja Nazm (Najm), probably the former.

harte, that all men thought that he had beene slaine; he strikinge the fellowe in the streete with a staffe, hee made noe more adoe butt stabd him; and thinking that he had slaine him, fledd; but I cawsed the gates to bee shutt, and tooke him the same night, and kept him within the howse two daies prisonner. But he was such an unrulie fellowe that the house was too little to hould him, soe that I was forced to deliver him to the Cutwall[1] of the towne to keepe him untill I sawe wheather the maister would live or dye; and perceiveing that his wound was not mortall, he was sett att libertie[2].

Aboute the end of October I receyved a letter from Captaine Hawkins, sent by his man Nicholas Ufflett[3], willinge mee to make present sale of all the leade, att what price soever, and bringe the money to Agra with all expedicion. But I had not aboute [above?] 20 piggs to sell; which I soone made dispatch of, and received in all my debts which I had made, and bought some cloves and baftas of Broche (accordinge to the Captaines order), and

---

[1] Superintendent of police (Pers. *kotwāl*, a commandant of a fort).

[2] About this time (Sept. 1610) Jourdain wrote the letter of which an unfinished copy is preserved in the *O. C.* series as no. 12. It has been printed in *Letters Received by the E. India Co.* (i. 35) but with a wrong date and without the name of the writer. There is no clue to the person to whom it was addressed, but it was perhaps intended for the English factors at Achin or Bantam, to be conveyed thither in some native vessel—possibly the one spoken of above as bound for Achin.

To this period must also belong the following incident, noted by Finch:—'October the twelfth, we were certified by letters of M. Jourdaine from Surat that thirtie frigats of the Portugals were cast away on the barre of Surat, hasting before the winter was broken up to catch more English. Many of the men escaped, and were glad to beg releefe at the English doore.'

[3] Possibly it was on this occasion that Ufflet followed the route described by Finch on p. 434 of Purchas's first volume.

Ufflet returned to England with Hawkins, but went out again to India in Downton's fleet. In 1617 we find him at Jakatra, in Java, and two years later he died on board one of the vessels of Sir Thomas Dale's fleet.

the rest of the money I passed by exchannge to Baramport with some gaine, aboute five pro cent proffitt. But before my departure I thought to have called Phillip Grove to accompt for money which he had taken out of John Johnsons chest. He dieing with eateing opium betwixt Cambaia and Suratt, leavinge his money in his chest at Cambaia, Grove tooke to himselfe to the value of 300 rialls of eight. He havinge some intelligence that I purposed to have it from him to give to other poore men which wanted, he secreetlie went his waie by night, giveinge out that hee was bound for Cambaia; but he went annother waye towards Mollalapottan[1]. But beinge lefte alone amongst strannger, and his ordinarie drinke failinge him by the waye, fell sicke and died within eight daies journey of Mossolopottan; and a Portugall benegado [renegado] inherited all that hee had, beinge supposed that he had poysoned him for his monie, as is likelie enough. To sett downe all the villanie done by Grove, both at sea and aland, were shamefull to be found in writeinge[2]. But his end by reporte was very desperate; which shewes that his life was accordinge.

Oct. 15[3]. This daie in the afternoone, havinge finished all buysines, I went to the Tanke of Suratt with all our provision for the jorney, accompanied with Nicholas Ufflett, Nicholas Bangam, Bartholomew Davye, and Thomas Stiles[4], Englishmen, havinge [leaving ?] in the howse at Suratt John

---

[1] Masulipatam is meant.

[2] Covert sums up Grove as being 'a Flemming and an arch-villaine and a'—something unmentionable.

[3] There is obviously an error in the date of this and the following entries, for Jourdain has just said that he received Hawkins' letter 'aboute the end of October.' It is pretty clear from his itinerary that he really commenced his journey on December 15.

[4] He started for Europe overland with Finch, and after the latter's death at Bagdad, fled secretly to Aleppo, arriving there early in October, 1613 (see *Letters Received*, i. 273).

WESTERN INDIA, SHOWING JOURDAIN'S ROUTES

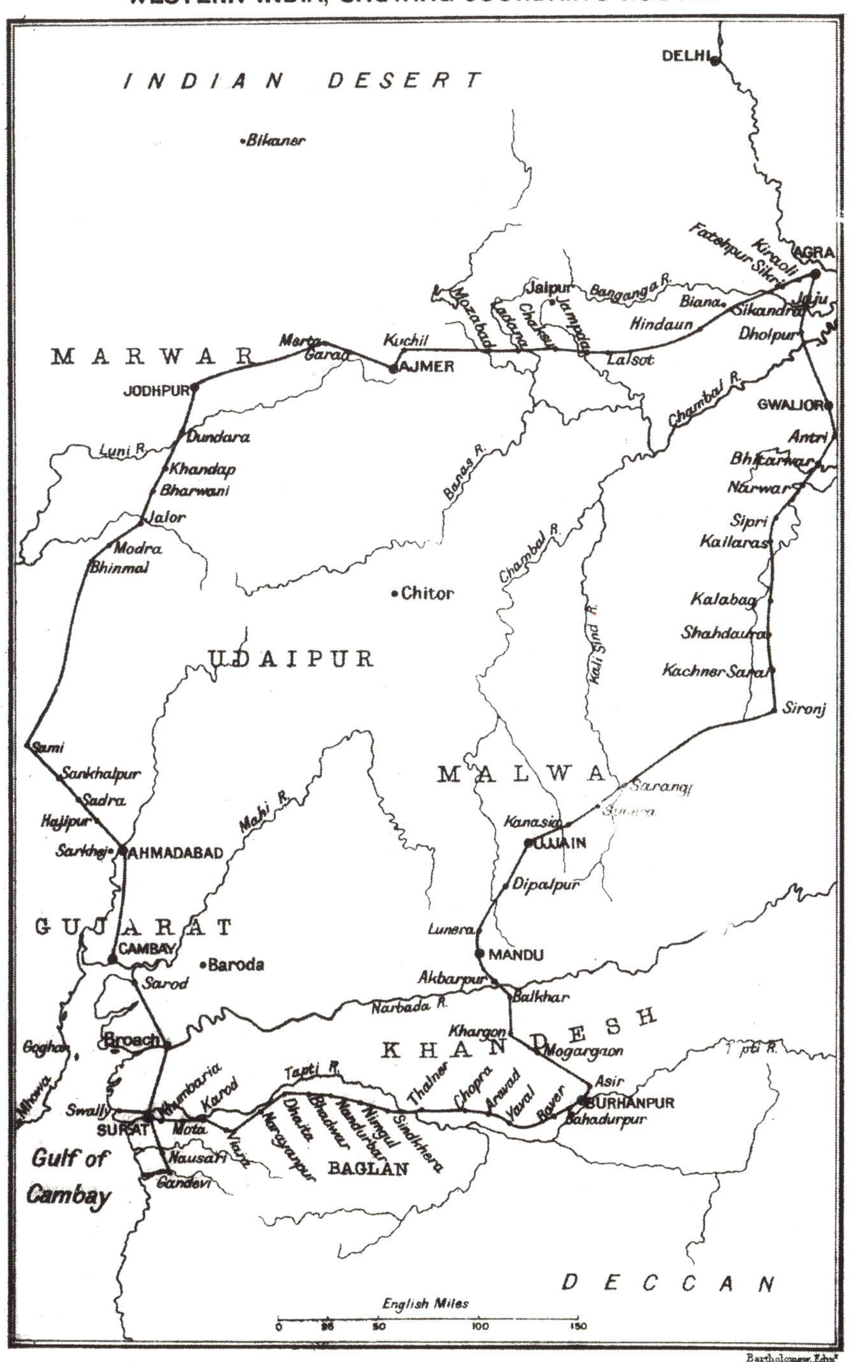

Hakluyt Society, Second Series, Vol. 16.

Winston, Thomas Mosgrowe[1], Herman Lane[2], and Thomas Senterell, with soe much money as would suffice for three monnethes diett, with the howse rent paid for soe longe; thinkinge by that time to have other order from Captain Hawkins from Agra. But within one monneth these men tooke their journey for Mossapatton, leavinge onelie Thomas Musgrow in the howse.

Our travaile from Suratt to Agra; our journeys dailie; with the names of the citties and townes where we laye, and what the townes affoard[3].

Oct. [*Dec.*] 16. In the morninge wee sett forward in our journey from the Tanke of Suratt, and came to a village aboute three coses[4] of, called Cossaria[5].

Oct. [*Dec.*] 17. We parted thence, and came att [an] aldea[6] or village called Mutta[7], aboute seven coses from Cossaria. It is a greate village, and we laye without the towne in the feild.

Oct. [*Dec.*] 18. Wee parted from Mutta, and came to a greate towne called Cossod[8]. This towne is a towne of

---

1 Master's mate of the *Ascension*.

2 Captain Saris found this 'disordered fellowe' in Nov. 1612 at Bantam, where he had been for some time. He and others offered their services to Saris, but drew back when they discovered that he was not willing to pay them their arrears of wages.

3 The general correspondence of Jourdain's account of his journey with Finch's itinerary suggests that the former wrote up his journal after his arrival in Agra, and used a copy of Finch's notes to refresh his memory.

4 The *kos* was about two miles; but it varied much in different parts of India. For the first part of the present journey it is to be taken as a mile and a half; later, as two miles.

5 Khumbaria, about four miles east of Surat.

6 A Portuguese term (of Arabic origin) for a village or an estate.

7 Mota, about eleven miles in a straight line from Khumbaria, in a patch of land belonging to the British subdivision of Bārdoli, but surrounded by Baroda territory.

8 Karod, on the Tāpti, ten miles E.N.E. of Mota, is meant. Finch calls it 'Carode, a great countrey towne, by which on the north

garrison of 200 horse, of Rashputts[1], and hath a castell on the topp of the hill, with water round aboute. These soldiars lye att this place to keepe the countrye quiett from theeves, butt they them selves will not sticke to take a good price[2]. It is seven coses from Mutta.

Oct. [*Dec.*] 19. I parted from Cossod and came to Birra[3], seven coses; a prettye towne with a castell; all laboringe people.

Oct. [*Dec.*] 20. I parted from Birra, and lodged in Corka[4], twelve coses; a ragged towne and poore.

Oct. [*Dec.*] 21. I parted from Corka and came to Narranporte[5], ten cosses; a pretty towne, governed by a Gentile called Pertabsaa[6], whoe is named amongst the Gentiles kinge but is tributarie to the Mogoll. This kinge hath many stronge holdes and castells, invincible by report.

Oct. [*Dec.*] 22. I departed from Narranporte, and came to Daytta[7], eight cosses. This towne is greate and belongeth likewise to Pertabshaa, and is his cheifest towne, standinge in a very fertill countrye by a river side very pleasant.

---

runneth Surat river. It hath a castle with two hundred horse, Patans, good souldiers.'

[1] Rājputs. [2] Prize.

[3] Vīara, in Baroda territory, about 13 miles south-east of Karod. In Finch's account, where the name is misprinted 'Beca,' it is described as 'a castle with a great tanke and a pleasant grove.'

[4] This is evidently Finch's 'Curka' ('a great village with a river on the south side'), but he makes it only five *kos* from Vīara. Tavernier calls it 'Kerkoa,' fifteen *kos* west of Navāpur. He says that the name had recently been changed to 'the Begum's *carvansera*,' as a fine building of that nature had been erected there by the Begam-Sahib, daughter of Shāh Jahān. The name is not found on modern maps.

[5] Nārāyanpur, in the Nandurbār subdivision of Khāndesh. Finch has 'Nacampore,' but this is doubtless a misprint.

[6] Partab Shāh, the ruler of Bāglān, a mountainous district of considerable extent. Akbar had failed to conquer it; but Jahāngīr was subsequently acknowledged as its overlord, and it was finally subdued by Aurangzīb.

[7] Dhāita. 'This towne hath a castle, and is almost encompassed with a river; seated in a fertile soyle' (Finch). 'This city yeeldes great store of drugs, fine pentathose [pintados] and calico lawnes' (Covert).

This towne is of greate trade for baftas and all kinde of handy crafte worke. In this place Mr. Revett, Gabriell Brooke and many other of our men died[1].

Oct. [*Dec.*] 23. I parted from Daytta and lodged at Badoxe, ten cosses[2]. It is an open towne, with manie rude and ungoverned people, with manye theeves. This towne alsoe belongeth to Pertabshaa, and is the farthest parte of his confines this way.

Oct. [*Dec.*] 24. I parted from Badorc[3] and came to Nunderbarr[4], seven coses. This is a stronge cittie walled, with a castell in itt standinge by a river side. There is made here much clothinge of the finer sorte, as birames[5] and serebaffe[6].

Oct. [*Dec.*] 25. I parted from Nunderbarr and came to Lingull[7], ten coses; a poore towne with a mud wall and castle correspondent.

---

[1] See p. 134.

[2] 'To Badur, ten c[os]; a filthy towne and full of theeves. Heere is made much wine of a sweete fruit called *Mewa* [mhowa], but I found it not wholesome, except it be burnt' (Finch). This town may be identified with the modern Bhadwar, which is fifteen miles from Dhāita and ten from Nandurbār.

[3] Jourdain often made his 'r' like 'x' or 'rc'; hence the many blunders of his copyist.

[4] Nandurbār, which is still a place of considerable importance. 'A great city of the Bannians called Netherberry, where is a great basar or market, and all maner of brasen wares to be sold, as pots, kettles, candlesticks, and caldrons of foure foot long, shirts of male, swords and bucklers, lances, horses in armour of arrowe proofe, camels, and all maner of beasts. There is also great store of cotten wools, cotten yarne, pentathoes, callico lawnes, shashes for turbants for their heades, limmons, potatoes [sweet potatoes, or possibly yams], three pound for a penny, and all maner of drugs. And surely cloth would be a very vendible commodity there, for course felt is there extreame deare. Also gold and silver is there very plentifull, and these are very good people to deale withall' (Covert).

[5] Fine cotton cloths of various colours. The name is from the Pers. *bairam*.

[6] 'Serribaff, a fine slight stuffe or clothe wherof the Mores make their cabaies or clothing' (*O. C.* 11).

[7] 'Lingull, 10 c[os], a beastly towne with theevish inhabitants and a dirtie castle; a deepe sandie way neare the towne' (Finch). The modern name is Nimgul.

Oct. [*Dec.*] 26. I parted from Lingull and came to lodge at Sinkerry[1], ten cosses. This is a very greate village; poore people.

Oct. [*Dec.*] 27. I parted from Sinkerry and came to Talnar[2], ten cosses; a greate towne, with a castle standinge by a river.

Oct. [*Dec.*] 28. I parted from Talnar and came to Chuppera[3], fifteen cosses; a greate walled towne, standinge by a river.

Oct. [*Dec.*] 29. I parted from Chuppera and came to a small village called Rawde[4], six cosses; where wee rest till the third of Januarye to ease our carriadges, as alsoe because wee had some raine and darke weather.

Januarie 3, 1610 [1611]. I departed from Rawd and came to Bewell[5], ten cosses; a very greate and stronge towne, with a castell. This towne is of greate trade for pintados of all sorts and many pretty stuffes and shasshes.

Jan. 4. I departed from Bewell and came to Raure[6], sixteen cosses; a greate village; all laboringe people.

Jan. 5. I departed from Rawrre and came to Badorpore[7], eight coses. This is a greate cittie borderinge upon Decan, and doth make much clothinge and pintados, and is a cittie of greate resorte of people.

---

1 Sindkhera, about 24 miles north of Dhūliā. Finch calls it 'Sindkerry, a great dirtie towne.'

2 Thālner, on the north side of the Tāpti. Here the road crossed the river. 'Ten c[os] to Taulneere, a theevish way; the towne faire, with a castle and a river, in time of raine not passable without boat' (Finch).

3 Chopra, on a branch of the Tāpti.

4 Arāvad, in Chopra subdivision.

5 Yāval or Byāval. The fort is in fair preservation. The town is somewhat decayed, but has a population of over 11,000. Finch calls it 'Beawle, a great towne, with a faire castle.'

6 Finch's 'Ravere,' *i.e.*, Rāver, a town about halfway between Sāvda and Burhānpur.

7 Bahādurpur, a town about four miles west of Burhānpur. Finch speaks of it as 'a faire city.' It was so called from having been built by Bahādur Khān, the last independent ruler of Khāndesh.

Jan. 6. I departed from Badorpore and came to Baramporte, ten[1] cosses; where I lodged in the campe without the cittie. Baramporte[2] is a very greate cittie borderinge upon Decan, and is of the kingdome of Hossier[3] the cheife cittie, but conquered by the Greate Mogoll Ecabar, this kings father. Here laye a campe of 200,000 horse to warre with the Decanines. Within the cittie there is a faire and stronge castell[4], wher the Mogolls sonne laye, beinge cheife governor of the cittye and campe for his father; his name is Soltan Pervise[5]. The armye laie round aboute the cittie, a mile without the walls, in a very plaine and pleasannt countrye full of trees and rivers. Here I remayned ten daies, as well to rest our beasts as to doe our buysines aboute receiveinge of our money passed from Suratt by exchange; which havinge received I delivered it out againe to bee paid in Agra, at seven pro cento profitt. As alsoe wee staied for a caravan which was to goe. This cittye is never without sicknes, by reason of the greate recourse of people[6]. Here I fell sicke of a flixe and fever; butt havinge ended our buysines I lett not to travaile. Many of the Assentions men died in this towne. Wee laye as secure in the campe as if wee had bene in our owne howses. I never sawe better government then there was in the campe, and plentie of all thinges. This cittie

---

[1] This is evidently a slip for 'two.'

[2] Burhānpur, on the Tāpti, in the Nimār district of the Central Provinces, was for two centuries the capital of the Farukī kings of Khāndesh, and after the conquest of that kingdom by Akbar in 1599 became the chief town of the Mogul province of Khāndesh. The ruins in the neighbourhood show that at one time the city extended over an area of about five square miles.

[3] Asīr (see p. 146).

[4] The *Lāl Kilā*, or Red Fort, built by Akbar.

[5] Sultān Parwīz, the second son of Jahāngīr. The reader will remember Sir Thomas Roe's account of an interview with him at this place.

[6] 'This citie is very great, but beastly, situate in a low, unholsome aire, a very sickly place, caused especially by the bad water' (Finch).

doth abound in makeinge of fine baftaies, bairames, serebafts, rich turbants and girdles of silke and gould. To this towne there is trade from all places of the India, and the Decanes may freelie come to buye and sell, although at warrs[1]. Here I staied till the 17th of Januarie; then with the carravan wee departed.

Jan. 17. I departed from Baramport and came to a village called Assier[2], eight coses. Upon the topp of a mountaine neere this village there is a very greate and strong castell, whereof the kingdome takes his name Assier, because that in times past the kinge of that countrie laye in itt, beeinge almost invincible, and cost the Mogoll kinge Ecabar more trouble to take this castle then all the countrie besides, for it is one of the strongest holdes in the Indies.

Jan. 18. I departed from Assier[3] and came to Magar Ganga[4], twelve coses; a greate village.

---

[1] 'This cittie is farre bigger then London, and great trade of all sorts of merchandise therein. It is one of the most famous heathen cities that ever I came in, and the citizens are very good and kind people, and very many gallants in the citie. Also fine rivers, ponds, orchards, gardens, pleasant walkes and excellent faire prospects as ever I saw' (Covert).

[2] Asīr, about twelve miles north-east of Burhānpur. For details of the siege by Akbar of the famous fortress of the same name on a neighbouring hill see the *Bombay Gazetteer*, xii. 579. Finch calls it 'the strong and invincible castle of Hassere, seated on the top of a high mountaine, large and strong, able to receive (as is reported) fortie or fiftie thousand horse. And on the top are many faire tankes and good pasture grounds. It hath had in the dayes of Badur Sha, late king thereof, some sixe hundred peeces of ordnance. The Acabar besieged it a long time, circling it on all sides, and at length tooke it by composition; for it is said that there bred such an innumerable sort of emmets or other small wormes in all the waters that the people swelled and burst with drinking thereof; which mortalitie caused him to compound and deliver it, being by meere humane force invincible.'

[3] There are some discrepancies between Finch's and Jourdain's accounts of the stages on this next section of the road, though their totals are fairly in agreement. The former makes the distance from Burhānpur to 'Magergom' 27 *kos* against Jourdain's 20, while from 'Berkul' to the river he reckons two *kos* instead of Jourdain's ten.

[4] Possibly the village of Mogargāon, about 33 miles N.W. of Asīr.

Jan. 19. I departed from Mogar Gange and came to Kergange[1], ten coses; a little village. These ten coses wee had stonye and hillie wayes.

Jan. 20. I departed from Kergang and came to a village called Becull[2], thirteen coses.

Jan. 21. I departed from Becull and came to Eccabarbore[3], ten cosses; a prettye towne standinge by a faire river, which cometh from Broche, neere Cambaia, and from thence yt falleth into the sea. It is a towne of garrison; soe that noe man of accompt can passe without leave of the governor of the castle; because many greate men leave the warres and goe to their howses; therefore none can passe towardes Agra without the Prince Pervise his passe. The river is as broad as the Thames. It is verye ill to passe with camells laden, for it is shole but at one place, which is very full of stones; and therefore the most parte doth passe in boats which are for the purpose; in which wee passed our horses.

Jan. 22. I departed from Eccabarpore and came to the cittie of Mando[4], nine coses. This is a very bad way, both steepe and stonye; soe that it is greate travaile for any beast to goe up laden. This cittie hath in times past bene the most famous cittie in all India, and is nowe ruinated and decayed. It hath within the cittie sixteen standing tanks or sestrons of water, because it standeth soe high upon a hill there is noe other water then whatt is of the raine in these sesterns. You may see the ruines of manie

---

[1] Finch's 'Kergom, a great village.' This may be identified with Khargon, on the Kundi river, 16 miles N.W. of Mogargāon.

[2] Finch calls it 'Berkul,' and it is perhaps Balkhar, 21 miles N.N.W. of Khargon.

[3] Akbarpur, on the Narbadā.

[4] Māndū, formerly the capital of Mālwā; see a note at p. 391 of *The Embassy of Sir Thomas Roe*, and the bibliography there given, to which must now be added two articles by Sir James Campbell and Capt. E. Barnes respectively in the *Journal of the Bombay Asiatic Society*, xix. 154, and xxi. 339. Finch's account (to which Jourdain is obviously indebted) will be found in Appendix D.

faire buildings and monuments. This cittie was taken by the ancestors of the Mogoll, by a kinge called Seer Shaselim, and by him ruinated[1]. In his florishinge time it could have made within the cittie 50,000 horse. There was greate store of treasure found hidden by the grandfather of this kinge the Mogoll. By the cituation of this cittie, the walls, castle and gates which yett are to bee seene, it seemeth to [have] beene one of the greatest and strongest cittyes in the world. From the gate which we came in att to the south (over which gate there is a plattforme for ordinance) to the north gate it is aboute six miles, and from the east to the west by reporte it is 20 cose[2], which is above 25 miles, waled round aboute with bricke; standinge on the topp on [of] an high mountayne, that the hill it selfe weare a sufficient defence if there weare people within itt. There are yett remayneinge twoe churches or missitts[3], wherein is buried four kings, laid in very faire and costlie toombs of rich stone. In one of these churches there is a very statelie tower of 170 steps to goe upp, built round aboute with many windowes curiouslie made. This tower hath six[4] storyes, and in everye storye chambers for men to lodge in, very pleasantlye contryved, and built all with greene stone like marbell. Att the north gate there are five gates, one within annother, very stronge, because att this side itt is not soe steepe as att other places, but men may easilie come att yt with burdens. By these gates the cittie was served with all kinde of victualls in tyme paste. Heere I

---

1 Cp. Finch's statements.

2 There is evidently a mistake here. Probably the copyist mistook Jourdain's '10' and '15' for '20' and '25.' Finch says four *kos* from north to south, and ten or twelve *kos* from east to west. As a matter of fact the extreme limits are 3¾ miles from north to south and 5½ miles from east to west. Malcolm estimates the circuit of the ramparts at 37 miles.

3 *Masīd*, the softened Indian form of *masjid*. Concerning these two buildings see the notes to Appendix D.

4 This should be 'seven.'

sawe the breech of a brasse peece the biggest that ever I sawe before. The suboorbs of this cittie without the north gate hath been seven miles longe; soe farr you maye see the ruines of itt. Towards the east gate of this cittye is all pasture and pleasannt land of corne and fruite. There are in the suburbs manie stronge sarrayes built of stone yett standinge for travellours to lodge in. The people of this cittie are Gentiles; and when any greate man of them dye their wives wilbee buryed [burned] with their husbands, and manye of his slaves, to serve him in annother world as they have done in this, and will thinke themselves happie if the master will chuse them before his death to accompanie him in annother world. But if the wife refuse to dye, shee is never more esteemed amonge them.

Jan. 23. Wee departed from the cittye of Manda and came to Connyhier[1], a small towne, four cosses.

Jan. 24. Wee departed from Connihier and came to Dolpore[2], fourteen cosses; where wee rest the 25th; beinge a prettye towne.

Jan. 26. Wee departed from Dolpore and came to the cittie of Augen[3], a greate and antient cittie, where lyeth a vizeroye for the Greate Mogoll, which makes the warres against the kingdome of Rana[4], that is in rebellion.

Jan. 27. Wee departed from Augen and came to a ragged towne called Conostia[5], eleven coses. Here is made much opium, and the best in the Indies, and is worth three ma[hmūdīs] per ser, which is 24 ounz.

---

[1] 'At 4 c[os] end lyeth Luneheira, a small saray' (Finch). Jourdain (or his copyist) has got the name wrong. It is the present day Lunera, a village eight miles north of Māndū.

[2] Dipālpur, 27 miles S.W. of Ujjain. Finch calls it 'Dupalpore...a small towne.'

[3] Ujjain, the principal city of Mālwā.

[4] The Rānā of Mewar (Udaipur).

[5] 'Conoscia...a little village' (Finch); probably Kanasia, about 24 miles E.N.E. of Ujjain, and three miles north of Maksi.

Jan. 28. Wee departed from Conostia and came to Sunearra[1], eight coses; a very hillie and stonie waye, and full of theeves. Here wee mett a carravan of pisas[2], bound for Baramporte to paye the soldiars, with a guard of 100 horse for feare of robbinge.

Jan. 29. Wee departed from Sunearra and came to Pimplgang, ten coses; but beinge a ragged place I went farther four coses, to a cittye called Sarampore[3], a greate cittie by the rivers side, with a faire castle in itt. Here is greate trade for all sorts of cloathinge which are made.

Jan. 30. We departed from Sarampore and came to Cuckra[4], seven coses; a place that yeilds much graine and opium.

Jan. 31. We departed from Cuckra and came to Delute, twelve coses; a great aldea or village.

Feb. 1. Wee departed from Delute and came to Burrou,

---

[1] Sunera, about six miles N.E. of Shāhjahānpur. 'Sunenarra...a small towne, short of which is a great tanke full of wilde fowle' (Finch).

[2] The small copper or brass coins called *paisās* (pice). 'The pice are heavy round peeces of brasse; 30 of them make our shilling' (Herbert, ed. 1638, p. 38).

[3] Sarangpur, in Dewās State, on the right bank of the Kāli Sind river. Finch calls it 'Sarampore, a great towne with a castle on the southwest side, with a faire towne-house. Here are made faire turbants and good linnen.' He makes it only four *kos* from Sunera (which is about right), on the way to 'Pimpelgom, a ragged *aldea*'; and Jourdain is clearly wrong in placing it beyond the latter town. 'Pimplgang' or 'Pimpelgom' cannot be identified with certainty; but the Indian Atlas shows a village (*gāon*) called Piplia in about the position indicated.

[4] 'Seven c[os] to Cuckra, a great countrey towne abounding with all sorts of graine, victuall and *Mewa* wine; at 4 c. lyeth Berroul, a great *aldea*....Twelve c. to Delout, a great *aldea*; the way for the five last coses theevish, hilly, stony; the other, pleasant plaines....Seven c. to Burrow, a small towne, but plentifull of victuall, except flesh, which is scarse all this way; the way dangerous....Seven c. to Sukesera, a small ragged towne....To Syrange nine c., a very great towne, where are many *betele* gardens' (Finch). These stages cannot be traced in the Indian Atlas; but evidently they were on a cross-country route from Sarangpur to Sironj, possibly following much the same line as the present military route, which goes by way of Biaora, Suthalia and Lateri. The road in many parts is still merely a rough cart track.

seven coses. This towne yeildeth greate plentye of corne and butter.

Feb. 2. Wee departed from Burrou and came to Suckerra, seven coses; a ragged village.

Feb. 3. Wee departed from Suckerra and came to the cittye of Sarrange[1], nine coses. This cittye is greate, and lyeth att the foote of a high mountayne, with a castell att the topp. It stands in a very fertile soile, and doth yeild very rich pintados[2] of divers sorts and rich shashes[3] with silke and gould, from 5 ma.[4] to 200 ma. a peece.

Feb. 4. Wee departed from Sarrange and came to Cuchinarque sarraye[5], where wee laye, the village not beinge past 20 howses.

Feb. 5. Wee departed from Cuchinarque sarraye and came to Sadura[6], five coses; a very stonie waie.

Feb. 6. Wee departed from Sadurra and came to Collybaye[7], seven coses; a very ragged towne with a ruinated castle.

Feb. 7. I departed from Collybaye and came to the cittye of Guallier[8], twelve coses; a pretty walled cittie, in a firtile and pleasant soile.

Feb. 8. I departed from Gualleer and came to Chipprie[9], seven coses; a theevish waye. This is a walled towne.

Feb. 9. From Capprie I came to Nerva[10], 12 coses.

---

[1] Sironj, in Tonk State, Rājputāna. It was formerly famous for its muslins and chintzes.

[2] See p. 25. [3] See p. 77. [4] See p. 135, note 2.

[5] 'To Cuchenary Saray, 8 c.' (Finch). This is the present Kachner Sarāī, about 22 miles N. of Sironj.

[6] Shāhdaura, 13 miles N. of Kachner Sarāī.

[7] Kālabāg, 17 miles N. of Shāhdaura. Finch calls it 'Collebage.'

[8] 'Twelve c. to Qualeres, a pretty small towne encompassed with tamarind and manga trees' (Finch). This is Kailaras, about 26 miles N. of Kālabāg.

[9] Sipri, 14 miles N. of Kailaras. 'To Cipry...way theevish, stony, full of trees, a desart passage; a walled towne, faire houses covered with slate' (Finch).

[10] Narwār, 23 miles N.E. of Sipri, on the right bank of the river

It is a greate walled cittye. And in these twelve coses there are manye sarrayes for travailours to lodge in, because it is a theevish countrie and noe villages in these twelve coses. There is belonging to this cittie a very statelie castle, a mile longe. It hath bene very famous, butt nowe decayed.

Feb. 10. Wee departed from Nerva and came to Gullica[1] sarraye, seven cosses.

Feb. 11. Wee departed from Gullica and came to Autro[2], twelve coses, a greate towne standinge by the side of a hill. Betwixt these two places is a fayre sarraye for travelours.

Feb. 12. I departed from Autro and came to a cittye called Gullier[3], six coses, a stonye and bad waye. In this towne there is a very faire and stronge castell, on the topp of a high mountayne of rocke which is aboute six miles aboute. It is very stronge both of people and ordinance, and verye faire buildings. There is noe water within ytt; onlie what doth rayne, they take itt in four greate tanks or sesterns. Att the gate of the castle, at the entry there is a carved stone made in fashion of an elaphannt curiouslie wrought. Within the castle is the Kings howse, very

---

Sind. 'The towne, at the foot of the hill, hath a castle on the top of a stony steep mountaine, with a narrow stone causey leading to the top some mile or better in ascent. In the way stand three gates, very strong, with places for *corps du guard*. At the top of all is the fourth gate, which leads into the castle, where stands a guard, not permitting any stranger to enter without order from the King. The towne within is faire and great, with a descent thereto, being situate in a valley on the top of a mountaine very strangely. As it is reported, this cliffe is in circle some 5 or 6 c., and walled round with towers and flankers here and there dispersed, without treason invincible. This hath been the gate or border of the kingdome of Mandow, and hath been beautifull, and stored with ordnance, but now is much gone to ruine' (Finch).

[1] Finch calls it 'Palacha.' It was probably near the present Bhītarwār.

[2] 'Antro' in Finch's account. It is doubtless Antri, 12 miles S. of Gwalior.

[3] Gwalior. Compare Finch's description in Appendix D.

faire, the walls of greene and blewe stone, with many towers ritch guilded with gould. All traytours are sent prisonners to this castle, because yt is very stronge; but whoe soever is committed to this place there is butt little hope ever to come out. The towne is cituated at the foote of the castell, and yeildeth all sorts of cloathinge and opium.

Feb. 13. I departed from Gullier and came to Mandabarr[1] sarraye, nine coses; a poore village joyneinge to itt, neere to two rivers.

Feb. 14. I departed from Madakarre sarraye, and came to Daulpore[2], ten coses. This towne is seated on a hill, and hath four gates, one within the other, by a river, where there is a faire bridge of stone for people to passe over.

Feb. 15. I departed from Daulpore and came to Jarowe[3], nine cosses, where Captaine Hawkins and Abraham[4], his wives father-in-lawe, and a Portugall called Miskitto, mett us; where we laye all night.

Feb. 16. I departed from Jarowe, in companie with Captaine Hawkins and the rest, and aboute noone wee came to Agra to Captaine Hawkins howse, where I found Captaine Sharpeigh and many other English of the Assentions companie; Mr. Finch beinge gone for Lahor to sell his indico which hee bought att Bianna for the Worshipfull Companie.

---

1 Not on modern maps. Finch calls it 'Mendaker.'

2 Dholpur, capital of the native state of that name. 'Ten c. to Doulpore. Within two c. of the towne you passe a faire river called Cambere [Chambal], as broad as the Thames, short of which is a narrow passage, with hills on both sides, very dangerous. The castle is strong, ditched round, and hathe foure walls and gates, one within another, all very strong, with steep ascents to each, paved with stone. The citie is inhabited most-what with Gentiles. The castle is three quarters of a mile through, and on the further side hath like gates to be passed againe' (Finch).

3 Finch has Jaiow, which may be Jaju, where the road crosses the Utangan river.

4 Abraham de Duyts, concerning whom see a note in *The Embassy of Sir Thomas Roe*, p. 442. By 'father-in-law' step-father is intended.

Of whatt passed in Agra in the tyme of my beeinge there, viz.—

Att my comeinge to Agra, I was presentlie informed that Captaine Hawkins was in some disgrace with the Kinge for three causes. The first was about Macrobean[1], he havinge made complainte to the Kinge that he did owe him money and would not paye it him; where upon the Kinge comanded his cheife secretarie, named Abdelasa[2], to cause Macrobean to paye him out of hand. This Abdelasah, beeinge a greate freind to Macrobian, advised him presentlie to paye Captaine Hawkins; which he promised to doe out of hand, butt as greate mens debts are slowest in payinge, soe his was delayed and putt of from daye to daie; but att length the money was ordayned to be paid, butt wanted of Captaine Hawkins demand accordinge to his bill aboute a quarter of the debt, Mocrobian alledging that the cloth which his brother had bought att Suratt was too deare by soe much, and therefore would give noe more[3]; which Captaine Hawkins refused to receive and departed, advisinge the Kings secretarie of whatt passed. This secretarie entreated Captaine Hawkins to receive his money, and that he would be worth him as much as that came unto and more in his jaguir[4] or land which hee was to have of the Kinge by the hand of Abdelasan the secretarie.

---

[1] See p. 135.

[2] Khwāja Abū-l Hasan, whom Hawkins styles 'the Kings chiefe Vizir Abdal Hassan, a man envious to all Christians.' About this time (1610–11) he was transferred to the *sūbah* of the Deccan, being succeeded as *Wazīr* by Mīrza Ghiāsuddīn, the father of Nūr Mahāl and Āsaf Khān. Later he returned to court and was made *Mīr Bakhshi*, or Paymaster-General (Elliot and Dowson's *History of India*, vi. 363). Roe, who describes him as 'captaine of all souldiers entertayned at court and treasurer to all armyes,' speaks highly of his character.

[3] Finch corroborates Hawkins regarding Mukarrab Khān's attempts to evade payment for the cloth he had bought, or at least to secure a substantial reduction in the price.

[4] *Jāgīr*, an assignment of land.

Captaine Hawkins refused to receyve the money, sayinge that hee would acquainte the Kinge therewith. He entreated him not to make motion any more unto the Kinge, butt to take his money. Notwithstanding all these entreaties he would not take itt, but againe acquaynted the Kinge. Soe the Kinge seemed to bee verye angrie that it was not paid, willing againe Abdelasan, his secretary, to cause it to bee paid, that hee might heare noe more thereof. Which Abdelasan the same daie performed, sendinge for Captaine Hawkins to his howse and paid him as much as was formerlie offerd him by Macrobian, and noe more would he paye him, and if he would not take it he might chuse; threatning him that it had bene better for him to have taken it before with quietnes. Soe that he was faine to take itt, and yett had both the secretaries ill will and Macrobians, and like to have the Kinges by Abdelasans meanes, who was most in favour of any man in the kingdome[1]. Nowe Captaine Hawkins looks for his land which the Kinge had promised him, and cannot be without the ayde of Abdelasan; which when Captaine Hawkins came to speake to him aboute it, he would hardlie affoard to speake with him, butt att length hee told him that there was nothinge for him; beeinge a marchannt, he might plye his marchandizinge and not looke for any thinge att the Kings hands, alledginge unto him that hee had sent to Biana[2] to buye the indico out of the Queenes Mothers[3]

[1] For all this see Hawkins' own narrative (*Purchas*, i. 211).

[2] Biāna, in Bhartpur State, 50 miles S.W. of Agra. It was at this time an important centre of indigo cultivation. Salbank calls it 'the cheifest place for indico in all the East India, where are twelve indico milles. It groweth on small bushes and beareth a seede like a cabbage seed. Being cut downe, it lyeth on heapes for halfe a yeere to rot, and then by oxen it is troden out from the stalkes, and afterward is ground very fine and then boiled in fornaces, and so sorted out into severall sorts. The best indico is there worth eight pence a pound' (*Purchas*, i. 236). See also Finch's account of the place and of its indigo manufacture (*ibid.*, i. 429).

[3] Jahāngīr's mother was a daughter of Rājā Bihārī Mal Kachhwāhā,

hand, her factour havinge made price for itt; for att the time of Mr. Finch his beeing att Biana aboute buyinge indico, the Queenes Mothers shipp was bound for Moucha, and therefore she sent her servannt to buye a parcell of indico to adventure in the shipp; which he had made price of; which Mr. Finch perceived, went and gave a small matter more then she should have given, and had awaie the indico; whereat her servannt seemed to be very angrie, and wrote Abdelasan that Captaine Hawkins had sent to buye up all the indico, and had taken a parcell that he was in price withall. Of this he advised the Queens Mother, whoe told the Kinge. These were two causes of his disgrace. The third was that the Kinge was informed that some of his greate men were bibbers of wine, that before they came to the courte daylie they filled their heads with stronge drinke; whereupon the Kinge comanded that upon paine of his displeasure that none of his nobles that came to the court should drinke any stronge drinke before there cominge. Nowe Abdelasan, knowinge thatt Captaine Hawkins was a great drinker, feed the porter to come neere to Captaine Hawkins (as is supposed) to smell if he had drunke any stronge drink, which is easilie discerned by one that is fastinge. Soe the cheife porter findinge that Captaine Hawkins had drunke, hee presentlye carryed him before the Kinge, in presence of the whole courte, where by the mouth of Abdelasan, being secretary, it was tould the Kinge thatt he had drunke stronge drinke. Whereat the Kinge pauzed a little space, and consideringe that he was a stranger, he bid him goe to his howse, and when hee came next he should not drinke. Soe, beeing disgraced in publique, he could not be suffred to come into

---

and after her marriage to Akbar received the title of Maryam Uzzamānī. Extensive trading operations seem to have been carried on by her, or in her name.

his accustomed place neere the Kinge[1]; which was the cause that he went not soe often to courte. These were the first occasions of his disgrace.

Nowe before my comeinge upp, Mr. Finch was gone with the indico which he had bought att Biana to Lahor, which is aboute 20 daies jorney from Agra, to make sale of the indico and soe retourne to Agra[2]. Butt Mr. Finch beinge there, and understandinge that there was good proffitt to be made of itt at Aleppo, where there was att present a caravan bound, as yearlie there is from this cittie to Aleppo, hee wrote to Captaine Hawkins, entreatinge him that, seeinge there was little hope of shippinge to come, that he might departe over land with the caravan, and carrie the indico with him for the Worshipfull Companies accompt, for that att Lahour there was noe proffitt to bee made; that if he would not consent that he might carry the indico for the Companie, that he would paye him his wages, and he would goe overland upon his owne charge. Which letter made Captaine Hawkins very fearfull least he would be gone before he could send thether; butt presentlie Captaine Hawkins went to the Portugall Jesuitts and entreated a letter to there factour that if Mr. Finch should ayme to departe with the carravan, that he would make staie of him and his goodes untill further order; and there withall sent a letter of attorney to the Portugall father there lyinge to that effect; which letter was to bee kept secrett unlesse they sawe him prepare to bee gone. Butt as soone as I came to Agra he acquaynted mee with all the buysines, and said that he would presentlie send

[1] Hawkins mentions that he was excluded, but ascribes it to the order of Abū-l Hasan. As, however, the latter would not have dared to take such a step without Jahāngīr's approval, the reason assigned in the text is probably correct.

[2] 'January the ninth I departed from Agra for Lahor to recover debts, and carried twelve carts laden with *nil* [indigo] in hope of a good price' (Finch).

downe Nicholas Ufflett to make staie of the goods, and if Mr. Finch would needes goe over land, that he should paie him his wages and goe at his owne pleasure. Soe that within a daie or twoe he dispatched awaie Nicholas Ufflett. Butt when he came to Lahour, he had but poore welcome of Mr. Finch, alledginge that if he had ment to have runne away hee would not have acquaynted Captaine Hawkins, butt, seeinge it was soe, that nowe, whatsoever came of itt, hee would be gone, and would paie himselfe his wages; of which he wrote to Captaine Hawkins, and by the same he wrote mee a letter to come to Lahour to goe overland together; which I had done, if I had not heard certaine newes of English shipps[1] which weare in the Red Sea; wherefore I made accompt that they would come for Suratt this yeare, and therefore determined with Captaine Sharpeigh to goe for Suratt, to be there in September to meete the shipps; and if they came not this yeare, that then to goe from thence to Mossopotan[2], which was butt 40 daies journey by land; of all which our determination, as likewise of the shipps being in the Red Sea, I wrote Mr. Finch at large, perswadinge him to come for Agra, and wee would goe for Suratt in companie; which he utterlie refused, sayinge thatt wee weare led awaie with fancies and idle words of shipping; that he knewe well the Companie would never send more shipps for Suratt, and therefore would nott lose this oportunitie, exclaymeinge very much on Captaine Hawkins and his disconfidence, sayinge that he would not come to Agra because he would not see the face of him, for that nowe he knewe of the letter of atturney which was sent formerlie to the Portugall father concerninge him[3].

---

[1] Sir Henry Middleton's fleet of the Sixth Voyage.

[2] Masulipatam.

[3] Finch started from Lahore in company with Captain Thomas Boys (who had reached the Mogul court overland shortly before

Nowe leavinge Mr. Finch with his determinacion, it followeth, vizt.—The Kinge all this time was not yet come from his huntinge, but was looked for within shorte time. Soe that wee determined when he came neere the cittie to meete him, which wee did aboute six miles of. Which amongst millions of people wee weare permitted to come where the Kinge might have sight of us, rideinge in the feild on an elaphant; which when the Kinge sawe us and knewe us to bee Christians, he staied his elaphannt till wee came at him, and demanded us if wee would have ought of him. Wee told him noe, but our comeinge was to welcome him to the cittie. Soe noddinge his head he went forward, and wee went to our horses againe. After the Kinges cominge to the cittie, havinge rested himselfe two or three daies, he beganne to sitt abroad, as he was accustomed, four howers every daie to heare all mens cawses, two howers in the forenoone and two howers in the afternoone. The rest of the daie he employeth in seeing elaphannts to fight, and other sports. One of his sports is to bringe forth a wild lyon and lett him loose amonge the people, to see if there be any soe hardie as to stand against the lion; which if there bee, he is a man for him, and will doe him greate favor. As at one time he brought forth a lion amongst the Portugalls to see if anie would resist him, but they all ranne awaie except one; butt the lion cominge towards him, he went to defend himselfe as he might, and struggled a good while with him untill they gate both into the river. Then his weomen, which through a lattis see the sporte, called to the Kinge to take up the lion; otherwise he would have suffred the lion to kill him, as it is thought, for he did not much affect the cheife man that

Finch's arrival there), Lawrence Pigot and Thomas Styles. The party got to Bagdad in safety, but there they all died from drinking bad water, with the exception of Styles, who, after being ill-treated by the Pasha, escaped to Aleppo (*Letters Received*, i. 273, 286).

was amonge them, whoe had longe time waighted at the courte for a reward of the Kinge; which when he sawe this reward provided for him, he came seldome after to the courte. Alsoe there was a greate soldiar, a Pottan, a man of a thousand horse and very well esteemed of the Kinge and nobles for his vallour. He came to the Kinge desiringe His Majestie to bee good unto him; that he was one that had served him longe time in the wars and had done him such services, and paie nothinge augmented, hee being at a greate charge with his contynuall lyinge in the feild, his paye not beinge sufficient to mayntaine his chardge. The Kinge demanded what his paie was. He awnswered: The paie of 1000 horse. And, said the Kinge, is not thatt sufficient to mayntaine one man? Sayinge further: What valour is there in thee more then in other men, that thou shouldest soe bouldlie demand more? Yee, he awnswered, that there was more in him then in other men; which if it pleased His Majestie to employe him he should see itt. Whie, said he, wilt thou fight with a lyon? He awnswered that a lion was a beaste that had noe sensible understandinge, and therfore not fitt to be fought withall. Naye, said the Kinge, thou shalt fight with a lion; and therewith caused a lion to be brought forth and the man must fight with him hand to hand, onlie a gluffe on his hand, and a little trunchion of a foote and a half longe. Soe he fought with the lion a prettie space and overthrewe the lion; yett it bruised and tore the man soe with his clawes that hee died within a little space[1]. These are some of the Kings sports. But itt hapned that in his last huntinge that his bouldnes had almost slaine him with a lion. For beinge a huntinge he espied a lion lyinge in a bushe as asleepe. He called for a peece, and laid itt on one of his noblemens shoulders and shott the lion. The lion, feelinge himselfe

[1] Hawkins tells the same story, but at rather greater length.

hurte, came very furiouslie to him. The nobleman seeinge the lion comeinge towardes the Kinge, he stept forwards towards the lion; butt the lion would nott meddle with him, but strove to goe to the Kinge thatt shott the peece; soe that by force this nobleman restrayned the lion untill many horsemen came to releive the Kinge, and killed the lion. This younge nobleman was sore wounded, butt died not. The Kinge made him 1000 horse per yeare, which is as good as 1000*l.* sterlinge per yeare. But the bruite was blowne abroad that the Kinge was slaine with a lyon; which if hee had, it had bene a just punishment for his sporte[1].

Nowe havinge spent two or three monnethes in Agra to little purpose, and knowinge that Captaine Hawkins would nott truste anie man to employe the Companies money to any proffitt, and the time begininge to drawe on to goe for Suratt to meete the shipps, I told him my determinacion was to goe for Suratt, and from thence to Mossopotan if shipps came nott. Hee was very desirous to have mee staye with him to goe for Goa; that seeinge hee could have noe meanes of the Mogoll, that he would goe for Goa with his wife and familie. I told him if he went for Goa

[1] Finch gives the following account of this incident: 'About the sixt of January [1611], the King, being on hunting, was assailed by a lyon, which hee had wounded with his peece, with such fiercenesse that had not a captaine of his, a Resboot, tutor of the late baptized Princes, interposed himselfe, thrusting his arme into the lions mouth as hee ramped against His Majestie, he had in all likelihood been destroyed. In this strugling Sultan Corom [Khurram], Rajaw Ranidas [Rāmdās] and others came in and amongst them slew the lyon, that captaine having first received thirty two wounds; whom therfore the King tooke up into his owne palanke, with his owne hands also wiped and bound up his wounds, and made him a captaine of five thousand horse in recompence of that his valourous loyaltie.' From the account in the *Tūzak-i-Jahāngīrī* it appears that the Rājput who was so severely mauled was named Anuprai. In recognition of his bravery the Emperor conferred on him the title of Anirai Singh-Dalan ['Lion-Cleaver'], presented him with a sword and increased his *mansab*, though not, of course, to the figure given by Finch. Roe mentions him twice (*Embassy*, 282, 293) as being then in charge of the captive Prince Khusrū.

his life would not bee longe, because hee had too much disputed against the Pope and their religion, and was apt to doe the like againe there if he were urged thereunto, which would cost him his life, and the sooner because of his goods. But he awnswered that the Fathers had promised him to gett him a passe from the Vizroye, as alsoe from the Bishopp and preists that he might use his owne conscience. I tould him that the same cause would be his destruction if hee went. Soe he was perswaded to goe that waye, and I was perswaded to goe the other waye[1], although he urdged mee very farre, promising greate wages; butt his promises weare of little force, for he was very fickle in his resolucion, as alsoe in his religion, for in his howse he used altogether the custome of the Moores or Mahometans, both in his meate and drinke and other customes, and would seeme to bee discontent if all men did not the like.

Of the Citty of Agra; with the territoryes of the Greate Mogoll. Of his forces and charge.

This Cittie of Agra is one of the biggest in the world. Itt is by reporte farre greater then Grand Cairo. It is well seated in a very firtill soile and by a river called Jeminy[2], which river goeth to Bengala, and into the river cometh parte of the river of Ganges, which is three daies journey from Agra. There is yearlie carryed from Agra to Bengala above 10,000 tonns of salte in greate barges of four and five hundred tonns apeece. The marchannts have there tents sett up in the barge as in a feild. These barges are very longe and broad and very well made accordinge to the manner. There are within the cittye manie faire buildinges, butt they stand soe scattered one from annother

[1] This seems to dispose of Downton's story (p. 176 *n.*) that Jourdain had asked the Jesuits at Agra for a safe conduct to Goa.

[2] Jumna.

as though they weare afraid one of annother; and the reason is that every greate man must have his howse by himselfe, because round aboute his howse lyeth all his servannts, every one in his owne howse, with their horses. Soe that by this meanes the most parte of the cittye is strawe howses, which once or twice a yeare is burnt to the ground, if they take not the better heed. The Kinge lyeth within the castle, which is a very faire and stronge castell, att least two miles aboute. The walls thereof are of very faire red stone, and at least five fathome highe, with battlements and towers round aboute. When you are within the castle you are as in a cittie, where all things is to bee sould. Within the castle lyeth the Kinges sonnes, each of them in their howse, and some three or four of the noblemen which are neere the Kinge lodge alsoe within the castle. The Kinge hath every 24 howers a fresh guard both of men and woemen. Every noble man takes his tourne to bee cheefe of the watch for 24 houres, and every daie aboute five in the afternoone they doe their dutie to the Kinge, and soe departe. The Kings elaphannts doe alsoe keepe watch, and come as dulie to the Kinge to doe their dutye as the men; for when the Kinge beholds them they all att once putt their truncks over their heads giveinge the salam to the Kinge; then they departe, for they will not be gone before the Kinge looks on them; then they march by degrees with their pages before them and there wives after them. Every elaphannt riall hath two or four younge elaphannts for their pages, and two wives which followe them, alias shee elaphannts. They are very ritchlie trapped with velvett, cloth of gould, and other ritch stuffes[1].

There is greate resorte of people to that cittie from all parts of the world, thatt you cannott desire any thinge butt you shall finde itt in this cittye. It is very populous, inso-

[1] Cp. the account of the muster of elephants given in Blochmann's *Āīn-i-Akbarī*, i. 213.

much that when you ride alonge in the streets you must have a man or two to goe beefore to thrust aside the people, for they are soe thicke as in a faire in our countrye. The cittie is 12 coses longe by the rivers side[1], which is above 16 miles; and at the narrowest place yt is three miles broade. It is walled, but the suburbs are joyned to the walls, that weare it not for the gates you could not knowe when you weare within the walls or without. There are many faire sarrayes in this cittie, wher travailours may lodge for little or nothinge. Every night the sarrayes are shutt, that none can goe in or out except it please the porter. This cittie is of greate trade from all places. Here you maye finde marchannts thatt will passe money to all places of the Indias, Persia, and Aleppo. A man maye bestowe 100,000 rialls in a weeke in diamonds; butt it must be very secreet, for that the Kinge hath comanded on paine of death that none presume to sell any diamond within his dominions that wayeth above five carretts; soe that you shall hardlie gett anie above five caretts except it bee by greate freindshipp and by familiar acquayntance with the brokers, whoe will helpe you from the hands of noblemen, who dare not to have it knowne for their lives. These doe secreetlie sell stones from 10 to 30 carretts, as in my time there weare five or six of that waight to be sold, and of the best sorts, which are growne in the countrye of Delly in the Mogulls dominion[2] and in the countrye where hee and his ancestours weare borne, the countrye beinge nowe decayed since the courte was brought to Agra, butt the Kinge, for the love that he beareth to his native countrye, comandeth the castell and citties to bee repayred. The Kinge is at greate charge in expence of his howse and for

[1] An over-statement. Finch says: 'The citie lyeth in manner of a half-moone, bellying to the landward some 5 c. in length and as much by the rivers side, upon the bankes whereof are many goodly houses of the nobility pleasantly overlooking Gemini.'

[2] This appears to be mythical.

his beasts, as horses, camells, dromedaries, coaches, and elaphannts. It was crediblie reported to Captaine Hawkins in my presence by the Kings purveyour for his beasts, that every daie in the yeare he spent in meate for them 70,000[1] ripeas, which is 35,000 rialls of eight. His wives, there slaves, and his concubines doe spend him an infinite deale of money, incredible to bee believed, and therefore I omitt itt. Hee hath but four principall wives, butt many concubines.

Haveinge passed five monnethes in this cittie, veiwing the strangenes of itt, the winter begininge nowe to end, wee determyned to speake with the Kinge before our departure, to have from him his passe to travayle to Cambaia and Suratt. We havinge acquaynted Can Juan[2], father-in-lawe to the Kinge, he appointed us a daie when wee should come to him. Soe at the daie appointed wee went; where as soone as the Kinge came forth and was sett on his throne, he called us to him, demandinge what our desire was. Wee told him that wee had lost our shipp, and that wee weare desirous to travaile to gett home for our countrie by the waye of Cambaia and Suratt; desiringe His Majestie that hee would favour us with his passe, as well for our quiett travellinge as alsoe for the free passinge of our stuffe without custome. He awnswered that his passe to travaile was needlesse, because his countrie was a free country for all men; notwithstandinge, wee should have his passe as wee desired. And being the custome, when he granteth any mans request, to give a reverence unto him

---

[1] Hawkins says 50,000. Elaborate details of the food, etc., of the various animals are given in the *Āīn-i-Akbarī*.

[2] By this is meant Khwāja Jahān, the title given by Jahāngīr (who married his daughter) to Dost Muhammad of Kābul, his former *bakhshi* (Blochmann's *Āīn-i-Akbarī*, i. 424, 477). Hawkins calls him 'Hogio Jahan, Lord General of the Kings Palace, the second man in place in the kingdome,' and a *mansabdār* of 3000. Jahāngīr employed him in superintending architectural work at Agra and Lahore, where he died in 1619.

in this manner, vizt. to laye your hand three times from the ground to your head, and then to kneele and putt your head to the grownd[1]; which the Kings father-in-lawe caused us to doe before he gave us the Kings awnsweare; then hee told us the Kinge had grannted our desire, and wee should come to him for itt. Wee gave the Kinge a peece of gould of our Kings quoyne, which he looked earnestlie upon and putt itt in his pockett. There are none that come unto the Kinge aboute anie suite whatsoever, be the partie never soe poore, but must bringe some thinge for a present, bee it never soe small; so that his daylie presents are worth much. There is accompt kept of every thinge which is given him, and is laid up in the treasurie. Hee delights much in toyes that are rare and hath not bene formerlie seene by him; in soe much that one thinge I will sett downe of his fancyes. The King had sent him from Caya[2], or by one which came from thence, two China dishes such as he had not formerlie seene, which he esteemed very much; delivered them to a noble man to bee laid upp. The nobleman chanced to breake one of them; which the Kinge understandinge sent for him, caused him to have soe many whipps before him; then he gave him 50,000 ropeas[3] to goe to Cattaya to fetch annother such dish, comandinge him presentlie out of his presence, and that he should come noe more to the courte untill he retourned with the dish. The noble man made speede to be gone, and had travelled some six months journey and was neere Cattaya, and some saie he was att Cattaya; but the Kinge sent post for him to retourne presentlie upon sight of his letter. Soe when hee

---

[1] A combination of the *taslīm* (salutation) and the *sijdah* (prostration), on which see notes in *The Embassy of Sir Thomas Roe*, pp. 135, 295.

[2] Cathaya (China).

[3] Hawkins, who tells the anecdote rather differently, says Rs. 5,000.

retourned the Kinge cared not for the breakinge of the dish, nor for his 50,000 ropeas, and the noble man was againe in greate favour; but was nott yett come backe when I came from Agra, butt beinge att Suratt I heard of his retourne. Alsoe there was a greate man of Cambaia that had two very fayre agatt dishes. He gave one of them to the Mogole, the other hee sent to the Kinge of Persia; which when the Kinge understoode, hee imprisonned the man and fined him to paye 200,000 ropeas; and by the Queenes entreatie, after he had bene one yeare in prison, was cleared for 50,000 ropeas.

Havinge finished all our buysines, and were to take our leaves of Captaine Hawkins, he out of his liberalitye gave 100 ma[hmūdīs] towards my expence downe, which is four pound sterlinge; which I would have refused butt that I thought itt better to departe in peace then ortherwise. Wee weare determyned not to goe the way wee came, because the winter is [was?] not yet ended; therefore wee went by the waye of Amadauar[1], which is the waye which goeth neere Sinda, as may appeare, vizt.—

Of our travailes from Agra to Cambaia by the way of Amadavar; the names of the cittyes wheare wee laye[2].

July 28. We departed from Agra, beeinge in companie Captaine Sharpeigh, my selfe, Derth.[3] Davye, the carpenter of our shipp, and Thomas Watkins. Captaine Hawkins brought us aboute six miles out of Agra, and he retourned; and wee came to lodge att Crowley[4], a prettye towne aboute six coses.

[1] Ahmadābād.

[2] Nicholas Ufflet travelled to Surat by a somewhat similar route, probably on the occasion when he brought down Hawkins' letter (see p. 139). His itinerary is given by Finch in *Purchas*, i. 434.

[3] A slip for Barth[olomew]; see p. 140.

[4] Kirāoli, about 13 miles W.S.W. of Agra.

July 29. Wee departed from Crowley and came to the cittye of Fettypore[1], a greate cittye, walled, with a very faire castle. The building within the cittie is much decayed. It hath bene the seate of a kinge in former tyme. The indico is made neere this cittie, att annother towne a side (*sic*) of, called Biana[2], where Mr. Finch bought his indico.

July 30. We departed from Fettypore and came to Primabado[3], a prettye towne, where there is alsoe made much indico.

July 31. Wee came from Primabado to Scandra sarraye; a prettye village[4].

August 1. We departed from Scandra sarraye and came to Hindone[5].

Aug. 2. Wee departed from Hindone and came to annother little village.

Aug. 3. Wee departed from thence and came to Lulsee[6] sarraye.

Aug. 4. Wee departed from Lulsee sarraye and came to Jampeth[7], a little towne.

Aug. 5. Wee departed from Jampeth and came to Churse[8].

---

[1] Fatehpur Sikri. Finch gives a good account of this famous mass of ruins.

[2] See p. 155. But Biāna is at a considerable distance from Fatehpur Sikri.

[3] Not identified.

[4] Finch's 'Scanderbade' (Sikandarābād), now called Sikandra, a village three miles to the south of Biāna Mundy describes it under the name of 'Shecundra.' For an account of it see Gen. Cunningham's *Archæological Reports*, vi. 74, xx. 79.

[5] Hindaun, in Jaipur territory, about 70 miles S.W. of Agra.

[6] Probably Lalsot, about 45 miles W.S.W. of Hindaun.

[7] This may be Jampda, about ten miles from Lalsot, where the Moril River would be crossed. Possibly it is Ufflet's 'Gamgra.'

[8] Chāksū, about 14 miles further. It is 22 miles south of Jaipur. Ufflet calls it 'Charsoot, chiefe seat of Rajaw Manisengo [Mān Singh] his prigonies' (*parganas*).

Aug. 6. Wee departed from Churse and came to Luddayna[1], ten coses.

Aug. 7. Wee departed from Luddayna and came to Muzaban[2].

Aug. 8. Wee departed from Muzaban and came to pitch in the waye, havinge much raine, soe thatt wee could nott avayle.

Aug. 9. Wee came to Sittill[3], thirteen coses; a pretty towne.

Aug. 10. Wee came from Sittill to Asmiere[4], seven coses. This is a citty where the Kinge hath a howse for his recreation when hee goeth a huntinge[5]. It hath alsoe a castle and is a walled towne, butt not stronge.

Aug. 11. Wee departed from Asmiere and came to Alsmura[6].

Aug. 12. Wee departed from Alsmura and came to Crowe[7], twelve coses.

Aug. 13. Wee departed from Crowe and came to Mertta[8], a pretty towne which doth abound with all sorts of druggs.

Aug. 14. Wee departed from Mertta and came to Berghee[9], thirteen cose.

Aug. 15. Wee departed from Berghee and came to Handolla[10], thirteen coses.

---

[1] Ladānā, on the Bandi R.

[2] Mozabad, 14 miles from Ladānā and about 30 miles east of Kishangarh.

[3] This may be Kuchil, a village about 14 miles N.N.E. of Ajmer. Tavernier calls it 'Coetchiel.'

[4] The well-known city of Ajmer.

[5] The Daulatbāgh, or Garden of Splendour, on the lake known as the Anā Sāgar.

[6] Not identified.

[7] Probably Garao, 11 miles S.E. of Merta. Ufflet calls it 'Cairo.'

[8] Merta, still a town of some importance, belonging to Jodhpur State. Ufflet says it 'hath a stone castle with many faire turrets, a faire tanke, and three faire pagodes richly wrought with inlayd workes, adorned richly with jewels and maintayned with rich offerings.'

[9] Not identified.

[10] Not identified.

Aug. 16. Wee departed from Handolla and came to Goodpore[1], nine coses.

Aug. 17. Wee departed from Goodpore and came to Donnara[2], twelve coses.

Aug. 18. Wee departed from Donnara and came to Tundacke, eleven coses.

Aug. 20. Wee departed from Tundacke and came to Conducke[3].

Aug. 21. Wee departed from Conducke and came to Imburrnie[4], being three coses.

Aug. 22. Wee departed from Imburnie and came to Gilburd[5], ten coses.

Aug. 23. Wee departed from Gilburd and came to Ingebor.

Aug. 24. Wee departed from Ingebor and came to Meerghee[6], twelve coses.

Aug. 25. Wee departed from Meerghee and came to Beerwall[7], twelve coses.

Aug. 26. Wee departed from Beerwall and came to Gundawe, fifteen coses.

Aug. 27. Wee departed from Gundawe and came to Cooga, fifteen coses.

Aug. 28. Wee departed [from] Cooga and came to Sarrand, fourteen coses.

---

[1] Jodhpur.

[2] Dundara, on the Luni River, seems to be meant; though that is 30 miles at least from Jodhpur.

[3] Possibly Khāndap, about 16 miles S. of Dundara; Ufflet's 'Canderupe.'

[4] This may be meant for Bharwāni, 6 miles S. of Khāndap, and 16 miles N. of Jālor.

[5] I take this to be Jālor, the well-known town in Jodhpur State. Ufflet gives a fairly long account of its famous fort.

[6] Ufflet's 'Mudre,' i.e., Modra, 16 miles S.W. of Jālor.

[7] Bhīnmāl, 16 miles S.W. of Modra. Ufflet calls it 'Billmall.' The next few stages are unrecognizable. They are probably small villages, and detailed maps of the district are not yet published.

Aug. 29. Wee departed from Sarrand and came to Bonnopp, fifteen coses.

Aug. 30. Wee departed from Bonnopp and came to Sarompore, eighteen coses.

Aug. 31. Wee departed from Sarompore and came to Serarpoore.

Sept. 1. Wee departed from Serarpoore and came to Semmee[1], ten cose.

Sept. 2. Wee departed from Semmee and came to Semmen.

Sept. 3. Wee departed from Semmen and came to Scolconpore[2], twelve cose.

Sept. 4. Wee departed from Scolconpore and came to Sodde[3], eighteen cose.

Sept. 5. Wee departed from Codde and came to Hoghepore[4], nine cose.

Sept. 6. Wee departed from Hoghepore and came to Doolpon, nine cose.

Sept. 7. Where wee stayed one day.

Sept. 8. Wee departed from Dolpon and came to Amadavar[5].

The 8 of September wee came to Amadavar, which is the principall cittye of Guzaratt, where there is a Vizeroy for the Mogoll. This cittie is one of the fairest cittyes in all the Indias, both for buildinge and strength as alsoe for bewtye, and scituated in a pleasant soile, and hath much trade by reason of much cloathinge which is made within the cittye, as baftas, birames[6], pintados and all other sorts of cloath. Likewise it is in the harte of the country for

1 This may be Sami, on the Saraswatī River, in Rādhanpur State.

2 Possibly Sankhalpur, about 20 miles S.E. of Sami.

3 Sadra, 22 miles S.E. of Sankhalpur.

4 Hājīpur, 14 miles S.E. of Sadra, and about 15 miles N.W. of Ahmadābād.

5 Ahmadābād.

6 See notes on pp. 95, 143.

indico, beinge neere the towne of Serques[1], where there is much indico made, as alsoe in many other villages neere adjoyneinge, which all goeth under the name of Serques.

Att our cominge to this cittye I found nott my selfe well. I desired Captaine Sharpeigh to staye to provide cartes to carrye our stuffe to Cambaia[2], and I would goe before to provide a howse, and take some phisicke in the meane time of his comeinge. Soe that I stayed nott above two daies in Amadavar, where wee paid our carriar for bringinge downe our stuffe, and departed for Cambaia, and lefte Captayne Hawkins [Sharpeigh], because wee could not soe soddenlye provide our selves of whatt wee wanted.

Sept. 14 The 14th of September I came to Cambaia, where I was extreame sicke of a fever and flix[3]; butt before the cominge of Captaine Sharpeigh I was reasonable well. Soe att his comeinge, the next daie wee went to visitt Macrobian[4] the Vizeroye, whoe seemed to welcome us in good manner, although hee weare angrye with Captaine Hawkins. Hee offered us all kindnes.

Sept. 30. The Vizeroye sent for us, and att our comeinge hee demanded us wheather wee had any newes of English shipps that weare come to the barre of Suratt. Wee told him that wee had noe newes of any. Then he tould us that there weare three ships and a pinnace come to Suratt[5]; thatt a friggott which came then to the porte mett with them and spake with them, and [they ?] demanded for the English men att Suratt; which the Vizeroye seemed to bee very

---

[1] Sarkhej, about five miles S.W. of Ahmadābād.

[2] Cambay, then the principal port of Gujarāt, situated at the head of the Gulf of Cambay, 52 miles S. of Ahmadābād.

[3] See p. 80.

[4] See p. 135.

[5] These were Sir Henry Middleton's ships of the Sixth Voyage, the *Trade's Increase*, *Peppercorn*, *Darling*, and a pinnace, named the *Release*, which they had put together at Mocha. The last-named was broken up at Swally early in December, 1611.

joyfull of their comeinge, wished us to provide our selves to bee gone as soone as wee might, and he would write a letter to his brother[1], which was his deputy att Suratt, to use us with all kindnes; and thatt he would provide two pallakins to carrye us to Suratt, because wee had sould our horses, and hee would send a dozen of his men to conduct us. Which the next daie, being the second of August [October], wee tooke our journey towards Suratt, and departed from Cambaia.

Although itt be somethinge tedious to sett downe every cittye with the circumstances of the trade of them, yett because this cittye of Cambaia is one of the best cittyes in all India for beautye and trade, I hould itt nott amisse to sett downe the principall traffique of this cittye, beeinge the staple towne where the Portugalls every yeare doe come with many friggotts out of all places, principallie from Goa, to fetch the comodities which are bought by Portugall factours which are leagers[2] in Cambaia, Amadavar, Broche, and other places; all which goods beinge bought in any place of India are brought to Cambaia and there shippd for Goa in friggatts, which come in fleets two or three times from September to December, guarded by the Portugall armatho[3] of friggatts; soe thatt you shall see 200 friggatts in a fleete goinge or comeinge from Cambaia to helpe lade the carricks att Goa. Their ladinge which they carrye from Cambaia is all sorts of fine cloath of cotton, much indico (which is brought from all places to bee shipped there as is aforesaid), all kinde of druggs, which are bought in Cambaia and many other places of India and sent hither against the time of the yeare. The countrye where the meaner sorte of indicoe is made is neere to Cam-

---

[1] Hawkins calls him 'Sheck Abder Rachim' (Shaikh Abdu'r-rahīm).

[2] See note on p. 2.

[3] Fleet (*armada*).

baia, as Barodora[1] and Saroll[2], as all the [alsoe ?] Serques; soe that there are in this cittie more marchannts that sell indicoe then att Amadavar; for it is to bee understoode thatt the indicoe beinge named Serques is not all made within the towne, butt round aboute the countrye of Amadavar and Cambaia; besides all the indico which is att Barodora and Saroll is the like. All which the most parte cometh to Cambaia to bee sould; as alsoe other thinges thatt are in India att the time of the caffolla[3] cometh, as they call them, which is the fleete of friggotts. Soe much for the trade of Cambaia. The strength of this cittie, weare itt in Christians handes, they would not care for a greate force; for that the walls thereof are very stronge, and at every gate there are two or three gates one within the other. In every streete is a castell, for after you are within the streets you cann see nothinge untill the porter open annother gate, where you must goe in att a little dore; then shall you see all thinges to bee sould within the cirquite; and soe is every streete throughout the cittie, that you may goe in the comon streete and scarce see a man before you enter into those little wicketts[4]. Soe that from their howses they may kill a multitude of people, if they are provided for itt.

October 2, 1611. The Vizeroye havinge furnished us with pallankins, and men to conducte us, and given us his letter

---

[1] Baroda.

[2] Sārōd, on the south side of the Mahi estuary, in Broach District. There is a ferry between this place and Dhuwaran, on the northern bank.

[3] Arabic *kāfila*, 'a caravan,' but also applied, as here, to a fleet of small vessels conveying merchandise.

[4] A similar arrangement at Ahmadābād is thus described in the *Imperial Gazetteer*: 'The peculiarity of the houses of Ahmadābād is that they are generally built in blocks or *pol*, varying in size from small courts of from five to ten houses, to large quarters of the city containing as many as 10,000 inhabitants. The larger blocks are generally crossed by one main street with a gate at each end, and are subdivided into smaller courts and blocks, each with its separate gate branching off from either side of the chief thoroughfare.'

to his brother in our favours, as likewise aboute the enterteynement of our shipps, wee departed from thence towards Suratt. Butt goinge over the river of Cambaia we wett all our stuffe, the water beeinge highe and the streame soe swifte that itt is very dangerous goinge over, because it is att least half a mile over, and deepe to the arme pitts; soe that the people are faine to hold hand in hand to gett over, otherwise the tyde would carrye them awaie, as itt hath manie, both horses, coatches and men drowned[1]. The reason of wettinge our stuffe made us staie one daye att Saroll, which is att the other side of the water, which is the place from whence the indicoe takes his name. Soe that it was the eighth daie before wee gott to Suratt. Butt beinge neere Suratt the Englishmen, hearinge of [our ?] comeinge, came forth aboute three miles to meete us; whoe advised us of Sir Henrye Middletons beeinge at the barre with three shipps and a pinnace; which did greatlie rejoyse us after our troubles and tedious journeys.

After our comeinge to Suratt wee presentlie went to the Governour, Macrobean his brother, and delivered his letter; whoe made unto us many promises of freindshipp, and willed us to write unto the Generall that any thinge which laye in him to pleasure us, that hee would to the uttmost performe itt. Soe for this time wee tooke our leaves and went home to write to Sir Henrie Middleton of our aproach, as alsoe of the state of the countrie; which letter was convayed to him by the shipps which rid att the barre[2], soe that within three daies we had awnsweare from him that if itt weare possible wee should repayre aboard; if not both, one of us; and that he would bee ready at the waters side to take us in, if wee did advise him of our comeinge. As alsoe he willed us to buye fresh

---

[1] Cp. *Della Valle* (Hakluyt Soc. ed., i. 63, 118).

[2] These were some native vessels which Middleton had detained.

victualls for him and send itt out by a boate of the countrye; and if the Portugalls did take itt, it weare no matter[1]. Soe wee bought wheate, rice and bread with other provisions, to the valewe of 200 rialls of eight, and sent itt out by the boates of the towne; butt the Portugalls tooke itt from them and mocked att us, bidinge them to will us to send them more refreshinge[2]. Notwithstandinge, our letters weare not taken, wherein wee advised Sir Henry that one of us would venter within two dayes to come to the waters side, intreatinge him to looke out hard for us when wee made a signe on the land, if by night with fire, if by daye with a white cloath[3]. Havinge given this advise, wee went

---

[1] A squadron of about twenty Portuguese frigates, under the command of Don Francisco de Soto Mayor, lay in the Tāpti, thus preventing the English from sending their boats up the river to Surat. Downton says that these frigates 'soe pestered the streames about us that none could nether out of the river nor anye other waye neere us but they would narrowly search and see that they had nether letters nor provisions that might comfort or releive our necessityes.' The letter which Bangham at last managed to smuggle through the cordon was 'conveied in a caine.'

[2] This occurred on Saturday, October 12 (Downton). In *Letters Received* (i. 138) will be found copies of two letters to Middleton, the first written by Sharpeigh and Jourdain on October 12, and the second by Sharpeigh alone on the 16th, together with a note of the provisions sent and their value.

[3] Middleton, despairing of Sharpeigh and his companions evading the Portuguese, wrote to the commander of the latter, 'requiring him that if he could not permitt him to trade heare, yet that he might take in the merchants and others his country men which were heare on shore in this country, and then he would be gone from this place. But the Portugall Captains answere to this was: Noe, for that he could carye them to Goa, and from thence they should be sent home. Also it seemed that John Jurdaine had bin flattering with the fathers both at Agra and Cambaia, and had obtained some commendations to the Viceroye, or request or hope of conduction unto Portugall, knowing at present no better meanes to gett unto his country; by which Sir H. M. could never expect anye safetye to such as continue firme to our state and countrye. And neare the time of this last letter from Sir H. M. Captaine Sharpeigh, by some principall Portugall then on land at Surat, made a motion ether by letter or otherwise to the Captaine Major to give him his *segure* or safe conduct for his safe passage abord the English ships; whereuppon the Captaine Major in scoff sent unto the English captaine and his companians his *segure* for his safecoming abord his galliote, without addition for there departure thence, the thing which he required; and further to shew the base accoumpt he made of our nation, added that if they would take

to the Governor and Hoghenazam[1], desiringe them to ayde us that one of us might gett saufelie to the shipps, and that wee might have some men of theirs to direct us. Soe havinge farther conference with them, they weare desirous to knowe whether the Generall did minde to settle a factorie and land his goods; which if he did, he would shewe us a place where the shipp might ride within muskett shotte of the shoare, in eight fathome water, and might land their goods att there pleasure without danger. Wee assured them that it was the Generalls onelie desire soe to doe, if he might have a place convenient. Then he tould us the place was called Swallye, aboute a league to the north of the place where nowe the three small shipps weare att anchour; which by sendinge of the small shipps they might easilie finde itt, giveinge us tokens uppon the land howe to finde itt promisinge alsoe to conduct mee to the waters side sal e, but thatt I must have on Magoll apparrell. Soe out of hand hee sent for the master of one of his owne shipps, willinge him to goe with mee with all his companie and bringe mee to the waters side neere the ships, and avoyed the Portugalls as much as he could, for their friggatts laye as then the one halfe att the barre and the other att Swallye, a little to the eastward; soe that by land in an hower they might goe from one place to annother. Soe wee weare to passe betwixt them. Wee departed by night and the next morninge wee came to Swalley, wheare

---

there passage along withim to Goa, he would use him and his companye with as much courtosye as he would doe to Turks, Moores and other nations that use these seas' (Downton's journal). The suggestion was made that the English at Surat should proceed overland to Dabul, where Middleton would meet them; but this idea was given up, partly on account of the trouble the journey would entail, and partly because the war in the Deccan made the ways dangerous.

[1] See p. 138. At this time Khwāja Nizām *was* the Governor (cp. p. 180 and Middleton's narrative), though he was superseded shortly after. Apparently Jourdain here refers to the Governor ('Captain') of the Castle (cp. p. 183).

the Portugalls weare washinge of their cloathes. Wee laye in the towne till the eveninge, that they went aboard. They knewe mee not because of my apparrell. After they weare gone aboard wee went by night and got neere the waters side, butt could nott come neere the shipps, because it was high water and there was an arme of a river where the sea flowed thatt wee could nott gett over, beeinge deepe and very oaze ground, that a man could not wade over if itt had bene drie. Butt wee swame over the river and came to the waters side right against the shipps, where behinde a bancke in sight of the shipps I made a weffe[1] with my torbant, and presentlie one of the shipps boats putt of; and the frigatt which they had taken two daies before from the Portugalls alsoe came with 50 men and Sir Henrie Middleton in her. The skiffe came neere the shoare, and I waded into her, and from thence to the friggott where Sir Henrie Middleton was, whoe kindlie welcomed me and carried me aboard the Peppercorne, where wee conferred with Captaine Downton and Mr. Pemberton; where I informed them of the place where shipps might ride att Swalley. The Generall understandinge thereof appointed Mr. Pemberton in the Darlinge to goe the next tide to search out the place, and found itt as

The 14 of October[2] I gott aboard the Peppercorne.

---

[1] Waft or wave.

[2] 'The 14th day, riding at this place within muskett shott of the shore, being two miles to the norwardes of the barr of Surratt, Mr. John Jordaine, merchant of the Assention, came aboorde' (Green's journal). Downton makes the date the 15th. 'Teusday the 15th in the morning the Genneral in the frigott went one shore, where presently came downe unto him Mr. John Jurdaine, accompanied with on Jadow [Jādū], a Benian who had sometimes bene Capt. Hawkins broaker. The rest of our countrimen also came furth of Surat with them; but the Portugals liing in wait in there passage, they esteemed it unpossible for so manye together to escape. Therefor they againe retourned to Suratt; but John Jurdaine and the broaker continued three nights in the feilds, watching there opertunitye to come downe when the Portugals should be gone who there lay in wait for them' (Downton's journal).

Hoghanazan had told me[1]. Soe the Generall knowinge the place went not presentlie thether with his shipps, butt stayed the cominge of Captaine Sharpeigh, whoe had wrote to Sir Henrie that he would bee with him very shortlie, but he stayed three or four daies longer then promise; butt att length hee came with the rest of the English men which were aland, all saveinge Nicholas Bangham, whoe remayned[2]. After thatt the Generall had conferred with Captaine Sharpeigh, wee went downe to the barre to the Trade and brought her upp to come to the place where wee weare to land our goods, called Swally. Where the Darlinge and the Release gott first within the barre; and the Peppercorne going in, the tyde beinge almost spent and the winde calme, came aground upon the bancke of faire sand, wheere shee laye all the ebb, and the Portugalls friggotts hard by her; yet none durst come neere her. For none of the other shipps could have done any good in rescueinge of her, because the tide was against us; butt, God bee thanked, the next flud without anie harme shee gott of againe and went in over the barre, where there is

[1] According to Downton it was not until Nov. 3 that Middleton sent Mr. Thornton in the *Release* to the northwards 'to discover out some place where we might bring in our ships to commaund the shore; but he soone retourned, pleading impossibilityes of what he sought for. Teusday the 5th, Sir Henry Middleton, impatient to receive such an answere uppon so little dilligence therein used, sent Wm. Pemberton, master of the *Darling* (in whose endeavours he had firme confidence) with his ship, the *Release*, and frigat againe to discover to the northwards as aforesaid; who there found a bard place whereunto not only all our smaller ships might at high water goe, but also the *Trades Increase*, being a little lightned, might also safely goe over the barr, and there ride within calliver shott of the shore.' The ships sailed thither on the following day. Green says the place was discovered on November 3, and the *Peppercorn* and *Darling* went over the bar on the 4th.

[2] From Downton's journal it appears that Thomas Watkins got on board on October 19, and was followed three days later by Thomas Musgrave [see p. 141], Bartholomew Davis and William Morgan, bringing with them Jourdain's and Sharpeigh's clothes and some provisions. On the 24th a boat was sent ashore, 'where presently came doune to them Capt. Sharpeigh with a hundred horssemen for his gaurd, all armed with bows and arrows and swords.'

att a high water 3½ fathome, butt in the right channell there was 4¼ fathome[1]. But the Trade as yett went not in, but rid without the barre in six fathome, aboute two miles from the place where the other shipps rid.

Nowe the Generall perceyveinge this to bee a good place to land our goods and send yt to Suratt, he sent to Nicholas Bangham that if anie would trade with him that hee should advise the Governor thereof; and that if itt pleased him to take the paines to come downe that they might conferre with him, that he doubted not but they should agree upon very good tearmes. Awnswere was retournd that the Vizeroye Macrobian was come from Cambaia, and that within two daies he would come downe to see the Generall and to conferre with him. Soe at the time appointed Hoghanazan came to the waters side. The Generall beeinge advised thereof, landed to speake with him, carryinge him a present. Soe att our landinge there weare manie complements betwixt them, as alsoe aboute landeing and sale of our goods; but the Governor told the Generall that the Vizeroye would bee with him in the morninge, and then they would conferre aboute that buysines att large; and soe departed, and sett up his tent a mile from us, stayinge for the Vizeroye.

The next daie[2] the Vizeroye came with his whole traine and pitched their tents in the plaine hard by the shipps. The Generall, perceiveinge his comeinge, landed and went into his tent, where they had much conference concerninge the sale of our comodities and landinge of our goods. After which the Vizeroye would goe aboard the

[1] Downton does not mention the grounding of the *Peppercorn*. According to Green, it happened on November 11, when the ships were re-entering the Pool after going to the assistance of the *Trade's Increase*, which was threatened by the Portuguese.

[2] The 24th November; see the accounts given by Middleton and Downton in *Purchas* (i. 269, 298). Jourdain evidently wrote this portion of his narrative from memory some time after; it is, however, generally correct.

shipps; which when he came aboard the Trades Encrease he wondred to see her, affirminge thatt he had bene aboard many Portugall carricks and that they weare nothinge in respect of this; as afterwards he affirmed the same on land in my presence to many Portugalls. In fine he liked the shipp soe well that he laye aboard her all night, with some dozen of his cheifest men; where he bought many things, as knives, hatts, lookinge glasses, stronge waters, cases of bottles, and many other things, which he paid well for. If itt weare a thinge that liked him he would have itt whatsoever itt cost. He gave many of the cheifest of the shipp presents of five or ten rialls worth of comodities to each, which he brought for the purpose. Soe the next daie att his departure the Generall gave him a good present, with a good peale of ordinance, and accompanyed him to his tent, where they conferred aboute the prices of goods and the landinge, which was agreed upon, vizt. that they should bringe a muster of every sorte of cloth to shewe us, and haveinge agreed a price wee should bringe our goods to the waters side, where they should take itt att the prices agreed upon, and they would bringe downe their goods to the waters side, where wee should receyve itt accordinge to the musters which remayned in our hands. Soe itt pleased the Generall to send Mr. Fraine[1], my selfe, and Nicholas Bangham to see the cloath, which was brought neere Swalley; soe wee went upp, and loosed many fardells[2] and tooke musters of each and retourned. And the next daie Hoghanazan and the Sabendar[3] came againe to the waters side to make an end of the prices of the comodities which was agreed upon. Then the Vizeroye departed to the cittie, leaveinge Hoghanazan and

[1] Hugh Frain, a factor of the Sixth Voyage. His death at Bantam is recorded later.

[2] Undid many of the bundles. This was on Nov. 28–29 (Downton).

[3] The *Shāhbandar* (see p. 59) at this time was Khwāja Hasan Alī.

the Sabendor to end that buysines[1], the Vizeroye makinge manie faire promises to the Generall aboute establishinge a factorie nott onelie att Suratt butt att any place of the India, havinge such aucthoritye from his master the Mogoll; which wee knewe to bee true, for att our beeinge in Agra Captaine Hawkins, haveinge newes of the beeing of these shipps in the Red Sea, by our procurement, went to the Mogoll to have his firma for their enterteynement. His awnsweare was that he would not give any more firmaies, but that he would write to Macrobian concerninge us in as ample manner as if he gave his firmae. By these meanes wee knewe that he had order from the Mogoll concerninge us.

Nowe Hoghanazan remayneinge aboute the perfourminge our agreement, ther was some difference aboute the waight of our lead, which wee weare to deliver him att 8½ ma[hmūdīs] the mane[2], butt when wee came to waye it he would have the greate mane, wee makinge agreement with him for the same ma[ne] that I had formerlie sold by in Suratt. But he would [not] agree to any thinge; except he had his desire there was noe dealinge with him; and in greate rage begann to lade away the goods which he had brought downe for us; whereof I presentlie went aboard to the Generall and advertized him howe matters past áland, whereatt he was very angrye. Nowe at this instannt there was the Captaine of the Castle and the Sabendour abourd with Sir Henrie Middleton to veiwe the shipp. Sir Henrie

---

[1] The date of Mukarrab Khān's second visit was December 8. He spent the night in his tents, and departed suddenly the next morning after receiving a letter from the Mogul Emperor (see the introduction).

[2] Maund (*man*). Later on Jourdain reckons the Surat maund at 28 lbs. Mitford in 1615 says that at Surat the small maund was 30⅝ lbs., and the great maund about 50 lbs. (*O. C.* 273). Green states that Khwāja Nizām was aggrieved 'bycause we would nott geeve him 46 kintalls for 36.'

This dispute took place on December 10; see the narrative of Middleton and Downton.

in his anger tould them howe Hoghanazan had dealt with him, and thatt he would keepe them aboard till the partido[1] made were performed, seeinge one of them was the cheife governor for the Kinge and the other the Sabendor, whoe was presennt at the bargaine makeinge and was interessant in the matter. Butt after hee had pawsed a little, hee cawsed the friggatt to bee mand and the longe boate, and tooke these twoe men into the friggott and carryed them aland, and by violence brought Hoghanazan abourd the Peppercorne, which was neere the shoare, and the Sabandour with him, and sett the Governour at libertie, havinge noe finger in the buysines. The General wilde mee to staye aboard the Peppercorne all night to keepe them companie. Butt Hoghanazan was in such a rage thatt wee thought hee would have killed him selfe; neyther would hee goe into the cabbin, butt laye all night upon the decke. The next morninge the Generall wrote to me to bringe the Sabendour and Hoghanazan aboard the Trade. I went to them, entreatinge them to goe aboard; butt Hoghanazan was in such a rage thatt wee might carrye him dead butt wee should never carry him alive to a man that had taken him prisonner in his owne countrye for standinge upon the buyinge of his comodities; which awnsweare I sent to the Generall, who sent mee word to come aboard and leave them. Soe as I was goeinge into the boate, the Sabandour sent to mee to staie a little; soe by his perswations Hoghanazan was perswaded to goe aboard the Trade. And when he came aboard and sawe the shipp, and all things in such good order, hee embrased the Generall, and tould him that nowe his harte was merry, thatt he cared not to dwell in such a shipp as that was. Sir Henrie used him very respectfullie, and tould him thatt whatt he did was to avoyed

---

[1] Ital. *partito*, 'a bargain.'

farther troubles, for if he should have gone for Suratt his buysines had bene much hindred by itt; therefore entreated him to take some course that the buysines might goe forward in freindshipp like lovinge freinds; which Hoghanazan promised should be perfourmed, and to thatt purpose he would leave his two sonnes aboard as pledges. His sonnes beeinge willinge to staye aboard were received by Sir Henry very kindlie, and Hoghanazan and the Generall went aland, after a present given him, to sett forward the buysines; where Hoghanazan and the Sabendour stayed in their tents untill the buysines was almost ended; his sonnes makinge merry aboard. Sometimes one of them by leave would goe home to their wives while the other staied; and soe retourne againe.

In the interim of this buysines the Portugalls, perceaveinge whatt we did, came by land aboute four or five companies from their frigatts, wherein was the Vizeroye[1] his sonne. They thought to intercept our men and goods; but havinge a good watch they were discried. Butt out of the greatnes of their valour some of them came on the sandes with there head peeces and costletts; where some of them lost their lives by the barre shott from the shipps. One of them wee tooke up and buryed; the others they dragged awaie, as wee might well discerne[2]. The people

---

[1] The Viceroy at this time was Ruy Lourenço de Tavora (see his letter on a later page).

[2] 'The 22th day [November], being the day apointed that the great mann Muccrebucan should come unto our shipps, lay in ambush behinde the hills right against our shipps 500 armed Portingalls, besyde slaves; who in the morning whenas our boates should come ashore and that the boates ging [crew] weare landed, came running towardes our men to entercept them. Butt, God be thanked, we had descried them in such tyme that all our menn gott into theire boates without any mann hurte, although they mad divers shott at them. In meane tym of their hott persut of our menn ashore, we on shippboord for their saveguard shott of divers peeces of great ordinance, which cast shott amongst them; in which conflict we killed them two menn owtryt and maymed a great manny more, as also we shott downe theire coulours hoyst. Which hott skermish being as unexpected of them, made them fly (as the proverbe is) faster then a parsonne for

of the countrye ranne awaye and lefte all to us. But against the next time of their retourne the Generall determyned to land and meete them with his companie. Within two or three daies after, they came within half a mile of us, and our men landed, aboute 200 men with their musketts; but the Portugalls would not abide. Our men followed them a prettye way; butt they beeinge come neere their friggotts, our people came backe againe; the countrye people standinge on the hills to see the fight, which was soone ended. Our people gave a volley of shott to Hoghanazan, whoe was upon his elaphant to see the sporte [1].

Wee havinge received all our comodities accordinge to promise, and our lead and other comodities delivered accordinglie, the Generall would have me to goe to Suratt to see whatt might bee done aboute the elaphannts teeth and broad cloth, which was not in the bargaine; onelie they bought all the leade and quicksilver, red leade and velvett. Soe I went [2] accordinge to order, accompanied with Heugh Fraine and Nicholas Bangham, with comission to sell these comodities aforesaid, as alsoe to feele the Vizeroye aboute his willingnes in setlinge a factorye, which he alwaies desired in outward shewe, as I advised

---

hast, leaving theire peeces, some theire swoordes, some their shooes and cappes to be gone' (Green's journal). See also Downton's account (*Purchas*, i. 298). He makes the date November 21.

[1] This happened, not two or three days, but more than three weeks, after the skirmish already related. According to Downton 'Monday the 16th [December], in the morning we saw uppon the hils to the southwards five Portugall cullours displayed; whereof the Genneral understanding, presently by his commaund were landed some 200 armed men with shot and pikes to meet them; which they perceiving retired. In which pursuit, being neere unto Swally, we mett with Coja Nazaun and all his troup, who was coming doune with some 20 packs more of India clothes. He informed the Generall that the Portugals were alreadye gotten over the muddy crookes and were neare unto there frigats; wherefor the Genneral gave over his pursuit and retourned abourd.'

[2] Dec. 30, according to Downton.

Sir Henrie Middleton; as alsoe aboute the sale of the L[1] teeth and cloth, they not cominge to the price which hee demanded; advisinge him that if his determynation was to settle a factorye, thatt then itt weare not good to sell itt att that rate, for that noe doubt in time it would yeild more profitt; but if hee determined not to leave any factorie, then our opinion was to take the money that was offred. Sir Henrie his awnsweare was that he purposed to leave a factorie upon conditions, if itt pleased the Vizeroye to take the paynes to retourne once more to the waters side to conferre with him; which as soone as I had advised Macrobean, hee seemed to be very willinge to goe downe to end that buysines, and appointed a tyme for the same; of all which I advised the Generall.

Nowe in the heate of this buysines there hapned two encounters, which was the cause thatt Sir Henrie had nott setled a factory. The one was that Captaine Hawkins was come to Cambaia with his familye, bound for Goa. And the Vizeroye of Amadavar[2] was come from the wars of Decan, with an overthrowe of 4000 horse, and was come within two daies journey of Suratt to goe to Baramporte, to renewe his armye. Macrobian, being his freind, must ride out in pompe to meete him to bewaile his losse and to comfort him; soe that att his retourne his minde was altered for goeinge to vizitt him. At his cominge home, hee demanded mee when our shipps would bee gone, sayinge that our marchandizing was nowe ended, that wee might departe, and the sooner the better, because thatt the Queenes shipp, the Beheme[3], was bound for Moucha, and

[1] Elephants'.

[2] Abdala Khān, who had distinguished himself in the war against Udaipur and had (1611) been rewarded with the *sūbah* of Gujarāt in succession to the Khān-i-Azam. For his defeat here referred to see Elliot and Dowson's *History of India*, vi. 332. His subsequent career is given in *The Embassy of Sir T. Roe*, 170.

[3] A mistake for 'Reheme,' *i.e.*, the *Rahīmī* ('The Merciful One's'). According to Saris she was 153 feet long by 42 feet broad, and of at

the marchannts would nott lade their goodes aboard untill wee weare gone from the countrie. I awnswered him thatt the Generall did looke for his companie att the seaside accordinge to promise, to conferre aboute setlinge of a factorie. Whereunto he awnswered that nowe it was too late to talke of thatt matter, for thatt Captaine Hawkins was come from the courte, he knewe nott in whatt sorte; therefore he durst not treate of setlinge a factorye untill he had further order from his master the Mogoll; willinge us to dispatch our buysiness and departe out of the towne with the rest of our comodities that was lefte; of all which I advised the Generall, and had present awnsweare thatt wee should dispatch and come awaie[1].

least 1200 tons burden. By 'the Queene' is meant Jahāngīr's mother, of whom see note on p. 155.

[1] 'The seven and twentieth [January] I sent John Williams and one of our factors to Surat upon businesse. This day Mockrib Can came to towne. He had been to meet a great commander which was comming from the warres of Decan and was to passe by Surat. Before his going out of the towne he sent for M. Jourdaine and willed him to commend him to me and to certifie me that he was to goe out of the towne, but would not tarry out above three dayes, and at his returne he would be as good as his word for what he had promised concerning our factory. Now at his returne he sends for him againe, and with a frowning countenance, contrary to his expectation, demands of him what he did there and why were we not all gone. He answered that hee staied upon his word and promise that we should leave a factory; otherwise he had not been there. He said againe we should have no factory there, and that the long staying of our shippes there had hindered him in his customes tenne hundred thousand manuveys [mahmūdīs]; and therefore in the Kings name charged them to be gone with speed out of the towne, for neither trade nor factorie was there to be had for us....The nine and twentieth I sent for the factors at Surat to doe as Mockrib Can commanded; to hast and come away, for that I would be gone' (Middleton). Green, who was sent with Jourdain on January 13, gives some further details: 'The 14th day we arived in Surratt, where we went unto Muccrebuccan, who as soone as he saw us asked what we made heere soe longe; althoughe himselfe with his faire promises was the cawse therof. We annswered that our Gennerall did now only stay the comming of Captain Hawkings....The 16th day we weare with Muccrebuccan, who shewed a letter which was sent him from Chaulle from the Shahbendor there, whereby he was geeven to understand that the Captaine of Chaul had embarged of his goodes to the valew of 28 thowsand mamodies, which was, as he said, bycawse he gave entertainement and trade to Englishmenn. Wherefore as yett he could

Butt in the interim of this buysines, while Macrobian was visittinge of the Vizeroye of Amadavar, the Generall, havinge received a letter from Captaine Hawkins from Cambaia, sent Captaine Sharpeigh, Heugh Greete and others to the towne to goe meete Captaine Hawkins and perswade him not to goe to Goa butt to come to the shipps with his wife and familie; willinge Mr. Fraine to accompanie Captaine Sharpeigh to Cambaia, to see the indico and to buye some store if he might at any reasonable price[1]. Soe that att the retourne of Macrobian, Cap-

---

nott resolve us yf we should have any more trade or nott....The 19th day we advized the Gennerall that for settling of a factory the people of the country weare most willing thereunto, for that as now Muccrebuccan had fermed the Kings letter and made us all the faire promises that might be....The 27th...comming before Muccrebuccan he asked why we weare nott gone, saying that our stay heere soe long had lost him a million of mamodies (butt never would say soe sooner) in his customes. We tould him that now our only stay was to know whether we should settle a factory ther (being we could nott sell our goodes) according as he had promised. Hee annswered we should have none, denieing all his former promises and speeches unto us, bidding and commanding us instantly withowt any delay to avoyd the country and town and nott to come there any more.'

[1] 'December 30...the Genneral received a letter from Captaine Hawkens at Cambaia, signifiing that his determination was with all his houshold to take his voyage to Goa and from thence to England. ...Thursday, the 2th Januarye, Capt. Sharpeigh and Hugh Greet were sent to Suratt, from thence to take along withem Mr. Frain to Cambay, with letters to Capt. Hawkens to alter his determination of going to Goa, but to come and take his passage with us unto England....Wensday, the 8th, Nic. Uphlet came doune from Cambaia with letters from Capt. Hawkins to the Genneral, certifiing him that by reason of his former letter he determined to come doune to our ships and take his passage with us. Thirsday the 9th Nic. Uphlett departed againe, with letters from the Genneral to Capt. Hawkens; also withim went Baly Ball, steward of the *Peppercorne*, hoping they should there have delt for much indico....Sonday, the 26th, Capt. Sharpeigh, Mr. Frain, Capt. Hawkins, with all there goods and familye, and the rest (Nic. Uphlett excepted) came downe, whom the Genneral with a troup of some 200 men went some three miles up unto the land to meet and guard from [the] Portugals, whose troup was not far of' (Downton's journal). According to Hawkins' narrative he quitted Agra on November 2, reached Cambay 'the last of December' (this is evidently inexact; see above, and Middleton's account), left that place January 18 and reached the ships January 26.

Green adds that Hawkins stipulated that Middleton should pay him the value of the goods (indigo and fine calicoes) he was bringing down, 'which was by estimacion the valew of 18 hundred powndes...

taine Hawkins was come with his wife and familie to Sually, and all his stuffe, with determination to goe for England with his wife; which was the cheifest cause that Macrobian made such haste for us to bee gone. And the Generall on the other side, beeinge somethinge incensed by Captaine Hawkins against the trade of this countrie, made the more hast to send for us to come aboard; which wee did with as much brevitie as wee could.

Soe the 5th of February Benjamyn Greene, my selfe and Nicholas Bangham departed from Suratt. The officers of the custome howse at our farewell serched our cabinetts and made us paie the custome of every riall of eight which wee carryed out, and of every thinge els, if the custome came but to one riall of eight. Thus after 15 [29] months beinge in the countrye of India I departed from Suratt, and came to the shipps to Sually the 6th dicto in the morninge earlie.

The kingdomes belonging to the Greate Mogoll; with the reason of his sodden settinge forth of an armye of 400,000 horse.

Cabull. Casmeir. Candahar. Ballucke. Delly. Cambaia. Sinde. Bengalla. Potann. Mandoa. Guallier. Hassier. Amadavar. Part [of] Decan. Pierb is 400 cose longe, and hath bene the seate of four kinges[1].

---

and that he might enjoy the same aboord withowt any detaine in the Companies behalf.' To this Middleton agreed.

[1] This list is a very rough one, and necessarily incomplete. By 'Ballucke' seems to be meant the country of the Balūchīs. 'Potann' may be intended for Patna; but is more likely to be a reminiscence of Finch's 'Potan [Pathān] kingdome,' which was evidently the district occupied by the Ghakkars on the northern frontier of the Punjāb. 'Mandoa' [Māndū] stands for Mālwā, and 'Hassier' [Asīr] for Khāndesh. 'Pierb' is the Hind. *Pūrb*, from the Sanskrit *Pūrba*, 'the east,' and seems to signify the country east and north of the Ganges, including Oudh, Benares, Jaunpur and part of Bahār. Finch calls Patna 'a great citie in *Purrop*'; and Hawkins speaks of Allahābād as 'the regall seate of a kingdome called *Porub*.'

In every of these provinces there is a vizeroye under the Mogoll; and the least of these hath the paye of 6000 horse, and some 12,000. Besides there are many other little countryes where there is onelie governours, men of 3000 horse to 1000 horse. Of these there are many; and haddyes[1], which are pentioners from the paye of one horse to ten, there are an infinite number. The paie of each horse is worth betweene 40 and 43 ropeas per monneth. All these men which have the paie of soe many horse allowed them are to have their full complement readye att any time that the Kinge comandeth them to goe forth to warrs; soe that his warrs cost him nothinge, for the paye of these horse is raysed upon the countrye whereof each is governor, accordinge to the number of horse. For it is to be noted that when the Kinge makes a man of 1000 or 2000 horse or the like, he giveth him a countrye that is sufficient for to paye whatt his horse amounts unto, and some times a greate deale more, as the parties are favoured by the distributour of the Kings jaguers[2] or lands, which was Abdelasan, Captaine Hawkins freind, in my time. This is the greatest office of honnor that is in the kingdome, to distribute the land accordinge to the Kings guifte. And sometime he will keepe the land in his owne hand half a yeare before the partie shall have itt, because he will receive the rents for soe longe himselfe; and yett the partyes are very well content to receyve itt in the end. Soe that the Kinge within one monneth is able to sett out 400,000 horse[3], besides elaphannts, if neede should soe require. I speake

---

[1] *Ahadī*, a gentleman-trooper or soldier of the body-guard. Numbers of them were attached to the imperial court, and were used to carry messages of importance and for other special services. Hawkins says: 'of horsemen, that receive pay monethly, from sixe horse to one, there be five thousand; these bee called *Haddies*.'

[2] See p. 154.

[3] Hawkins says 300,000.

a greate deale within compasse of whatt I have heard crediblye reported, and some thinge I have seene my selfe.

Our course from Sually roade to Dabull.

Feb. 9. The Trades Encrease[1] warped over the barre of Sually, wee havinge stayed two daies for the cominge of Nicholas Ufflett and Jadoo[2], that was att Cambaia aboute some buysines of Captaine Hawkins[3]. Being without the barre, wee stayed till the 11th, fittinge all things pridie[4] to sett saile. In the meane time wee mett with a friggott laden with rice and pitch bound to the Queenes shipp the Beheme [Reheme], ridinge att Gogo. Wee tooke such things as wee wanted from them, and Captaine Hawkins passed a bill of exchange upon the deptours att Suratt to paye them for itt.

Feb. 11. In the morninge wee sett saile from the barre of Sually, and in the eveninge wee anchored at the barre of Suratt, where wee found a shipp of Suratt that was come over the barre to take in her ladinge for the Red Sea. Wee tooke some wood from them; as alsoe this daie wee tooke a boate laden with coale[5]. Wee tooke whatt wee needed, and Captaine Hawkins passed annother bill of exchannge upon his debtours.

Feb. 12. Wee sett saile from the barre of Suratt, and wee mett with twoe Mallabar shipps laden with coker nutts and racke[6] bound for Suratt. From one of them

---

[1] Evidently Jourdain was with Middleton on board the flag ship.

[2] See note on p. 178.

[3] From Downton's journal it appears that Hawkins and Sharpeigh 'left Nic. Uphlett and Jawdowe the broaker in pawne for money by them taken up at Cambaia for their present use.'

[4] A sailor's term for getting a ship ready to sail.

[5] Charcoal.

[6] Arrack.

wee tooke a pylott to carry us to Dabull. In the eveninge wee ankored aboute three leagues of the barre, the tyde beeinge soe stronge against us that wee could nott gett ahead.

Feb. 13. Wee sett saile aboute seven in the morninge, and wee mett with two Mallabar shipps more, laden with coker nutts as the other. Wee spake with them and lett them departe. This daie wee had the winde att N.W., a fresh gale, and wee steered awaye S.W. & by W. and W.S.W. Aboute three in the afternoone wee fell into shoald water from 8 to 6½ fathome. Then wee stoode more southerlie a glasse or twoe, and wee had 19 and 20 fathome. Then wee steered all night S.W. & by S. Wee had one cast 13 fathome; butt standinge more westerley wee had our ould depth, 19 and 20 fathome.

Feb. 14. Wee had sight of high land, and wee steered S.S.E., the winde att North and N.N.W. Aboute three of the clocke wee sounded and had 13 fathome, beeinge neere the land as wee suppose of Basaim. This day wee mett with three Mallabar shipps bound for Suratt, laden like the former. Wee medled not with them.

Feb. 15. Wee had calme untill noone; then a fresh gale at N.N.West, and wee stoode away S.S.E. to seaze the shoare. At evening wee weare two leagues shorte of Chaule[1], havinge all night a fresh gale att North. Wee steered alonge the shoare.

Feb. 16. In the morninge wee weare neare the shoare, which our pilott made to bee Dabull, butt after speaking with a fisher boate tould us thatt Dabull was seven leagues further ahead, and thatt wee weare nowe half the waye betweene Chaule and that. Soe wee steered alonge the shoare till eveninge, att which time wee anchored neere Dabull, havinge had a fresh gale at N.N.W. all daie. Wee

1 Chaul is about 30 miles south of Bombay.

might discerne the castle on the hill and some howses, butt not the towne[1].

Feb. 17. Wee tooke a fisherman, by whome the Generall sent letters which hee had brought from Moucha from a captaine of a shipp to the Governour in the Generalls behalfe; and the same daie the Governor sent to vizitt the Generall, with a present of fresh victualls in greate plentye. The Generall retourned him annother by four of the marchannts, which he sent aland with itt, willinge them to knowe of the Governor if hee would give us trade. Hee awnswered very kindlie thatt himselfe would give money for all our cloath; with many other promises and complements.

Feb. 18. The Generall havinge receyved these kinde words from the Governor, sent Mr. Fowler and my selfe the 18th daie in the morninge to conferre with him aboute our buysines, carryinge with us the musters of cloath; which when the Governor had seene, hee seemed as though hee cared not for the cloath, onelie he was desirous of our lead, with some of our cloath, which he would chuse by the coulours; butt hee offred such a lowe price for the cloth thatt it shewed noe greate willingnes to buye any. Notwithstandinge, wee lefte him the musters and went aboard to advise the Generall of whatt passed. The Governor had many complements with us, with many comendations to our Generall.

Feb. 19. The next daie we landed againe to knowe the Governours ultima concerninge our cloath and other comodities; where wee found him sittinge in his state at his howse, with many cheife men of the towne with him. Wee demanded our musters of him, entreatinge to knowe his awnsweare whether he would buye any of our comodities or nott. Butt wee perceyveinge noe greate willingnes in him, wee entreated him to give order thatt wee might buye

[1] Dābhol, 85 miles S. of Bombay, was the principal port of the Bījāpur kingdom.

for our money such thinges as wee wanted and wee would departe; which he very kindlie granted, and sent one of his men with our purser to see thatt hee paye noe more then ordinarilie itt was sould for in the markett. This daie the winde blewe soe hard thatt wee could nott gett aboard, thatt wee were forced to staie aland all night. Soe wee went to the Governour to entreate him to ordaine us a house to lodge in all night; which he presentlie gave order for, and told us that he was sorry wee would departe soe soone without sellinge any of our comodities; sayinge farther that because wee should knowe thatt he was willinge to deale with us, hee would give us four royalls of eight for a covedo of such broade cloath as he liked, and two rialls for a covedo of the kersey, and 38 rialls of eight for 25 ma[ns] of leade, which maketh Suratt weight 20 mans[1]. Att thatt price he would take 14 peeces of broad cloath and 8 peeces of kersey (but he would chuse the colours), and he would take all the leade. Wee demanded more of him, puttinge him off untill wee had acquaynted the Generall. Soe for this time wee tooke our leaves and departed to our lodginge, which was the sarraye of the towne, causinge itt to bee made very cleane and putt out those that lodged in itt. He sent greate store of victualls, and his servannts to attend us untill wee had eaten.

Feb. 20. The next morninge early wee went aboard and acquaynted the Generall with his offer for our comodities, leaveinge the purser and other aland to provide such provision as was necessary for the shipps. The Generall beinge willinge to sell him the comodities for the price which he had offerred, sent Benjamyn Greene and other the factours to end with him; which beeinge done Benjamin Greene came aboard for the comodities to deliver him, and brought two pledges of the Governours servannts,

[1] Green states that the local 'covado' was 29 inches, and the local maund 25 lbs.

as pledges to remayne aboard untill the mony weare paid; which the Generall retourned againe aland, sayinge that he doubted nothing of the performance of his word. Soe they carryed all the comodities aland, where they remayned till the 24 dicto, measuringe out the cloath and wayinge the leade; butt the Governor tooke butt the very choise of the stamell and Venice red. Alsoe he bought the red leade that was in the shipp. Havinge neere done all there buysines aland, the maister went aland in the skiffe and brought aboard the money which they had received of the Governor. And the next daie the marchannts came all aboard; with whome came some of the Governours men to buye some more cloath, with manie complements from the Governor to the Generall, that if itt pleased him to leave a factorie in the countrie they should be well entreated. The Generall excused the matter for this time, sayinge he was not provided for itt, but some other voyage it might bee effected.

Feb. 25. Benjamin Greene and John Williams went againe aland to see if they could sell some more cloath and a parcell of red capps. They beinge aland the Governor refused the red leade, because it had bene wett, and detayned Benjamin Greene untill he had wrote aboard to the Generall to knowe whether he should take itt or nott. Soe the Generall willed them to staie untill farther order; but the next daie he wrote for them to bringe the red leade with them, if the Governor would not have itt. Soe they came aboard the 29th dicto, and brought a present from the Governour to the Generall.

In the interim of this buysines, wee discryed a saile to the offinge, a good tall shipp[1]; and beinge calme they

---

[1] 'The 26th of February was taken a Portingall shipp called the St. Nicholas, who came from Cochinn, bownde for Chaule and from thence for Ormuse, laden with tinn and other groce commodeties' (Green). Downton adds that she was of about 300 tons burden.

ankored two leagues of. Soe the Generall caused the Peppercorne and the Darlinge to goe of by night to them to see what they weare, and if they were Portugalls to bringe them into the roade. In the companie of the ship there was a great frigatt laden with rice, bound for Ormus. They tooke both the shipp and the friggott, and brought them to the roade the next daie; at which time the Generall went aboard to search the shipp, and found her to bee laden with coker nutts, except some 52 c[wt] of Lankin[1] silke and some cinamon of Selan[2]; all which the Generall tooke from them, in satisfaccion of parte of the wronge there countryemen had done him att Suratt; as alsoe he tooke as much rice out of the frigatt as hee needed, as alsoe other provision; for all which he gave them a noate of his hand, and they gave him annother wherein was sett downe all things which was taken from them. The friggatt was suffred to departe the same daie, and she went into the porte of Dabull, thinkinge themselves well dealt withall. The shipp had likewise leave to departe, butt they would not parte from us for feare of the Mallabars which were some four daies before past towards Chaull, whither this shipp was bound, and came from Cochin in company with the friggatt. Soe the shipp rid still by us untill wee sett saile.

From the 16th [26th] of February to the 4th of March wee weare buysied aboute the sale of our goods and aboute the Portugall shipp; which buysines beeinge nowe at an end, the Generall called councell concerninge his farther proceedeinge in his voyage. His demands weare these, vizt. Whether wee thought it meete to goe to the barre of Goa to demand satisfaccion of the Vizeroye for the damage sustayned by him, and to render up the goods taken for [from] the shipp[3] if he gave us any reasonable content; or to proceede in our voyage (accordinge to comission) for

---

[1] Nanking. [2] Ceylon.
[3] The Portuguese vessel just captured.

Bantam; or else to retourne into the Red Sea from hence directlie, there to staye for the Indian shipps and barter our goods with them in parte of recompence of the wronge offred us att Suratt, as alsoe of the Turks in the Red Sea. The most voyces was to goe directlye to the Red Sea, where wee should be sure to have whatt satisfaccion wee would. Some weare of opinion to followe our voyage for Bantam, accordinge to comission; butt it was resolvd for the Red Sea, and in the morninge to sett saile[1].

A discription of Dabull, the towne and porte.

Dabull standeth in 17 degrees, 34 minutes; variation 17 degrees. Itt is a bard harbor, and narrowe att the entrannce of the barre; there 2½ fathome water att a lowe ebb, and att full sea 4½. The goinge in is at the souther side. You may goe close by the rocks and there is the deeper water. The breadth of the barre att entringe is not above a cabells length, butt presentlie itt goeth broader and broder untill you come to the towne, which is aboute two miles within the barre. When you come before the towne there is a goodlie harbour, where a shipp may ride in eight fathome with a fishinge line for any winde that hurte.

The towne standeth in a valley environed aboute with highe mountaines; soe that it is very hott to them which are not used to itt. The Governor and greate men have faire houses; the rest are poore cottages, as in all other parts of India, which lives like the fishes in the sea, the greater eate the lesser. The Governor liveth in greate

[1] Green says that the council was held on March 5, and that the chief arguments used against proceeding to Bantam and the Moluccas were the want of provisions and the probability that they would find themselves anticipated by a ship of another Voyage and would be unable to obtain enough pepper to lade their vessels. Middleton gives February 24 as the date of the council, while Downton makes it March 4.

state. His name is Agaa Mahomett Roza[1]. The kinge of this countrye liveth att Vizapor[2], in the countrye of Decan; his name is Adelshaa[3]. Vizapor is aboute six daies journey from Dabull. This kinge is the cheife of five kings which maynetaine warre with the Mogoll. This countrie is very firtill, and yeildeth store of all sortes of fine cloathinge, as baftas, birams, shasses and many other sortes; as alsoe indico, and diamonds, greate store of the newe rocke, and many other stones of little valewe. From this towne every yeare goeth two or three shipps of greate burthen to the Red Sea, farre richer then those that goe for [from ?] Suratt, beinge supposed that the Portugall[s] are adventurers with them. Their ships are made Christian like, with topps and all their tacklinge accordinglie. Alsoe they send two ships yearlie for Ormus from this towne very ritch. In this towne of Dabull lyeth a factour for the Portugalls contynuallie, who giveth passes by the Vizeroyes aucthoritie to all their shipps which goe for the Red Sea, Ormus, and other places; butt if they bee found carryinge powder, shott or any other munition, or pepper, cinamon, with divers other comodities, it is confiscated; butt much of these comodityes doe passe with a bribe given to the factour, which is the cheifest of his vailes. This factour hath 2000 pardas[4] of the Kinge of Spaine per yeare, butt his vailes, alias bribes, are greate. Alsoe he hath license that none may sell racke or reason wine within the towne butt himselfe, which is good proffitt to him, butt for his license he giveth the Governour 2000 laruns[5] per yeare.

---

[1] Āghā Muhammad Razā.

[2] Bījāpur.

[3] Ibrāhīm Adil Shāh II.

[4] There were two *pardaos*, one of gold and the other of silver. For a long note on their value, etc., see *Hobson-Jobson*, 2nd ed., p. 672.

[5] A peculiar kind of money much in vogue on the Malabar Coast and in the Persian Gulf. It was made by stamping a small rod

It is butt a base factory, for hee is no better then the hoste of an alehowse, for he selleth both drinke and meate, as all kindes of fruits which hee hath growinge within his garden. Butt he was much ashamed that wee should knowe that hee sould these thinges, butt the saylours were never out of his house. With these pettye matters it is worth by reporte 15 or 16,000 pardoas per annum. This towne hath of all nations tradinge in itt, and is very populous of itt selfe and greate. It hath a small castell standinge by the waters side within the towne; it hath two small peeces in itt, and is of noe force[1].

Our course from Dabull to the Red Sea.

March 5. Wee sett saile from Dabull, with the winde at E. and E.S.E.; butt in the eveninge, beeinge calme, wee ankored neere the shore within seven leagues of Dabull

---

of silver and then doubling it up (see a note by Mr Albert Gray in his edition of *Pyrard de Laval*, i. 232). Its value at this time was a little under a shilling.

[1] Compare Green's description: 'Dabull hath two miles withowt a barr, upon which we have sownded and fownd at most 15 foote water. The going over the said barr is narrow, yett nottwithstanding they have 9 shipps of great burthen and draughts belonging to this place, the least of them drawing 18 or 20 foot, being laden; and they lade before the towne, and being laden bring theire shippes over this barr upon a spring tide. After you are over the barr, which is halfe a cables lengthe over, you may ryde in 7, 8, 9 or 10 fatham withoutt any commaunde of ordinance....Dabull hath only a small rownde forte in the north end of the towne, in which appeereth noe more then 3 or 4 small bases, nor noe other fence for the towne, being very low and small cotteges, the walls of stone and covered with canes. Only the Governer hath a very faire and large howse built of stone on the norward parte of the towne, which showeth more like a fort then a howse. Yt may contain 1000 menn in armes very well. They are good souldiers, and their strengthe lieth in them more then in fortifications. These shipps yeare[ly] sally owt with very riche commodeties, as indico of Gulcunda, in Cuttuppshas [Kutb Shāh's] countrie, who is king of Muselepatan, and is 15 dayes jorney from Dabull to Gulcunda. The king of this contryes name is Abraham Adelshaw and is residinge at Visapour, 4 dayes jorney from Dabull. And from thence yearely the Portingalls hath to the valew of twenty hundred thowsand rialls of eight in diamondes and other jewells, of which twyse a yeare [? t]heere is a great mart or faire at the Kings coorte.'

roade in 7½ fathome. Wee kept neere the shore because the Portugall shipp was afraid of the Mallabars. Wee conducted him neere to his porte, for that wee would not that any should injurye them but ourselves.

March 6. With little winde of the shoare wee steered alonge in company of the Portugalls shipp untill four in the afternoone. Then the maister went aboard them and tooke leave of them, beinge in sight of Chaulle aboute five leagues off. Then wee stoode our course att West and W. & by S.; the winde at N. and N.N.E.

. . . .

March 20. Winde E.N.E.; our course as before. This daie Captaine Hawkins and Mr. Pemberton came aboard to take their leaves of the Generall, because it was concluded that the Darlinge should stopp att Soccatora, to understand of shippinge, if any had bene there. They stayed not longe aboard, butt retourned to make all the sayle they could to gett Soccotora, and meete us againe neere Aden.

. . . .

March 24. A pretty gale at East; course W. and by N. Aboute nine in the morninge we had sight of the east parte of Soccatora, bearing off us S.S.W. Then wee steered N.W. till night, and after W. and W. & by N.

March 25. A faire gale at E.S.E. In the morninge wee weare faire by the iland of Soccatora, the west parte. Then wee steered N.W. And this night we came betwixt the iland of Soccatora and the rocke which lyeth aboute three leagues of. It fell calme; and the current settinge upon the rocke, weare forced to anchour till the morninge in [*blank*] fathome half a mile from the rocke.

March 26. Winde at S.E., a leading gale. Then we sett saile from betweene the rocke and the iland and steered W. & by S. and W.S.W. In the eveninge wee had sight of Abdelcura[1].

---

[1] Abd-el-Kuri.

March 27. A fresh gale at S.E. In the morninge wee had the wester parte of Abdelcura E.S.E. of us. Wee steered Weste by S. and W.S.W. Att sonne settinge wee sawe the mayne land of Abex[1] neere Cape Guardefu; and then wee steered all night W. & by N. with a shorte saile, beeing neere the land.

March 28. In the morninge wee weare hard aboard the shoare, betweene Cape Guardafu and Cape Felix. Then the Generall cawsed the friggott to be manned, and the skiffe to attend her, and went himselfe in the friggatte, accompanyed with Captaine Sharpeigh and my selfe. The Generall appointed the shipps to come to anchour wheare they sawe us anchour, neere the shoare. Approachinge to the land, wee landed betweene the twoe capes to see if wee could finde water or other refreshing; where wee spake with some of the countrye people, whoe told us that four Indian shipps were already passed into the Red Sea; which after wee perceived to bee Generall Sarrys fleete[2]. They tould us that there was not any water at this place, butt att the westward of Mount Felix there was fresh water and other refreshinge; and they came into the friggatt and went with us to the place. Butt these are a kinde of savage people, for they tooke us to bee Indians and of Mahometts lawe[3]; otherwise they would not have come neere us. Butt comeinge to the place wee could neither finde water nor any thinge elce, onelie a little hole that was digged in the grownd above a mile up, which was digged for cattle to drinke and was very brackish. Wee had this afternoone soe much winde that the poore friggott could hardlie beare any saile; therefore wee ankored neere the shoare, and the shipps came to anchour to the offinge

[1] See p. 106.

[2] The ships of the Eighth Voyage, under John Saris.

[3] Green says that those who landed told the natives they were 'Mussellmen.'

of us, in nine fathome water. It seemeth at this place as if there weare a river, butt itt is the arme of the sea that cometh within the land and maketh an iland[1]. There is good shoaldinge all alongst the coaste; a lowe land by the waters side, and white sandy strand. Wheare wee landed is aboute half a league to the westward of Mount Felix. This Mount Felix, or Mount Elaphant[2], is a pointe of a land very high, in fashion like an elaphant; therefore it is called Fill, which is the Arab word for elaphant. The Indias called itt Hattee[3], which is likewise elaphant in their language; and the Portugalls call itt Elaphante. It seemes before you come att itt to bee an iland distant from the mayne, because onelie the pointe is highe land, and the land within itt very lowe. The Generall havinge seene what might there be done, and left a letter to deliver to the next shipp that came, supposinge the Darlinge would come that way, wee departed in the eveninge to the shipps. Captaine Downton beinge nowe come with his pinnace to

---

[1] Peninsula (see note on p. 75).

[2] Ras Filuk (Ras-al-Fīl), the ancient Mons Elephas, a rocky mass 800 feet high, about 40 miles west of Cape Guardafui. It is generally called by the natives Ras Belmūk. 'A great hie hummack, which standeth upon a low point upon the sea syde, which our Gennerall called Mount Felix, and is called by the inhabitants Fileack. Right against the water as aforsaid is a small river going in, in which river, butt sault, the boate may enter an arrow shafte; and thether the Indias bring their water by cammells. Butt the river streacheth 4 miles along the shore, and maketh an iland of low white sandy grownde. In this place you cann see noe manner of green thing, butt all white sandy banques' (Green). Saris, who had anchored in the same place a few weeks earlier, calls the mountain 'Feluke' and says: 'In this place is great aboundance of severall sortes of gomes verye sweet in burning, wheareof some samples I have, as gume Arrabeck, insence and others which we knowe not. They have allso fine matts well requested at Aden and Moha and in the Indyes; for ordenaryly the Indya juncks touch heare boath inward and outward to buye thereof and of the gumes for manye uses; allso victuall, viz. sheepe and butter, which is far better cheape then at Moha, for daylye boates goe over laden with victuall to sell at Aden and Moha. But they will not barter for anye thing but lynin cloath' (*I. O. Marine Records*, no. xiv.).

[3] Hind. *hāthī*.

the Generall, wee lefte the friggatt and went aboard in the pinnace. There blewe soe much winde that wee weare like to be oversett goinge aboard, and the friggatt had much adoe to gett aboard. This night the people aland promised us sheepe and goats against the morninge if wee staied; and because the Darlinge was to come that waye from Soccatora, wee made noe greate haste to bee gone, butt to staie till the morninge to gett some fresh victualls.

March 29. The skiffe was sent aland for sheepe and goats which were promised, and retourned aboute noone and brought aboard 25 sheepe, which cost a matter of 3½ rialls of eight in Indian cloath. And aboute two in the afternoone wee sett saile and steered awaye N.W.; the winde at E.N.E., a faire gale.

March 30. The winde at E.S.E.; course N.W. Little wind till noone; then we had a stiffe gale at E. and E. & by N. After midnight wee went with a slack saile, beinge neere, as wee supposed, the land of Arabia, at the other side.

March 31. In the morninge wee weare aboute five leagues of the shoare; the winde East. Wee stoode alonge the shoare all daie and night, keepinge the lead, and had from 20 to 24 fathome aboute three leagues of shore.

Aprill 1. Winde E. and E.S.E. Wee stood alonge the shoare aboute 3½ leagues of, and had betwixt 35 and 40 fathome; a little farther of, noe ground.

Aprill 2. Att sonne rizinge wee had sight of the Darlinge right ahead us some two leagues, riding att an anchour, aboute six leagues of Aden, in 15 fathome water. As soone as they discryed us they sent of their boate to meete us, wherein came Captaine Hawkins and Mr. Pemberton, whoe brought the coppie of a letter lefte att Soccotora by Captaine Saris, Generall of three shipps vizt. the Clove, the Hector and the Thomas, by which wee understood that they were gone into the Red Sea before us[1].

It was then concluded that the Peppercorne should staie att an anchour in this place, to staie for shipps which were bound for Aden, and suffer none to goe to Aden but putt them of to come to Moucha within the Red Sea, where the Trades Encrease and the Darlinge weare to staie for them at the mouth of the Red Sea, att Babelmandell. For soe wee in the Trade and the Darlinge steered awaie S.W. & by W. and W.S.W. with a little gale at East, saileinge alonge the shore within half a league of Aden in 20 and 22 fathome.

Aprill 3. Winde at E.N.E. Wee stood alonge the shoare; by our leade in 18 and 20 fathome. Att one place wee had butt 10 fathome; then edginge of wee had deeper water, and noe ground in 40 fathome. In the eveninge wee had sight of the mouth of the Straicts. Much winde at E.S.E.; but beeinge night wee ankored aboute two leagues to the eastwards of Babelmendell in 20 fathome.

Aprill 4. Wee wayed and stoode in for the Straicts with the winde at E., a fresh gale. And aboute ten in the forenoone wee passed it, and ancored within the iland neere the mayne, in nine fathome water, half a league of the shore, neare a miskett[2] and village which is on the sea side. Presentlie there came a boate of the shoare with four Turkes, thinkinge that wee had bene the Indian shipps which they expected; butt when they knewe the shipp they weare in greate feare, because some of them were actours aboute the emprisoninge of our men with Sir Henrie Middleton. But the Generall gave them good enterteynement and sent them aland with letters to the

---

[1] The letter is given at length in *I. O. Marine Records*, no. xiv.

[2] Mosque.

English att Moucha, the[y] promisinge to retourne with awnsweare within three daies.

A discourse of what passed att Moucha after our arrivall in the Red Sea the second time.

Aprill 7. The fourth daie after our arryvall att Babelmendell, Richard Wickham[1], one of the marchannts of Captaine Saris fleete, came to us with letters from Generall Saris. The drogaman which came with him retourned the same daie by land with awnswer from our Generall to Captaine Saris. This drogamon was an Italian renegado that was with me at Senan[2]. This daie came an Indian shipp from Mangellor, laden with cinamon and rice and other comodities. The 9th of the same monneth came annother Indian shipp from Dieu, laden with Indian comodities, some nill[3], some cloves and druggs. Their sailes were taken from the yard, and the 10th dicto the Generall went aboard and unladed what goods he liked, viz.:—cinamon, cloves, indico, olibanum, lignumaliais[4], turbett[5] and other druggs. And in the eveninge arrived annother small vessell, from Caixen[6], laden with olibanum[7].

---

[1] He had been one of the merchants of the *Union*, but had been captured by the Portuguese at Zanzibar and sent to Goa. Pyrard de Laval met him there (*Voyage*, Hakl. Soc. ed., i. 45, ii. 264) and they sailed for Lisbon in the same fleet (1610). On his return to England, Wickham was appointed a factor in Saris's fleet. He was left at Hirado, in Japan, when the factory was established there under Richard Cocks, but in 1618 returned to Bantam, and died at Jakatra not long after.

The letter brought by Wickham is given at length in Saris's journal (*I. O. Marine Records*, no. xiv.).

[2] See p. 65. Saris gives his name as 'Mustafa Trudgeman' (Mustapha the dragoman).

[3] Indigo (Hind. *nīl*, 'blue').

[4] Lignum aloes, or eagle-wood.

[5] Turbith, turpeth, or Indian jalap, the root of a convolvulus found in India and Ceylon, which has cathartic qualities.

[6] Kishin, on the southern coast of Arabia, a little to the west of Ras Fartāk. Socotra belonged to the Sultan of Kishin.

[7] Frankincense.

And att night came the Cloves skiffe from Moucha and brought letters from Captaine Saris[1], and the next daie departed with awnswere, and Richard Wickham in her. Beinge the 11th of Aprill arrived the fourth shipp of India, from Sinde, laden with cotton woll and other Indian comodities. This daye wee had soe much winde at N.N.W. that the Indian shipp began to drive, that wee were faine to helpe them from driveinge ashore. And in the eveninge, being the 12th dicto, wee made an end of takinge out the cinamon, which was 373 sacks.

Aprill 14. Captaine Saris with his three shipps came up to us, and shott 21 peeces of ordinance, salutinge Sir Henry Middleton, and was awnswered by 15 peeces. Captaine Saris and Captaine Towerson[2] with the maister and some of the marchannts came aboard and dined, and staied till night and soe departed.

Aprill 15. The next daie, beinge the 15 dicto, wee weare invited with the Generall abourd the Clove; where the Generall staied with Captaine Saris conferringe aboute buysines till ten at night, butt they did not well concurre together aboute their affaires[3].

---

[1] See his journal, as above.

[2] John Saris requires no introduction to readers of the Hakluyt Society's publications. Gabriel Towerson was the commander of the *Hector*. He went out in the Company's first voyage, and was chief of the Bantam factory from 1605 to 1608. After Hawkins' death his widow married Towerson and they both went to India (see *The Embassy of Sir T. Roe*, 438 *n.*). In later years he became head of the English factors at Amboyna, and was there put to death by the Dutch in the so-called 'massacre.' In Saris's journal he calls Towerson his 'brother,' but the actual relationship between them has not been traced.

[3] Saris's account is as follows: 'Dinnor ended, I desired to knowe yf he had considered of what we yesterdaye had speech of. He said he had, and would take out of all the Indya shipps which should com in heare what he thought fitting, and then yf I would I might take the rest. I tould him I held that no indifferent course, intreating him to consider better of it; otherwayes I should be inforsed to take my leave of him. He asked me wheather [whither] I would goe. I tould him to wyndward, and trye my fortunes; wheareat he swore most deepelye that yf I did take that course he would sinke me and sett fire

Aprill 16. Came two Indian shipps more, one from Callicut, laden with cotten woll and other comodities, and the other from Achin, laden with pepper, and belonginge to the Governor of Dabull. In the eveninge the shipp of Mangallour was sett att libertie, and went for Moucha.

Aprill 17. Generall Saris and Captaine Towerson retourned aboard to conferre upon a certaintie whatt parte of the Indian comodities each should have; but they could nott agree. Captaine Sarys desired to give him leave till the next daye to awnsweare Sir Henryes propositions. And the next daie Captaine Towerson and Mr. Cocks[1], the cape marchannt, came aboard and brought awnsweare from the Generall that he was content to accept of Sir Henries offer to take a third parte of what was received from the Indian shipps, and that the Generall should have two-thirds. And in the eveninge came annother greate Indian shipp, from Cananor, laden with pepper, cinamon and other Indian comodities.

Aprill 19. Captaine Saris retourned aboard, and made a writeinge betwixt Sir Henrie and himselfe of the agreement made for the one-third parte, and tooke his leave, and departed with the Clove for Moucha[2]. And the

---

of all such shipps as traded with me. But, not willing to put flax to fire, I sought by milde speeches to wyn him to rememberance of the love he had borne me and not to faule out with me in this accion, seeking but to advance the bennifitt of the undertakers of my voyage, his unexpected retorne having much impared the same; and for himselfe, I honnored him as one that had and shall commaund me; desiring that as I was com unto him to confer and contrive what shalbe fittest to be done, so that he would be pleased not to be offended yf I shall not assent to unprofitable projects. He tould me I should not meddel with anye shipp that came in heare, nether goe to wyndward of him; and so parted.'

[1] Richard Cocks, whose entertaining diary of his experiences in Japan was edited for the Hakluyt Society by Sir E. Maunde Thompson in 1882.

[2] The agreement related only to future captures, and it was also decided that the 'Graund Signior' should 'have his customs paid.' Thereupon Saris left two of his ships to join in the blockade, while he himself departed for Mocha, in the hope of purchasing a parcel of indigo which had been offered to him there (Saris's journal).

Hector and Thomas sett saile in the eveninge to goe to the Abex shore to fill water, which they wanted; as alsoe to staie in the other channell to stopp the [ships that?] should come thatt waye. And in the eveninge came two greate shipps of Suratt, one of them a newe shipp[1] belonginge to Abdelasan, Captaine Hawkins freind, and the other to Hoghanazan, our ould freind the Governor of Suratt; the biggest of them 600 tonns, thother 200 tonns. Presently came the captaines aboard and many other of our ould acquayntance. These shipps were richlie laden with indico and all other Indian comodities. They brought us newes that the Reheme[2] was comeinge, the Queenes Mothers shipp.

Aprill 20. Came in annother shipp, laden with pepper, rice and cinamon from Callicutt; and this eveninge went four of the countrye boats for Moucha with passengers which came from Suratt in the twoe shipps. In the biggest shipp came 800 personns, att [that] had bene 38 daies att sea.

Aprill 21. The Hectours boate came roome from the shipp with 40 men in her and brought a peticion to Sir Henrie Middleton, signed by most of them, in the manner of a circle, because itt should not bee knowne whoe was the principall of the mutiny[3]. The effect of there peticion was to have more victualls, for that they weare almost starved, and some had already perished for wannte of foode; and that rather then they would endure itt any longer they would runne to the Turkes. Presentlie after Captain Towerson sent the skiffe aboard the Trade, with a letter to Sir Henry entreatinge him to come aboard the Hector to pacifie the company; which presentlie Sir Henrie perfourmed; and havinge promised them to have redresse

---

[1] The Hassanī.

[2] See p. 186.

[3] An early instance of a 'round-robin.'

when the Generall came, they rested satisfied on Sir Henries word, entreatinge Captaine Towerson that in the meane time they might have better allowance. And in the eveninge hee retourned aboard with Captaine Towerson. This daie at night came two more Indian shipps, the one from Dabull, the other from Dieu. Beinge night they thought to have past without lett, they discryinge us before night thought wee had not seene them; but at night the Hector sett saile and laye in the mouth of the Straict neere the iland, and our boats went off to the Indian shipps, making falce fires neere her; soe when they sawe noe remedy they ankored by us. These two shipps weare laden with Indian comodities very ritch, with store of indico, pepper, and all other sorts of fine comodities of cotton woll.

Aprill 22. In the morninge wee had sight of two sailes cominge into the Straicts. One of them anchored by us; the other, thinkinge to passe by the souther channell, was taken by the Darlinge, who rid there for thatt purpose. These two shipps, one of them was of Caixen, belonginge to the Kinge of Soccotora his father[1], and the other came from Goga and Dieu. The Caixen shipp had olibanum, and the other Indian comodities.

Aprill 23. In the morninge came in the Reheme, the Queenes Mothers shipp, one of 1000 tonns or more, and came from Goga laden with indico and other Indian comodities in aboundance. We shott three peeces at her before shee would ancour. Shee had in her 1400 persons[2]. This is the shipp which wee soe much expected; which (*sic*) the Darlinge, beeing to the offinge, perceived that shee was come, sett saile and came to us to understand Sir Henries farther pleasure. The captaine and cheife of the Reheme came aboard the Trade, where Sir Henrie comforted them as hee might.

---

1 See note on p. 205.

2 Middleton says 1500.

Aprill 24. Havinge nowe as many shipps as wee could well tell whatt to doe withall, wee sett saile towardes Asabb[1], a place of refreshinge at the other side on the coast of Abex, the Trade goinge ahead the fleete, and our prizes in the middest, the Hector followinge for convoye; the Thomas and the Darlinge remayneinge to take the rest thatt should come after, and to bringe them to Azabb with the Peppercorne, which was lying att Aden. Some of the Indian shipps which were better of saile then the other would strangle[2] abroad thinkinge to escape, but the Hectour sent three peeces after them and made them keepe together, being in all twelve saile of Indian shipps, besides those which wee had lett goe. We came soe neere the coaste of Abex that we were in five fathome water of a sudden, and 1½ leagues of the shore; soe that the captaine of the Reheme cried that his shipp would bee aground. Soe wee made a signe to them to edge farther of, as wee did the like, and had presently 15 fathome. This place was onelie a shoale which laye ther. Soe in the eveninge wee all anchored in the Baye of Asab, but somethinge farre of; soe that the next daie, beeinge the 25th dicto, we wayed and went farther in, and moored all our vessells, except a small shipp of Cashen which the Generall gave leave to departe, not medlinge with any thinge they had in them. They went directlie for Moucha.

Aprill 27. The Clove came from Moucha att night; and this daie the Generall cawsed the Guzaratt shipp to make waye to have out there indico.

[*Aprill* 28.] And the 28th dicto General Saris sent aboard to Sir Henrie, entreatinge him to come aboard the Hectour to helpe pacifie their men, whoe were in a mutiny

---

[1] Asab Bay, an excellent anchorage opposite to Mocha. It is now in Italian Somaliland.

[2] Straggle.

when the Generall would have punnished some of them, the mayster of the Hectour[1] resistinge the Generall aboute his sonne, which was one of those that had signed the peticion to our Generall. Captaine Sairis would have sent [him] aboard the Clove to have punnished, butt his father would nott lett him goe, and drewe his dagger at Captaine Saris. Soe thatt at the cominge aboard of Sir Henrie, Mr. Fuller was sent for, whoe seemed to excuse himselfe and his sonne; butt Sir Henrie perswaded him to submitt himselfe to his Generall and goe aboard the Clove with his sonne, and the Generall would bee good unto him; where they were comitted to the bilboes, and the rest were pardonned and promised to have all things thatt weare fittinge for them as in other shipps; soe they rested satisfied for that time. Butt the companie generallie exclamed very much on their Generall to deale soe hardlie with men, havinge such plentie of victualls in his shipp that was like to be spoyled for wante of eatinge, and the men starve for wante thereof, beinge forced to eate the tallowe from the tyes[2] with hunger; with many other tyrannies which I cannott beleive that soe wise a gentleman would doe to Christians; which I omitt to repeate, because I knowe that there are many bad tongues which will make itt worse then it is.

Aprill 29. Generall Saris came aboard the Trade and stayed all daie conferringe with Sir Henrie Middleton

[1] Thomas Fuller. His son was one of the boatswain's mates. There is a long account of the affair in Saris's journal. The men complained specially of their not being supplied with fresh meat, as Middleton's crews were; but Saris declares that he was unable to purchase meat as he had neither rialls of eight nor Indian calicoes to offer in exchange. Later on he protests in his diary (Oct. 24, 1612) that his economy of victuals is only because he fears 'an heareafter scarsitie, which is not pleasing in an homeward bound voyage,' though he knows that the evil-disposed think 'that my sparing is to purchas myselfe a good conceite of the Companye by favoring of there purses.' Fuller was dismissed and sent on board the *Thomas*.

[2] The runners of thick rope or chain used in hoisting topsails.

aboute the ships which weare in our custody; that our Generall should not sett any of them att libertie without his consent, affirminge if hee did he would take them into his custodie and take their comodities att his pleasures fittinge for Achin and other places where he was bound, and for England; soe that there passed many unkinde words betweene them, which I omitt[1]. Notwithstanding, they went forward in there buysines all well, in sortinge out the indico and cloathing, thatt each might take his parte accordinge to agreement; while the Guzaratts and other of the Indians stoode by to see their goods parted before their faces, and knewe not whether they should have any thinge for itt or not.

Maye 3. Came two boates of Moucha called gilbaies[2], with a present of eatinge comodities to the Generalls and Captaine Sharpeigh, with letters from the Governour and Captaine of the Gallies to entreate of some agreement to deliver the Indian shipps and to trade att Moucha in peace. Captaine Saris beinge aboard the Trade all this daie, and att night went aboard his owne shipp.

Maye 6. And the 6th dicto he retourned againe aboard to conferre with Sir Henrie Middleton aboute some buysines, where hee dined and staied till night; and after supper

---

[1] According to Saris, Middleton (who had procured a stock of calicoes at Surat) declared that 'he would meddell with nothing but indico' and would then release the junks; and that Saris should not take any calico from them 'to spoyle his market in places wheare we shall com.' Saris on the other hand claimed his third share of whatever was on board, and threatened that if Middleton released the ships without satisfying him, he would follow and re-arrest them. Middleton told him that he 'would not suffer it; againe swearing that he scornd I should doe him that discredit, to come out a yeare after him and be further forward in my lading then himselfe, which had beene out two yeares.' So they parted. On the first of May, however, Middleton so far modified his refusal that he insisted only on taking out the indigo first, hoping that there would be enough of this to make up Saris's proportion; and on the fifth he at last consented to allow the calicoes to be shared, 'and now was willing to take his two-thirds.'

[2] *Jalbas*, small boats used in the Red Sea ports.

there was some discontent betweene Sir Henrie and Captaine Saris, and very grosse speeches not fittinge for men of their ranke. They were from this time forward soe crosse thone to the other as yf they had bene enymies; yet still they conferd together, but alwaies att square.

Maye 7. The Thomas and Darlinge came to Asabb, the time which was limitted for their staie beeinge expired. We went contynuallie openinge of packes to choose out the best goods, and sortinge and weyinge the indico. And because Sir Henrie would avoyde troublinge with Captaine Saris, he wild me that his marchannts should chuse whatt comodities they would have, whereof I should take two-thirds parts, and leave them one. Soe wee contynued sendinge of goods aboard the shipps till the 12th dicto, at which time came the Captaine of the Gallyes of Moucha aboard the Trade, to conferre with the Generall aboute the buysines of the Indian shipps. Soe the Captaine of the Gallies made faire promises to the Generall thatt he should have whatt he demanded. Soe the Generall gave him some present; and the next daie, beeing the 13th, he departed for Moucha, to advise the Governor of the Generalls demannds[1].

Maye 14. Came the Peppercornie from Aden, the time of staie beinge eight daies past expired. She brought with her a prize, a shipp of Sindee[2]. This daie I was aboard the Clove aboute partinge some Indian clothinge; where Generall Saris tooke mee into his cabbin, tellinge me that Sir Henrie Middleton did not accomplishe his promise with him; to which I awnswered what I knewe and departed.

---

[1] Saris says that Middleton demanded 100,000 rials of eight from the Turks as 'satisfaction for the losse of his mens lives and for his tyme spent, having lost his monsone to the overthrowe of his voyage.' At the same time Saris intimated that he too must be satisfied before the Indian ships were released.

[2] See note on p. 103.

And in the eveninge wee had newes that the kinge of the countrie neere Asabb would come downe to the waters side to see the shipps. The Generall sent word thereof to Generall Saris, to knowe whether he would goe aland in the morninge to meete him. Soe they concluded to land in the morninge with as manye men as the shipps could convenientlie spare, with their furniture.

Maye 15. [Came?] the Kinge of Rahitta[1] and his sonne, with some 200 men with him. As soone as the Generall sawe him comeinge he landed, accompanied with Generall Saris, Captaine Sharpey, Captaine Hawkins, Captaine Downton, and Captaine Towerson, with the maisters and marchannts of all the shipps; soe that wee made in all aboute 200 armed men. Soe the Generall went to him and saluted him, and gave him and his sonne with other of his followers presennts. After much conference he entreated that the Generall would use some meanes that these Indian shipps might give him somethinge as acknowledgment for comminge into his countrye. Our Generall awnswered thatt hee could not comand them to any thinge, but hee would intreate them to bee liberall to him. He used many complements with our Generall, tellinge him that the whole countrye was his and himselfe and all his people at his service, and from henceforwards that he would accompt him as his brother. The Kinge himselfe with his sonne and the rest of these people are very blacke, with curled haire, as the ordinarie neg[r]oes of Guenea. He brought with him four horses for himselfe and his sonne, and two of his nobles, with two camells with provision; the rest were all on foote with lances. All naked above the girdle, except the Kinge, his sonne, and two more of the principall; these had coates after the

---

[1] Raheita, the district round Asab Bay. The present Sultan resides at Mergabela.

Turkish manner[1]. They dranke wine and aquavitee very hard; yett weare not any thinge moved with itt, that any could saie that they weare drunke. Soe havinge ended their complements, they tooke their leaves of the Kinge of Rahitta, and came aboard the Trade, where Generall Saris and the rest of the captaines supped; and after meate they began to conferre aboute the buysines in hand. Sir Henrie and Captaine Saris disagreed in some matters which was handled aboute the Guzaratts. The cheife matter was that Captaine Saris would receive the goods from the Guzaratts and would paie them att his pleasure, and that Sir Henrie should nott be acquainted therewith, whether he paid them ought or nought, sayinge thatt he would not acquainte any man with his dealings; whereunto Sir Henrie and all the rest awnswered that seeing they jointlie tooke their goods from them and weare acquainted with one annothers receats, it was reason alsoe that one should bee acquaynted with the others payment, because the Guzaratts did whollie depend upon Sir Henrie Middleton, whoe had taken the most parte of them. Captaine Saris held his owne opinion to be best; whereupon there were most bitter wordes betweene them, Generall Saris intent beeinge to take a goose and sticke downe a feather, as was understoode by his speeches, that he ment to give them little or nothinge for their goods, puttinge of his goods att unreasonable rates, contrarie to the agreement made betweene Sir Henrie and him; theffect of which writinge

---

[1] Saris (*Purchas*, i. 349) says that the Sultan 'came riding downe upon a cow to visit Sir Henrie and our Generall. He had a turbant on his head; a piece of a periwinkle shell hanging on his forehead instead of a jewell; apparelled like a Moore, all naked saving a pintado about his loines; attended with an hundred and fiftie men in battaile after their manner, weapond with darts, bowes and arrowes and sword[s] and targets....They presented him with divers gifts and (according to his desire) did give him his lading of aquavitae that he was scarce able to stand. They are Mahometanes; being a blacke hard-favoured people, with curled pates.'

was that nothinge should be done in this buysines concerninge the Guzaratts without the consent of them both. This contention lasted till midnight, with most vile words betwixt them[1]. Captaine Saris departed; and the next morninge, beinge the 16th of Maye, Sir Henrie Middleton sent aboard his cape marchannte to Captaine Saris with a letter certifieinge him that if he woulde stand to the agreement made betweene them, they woulde proceede forward in the buysines as before; which if hee refused and would bee his owne carvar, contrarie to the agreement betweene them, that then he should have noe parte of their goods more then he had receyved alreadye, for that if the condition weare broken Sir Henry would keepe all to himselfe, and he should have nothinge to doe with what he had taken, the shipps beeinge att his disposinge. Whereunto he awnswered that he would send Captaine Towerson in the afternoone to declare his minde therein and to conferre with Sir Henrie and his marchannts.

This daie in the afternoone Captaine Saris, accordinge to promise, sent Captaine Towerson and the marchannts of his fleete to conferre aboute the prices of the Indian comodities as alsoe of our English; which prices Sir Henry

---

[1] Saris says that Middleton 'gave me good cheere but most vild words; telling me he marveled I would be so sawsie as to stand out with him for the advansing of my voyage; asking me yf I thought myselfe as good a man as he; saing that the King of England knew me not, etc.; with manye other strange words in his chollor....[I] onely answered that what composityon was made or monye paid for the release of these Indya shipps, I would have at least the one third thereof or I would carrye one third of the junckes out of the Redd Sea with me; to which he swore he would thrust his dager into my throate before.' From Downton's account (*Letters Received*, i. 166) it appears that the dispute ranged over a variety of topics: whether the sum demanded for compensation might be levied from the Indians if it could not be got from the Turks: at what advance on cost price the English goods were to be rated in bartering for Indian commodities: whether Middleton had a right to control those rates: whether 'our friends of Dabul and Malabar' were to be rummaged as well as the Gujarātīs; and so on. Downton and Jourdain naturally take Middleton's side in these quarrels.

wild us to goe privatelie together and to sett downe the prises as well of our English as the Guzaratt comodities[1]; which prizes sett downe by us was as appereth, vizt.—

Indico, the three worst sorts, Serques, Baradora and Seroll[2]: the first att 14, second at 12, third at 8 ropeas the greate man of Agra, containing 55 *li.* English[3]; allowinge them ten per cent for fraight and charges.

Indico of Biana, comonlie called Lahor, whereof there is three sorts: the best rated at 36, second 30, and the third sorte 28[4] ropeas the greate man of 55 *li.*, allowinge them twenty per cent fraight, custome, and bringing from Biana to Suratt. Every ropeas (*sic*) is 2*s.* English.

Broad cloath, one with the other, 20 mamuds (which is five rialls of eight)[5] per covedo of Equabar[6], which is a just yard; the cloathes beinge from 23 *li.* to 13 *li.* per peece.

Kersyes at seven mamudes per covedo Equabar.

Leade at 7¾ mamudes per mane of Suratt, which is 28 *li*[7].

Tynne at 120 rialls of eight per bahar of Moucha, which is aboute 380 *li.*

For their clothinge, they must be prized accordinglie per the musters.

These prizes beinge concluded betweene us, his marchannts would nott agree unto before they had acquaynted their Generall. Soe they departed; butt sent noe awnsweare of any thinge not within two daies, for wee weare busie makinge peace betweene the Arabs and the Guzaratts, the Arabs haveinge hurte some of them because they would not agree to give them some acknowledgment

---

1 It appears from Saris's journal that these were the prices recently given or obtained at Surat.

2 See p. 174.

3 Saris says 'the maunde of 33 lb.'

4 24, according to Saris.

5 'Five mamoodyes is a rial of eight' (Saris).

6 Akbar. Saris says 'the covido of 35 ynches.'

7 'The greate maunde, 33 lb.' (Saris).

for beeinge in their countrye. Soe that Sir Henry sent aland for one of the Kinge of Rahittaes men, and sent the maister with him from shipp to shipp to give the Kinge somethinge of each shipp, to which for quietnes sake they agreed unto; soe that after they rested in peace, and weare greate freindes.

In the interim of this troublesome buysines, Sir Henrie determined to send the Darlinge with a good cargason of cloath to Tecoo and Priaman[1], to provide pepper against his comeinge, knowinge that this intricate buysines would cost him longe time to end itt in good sorte. Therefore with all secreete and expedicion he hasted awaie the Darlinge. My selfe havinge notice thereof, and beinge weary to see and heare dailie such controversies betweene the two Generalls, I desired Sir Henrie that I might goe in the Darlinge; which, although he weare loth because of buysines in hand [which?] was better knowne to mee for the prises of comodities then to any, yett hee grannted mee, willinge mee to leave a noate of all the sortes and prises of Guzaratt comodities; which I performed accordinge to his order, and fitted my selfe to departe the next night. Butt before my departure he caused me to translate a letter into the Portugall tongue, which he had wrighten to the Greate Mogoll, certifyeinge him the cause of stayinge his shipps; the coppy whereof is viz.—

A Coppy of a Letter written by Sir Henrie Midleton to the Greate Mogoll out of the Red Sea, in the Portugall tongue, vizt.—

Most high and mightie Emperour, itt is well knowne unto your Emperiall Majestie that fewe yeares since the most highe and mightie Kinge of England, Scotland,

[1] Tiku and Priaman, pepper ports on the west coast of Sumatra. The former is now of little importance.

Frannce and Ireland sent William Hawkins his servannt as embassadour to entreate with Your Highnes concerninge peace and amitie, and to establish a factorie for the good of both your subjects in Your Majesties dominions; and by Your Majesties admittance the said Hawkins, alias Engrezcan[1] (soe named by Your Highnes), was brought to your presence, havinge bene kindlie received and well enterteyned by Your Majesties subjects at Suratt, where he landed, promisinge him many favours, which they performed as longe as his shipp was remayneinge att the barre of Suratt. But when the shipp was departed, he remayneinge amongst your subjects att Suratt, contrary to Macrobians promise and his expectacion, he could not be master of his owne goods, they takinge it from him perforce by order from Macrobean, takinge them at his owne price as he would himselfe; in the which there were greate losse received by our marchants in the prises, besides manie other injuries done by the said Macrobean to Captaine Hawkins and with much trouble and vexation. In the end he gave him leave to goe for Agra with the Kings Majesties of Englands letters directed to Your Highnes aboute setling of a factorie to trade in Your Majesties dominions, with determination to complaine to Your Majestie of the affronnts and injustice which he had received at Suratt. And cominge to Your Majesties presence, was much honnored at the receiveinge of His Royall Majestie of Englands letters, beinge much respected by Your Emperiall Majestie, granntinge him althings which the letter did treate of, and gave him all things that his harte could desire, giveinge him a firmaa for peaceable and quiett trade, with a letter to Macrobean advizinge him

[1] *Angrez Khān*, 'the English lord.' Hawkins says that 'because my name was something hard for his [Jahāngīr's] pronuntiation, hee called me by the name of English Chan, that is to say, English Lord.'

to entreat our nation kindlie and not give us cause to complaine, which in doinge the contrarie he should awnsweare itt to his uttermost perill.

And after all these favours grannted by Your Majestie, it was your pleasure to detaine Captaine Hawkins in your emperiall service, assuringe him that it was the best course for him to bee neere your Majestie to advise of any injustice that might bee offred to our nation in any place of Your Majesties dominions where wee traded. This beeinge Your Highnes pleasure, the said Engrezcan accepted of Your Majesties favours; which was presentlie published in all Your Majesties dominions; as likewise the said Hawkins advised the Kinges Majestie his maister of Your Highnes kinde dealinge with him. Upon which kindnes the said Captaine Hawkins advised into England to send yearly two or three shipps with such goods as the marchannts of the country should advise to bee most vendible in those parts, accordinge to Your Majesties direction. Upon which advise that was sent, there came first two shipps out of England[1], one of them beinge cast awaie upon the shoaldes of Cambaia, with all their goods lost; onelie the captaine and the rest of the people saved themselves in their boats, and came to Suratt, hopinge to have had good enterteynement after their troubles. But the Governor and the rest would not permitt them to enter within the cittie; soe that the captaine with his people were forced to come for Agra, where he remayned 20 monnethes, beinge promised at his first comminge to the courte many favours, but in the end, when he had spent the most parte of the poore meanes that he had, was forced

[1] The suggestion that Sharpeigh's and Middleton's fleets were despatched in consequence of Jahāngīr's promises to Hawkins was of course untrue. The *Ascension* and *Union* left England a year before Hawkins reached Agra; while, as regards Middleton's ships, it is clear that the Company, when drafting his instructions, were not even aware that Hawkins had left Surat (see *First Letter Book*, 328).

to seeke some remedye to gett into his countrye, because it was not accomplished thatt was promised him att his first comeinge.

Secondlie, the Kings Majestie my maister beeinge pleased to send mee as embassador with three shipps and letters to Your Highnes, with a present of greate emportance from the Kings Majestie my sovereigne, the present beeinge of ballast[1] rubies and other the like which our country of Europe doth affoard, which would have given Your Highnes greate content, beinge things of greate esteeme and rare, fitt for such a monarke; nowe att my arryvall with the three shipps att the barre of Suratt, beinge laden with ritch comodities of all sortes of Christians, supposinge to have had good and freindlie enterteinement, butt contrarie wise I was nott suffered to land, nor my people to take as much as water and other refreshinge which I expected, havinge beene two yeares att sea since I departed from my countrie, beeinge come upon advise of Captaine Hawkins haveinge sent the coppie of Your Majesties firmaa; the Governor of Suratt commandinge, upon paine of death, that none should presume to bringe mee any kinde of refreshinge, the which was to mee very strannge, seeinge that Your Majestie had granted by firmaa free trade in all your dominions, and they to esteeme the

---

[1] Balass. The term is generally supposed to be a corruption of *Balakhshī* or *Badakhshī*, 'from Badakhshān,' the source of supply. The presents sent in Middleton's fleet for the Mogul consisted in reality of velvets and gilt plate; and the statement that the fleet had brought a quantity of rubies was (like the story of Middleton's embassy) a fiction invented for the occasion. It was probably suggested by Hawkins, who would remember that one of the baits held out by the Portuguese to secure his dismissal was the story of 'a very faire ballace ruby, weighing 350 rotties.' Jahāngīr was so eager to obtain this jewel that he sent Mukarrab Khān to Goa to purchase it; but that cunning individual returned without it, declaring it to be false, though in Hawkins' opinion the real reason was that he feared the Emperor would not approve the price and would force him to pay the excess.

command of soe greate a monarke of soe little valewe; by which occasion there doth redound greate losse to many of our English marchannts to whome the goodes doth belonge, as likewise itt maye redound to the prejudice of Your Highnes and subjects. The third lose and reason of our complainte is that upon the same advise of Your Highnes firmaa, there came three ships the yeare after, which att present are here att Moucha in my companie; and this next yeare there are three more to come by vertue of the same firmaa; soe that in fine there are yearelie to come three shipps which bringeth greate ritches, all which are in danger to lose their voyages, as my selfe and others have, to our greate losse and utter undoinge of many marchannts; and my selfe in particuler have adventured in these shipps my whole estate, soe that itt would bee a greate shame and dishonnour, besides the losse for mee to retourne to my countrie in poore estate, my selfe beeinge in my countrie of good esteeme and creeditt. For these reasons before mentioned and for satisfaccion of parte of the injuries receyved of your subjects, and espetiallie of Macrobean and Hozanazan with manie others, as alsoe for the injuries which Captaine Hawkins hath receyved, beinge come to my ships with desgrace with Your Highnes, havinge formerly soe much honnored him, nowe beeinge glad to escape with his life, complaineinge very much of the unjust dealinge of Abdelasan and Macrobean, they beeinge the cause of his undoinge and disgrace with Your Highnes, they havinge eaten that which Your Majestie bestowed franklie upon him, nott beeinge content therewith butt have likewise taken his goodes which he brought from his countrye, notwithstandinge Your Majesties comand to the contrary, all which they have parted and eaten betweene them, he havinge spent the most parte of his meanes which was lefte in Your Majesties service att courte upon hope of faire promises, and delayes, hee followinge the courte, which cannott bee done without great coste; soe thatt hee hath spent all or the most parte of the goods which hee landed, and att last thrust out both of courte and Your Majesties favour, att the suite of falce Jesuitts and their deceiptfull promises, with the helpe of Abdelasan, upon hope of a rich jewell which was said to bee att Goa, which in the end Your Majestie found to bee falce, as are the Jesuitts, for they are like serpents which thrust themselves in princes affaires with their false reportes, thereby to induce them to warre one against annother; wondringe much that Your Highnes, beeinge soe greate a monarke, to live as it weare in slavery to the Portugalls, in such sorte that your subjects shipps cannott make any voyage any where butt they must first paye tribute to the Portugalls; which if they should doe otherwise, and goe to sea without their passe, or cartax[1], they confiscate their shipp and goods to there owne uses and ransome the men of the shipp as their slaves; which is a greate disgrace to the greatnes of your monarchie; much marvellinge that it can be sufferred by Your Highnes, such open injuryes within your owne land.

Nowe to conclude and make knowne to Your Highnes of a greate injurie done by Your Highnes to the Kinges Majestie of England in disdaineinge to write him awnsweare of his royall letter sent you, sayinge that you did not use to send awnsweare of letters to any except to your equall, deeminge the Kinges Majestie to bee some pettye kinge, he beeinge one of the greatest monarkes of Europe[2]. In this manner he was esteemed by Your Majestie. For

---

[1] Port. *cartaz*.

[2] Hawkins says that upon his requesting an answer to King James's letter, 'Abdall Hassan, comming unto me from the King, in a disdainfull manner utterly denyed me, saying that it was not the custome of so great a monarch to write in the kind of a letter unto a pettie prince or governour.'

which cause and for others beforementioned I was forced to take occasion to deale in this manner heare with Your Highnes subjects within the Straicts of Moucha. Butt whatt is done unto them is nothinge in respect of the bad dealinge that I finde in Your Highnes dominions; havinge taken nothinge from them butt whatt I have paid for in other comodities, beeinge in my handes to have taken it for nought. Therefore I thought good at present to advertise Your Highnes that if it shall please you to have a care of your subjects and their goods, that you would bee pleased to send to the Kinges Majestie of England to entreate of peace, before hee send his armadas and men of warre to bee revenged of the wronges that to His Majestie and his subjects hath bene offred within your dominions unjustlie.

From the Straicts of Moucha, in the Red Sea, the 18th of Maye, 1612.

Henrie Middleton.

Theffect of this letter was translated into the Pertian tongue and was made up with the other which was in Portugues, and was delivered to the Mogoll, as afterward I understoode for certaine; for when the marchannts of Suratt made their complainte to the Kinge that they weare undone by the Englishmen, hopinge thatt the Kinge would have pittye of them and have given them a meanes to live, he awnswered them that if the English had taken ought from them, thatt itt was their owne faults for dealinge roughlye with them att Suratt, and made peticions to him to putt the English out of the countrye; sayinge farther that the English had used them better then they deserved in giveinge them of their comodities in payment. Soe with this awnsweare they departed with shame, when they perceived that the Kinge knewe of the goods that they had received in recompense of their goods taken.

The coppy of a letter written by the Vizeroye of Goa to the Sabendor of Suratt, in applaudinge him for nott enterteining of the English, entreatinge him to contynue his constancie.

By a letter received from the Captaine Major Don Francisco de Souto Major I understand howe you have and doe contynue to this time constant in conserveinge our amitye, in nott consentinge trade and comerce with those English shipps that are there; hopinge that you will goe forward in your honest proceedinges, that they maye goe resolved not to retourne; that therby I may remayne the more bound to gratifie you for this and other thatt you have done in our behalfe; which by this my letter (in the interim) I doe in the behalfe of His Majestie Don Phillipp my maister yeald you manye thankes. And because there is noe other matter of emporte at present I rest, prayinge God to enlighten you with His divine grace, etc.

From Goa, the 28th of November, 1611.

Ruy Lorenca de Tavary[1].

This letter was sent unto mee by the Sabendour to reade and enterpreete for him[2]; whereof I tooke the coppy.

Maye 18. Havinge bene aboard the Trade to supper and taken our direccions from Sir Henrie Middleton, wee tooke our leaves of him, leaveinge them with their dissention and their prizes together. Aboute midnight wee went aboard the Darlinge, and att three in the morninge wee sett saile and stoode of aboute 1½ league. The winde came contrary, and wee anchored. Then the Generall shott of a peece, and the maister[3] and Mr. Fowler[4] went

[1] See note on p. 184.

[2] Middleton states that the Shāhbandar showed this letter to him on Dec. 19, 1611 (*Purchas*, i. 270).

[3] William Pemberton.

[4] John Fowler, a merchant of the Sixth Voyage. He died at Tiku a few months later (p. 235 *n.*).

aboard; and at there cominge they conferred with the pilotts of the Guzaratts which was the best waie to goe, within or without the Maldives. Soe it was concluded that to goe within was the neerer and the better waye. Soe in the eveninge they retourned aboard.

Maye 20. Wee sett saile and stoode of as the winde would permitt us, beeing easterly. Wee anchored neere Crabb Iland[1] till eleven att night the winde came at N.W., and wee stoode awaye betwene the E. & by N. and E. & by S. till the morninge. Then it fell calme.

Maye 21. In the morninge aboute nine wee had a fresh gale at N.N.W. Our course E. & by S. and E.S.E. And aboute four in the afternoone wee passed the Straights of Babelmendell.

Maye 22. In the morninge wee sawe a saile ahead us, standinge as wee did; and aboute eight wee came neere her and shott a peece; and presentlie they strooke their sailes and sent their boate aboard us with their nocoda[2] or captaine. Shee was belonging to Shaher[3] and came from Zida[4]. Soe they departed abourd their shipp, and wee stoode our course at E. and E. & by S., with a stiffe gale at W.S.W. till night; then itt fell calme till midnight.

. . . .

Maye 29. ...Wee had sight of Cape Felix, which bare of us S.S.E. With the former calmes wee have been driven by the current into the Red Sea[5] aboute ten leagues....

Maye 30. ...Very hazye weather, thatt wee passed within three leagues of Abdelcara and could not see itt.

---

[1] One of the islands on the eastern side of Asab Bay, possibly Jezirat Fatma. Downton speaks of it as 'an iland which, for the abundance of great crabs thereon, wee called Crab Iland' (*Purchas*, i. 288).

[2] *Nākhudā*, 'ship-master.'

[3] Ash-Shehr, on the southern coast of Arabia, about 28 miles eastward of Makalla.

[4] Jiddah.

[5] *I.e.*, towards the Straits.

At night soe much winde that wee steered with our fore-course, S.E. and S.E. & by E. Wee had a much growne sea. Att eight att night wee weare aboute twelve leagues to the eastward of Abdelcara.

Maye 31. Wee had very much winde and darke weather. Our course as before; and by supposition wee passed within two leagues of Soccotora, butt could nott see itt. Wee had nowe a sett storme, steeringe awaie still with our fore course half maste highe, at S.E. and S.E. & by E.

. . . .

June 6. Winde at W. Faire weather. Our course E.S.E. till eight at night; then observinge both the North Starre and Croziars[1], found the shipp in 8 d. 40 m.; suspectinge some corent settinge to the southward, wee steered E. and E. & by N. Note to this daie wee had sight both of the Croziars and North Starre.

June 7. The winde at West; a pretty gale. Course E. & by N. till eight att night; then observed the starre, and found her to bee in 9 d. 10 m. Then wee steered E. & by S. and E.S.E.

June 8. Winde at W. Faire weather. Course E.S.E. till eight att night. Then wee tooke in our sailes and laye ahull till three in the morninge, supposinge to be amongst the ilands which are laid in the platt betweene the Maldives and Cape Comorin.

June 9. Att three in the morninge wee sett saile. Winde west. Wee steered E.S.E. with a fresh gale till seven at night; then wee tooke in our sailes and laye ahull till five in the morninge, because of the fore said ilands, the maister beeinge desirous to see them.

. . . .

---

[1] The old name for the Southern Cross; cp. Fryer, 11: 'the Crosiers, a South constellation, taking its name from the similitude of that pastoral staff.'

June 12. Aboute five in the morninge wee sett saile, with a faire gale att N.W. Wee steered S.E. This daie wee had some gustes, butt little winde, and some raine. At night by observacion 8 d. 20 m. Then wee steered E.S.E. till midnight; then wee sounded and could finde noe ground in 100 fathome. Then supposing to be past the ilands, we stoode away our course the rest of the night at E.S.E.

June 13. Winde W.N.W. Course S.E. and S.S.E. Att five in the morninge wee sounded, but found noe ground in 100 fathome. At eight in the night having observed, weare in 7 degrees. Our course S. and by W. all night, to avoide to come neare Seilan, because of currents.

. . . .

June 18. Winde at W., with much raine. Course E. & by S. and E.S.E. till eight att night. Wee laye ahull till the morninge, because wee would see the iland Douro[1], which we supposed to bee neere us. By observation att night 2 d. 00 m.

June 19. Aboute five in the morninge wee sett saile. Winde W., a fresh gale. Course S.E. & by E. till eight at night; then we lay ahull, because wee would see the iland of Ouco [Ouro ?]; having much winde and raine att night.

. . . .

June 27. ...At night were directlie under the equinoctiall.

. . . .

June 30. Thicke weather and much raine. Winde N.W. Aboute eight in the morninge betweene the showers wee had sight of two small ilands, the one of them S.E. of

[1] In Linschoten's map of the Indian Ocean (Eng. ed., p. 12) *three* imaginary groups of islands named 'De Ouro' are shown to the southwards of Ceylon, between the Maldives and Sumatra. Valentyn's map of the E. Indies (1724) has them in the same position; and they appear (though marked as 'uncertain'), under the name of 'Owra,' as late as 1787 (Dunn's *New Directory for the E. Indies*).

us, thother N.; but the weather beeing darke wee doubted whether they were ilands or the mayne[1]. Butt we stoode towards the lesser of the twoe; and aboute three in the afternoone wee came to anchour within half a mile of the shore in 28 fathome. This iland is a smooth land, thicke of coker nutt trees and other. Wee could not land, because our boate was soe leake that wee could not keepe her above water. At the souther parte of this iland there is a shoale which lyeth a league of shore, trendinge from the pointe to the seawards N.N.W. Where wee ankored was good ground, butt neere the shoare were corall rocks. This iland is in 10 minutes South.

Julye 1. This daie wee spent in mendinge our boate; beinge calme and gusty weather, the wind N.N.W.

Julye 2. Aboute four in the morninge wee sett saile. Winde N.W. Course S.S.E., and sometimes S.E., till noone; then observinge, weare in 15 m. South lattitude, neere aboute the lattitude of Tecoo. Then wee steered E. & by N. and E. In the afternoone gustie weather and raine. At night little winde.

Julye 3. In the morninge wee weare neere the land in a greate baye amongst many ilands, supposinge itt to have bene the mayne of Sumatra, beinge in the true lattitude of Tecoo; butt wee soone perceived itt to be an iland of 15 leagues longe, with many small ilands aboute itt[2]. Soe wee stoode awaie S.S.W. to double the souther parte of the iland which was S. of us[3]. Winde att N.W. And the pointe was aboute seven leagues of us. The iland stretcheth N. and S. Wee weare in the very codd[4] of the baye neere the land, but could find noe ground.

---

[1] Apparently they had reached the Batu Islands, on the W. coast of Sumatra.

[2] Tanah Masa, the central island of the Batu group.

[3] Tanah Balah.

[4] Inmost recess.

Julye 4. In the morninge wee had doubled the souther parte of this iland; then wee stoode our course N.E. Wee passed by night betwixt two ilands which wee could not discrye before night. From this iland from whence wee last came there is annother[1] as bigge as thatt, some five leagues distant, bearinge E.S.E. from itt. The souther parte of this iland which we passed lyeth in 40 m. South lattitude. This daie aboute noone wee sodenlie fell into shoald water two leagues of the easter parte of the iland which wee passed. Wee weare in four fathome, and rocks that wee could perceive neere us, the topps of the rockes brimingе above water and the current settinge towards them; butt haveing a little gale wee steered N.E. a good birth of the shoare. And att night itt fell calme; and because of the corrent settinge on the iland, wee anchored in 60 fathome.

Julye 5. In the morninge calme till noone. Then wee had a little gale att N. Wee sett saile, and steered E.N.E. Then wee sawe the mayne of Sumatra N.E. of us, very highe land, which wee supposed to bee neere Tecoo. In the afternoone gustie weather, the winde at N.N.W. Wee stood all night N.E. towardes the land; soe thatt before the morninge wee weare neere the mayne.

Julye 6. Wee weare neere the mayne of Sumatra, aboute eight leagues to the north of Tecoo. Then itt fell calme till the eveninge. Then wee steered E.N.E. and E. & by N. till ten att night. Then wee anchored in 28 fathome. Wee found faire shoaldinge all alonge the shoare, although there be many rubbs in the way which wee knewe not of till afterwardes. This night much raine.

Julye 7. In the morninge we sett saile. Winde N.N.W. Wee stoode S.E. alonge the shoare of Sumatra till eight in

---

[1] Siberut. They passed through the Siberut Strait, between that island and Tanah Balah.

THE MALAY ARCHIPELAGO

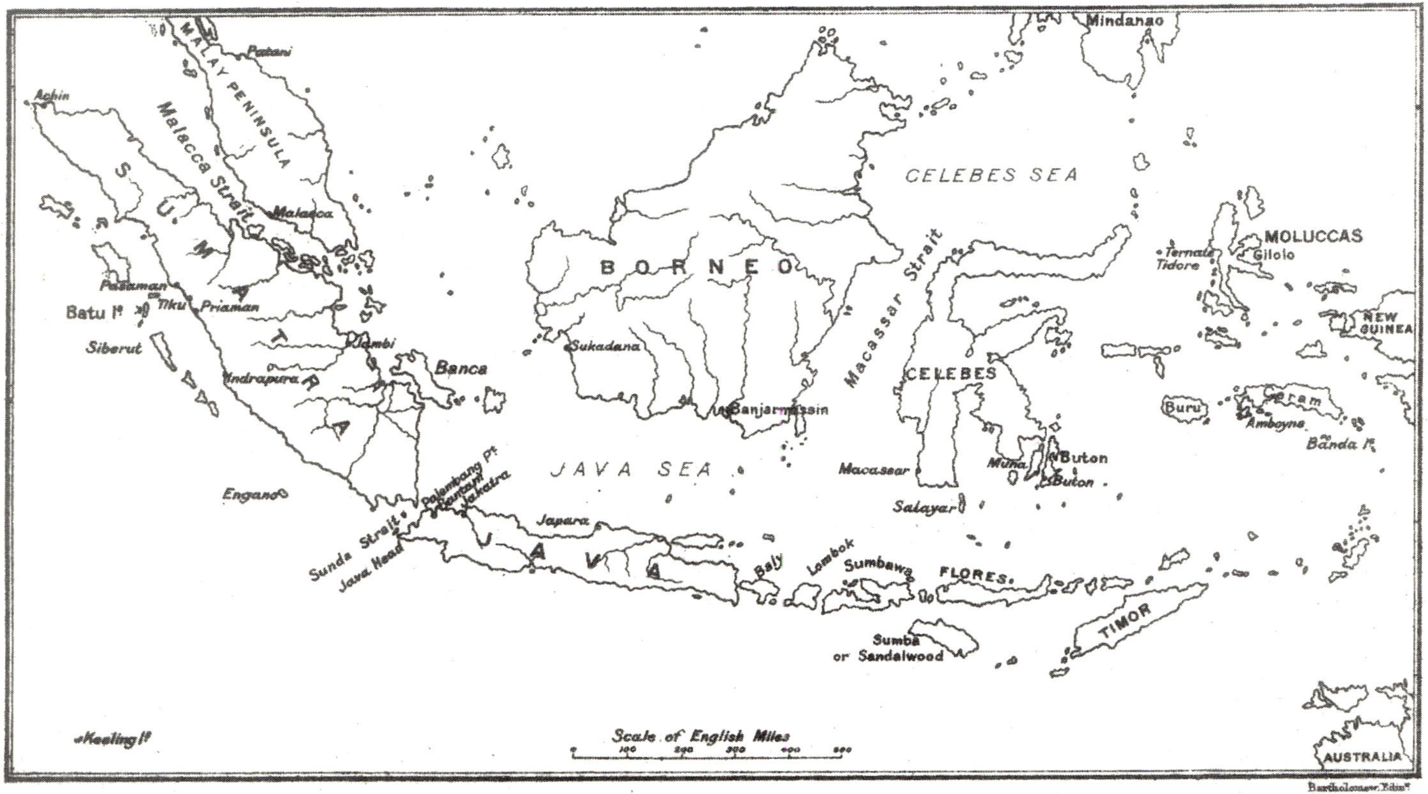

Mindanao
Patani
Achin
MALAY PENINSULA
Malacca Strait
CELEBES SEA
SUMATRA
Malacca
BORNEO
MOLUCCAS
Ternate
Gilolo
Tidore
Pasaman
Tiku
Priaman
Batu Is
Jambi
NEW GUINEA
Siberut
Sukadana
Banca
Macassar Strait
CELEBES
Indrapura
Banjarmassin
Buru
Ceram
Amboyna
Banda Is
Muna
Buton
Buton
JAVA SEA
Macassar
Engano
Palembang Pt
Bantam
Jakatra
Salayar
Japara
Sunda Strait
JAVA
Java Head
Baly
Lombok
Sumbawa
FLORES
TIMOR
Sumba
or Sandalwood
Keeling Is
Scale of English Miles
0 100 200 300 400 500
AUSTRALIA

Bartholomew, Edin[r]

Hakluyt Society, Second Series, Vol. 16.

the forenoone; then wee sawe the three ilands of Tecoo, and aboute ten before noone we came in betweene the norther iland[1] and the two souther ilands[2]. Wee mistaking the channell, wee came upon a bancke of currall rocks, where our shipp gave two knocks with two dangerous seeles[3]; butt havinge a stiffe gale, brake thorough the corall, and by Gods providence passed without any hurte; which after wee went againe to sound with our boate we could hardly finde six foote water where our shipp passed. The direccion which were given Mr. Pemberton weare mistaken, for itt did belonge to the iland[s?] of Priaman, for wee should have come betwixt the mayne and the norther channell. Neere the iland there is nott lesse then 4½ fathome, which is the comon channell for shipps, for att the place where we came with our shipp there is not passinge for a boate at lowe water. Yett, God bee thanked, wee escaped, and came to anchor aboute eleven in the forenoone in 3½ fathome water hard by the iland; butt not in the best roade, which is farther in. Att our entringe neere the ilandes wee had sight of twoe ships which came from within the iland. One of them was the Thomas and the other a Guzaratt, which were not granted trade, and sett saile the same morninge, one for Achin, thother for Priaman. For as soone as Generall Saris knewe certeinly thatt the Darlinge was bound for Priaman, he made all the haste might bee to dispatch awaie the Thomas, to hinder our proceedinges at Tecoo as he had done in the Red Sea. Soe that, by reason of our lyinge ahull[4] some five or six nights, shee was gotten to Tecoo before us; but could not bee enterteyned at Tecoo [and?] went for Priaman, thinkinge

---

[1] Pulo Tapies.

[2] Pulo Tenga and Pulo Oujong.

[3] Rolls.

[4] To hull, or lie a-hull, was to furl the sails and simply let the vessel float on the waves.

to finde us there. Butt although the heads[1] could not agree, yett without them we had correspondencie one to annother from Diamon [Priaman] to Tecoo, because wee would not spoile one annothers markett. What wee did at Tecoo we advised them, and they the like to us. The cape marchannt of the Thomas, Tempest Peacocke[2], brought a letter from Sir Henry in secreete to us; butt he had taken the paines to open itt, and tooke the coppye and cunninglye sealde itt againe, as wee perceived by his owne speeches. Notwithstandinge wee proceeded in our buysines like loveinge freinds.

From the 8th of Julie to the 7th of August wee were in Tecoo without any trade, beinge putt of from daie to daie with delayes, the people beinge soe unconstant in their resolutions that one daie they would trade with us, and putt us to three or four daies longer; then wee should have them of annother minde, askinge an extreame price for their pepper, and nothinge for our cloth; and some times they would have money for their pepper, and within two or three daies cloth was better then money. Thus they led us a monneth before wee could gett one bahar of pepper, beeinge loth to suffer us to departe and afraid to trade with us[3]; butt att length, with a fewe bribes to the cheefe men, with promise to give them somethinge more then ordinary for there pepper, wee made an end with them at 20 rialls the bahar of pepper, and the price of our cloth agreed upon. But after wee had begunne to trade with

---

[1] Saris and Middleton.

[2] He went afterwards to Japan with Saris. Later on he was sent from thence in a junk to Cochin China, where he was murdered by the natives.

Peacock was severely censured by Saris for conveying these letters of Middleton's (Saris's journal, Nov. 23, 1612).

[3] Probably owing to the fact that the English had not obtained a special license at Achin. Both Tiku and Priaman were under the rule of the King of Achin, who kept a tight hand on their trade with Europeans.

them we had many breakings of, soe thatt a peece of bafta or two for a bribe would bringe us freinds; butt they are the basest people thatt I have seene (of civill people) in all the Indias. Soe that from the time that wee beganne to deale with them to the 19th of October, we gott [*blank*] bahars of pepper, which wee sent dailie as we brought [bought?] it to the iland neere the shipp, where wee had made a howse and a tent to keepe itt till the cominge of the rest of the fleete from the Red Sea. Butt in the meane time wee had newes of the arrivall of annother English shipp att Priaman. Therefore I tooke a small proa of the countrye, and went thither to see whatt she was; and comeinge thether I found her to bee the Pearle, not sett out by the Companie, butt a pillaginge shipp, wherein was cheife commander Captaine Samuell Castleton, and master John Totton. They sett up a pinnace upon the ilandes of Priaman, and then they came to Tecoo, and stayed one daie, and departed the 27th of August, bound I knowe not whether, but they vowed not to doe any injurie to the Worshipfull Companie[1]. Alsoe the James[2] came into Priaman bound for Bantam; and not longe after came the Hectour[3], whereof wee had newes att Tecoo. Mr. Pemberton tooke the boate and went aboard to understand newes of our fleete; but Captaine Towerson, havinge had his Generalls lesson, made him doubt much of the Generalls[4] comeinge, sayinge that he heard that hee was to lade pepper and indico at Dabull and to departe for England

---

[1] The voyage of the interloper *Pearl* is briefly narrated in *Purchas*, (i. 328); see also Brit. Mus. *Cotton MSS.*, *Otho*, E viii. no. 102, and an undated broadsheet in the Guildhall Library entitled *The Petition to Parliament of the Adventurers in the Ship called the Pearl*. An account of Captain Castleton will be found in the introduction to vol. iv. of *Letters Received*, p. xvii.

[2] Of the Ninth Voyage (see p. 240). The date of her arrival was September 26.

[3] Another of Saris's ships. She had left Mocha on August 8.

[4] Middleton.

from thence; urginge him to sell the pepper which he had bought to him, and to goe with our shipp in his companie to Bantam, because our shipp was soe leake, eaten with wormes, thatt wee durst nott adventure to lade her with pepper, beinge very leake betwixt winde and water; which Captaine Towerson understandinge, used this pollicy to gett the pepper from us. Butt wee nothinge doubtinge of the comeinge of one of the shipps, wee tould him that that shifte would not serve his tourne to gett our pepper. But he would not spare us any thinge which wee wanted, although wee stoode in greate neede of many things, as well victualls as other. The Hectour stayed not longe att Priaman, but departed for Bantam in company of the James[1], leaveinge the Thomas at Priaman, and the Darlinge at Tecoo, very leake, many of our men dead and many remayneinge sicke, with small store of victualls.

The Thomas beinge at Priaman, as is before specified, understandinge of our distress, the 18th of October they sett saile from Priaman and came to Tecoo, havinge bought as much pepper as was there to be sould, for thatt all men brought the pepper to Tecoo. Butt the occasion of the cominge of the Thomas was to see in what case wee weare at Tecoo, thinkinge our shipp to be soe leake that wee had not bene able to lade our pepper; which indeede wee could nott untill wee had found our leake, and our men beinge soe weake that they were not able to search for itt. Butt, as some of their marchants tould me, that their cheife cominge was to buye our pepper and to carry us to Bantam, and to leave the shipp, being unserviceable. But it pleased God that before the Thomas came within the ilandes, Sir Henrie Middleton, with the Trade and Peppercorne, weare in sight, being the 19th of October[2]. In the morn-

---

[1] October 9.

[2] 'October 19. At three a clock afternoone we anchored in the roade of Tecoa, where we found the *Darling*, who had continued

inge wee sawe them aboute two leagues of, to our greate comforts; which the Thomas havinge espied came not to Tecoo, butt went aboard to speake with Sir Henry Middleton, and presentlie departed againe for Priaman. The Trades boate came presentlie to the iland, and from thence came aland to fetch me, and I went aboard to speake with Sir Henrie; and the same daie Sir Henrie came to the iland to comforte the sicke men, the shipps beinge att anchour to the offinge.

Oct. 21. The next daie, beinge the 21th dicto, the Generall came aland to conferre with the Governours, and gave presentlie to every of the cheife men a small present. Hee dined aland, and after dinner departed and went aboard to provide himselfe to goe for Bantam in the Peppercorne; whoe departed the same [next?] day att night, leaveinge Captaine Downton in the Trade for the ordayneinge of the shipps buysines aboute takeinge in the pepper[1], and my selfe aland aboute buyinge the rest of the pepper which was there in the handes of the Achin marchanntes; ordayneinge that the Darlinge should spend some ten daies att Passaman[2] to see the countrye and buye whatt pepper was there to bee had; wherein went Benjamin

---

there from July (unto our coming in) in a great part of the raines, which is not yet ended; they having before our coming buried three merchants and three sailers, to witt John Fowler, Francis Glanfeild and William Speed; also they had most of there men sick, and had gotten but little pepper, which remaineth on the iland; and little more is heare to be had untill the next season, which wilbe in Aprill and May; but the civill wars is a hindrance to our trade' (Downton's journal in I.O.).

[1] Downton says that Middleton departed the 22nd, leaving him behind in the *Trade's Increase*, 'partly to stop a great leake in the ship which would require much time in rumaging, landing and relading of goods, also to relade unto the ship such pepper as remaineth on the iland in tents, and what els we should buy from the maine in our time limited; also in the meane time to [send to?] Passaman, nine leagues to the northwards, to try what pepper may there be gotten; and then with most expedition to follow after him to Bantam.'

[2] Pasaman, a village at the mouth of a river of the same name, a few miles north of the equator.

Greene and other of the factours, where they bought aboute 30 bahars of pepper[1]; and within the tyme they retourned with manie of their men sicke, soe that within shorte time they all dyed, as many as had layen aland att Passaman. Onely Benjamin Greene remayned sicke untill he came to Bantam, and there died. It is a very contagious place for our men, yet very pleasannt and fruitfull.

After the departure of the Generall, wee spent a full monneth aboute buyinge a small quantitie of pepper which was remayneinge, and in ladinge the pepper which was on the iland aboard the Trade, with other necessarie buysinesses aboute the repayringe of the Darlinge. And havinge brought all remay[n]ders from the shoare, and taken my leave of the Governours and cheife men of the countrie, I came aboard the Trade to sett saile for Bantam, haveinge bought in all since our first comeinge [*blank*] bahars of pepper, with much labour and vexation with these unseasoned Mahometans. Although they are all bad enough, yet these are the worste that I have seene.

November 20. This daie aboute eleven att night, with the winde of the shoare, wee sett saile from Tecoo with the Trade and Darlinge. And aboute two in the morninge wee came aground with the Trade upon a rocke, aboute three leagues S.W. and by W. off the iland where wee ridd; where she stucke fast untill five in the morninge. Then layinge our anchour astarne, beeinge deepe water, the shipp went easilie of; but her foreshipp and starne being afloate and the midshipps aground, she wronge soe much that she was very leake. Wee beeinge aground shott a peece, because the Darlinge was half a mile astarne, where shee anchored when shee perceived us to bee aground. It pleased God that it was very smooth water and little winde, otherwise she had left there her bones;

[1] 'Twenty-eight bahars, or ninety-three hundred weight' (Downton).

and at her goinge of from the shoale there came a puffe of winde in a gust off the sea, which was a great helpe in her gettinge of from the danger. But her leake began soe much that our two chaine pumps were hardlie able to free her with contynueall pumpinge; soe thatt wee were forced to beare roome againe for Tecoo, where in the eveninge shee ancored where the Darlinge was before anchored, hard aboard the iland, in four fathome water, within a butt shott of the norther iland of the three. Soe that the next daie all handes went to worke, some keepinge the pumpe, and others unladinge of the shipp to lighten her, keepinge the pumps goeinge contynuallie daye and night, doubtinge much of her goeinge to Bantam this monsonne except wee could finde where the leake was. Therefore it was determyned forthwith to buye a small juncke thatt was aland, to send to Bantam for provision and to advise Sir Henrie therof; aboute which buysines I was sent aland, as alsoe for provision to make a howse to keepe the indico and other comodities drie; in the meane time there was made a tent with sailes. This small juncke beeinge bought, the carpenters went aboute to fitt her. In the meane tyme of this buysines, most parte of the light goods beeinge landed and the shipps hould beeinge att some places cleare abaft the maste, wee might discerne where the leake was, neere the rimme of the shipp; which beeinge found, although wee could not come at itt, wee were in some hope of remedy to stopp itt; which with greate labour the roombes abafte the mast weare cleared, and the seelinge of the shipp broken upp to finde where the water came in, which was neere the garbar streeke[1] in the starne shuttes. Soe usinge some meanes to thrust in okam without board, itt did stopp out some of the water, soe that they might come to the leake; for nowe, with this little stoppinge out

[1] The garboard-strake or streak is the first range of planks above the keel.

of the water, the pumps might easilie free itt[1]. Soe in cuttinge awaye a peece of the kilson[2], wee might easilye free itt, soe in with in board (*sic*); which was with greate dilligence soone effected to all our comforts. Gods name be praised for itt. Soe that the next daie, beinge the 30th of November, wee begunne againe to beginne to lade our goodes againe which was on the land, and to fitt all things to make hast to bee gone, fitting the small juncke with crosse sailes to goe in companie with us.

In the interim of this buysines, I bought aland aboute 100 bahars of pepper more, and brought it aboard, which was a marchannts pepper of Achin, which formerlye he would not sell. I paid some cloath, some money for itt. Soe nowe all things beinge againe aboard, the shipp ready to departe,

Dec. 8. Aboute five in the morninge (beeinge nowe taught not to worke by night in soe dangerous a place) wee sett saile the second time (the Lord in His mercy guide us), with little winde of the shore at E.N.E., and wee steered W. and W. & by N. Aboute noone it fell calme untill two in the afterward [afternoon]; then wee had a prettye gale at W.N.W. Wee stood to the offinge upon a tacke S. & by W. and S.S.W.; and aboute noone there came a fisherman aboard us and tould us that wee should not keepe much westerlie to the offinge, butt keepe in thatt berth of the shore, and then wee weare aboute three leagues of; for, said hee, that of each side, both a seaboard and to the landward, were many dangers not seene, and that wee should keepe S.S.W. awaie, beinge aboute three leagues off as aforesaid, the norther iland of Tecoo bearinge N.N.E.

---

[1] Downton gives a long account of their running on the rock, their search for the leak ('being an open seame 6 inches long, and 10 inches above the keele on the larboord side') and their success in stopping it temporarily.

[2] Keelson, or internal keel.

of us. This poore fisherman told us that there weare betweene Priaman and Passaman (which is nott above 15 leagues distannce) more then 60 sholes, moste parte under water, and some seene. I take this to be the most dangerous place that is in all the Indias. Yet wee went in with the Darlinge without feare, seeinge none of these sholes; butt after, when the Darlinge went for Passaman, Mr. Pemberton discovered manye, wondringe much howe wee had formerlye passed them and nott seene any untill we came agrownd betwixt the ilandes.

Dec. 21. Wee fell with the Salt Hills[1], and wee stoode towardes the Straicts of Bantam; but beeinge night before wee could passe them, Thomas Herod[2] tooke upon him to carry the shipps as farre as Palembam Pointe[3] by night. Butt aboute eleven at night wee steered E.S.E. [and?] came into a deepe baye, where wee had butt seven fathome water, and the Darlinge being ahead us, havinge butt four fathome, came to an anchor; so that presentlie we chopt to an anchour all sailes standinge, little winde; Harwood [Herod] being still very constant that it was the goinge into Bantam. Butt when the morninge came wee per-

[1] The old name for the Krakatoa group in the Sunda Straits; see marginal note to 'Cracatawe' in *Purchas*, i. 620: 'the blackes call the Salt Hill so.' John Davis in his *Ruter* (*Purchas*, i. 444) mentions, in his account of the Straits, 'the three Salt Hills, which are three islands that lye south and north one from another...the latitude of the S.E. Salt Hill is sixe degrees, ten minutes; the longitude from the Cape of Good Hope eightie one E., the variation three degrees, twentie minutes. These Salt Hills stand nearer Java then Sumatra by two leagues.'

[2] Thomas Herod was originally a master's mate on the *Pepper-corn*, but on the outward voyage Middleton transferred him to his own ship. In Sept. 1613 he was made master of the *Darling* in her abortive voyage to Masulipatam (see later); and afterwards was sent with her to Sukadana and Patani. The ship was laid up at the latter place as past repair (June 1615). According to Peyton (*Purchas*, i. 533) 'Herrold the master was reported to have intended to runne away with her to the Portugals; which being prevented, he yet went himselfe.'

[3] The N.W. point of Java, now called St Nicolas Point.

ceyved itt to bee a deepe baye, att least ten leagues of Bantam; soe that wee weare faine to laye out a warpe of 200 fathome to gett out, the winde hanginge in our teeth and wee beeinge within a mile of a lee shore with sholes and rocks within two cables length. Soe the maister, Giles Thornton, named this place Bussards Baye[1]. Butt aboute eight in the morning itt pleased God, before they had made an end of layinge out the warpe, the winde came of the land and caryed us out. And this daie aboute nine att night wee anchored within Palembam Pointe, where wee found three Dutch shipps att anchour bound for Holland.

Dec. 22[2]. Wee passed betwixt Pulla Penjange[3] and Pulla Lima[4]; att which time our Generall, with Captaine Marlowe[5], came off unto us in the James skiffe, and willed the maister to goe for Pulla Pengan, where the James was att anchour bound for Musapotan, and the Peppercorne on the careene. Captaine Saris with his fleete and the Soloman[6] weare in Bantam Roade; the Hector, Thomas

---

[1] The buzzard was an inferior kind of hawk, useless for falconry, and from this the term was transferred to a silly blundering person. Goldsmith in his *Natural History* says: 'It is common to a proverb to call one who cannot be taught, or continues obstinately ignorant, a *buzzard*.' The application in the present instance is obvious.

[2] '21' in the MS.—an evident error.

[3] Pulo Panjang, an island about two miles in diameter, lying in the entrance to Bantam Bay. Here the English usually careened their ships.

[4] Pulo Lima is a little island close to Bantam.

[5] Edmund Marlow, captain of the *James* in the Ninth Voyage (1612–15). He sailed in her from Bantam, homeward bound, in Jan. 1615, but died on the voyage. John Davis (of Limehouse), who was master of the *James* and wrote an account of the voyage which is given in *Purchas* (i. 440), says that Marlow was 'an excellent man in the art of navigation and all the mathematicks.' He seems also to have been a contentious person and a rapacious private trader. In the index to the *Calendar of State Papers, E. Indies*, 1513–1616, Edmund Marlow has been much confused with Anthony Marlow.

[6] The *Solomon* (Eleventh Voyage) reached Bantam Nov. 4, 1612. She was commanded by Robert Ward, who died on Jan. 28, 1613, just after leaving Bantam for England. Brief accounts of the voyage will be found in *Purchas* (i. 486) and *Letters Received* (i. 287).

and Solomon beinge almost laden to goe for England, and the Clove for Japan. Alsoe there weare in Bantam Roade four greate Dutch shipps, which weare taken in their ladinge to goe for Holland, the other three stayinge for them at Palembam Pointe.

This daye att night Sir Henrie Middleton, Captaine Hawkins and my selfe landed at Bantam, where wee found Heugh Fraine[1] very sicke, and the 27 dicto died. I havinge given Sir Henry my word to staye after his death with him as longe as he stayed in the countrye, by his perswation and Captaine Sharpey his letter which he had lefte with Sir Henrie att his departure for Saccadania[2], I was content to staie, provided alwaies that I would not be bound to staie in Bantam longer then Sir Henrie stayed himselfe: upon which condition Sir Henry delivered mee the charge of the house and goodes, and presented me to the Kinge of Bantam as cheefe factour, and Mr. Jones[3] as deputy to Captaine Sharpeigh, whoe was elected to staie as Consull or Governor over all the Englishe[4]; the which the Kinge accepted and tooke notice thereof.

---

[1] See p. 181. For an account of his death see *The Voyages of Sir James Lancaster*, p. 218. Both Downton and Saris make the date of his decease Dec. 26.

[2] From Saris's journal it appears that Sharpeigh sailed on Dec. 10, 1612, in a small junk for Sukadana, in Borneo. This was a trading venture undertaken at Middleton's request on account of the Sixth Voyage. We hear no more of him except that at Jakatra the Dutch searched his boat (*Letters Received*, i. 230; *Voyage of John Saris to Japan*, p. 4); and probably he died either at Sukadana or on the way thither.

[3] He seems to have died shortly after (see later; also *Letters Received*, ii. 122). Possibly he was the Thomas Jones whose widow was petitioning the Company in October, 1614.

[4] Saris, in his journal, tells us a little more concerning this interesting attempt to establish an English Consul at Bantam: 'The 13th [Dec.] Sir Henrie caused a meeting at Pooloo Panjang for the displasing of Mr. Camden and plasing a Consull in the howse to command the marchants and marchandies, as well of the Eighth Voyage as of all the rest. But no man was nomynated for the Consull this meeting; onlye a writing drawne, subscribed by Capt. Ward, Mr. Jones and Capt. Marlo, appoynting 120*li.* yeare

Sir Henrye Middleton the most parte of the time of his beeinge remayned att the iland of Pulla Pengange aboute the sheathinge of the shipps. The Peppercorne beeinge ended, the Darlinge was laid in the careene, the Trade beeinge alsoe within the two little ilandes where the shipps weere careeninge, to take her turne when the others were ended; soe that Sir Henrie had much travaile aboute it. Soe nowe the Peppercorne beinge laden with indico and other ritch comodities, Sir Henrie, havinge written his letters, sent them to Palembam Pointe, where the shipp was takinge in of water; which beeinge ended shee departed from thence.

Feb. 9 [1613]. Departed the Peppercorne from Palembam Pointe; which God grannte saufelie to arrive in England[1]. And this daie att night Sir Henrie came for Bantam, and brought newes of the departure of the Peppercorne and of the death of Giles Thornton, the maister of the Trade, whoe upon some disgest taken against Captaine Downton

---

wages to this unknowne Consull to be paid to him heare, viz. 80*li.* out of the Sixth Voyag and 20*li.* a pees per yeare of the *Solloman* and *James*.' A few days later Middleton demanded Saris's concurrence in the scheme, but he refused on the ground that he had already appointed a competent merchant Edmund (Camden) to look after the affairs of the Eighth Voyage and 'had no order to put the Companye to frivilous charge.' Richard Cocks, writing from Bantam to the Governor of the Company on Jan. 12, 1613, says that Middleton was annoyed to find Camden appointed 'and would have had our Generalls ordenance frustrated and Capt. Sharpigh elected Consull to remeane over all in the generall busynes. But our Generall wold not condecend therunto, havinge formerly made a legittimate or rightfull election, as alsoe aleadginge that he helde it not suffitient nor reasonable to frustrate his owne marchants of their due, except Ser Henry or others could prove their insuffitientye. But all this wold not serve; for (as I understand) Ser Henry hath proceaded accordinge to his owne determenation without advice of our Generall' (*O.C.* 97). The scheme, however, fell through, owing to the death of all the persons principally concerned; though (as will be seen later) it was revived by Captain Best, Jourdain then being chosen for the post, though without the title of Consul.

[1] For Downton's account of the homeward voyage see his journal in *I. O. Marine Records* and *Purchas*, i. 312; also *Letters Received*, i. 241, 259, 290, and *The Voyages of Sir James Lancaster*, p. 221.

and Sir Henry checkinge him for itt, died, not beeinge sicke to any mans seeminge. Butt Sir Henry was a very sorrowfull man for him and knewe not whome to make maister of her, demandinge my opinion whome I thought most fitte. I awnswered him thatt I thought Mr. Pemberton to bee the fittest man for that greate buysines of careeninge the Trade; whereunto Sir Henrie awnswered that hee was to goe for the Molluccas in the Darlinge; which if hee were maister of the Trade, hee had none to send in the Darlinge for comander of that buysines, except I would take it upon mee; to which I awnswered that I was not weded to Bantam; which if it pleased him, and that hee thought I would doe better service in her then at Bantam, I was content to goe at his pleasure to doe the Worshipfull Companie any service. He deferred it till the next daie that hee had talked with Mr. Pemberton; then hee demanded mee againe whether I was of the same minde as before to goe in the Darlinge to the Mulluccas. I awnswered: Yea, if it pleased him. Soe then he concluded that I should goe in the Darlinge, and Mr. Pemberton to bee maister of the Trade, and himselfe would staie att Bantam untill my retourne from the Mulluccas; willinge mee to provide my selfe to departe within three daies, for that the Darlinge was nowe ended. And he went to Pulla Pengange to make all thinges ready against my comeinge; and caused mee to deliver all thinges to Robert Larkin[1] untill his retourne to Bantam, because Benjamin Greene laye sicke aboard the Trade of his Passaman disease.

Sir Henry Middleton haveinge in the meane time fitted the shipps and made his comission to mee, haveinge brought him accompt of whatt passed att Bantam in that little time that I had the charge, haveinge appointed for my assistance

[1] Engaged as a factor in January, 1610. He was afterwards chief at Patani, where he died May 12, 1616.

Georg Cockayne[1], Nicholas Bangham, and a Spaniard as juribasse[2] and our pilott for the countrye, beinge well acquaynted; alsoe Benjamin Farrie, the purser, was appointed one of the assistants. All thinges beeinge ordered, wee sett sayle.

Feb. 15. Wee sett saile from Pulla Pengan aboute three in the afternoone, Sir Henry, Mr. Pemberton, the preacher, Mr. Adams, beeinge aboard; where Sir Henrie made a speech to the whole companie, and espetiallie to Cornelius Billinge, whoe was appointed maister of the Darlinge; which beeinge ended they departed.

Nowe the daie before my departure the Kinge of Bantam and the Protectour his unckle, with many of his nobles, came to the iland to see the Trade, and brought with them above 50 greate proas or friggotts armed. The Kinge and the Governor came abord the Trade, where he was afraide to staie longe, not beeinge used to see such shipps. The Generall gave him a good present and tooke itt for a greate favour of the Kinge to adventure to come aboard his shipp, knowinge that none can come to talke with him butt whome the Protectour pleaseth. Soe when they departed, they desired the Generall nott to shute before the Kinge was out of sight of the ordinance, for that he was afraid. Soe the Generall gave them all the ordinance of the Trade and the Darlinge, which the Kinge and Protectour tooke very kindlie. And this daie two Dutch captaines and two maisters dined at Pulla Pengan with Sir Henrie Middleton, they beinge two ships newlie come

[1] Engaged as a factor in December, 1609. Jourdain left him at Macassar on the return voyage. He took a prominent part in the voyage of 1615 to the Bandas, and was afterwards chief at Sukadana, in Borneo. He was murdered while on his way from that factory to Bantam about May, 1619.

[2] Malay *jurubahāsa*, 'language-master,' *i.e.*, an interpreter. From a passage on p. 263 it would seem that this Spaniard's name was Philip Badnedge. We hear of him at Macassar in December, 1613, and later as being at Bantam in April, 1619.

out of Holland. The President[1] was likewise invited; butt beeinge sicklie could not come.

The 15 of February wee sett saile in the Darlinge from the iland of Pulla Pengan neere Bantam, as is before specified. And the same daie in the eveninge wee mett with a greate juncke come from China bound for Bantam, of whome wee bought some gamons of porke and other provision. And we steered awaye East and by North.

Feb. 16. Wee had little winde W.N.W., and at night of the shoare and calme.

Feb. 17. Wee had a pretty gale at W., which came aboute noone. Soe steered for Jacatra[2]; and in the afternoone wee anchored hard by a Dutch shipp that was in the roade, and I sent a booate on the land to provide fish and racke[3] for the shipps provision, and racke to send for Bantam in the juncke which wee bought att Tecoo, for the Trades companie att Bantam, the juncke cominge with us for that purpose.

Feb. 18. I went aland at Jacatra, and in the afternoone wee anchor[ed] hard by a Dutch shipp that was in the roade[4]; and presented the Kinge with a peece and other trifles, which hee kindlie accepted with many complements; where I provided racke, rice and fish for our provision, as alsoe bought 15 butts to send for Bantam in the little juncke, which was to bee delivered within three

Feb. 19. daies. And at night I retourned to the shipp, leeveing the ladinge of the racke to [*blank*], whoe came purposly for itt.

Feb. 20. Wee sett saile from Jacatra aboute nine in the morninge; and in the eveninge, fallinge calme, wee

---

[1] Matthys Coteels was then the Dutch President at Bantam.

[2] The native town on the site of which the Dutch afterwards built the city of Batavia (Nova). It was about fifty miles east of Bantam.

[3] Arrack.

[4] Apparently this has been repeated in error from the previous entry.

anchored neere a little iland three leagues of Jacatra, where wee tooke wood for the shipps store.

The course from Bantam to Ambonia is sufficientlie knowne to most men that travaile this way; therfore I hold itt needles to repeate the particulars. Onelie I will in breife sett downe what passed in our voiage of all things worthie the writinge, vizt.—

Inprimis, Sir Henry Middleton havinge a good opinion of John Darby, one that was lefte of Captaine David Middletons companie, placed him to be pilott in the Darlinge, to goe to Macassar, Ambonia, Lugho and Cambella, and homewardes bound for Benjarmassom[1] and Sacadana, hee haveinge bene at all the places latelie, makinge a shewe of some understandinge in his silence (*sic*) cariage; for I remember Sir Henrie told me that although he weare a man of fewe wordes, yett he was very sufficient for these places. Butt before we passed the Straicts of Disslein[2], he was like to cast us awaye upon the shoales neere Macassar; where by night beinge amongst the shoales, I cawsed to lett fall an anchor in ten fathome water, he and the most parte beeinge asleepe, myselfe hearinge a ripplinge of water cawsed to throwe the leade, and findinge shoald water, ankored amonge a world of ilandes and shoaldes, which the next morninge wee might discerne. Soe that beeinge within ten leagues of Macassar he would not take upon him to carrye in the shipp, butt stoode of south untill wee had past all the shoaldes, and then wee stoode directlie for the Strayghtes of Disselin; where wee mett with two Dutch shipps, bound as they said for the Mulluccas to Tornato and Tedore, but entringe the

---

[1] Banjarmassin, on the southern coast of Borneo.

[2] Deselem or Desolam is an old name for Salayar, an island lying off the south-eastern end of the south-western peninsula of Celebes. The strait between them, which was also called the Strait of Celebes, was the usual highway to and from the Spice Islands.

AMBOYNA

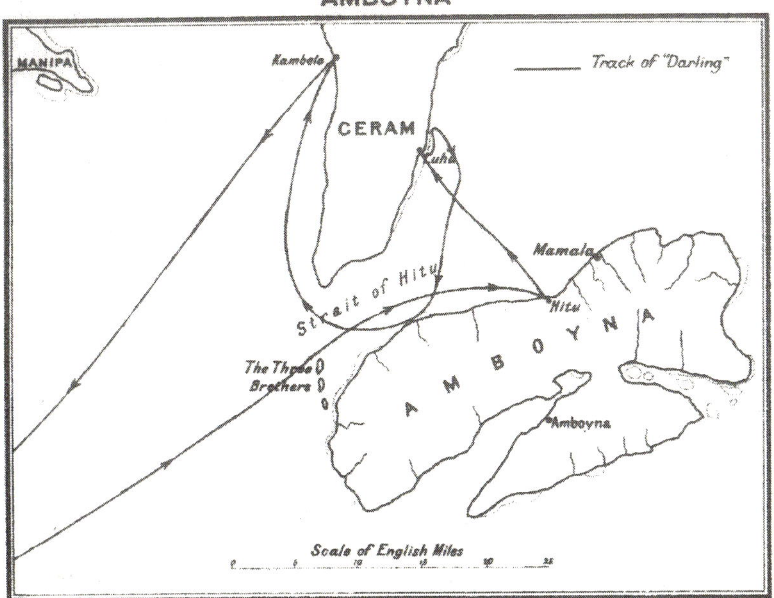

BUTON

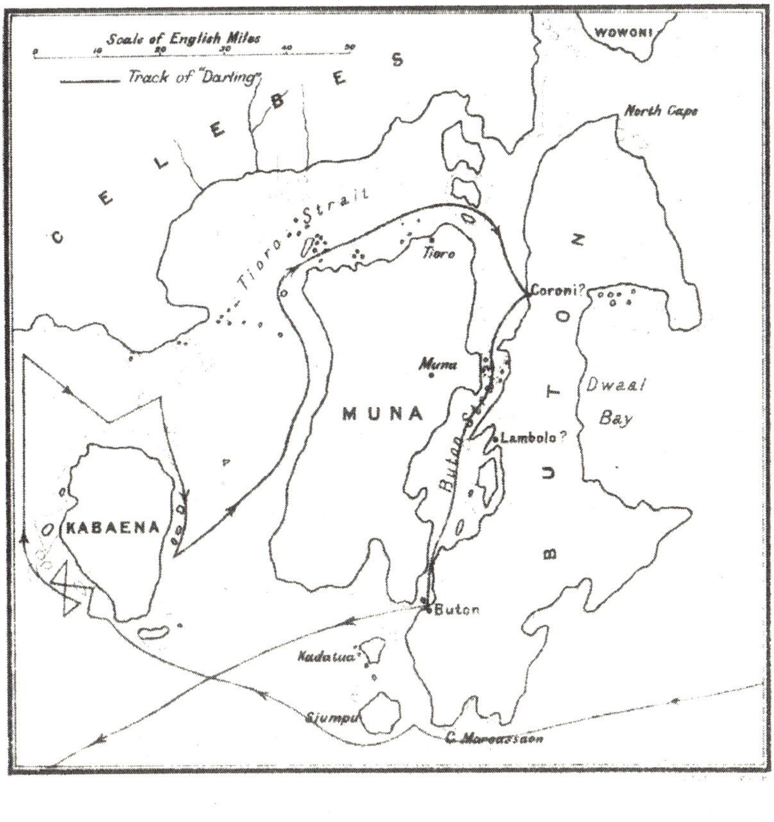

Straicts of Hitto uponn Ambonia, wee sawe them goe into Ambonia Castle or Roade, where wee arryved the 21th of March and anchored within the straightes att a towne called Hitto[1], pistoll shott of the shore, where the Dutch hath a factory and a faire howse. Wee weare noe sooner att an ancour but a proa came off to us from the Flemish house, whoe tould us thatt they every day expected ther Generall[2] from Turnatto, supposinge us to bee the shipp that he was to come in.

March 22. The next daie, being the 22th of March, I sent George Cockaine, Nicholas Bangham and the Spaniard aland to talke with the Governor[3] to provide us a howse; butt the Governor nott beeinge at home, could doe nothinge; and the people of the countrye durst not to bee seene to talke with them. Yett the same daie the Governor [of] Lughu[4], a place on the iland of Seran, aboute four leagues from Hitto, understandinge of our arrivall att Hitto, sent over a proa to us to knowe whatt wee weare, invitinge us to come over with our shipp and they would sell us cloves. I told him that as soone as wee had done att Hitto wee would, God willinge, come to Lugho, aboute 15 daies, or happilie in lesse tyme. Soe he departed to acquainte the Governor of Hitto[5] of what comodities wee had brought, as alsoe to entreate him from mee to provide us a parcell of cloves against our comeinge. And this daie in the afternoone the Dutch factour, whose name is Stephen

---

[1] Hitu, on the northern side of Amboyna.

[2] Pieter Both, the first Dutch Governor-General of the Indies, was at this time on his way from the Moluccas to Amboyna.

The account which follows should be compared with Jourdain's further narrative given later on, and also with Coen's version in Appendix E.

[3] The native chief of the place, generally called the Captain of Hitu. According to Valentyn his name was Tepil.

[4] Luhu, on Ceram. Valentyn gives an account of it, with a view, in his *Beschryvinge van Amboina*.

[5] A slip for 'Lugho.'

Cottelas[1], and is cheife factor at Hitto, Lugho, and Cambello[2], came aboard with the marchannts; where after many complements hee desired that wee would not make any motion to buye cloves of the country people, for raisinge of the price; that if wee would buye any, they would sell them us as good cheape as the countrye people, and that he had already wrote to the Governor of Ambonia Castell[3] to that effect, and that within two daies he should have awnsweere; desiringe to knowe howe many bahars[4] wee would buye. I told him that I would bee loth to raise the price; which if they would provide us a parcell of 200 bahars or there aboute, wee would not deale with the countrie people for one bahar; and that wee would give them 5 rialls of eight in every bahar more then they paid for them, and that I would staie these two daies for his awnsweare. Hee seemed to bee well satisfied, and wee well content, because that wee could not doe any thinge untill the Captaine of the towne came, whoe was at the warrs at the other side of the iland of Seran[5], and was looked for dailie, every houre. Soe with this the Fleemings departed, promisinge to send us word as soone as they had awnswere.

March 25. The Captaine of Hitto came from the warrs, with two greate carracores[6] and two greate proas, and anchored hard by us, betwixt the shoare and us by night. And in the morninge. I sent our boate aboard to

---

[1] Steven Coteels.

[2] Kambelo, on the western coast of Ceram.

[3] Jasper Janssen, Dutch chief at Amboyna, 1611-14. Valentyn gives a short account of his previous career in his section on *Ambonsche Zaaken*, p. 37.

[4] In *O.C.* 240 Jourdain defines the bahar as '628li. suttle [net].' Saris makes it 662 lbs. 8 oz., avoirdupois, also net.

[5] He was at war with the chief of Kambelo.

[6] *Cora-coras* were large vessels carrying from 50 to 70 men, and propelled with sweeps. They were sometimes fitted with a platform for ordnance (see plate 6 in Corney's *Voyage of Sir Henry Middleton*).

knowe if the Captaine of Hitto were there. And presentlye hee with his sonne and some of the Arancayes[1] came aboard our shipp, where wee enterteyned them in the best manner wee could, and they seemed to be very joyfull of our comeinge to the countrye. I conferd with him concerninge trade with them for cloves, acquayntinge him with our sorts of comodities and money to buy them; whereunto he awnswered that wee might buye and sell att our pleasure, but he would intreate us to have the good will of the Dutch Governor of Ambonia Castell first, that he might the better favour us in our buysines. I awnswered that this country did nott belonge to the Dutch, but to him; which if itt weare soe, whie should I seeke there good will to trade? For, said I, if the countrye did belonge to the Hollanders I would conferre with them aboute ytt, for that wee are freinds with them and they cannot deny us trade in any of their dominions, except they will breake the league which is betwixt us. But if they were free, and not subject to the Dutch, they mighte freelie deale with any that came to their countrye. He awnswered that there weare more of the Arancayes aland, as alsoe the Kinge of the countrye; with whome hee would conferre and give us awnsweare the next daie. Soe I gave him and his followers a small present, and they departed with many complements.

March 26. I landed to conferre with the Captaine of Hitto; but I was mett by the Dutch factours, whoe carried mee to their howse. And because I would nott bee seene to have conference with the Captaine of Hitto, I sent Nicholas Banham and the juribassa to speake with him to knowe his awnswere, while I remayned at the Dutch house; whoe haveinge conferred with him, [he] told them that he had according to promise acquainted the rest of the Arancayes aboute our buysines, who awnswered that

---

[1] Malay *orang-kaya*, 'a great man,' 'a chief.'

wee might leave a factory in the countrye and freelie buye and sell att our pleasures, as the Dutch did. The Dutch factours would not leave mee; soe that I could have noe time to conferre with him my selfe, for the Captaine was not willinge that the Dutch should knowe that I had any conference with him concerninge trade or buyinge of cloves; the Dutch still urginge me not to motion any thinge aboute buyinge of any untill hee had awnswere of his letter from Ambonia Castle, assuringe mee that itt would be grannted to sell mee cloves, alleadginge many reasons, cheiflie that if wee should raise the price itt would be more losse unto them then our shipps ladinge of cloves were worth; with many other words, thinkinge to delude me therewith; to all which I gave eare, and awnswered that I should be very sorrye to hinder them in any thinge if I might otherwise chuse, and therefore I would staie one daie longer for their awnswere. Yett I did not lett slipp the kinde offer of the Captaine of Hitto. And soe at night I went aboard.

[*March* 27.] The next daie in the eveninge Stephen Cottellas, with others of the Dutch, came aboard and brought awnswere of the letter that he had sent to the Governor of Ambonia Castell, beinge comanded by the Governor to reade itt unto mee. The effect thereof is vizt.—The first article of his letter was that he much marvelled that wee would presume to thrust ourselves into a countrye where they had made contracte with the people for all the cloves growinge upon the iland and had paid for them. Secondly, thatt they did nott thrust themselves into any place where wee had to doe, to buye to raise the price of comodities to hinder us; advisinge us nott to deale with the countrye people for any cloves; which if wee did the[y] would seeke there uttermost to prevent us, they beeinge protectours of the countrye and people, and bound to them not to sell any cloves to any other nation; alledginge farther that they had bene at an extreame charge in buildinge and mainetayneing castles to defend them against their enemyes, and wee to come to reape the fruite of their labours. Whereunto I awnswered that wee sought not to breake the contract, for that wee knewe of none they had made with them; which suppose they had, it was never in their contract with the English that they should not trade in Amboyna, Lugho and Cambello, beeinge a countrye free for all men, they not beeinge in anye subjection to the Dutch, but onelie as marchannts to trade with them; which if the country people had broken any contract they might take the forfecture of them, and if they had trusted them with a fewe rotten comodities it should be noe cause to restraine us from buyinge and sellinge with them, for that every debtour is not a slave; therefore might as freelie deale with us as with them. And whereas in a skoffinge manner they alledged that they did nott hinder us of our trade where wee had factories, it is well knowne that wee have noe factorie in the Indies where they have not likewise; therefore a frivolous question. But putt case wee had factories where they had none, would they thinke themselves well dealt withall in usinge such hard measure towardes them as they doe towards us, rather consentinge that infidells and Moores should trade where they have their factorie then the English, which are Christians of their owne religion and neere neighbours, to whome they have bene much beholdinge? Notwithstandinge these reasons allegd, if the countrye people will confesse themselves to bee vassalls to the Hollanders, then wee would desire them by waye of entreatie to suffer us to trade; but if they dare not avouch to their faces that they are their vassalls, and they alledginge to us that they are free, I see noe cause butt that wee may buye and sell with them if they are soe content, as they are. And whereas they saye that wee goe aboute to reape the fruits of their labours, it is rather contrarye then as they alledge, for that they seeke to barre us of our libertie to trade in a free countrye, havinge many times traded in these places, and nowe they seeke to defraude us of that wee have soe longe sought for; and therefore I conclude that they goe aboute to reape the fruits of our labours, and not wee theirs. And for your charge in buildinge and mayntaineinge castles in other countryes where you have little thanke[s] for your proteccion which you alledge, for that with your forces you seeke to bringe these people to bee your subjects against their wills, and [they] would if they could debarre you from buildinge of castles.

Havinge[1] nowe bene putt of by the Captaine of Hitto for our trade, as alsoe by the Hollanders deluded till they had gotten the moste parte of the cloves into their handes, I determined to knowe of the Captaine of Hitto his ultimo determynation, whether hee would deale with us or nott. Butt in the interim of this buysines came awnswere from the Governour of Lugho, desiringe us to come thither, that wee should have all the cloves of the countrye, although not many, because it was a bad yeare and the Hollanders had already receyved the most parte; butt for the next yeare wee should have all that was in the countrye; with many other hopes of good usage, seeminge as if they had beene weary of the Hollanders dealings. As alsoe a Guzaratt that was bidinge att Hitto enformed us att full of the state of the countrye, and that the people were very desirous to deale with us, and that the Hollanders had threatned them to burne their howses if they dealt with us; as alsoe since our comeinge that they had entred many mens howses perforce and

[1] In the MS. this paragraph is headed 'Aprill 4,' which is obviously wrong. Apparently it is but a continuation of the entry for March 27.

taken their cloves from them, for feare lesse they should sell them to us. Soe that with the buysines of the Arancayes of Lugho, and the hopes of this Guzaratt, made us staie longer then wee would have done in this place; butt seeinge wee weare nowe heare, I determined to see the event for eight or ten daies longer more or lesse. With this awnsweare I dismised the Arancaye of Lugho, promisinge to bee there, God willinge, within ten daies att farthest; giveinge to each of them a small present, with which they departed.

[*March*] 27[1]. I sent Nicholas Bangham aland with the juribassa to knowe the Governours determynation. And at their comeinge aland havinge conference with the Sabendour[2], who is a Guzaratt, whoe tould him, as the Governor or Captaine of Hitto had formerlie, that it was concluded to permitt us a howse and factory, butt they did not give us absolute awnswere untill they had newes from Ambonia Castell from the Holland Governor, they havinge sent a man of purpose. And before there comeinge from ashore they had awnsweare (that they should not give us trade nor enterteynement in the countrye) from the Governour of the Hollanders, except we would be bound unto them to defend the countrye from the Portugalls, Spaniards and all other nations; which if they did give us trade upon any other condition, they would build a castle att Hitto and burne their towne. Soe these threatninges made them soe fearfull that they durst not give us any enterteynement. Notwithstandinge the Captaines sonne and other Arancayes at night came aboard and brought the Kinge of Hitto, who because he is butt a simple man, the whole government is comitted to the Captaine of Hitto. Att their comeinge aboard they desired me not to bee offended with them for puttinge us

---

1 This should probably be '28.'

2 See note on p. 59.

of soe longe; the cause, said hee, was for that the Hollanders had threatned them, if they enterteyned us but upon these conditions above specified, that they would build a castle instantlye in there towne, soe that they should not bee able to doe us any pleasure, nor wee able to resist their forces, to protect them. Therefore they all desired us to bee content for this time; and that if wee would goe for Lugho, hee would cause his people secreetly to carry cloves to us thether, and that he had conference with the Arancayes of that place to give us enterteynement. Butt this, I perceived, was butt a shifte of them to gett us gone from hence, as after it proved. Notwithstandinge, he went presentlie to talke with the Arancaye of Lugho, that was there ridinge by us in a small proa, promisinge faithfullie to send at least 100 bahars of cloves theather. I would have agreed a price for his cloves, but he would nott, sayinge that if wee gave more then the Hollanders wee should have them; which shewed plainely that his desire was onely to have us gone. Yett seeinge noe remedy, we gave him good words, hopinge the best. Butt they expected annother present; butt, doubtinge of their promise, I promised them faire, when they had performed with us; soe they departed.

This daie came the Dutch factour againe aboard, tellinge mee that hee had sent my awnswere to the Governor and expected retourne the same eveninge. I tould him of the injuries done us in threatninge the country people and takinge their cloves perforce, because wee should not have them; all which he denied, onlie that he willed them to remember their contract made with them; with much other disputacions which is too tedious to sett downe.

[*March*] 28[1]. This day in the morninge the Captaine

---

[1] Probably the 29th.

of Hitto and his sonne (which had bene in Holland[1] and could speake Dutch) retourned aboard againe, assuringe mee they would bee as good as there words if wee would goe for Lugho, affirminge that [they] had taken that course that wee should have all the cloves that were there, besides those which he would send us from Hitto and Mamello[2], which is annother towne upon Ambonia; and to animate him to performe his promise I gave him and his sonne a small present, assuringe him that I would sett saile for Lugho the next daie.

And in the afternoone retourned the Dutch factour Cotellas and tould mee that he had written to the Castle to the Governor to sell us cloves, and he doubtinge nothinge but that the Governor would yeald unto itt; which if hee did, wee should have all that hee had in the howse, as alsoe those that weare at Lugho and Cambello. But I made little reckoninge of his promise, tellinge him that where I had bene once deceyved I would believe noe more; shewinge him that hee had nott learned his lyinge tongue att London, butt amongst the Portugalls; for hee had spent the most parte of his youth in London and in Portagall, and could speake both languages perfectlie. Soe I bid him to keepe his cloves, for I would none of him; that in the morninge I would sett sayle, God willinge.

[*March*] 29[3]. This daye in the morninge the Governor of the Hollanders and the comander of the two shipps which came from Bantam came to Hitto, within two miles of the towne, and Cotellas retourned againe aboard, entreatinge mee to staye till night till they came to the towne; assuringe mee that they would deale with mee for

---

[1] See Valentyn, *Ambonsche Zaaken*, 32.

[2] Mamala, on the coast of Amboyna, a few miles to the N.E. of Hitu.

[3] Read '30.'

some cloves. And at night I understoode by shootinge of some peeces aland that they were come.

March 31. As wee were settinge saile for Lugho, the Dutch marchant came againe aboard with other marchanntes, who told us that the comander of the two shipps, which were aland, beinge come to see the countrie, would willinglie speake with mee. I demanded of them aboute whatt buysines. They awnswered that they knewe nott, butt that they were comanded by their superiours to tell us soe much, and alsoe to advise us that if wee went for Lugho they would followe us, to prevent us of trade; whereunto I awnswered Cotellas that I had formerlie told him where he had learned his lyinge tongue, in urginge mee so earnestlie to staie, with faithfull promise of sellinge us a parcell of cloves, and now come with this sleeveless awnswere; that hee neede not followe us, that if they pleased I would carrye them in the shipp; butt without further repetitions they departed, and wee sett saile aboute nine in the morninge, the Dutch threatninge us to bee att Lugho before us, to make our bedds against our comeinge. I bad them doe their worst.

Aboute three in the afternoone wee anchored att Lugho, in 40 fathom water, within a butt shott of the Flemish howse. Our anchour laye in 60 fathome, faire ground, but soe neere the shore that with the winde of the sea[1] our shipp starne was within a ships length in 2½ fathome; but a man neede not feare his ankour, because it is very firme ground, and against the hill, that hee cannott come home. And as soone as I ankored I went aland with the marchannts and juribassa to conferre with the Governor concerninge our tradinge with them, shewinge him what comodities wee had besides money. Hee seemed to give us a kinde welcome, awnsweringe in this forme, vizt.—That although

[1] *I.e.* when the ship swung round with the tide.

hee were cheife and head, there were others alsoe which were the armes and leggs, with whome he would first take advise, and in the morninge give us awnswere. But this same night came our persecutors the Hollanders, vizt. the commander of the two shipps[1] and Cottelas, with two or three more of the principall marchants of India; whoe att their arrivall had private conference with the Governor, as I understood the next daie by one which I had hired aland for the purpose.

Aprill 1. This day in the morninge from our shipp wee might perceive the Governor and Arancayes to goe into the Dutch house, and from thence he went to the towne house to conferre with the Arancayes; and present[2] us word aboard that he would come aboard in the afternoone to give us awnswere of our demand. But he came not aboard accordinge to promise; but in the eveninge he came to the waters side to the Sabendours house and sent abourd to have the juribassa come aland to speake with him. Soe I sent him, accompanied with Nicholas Bangham; whoe gave this awnswere, vizt.—That hee could not permitt us to settle a factory, because the countrye did belonge to the Kinge of Turnatto[3], with whom the Dutch had greate league; whoe would not give consent to enterteyne us, threatninge them to build a castle if they did trade with us, and they durst not to displease them without order from the Kinge of Turnatto; but if wee could procure a letter from the Kinge, they would with all their harts give us as kinde enterteynement as might bee. With this awnsweare they retourned aboard; whome I presently sent aland againe, tellinge them that this was contrarie to the promise

[1] The future Governor-General, Jan Pieterszoon Coen (see Appendix E).

[2] Presently sent?

[3] The Sultan of Ternate, who was acknowledged as suzerain by the chiefs of Amboyna, Ceram, etc.

that was made unto mee att Hitto, perswadinge me to come with the shipp, and nowe to putt mee off with this awnsweare; demandinge them if they would permitt us to take a howse for the time thatt the shipp was to staie, to drye some of our goods that were wett and ill conditioned; to all which they awnswered that it was true that they sent us word to come over with our shipp, because they thought that wee had bene freinds with the Hollanders, but nowe they perceived by them that they were rather our enemyes then other, and they durst not displease them, alledginge their greate force of shippinge at Ambonia and Turnattee. And for our howse in the meane tyme to drye our cloth, they would take counsell aboute itt, and in the morninge give us awnswere. And at night there came two of the Dutch factors, of the cheefest of them, which began to wonder that wee would seeme to come to trade where they had to doe, jestinge att our little shipp[1] and tellinge of their greate forces. I awnswered little [to?] them; onlie I told them of their followinge us, as the Jewes did Christ, doinge us manie injuries, which one day they might awnswere for betwixt Dover and Callice; with many other wordes which I omitt. Att the tyme of the Hollanders departure, there came aboard the Sabendour with four more of the cheife Arancayes, as excusinge themselves and the Governor, tellinge us that the Governor was a Turnatan[2], sett in by order of the Dutch to prevent tradinge with other nations. Notwithstandinge, both he and they were desirous to trade with us; but the Hollendours had threatned to burne their towne and carry the cheife of them prisonners to the Kinge of Turnatto if they enterteyned us; sayinge further: Whie will you enterteyne the English, that are

[1] The *Darling* was only 90 tons burthen.

[2] The Kimelaha (chief) Sabadin (according to Tiele).

a petty nation that can doe you noe good to defend you from your enemies, they not beeinge able [to] sett out above six shipps? Notwithstandinge, said they, wee knowe the contrary, by reporte of the Portugalls, that the Dutch have beholdinge to the English, in soe much thatt if the English had not ayded them there had bene noe Hollanders livinge; therefore they rather desired trade with us then with them. And because wee should not thinke that it were their faults, they would speake soe much before their faces, that they weare willinge to enterteyne us weare it not that they had threatned them; desiringe mee to come aland and I should heare what they would saye to the Hollanders; that in the morninge they would call all the cheife of the countrye; then I might make my demands, and I should see what they would awnswere before the Hollanders. I promysed to bee with them in the morninge; and att their departure they said that although the Dutch would not consent that wee should have a house, yett they would sell us all the cloves which were to bee had in the countrye; and soe they departed.

Aprill 2. This daie in the morninge I landed to conferre with the Arancaies. The Hollanders, perceive-inge mee to land, came to mee, desiringe me to goe to there house; where I was received by their comander and the rest with a fained welcome, which might by their gesture bee easilie discernd; where the camander in a chollericke manner beganne to accuse me of misbehavinge myselfe in offringe to buye cloves in the countries that were under their proteccion, as itt were in dispight of them; which he said was contrarie to comission given by Sir Henrie Middleton; whereunto I replyed that I wondred much that hee should bee soe well acquainted with my comission; but seeinge he knewe it soe well, his long beard (for he had none att all) could not teach me to followe my comission[1]; advisinge him to looke well to his owne buysines and comissions, for if I had done otherwise then my comission I was not to yeild accompt thereof to him, but to his betters; and therefore, if hee had noe other thinge to talke of, hee needed not to have sent for mee; but that they had not onelie abused mee butt our whole nation, in disablinge us amonge the countrie people, threatninge them to burne their howses if they gave us any enterteynement, as alsoe in followinge us from place to place, persecutinge us, giveinge us a Judas kisse with faire words when behinde our backes they sell us; thus it was plaine that they had abused us, which they could not denie; entreatinge him quietlie to shewe wherin wee had wronged them. Whereunto hee awnswered that the word of persecutinge was not propper to them, for that they were not Judas; but the matter was that at my first comeinge to Hitto I made out to buye cloves, where they were contracted with the countrye people before for all that groweth yearly in the land, and that I had offred them 15 ryalls in a bahar more then they gave, sayinge that I would have cloves althoughe they cost 100 rialls per bahar; all which I did malitiously to make the countrie people breake their contracte made with them; affirmeinge that whoe soe ever bought any cloves in these countries without their consent it was soe much stolne from them; and therefore they would prevent itt, if by any meanes they might. Whereunto I replyed that it was true that I came to buye cloves if I might gett them, and had offred money for them; which I might have had, if I had not given some creditt to Cottelas words, whoe had promised that I should buye of them, entreatinge mee not to offer money for any untill awnswere from the Governor of Ambonia; by which delayes I had spent 15 [10?] daies

[1] Jourdain was of course jesting at Coen's youth. The latter was only twenty-six at this time.

without doinge any thinge, and in the end I had a flopp with a foxetaile, as the old proverbe is[1]. Besides, I offred unto Cottellas (whoe is here present) 16[2] rialls of eight in a bahar to you more then you paye to the people of the countrie, because I knowe it would be a hindrance to you if wee raised the price. I was putt of from day to daye to the last hower that I came from Hitto; and when you sawe that I would be noe longer delayed you sent mee word that you would pursue mee wheresoever I went; and therefore accordinge to your owne speeches I might rightlie terme it persecutinge. And as for their contract, I did nott take any notice of their buysines as they did of ours; butt I understood that the countrye was as free for us as for them, if the people of the countrye would deale with us; which they were willinge to doe were it not for the Dutch threatnings to burne there townes and build castles and carry them prisonners to Turnattee, if they dealt with us. All which hee denied, sayinge that the countrye people were noe way willinge to deale with us butt would be glad that wee weare gone. Wherewith I concluded that if itt pleased him to send for the Governour and Arancayes, if they said that they will not trade with us, wee will, God willinge, in the morninge sett saile and not trouble you anie farther in this place. Tah, said hee, will they come at my sendinge for? If not, said I, lett mee goe for them; or lett us goe to the towne howse, where they have promised to bee this afternoone. If you will not goe thether, nor suffer them to come to your howse, I will send for them to your bally[3]

[1] For instances of this proverb see the Oxford English Dictionary *s.v.* 'flop' and 'flap.' The origin is obscure. It seems to have derived from some simile of a fox who not only evades an attempt to capture him but in so doing deals his would-be captor a blow with his tail.

[2] 'Five,' according to p. 248. Perhaps Jourdain had subsequently increased his offer.

[3] Malay *bālai*, an audience-chamber or public meeting-place; in this case probably a large verandah outside the Dutch factory.

without the dore, where wee will speake with them. To none of these would they consent, sayinge that they had nothinge to doe at present with the Governor and Arancayes.

Seeinge that they would not consent to nether of these, I tooke my leave of them, and went to the place where they had appointed mee to come; where I found the Governor and the cheifest Arancayes, with manie other. To whome I said that I had bene putt off these many daies by delayes, they alledginge that the Hollanders would not permitt us to trade with them, threatninge to burne their townes and emprison them if they enterteynd us, all which the Dutch denied, sayinge that your selves are not willinge to deale with us; which if it bee true, I am come to crave your awnswere, that I maye departe with the message to whome sent mee. In awnswere of which they all with one accord stoode up, sayinge: Our onelie desire is to deale with the English, butt wee are daylie threatned by the Hollanders, as wee have formerlie told, soe that wee dare not almost to speake with you for feare of their forces which are neere; and because you shall see that it is true, wee will send for them, and will saye soe much to their faces. Soe presentlie they sent for the Hollanders to come to the courte; which they refused. Butt they all with one voyce retourned the messenger to them, sayinge: If you refuse to come to our courte, wee will forthwith ordayne a place for the English to build a howse and trade with them, for that they are our freinds. Att which message they all presentlie came, the comander in greate collar; to whome the Governor and Arancayes said that the English were come to their countrye to trade with them as marchannts; which they all were willinge to enterteyne, butt they feared their displeasure, whoe had soe often threatned them to burne their towne and to build a castle and emprison them if they enterteined us;

and therefore they had sent for them to the intent to cleare themselves, there [that?] wee might see that they were not in fault of enterteyneinge us. To which words all the countrie people made a greate shoute, sayinge: Wee are willinge to deale with the English; demandinge the Hollanders what they said to itt; whereunto they were silent, awnsweringe neither yea nor naye. The people did the like the second time, requyringe the Dutch to awnswere, butt noe word nor awnswere could be had. Soe then I tould the commander that it was approved to his face that they weare the cause that wee could not bee enterteyned; thatt nowe they could not denie itt. But he awnswered me with silence, as hee had them. Seeinge I could gett nothinge from him, I tould the countrye people that I sawe their willingnes and perceived that the Hollanders were the cause that they did not enterteyne us, as they desired. And soe I departed, leaveinge the Hollanders with them. What passed after my departure I knowe nott, but they staied not longe after mee. Of all that passed this daie I tooke witnes by our English-men that weare present, vizt.—George Cockaine, Nicholas Bangham, Benjamyn Fary, Phillipp Badnedge, juribassa, Abraham the cockson, and other standers by of the shipps companie.

Aprill 3. This night the Governor sent aboard word to have the juribassa to come in the morninge to him. Soe the next daie I went aland, and sent the juribassa with Nicholas Bangam to the Governours, while I was talkinge with the comander; for that alwaies att my landinge I had soe many wayters on mee that I could goe noe where but some of them weare at my heeles; therefore I was content to entertaine the time with them while they went to knowe the Governours minde; which was to this effect, vizt. that hee and the Arancaies would come aboard at night to conferre with mee; makinge a shewe of greate sorrowe that he could not freelie deale with us, but that hee would with the rest of the Arancaies write to the Kinge of Turnattee concerneinge us, not doubtinge by the next monson to have order from him to enterteyne us in despite of the Hollanders; willing us not to faile to come the next yeare, which was the greate monsone of cloves[1]; and in the meane tyme of our beeinge, he would give secrett order to sell us as manie cloves as weare in the countrye.

Aprill 5. The next daie, beeinge the fifth daie, aboute noone there came two or three Arancaies sent by the Governor [to say?] that they had some 30 bahars of cloves, which they would bringe aboard if wee agreed a price. They demanded 100 rialls of eight per bahar, and would not abate any thinge thereof; for, said they, wee endanger our selves to bee taken prisonners by the Dutch and carried to Turnatto, if they should come to knowe itt, and therefore wee have not reason to sell them to you upon soe greate a hazard except we may have some profitt by them. Soe I offred them 70 rialls per bahar, which was 20 rialls per bahar more then the Dutch gave them, assuringe them that I would give noe more whether I had them or nott, and that if they brought them nott aboard the next daie I would sett saile and begone.

And this daie the Governor sent againe for our juribassa to come aland to talke with the Sabendour, because himselfe would not bee seene to conferre with us. And at there cominge aland, Nicholas Bangham beinge present, the Sabendour began a greate discourse concerninge the Dutch, sayinge that at their first comminge to the countrye they made agreement with them for 95 rialls per bahar

[1] 'Theare groweth aboundance of cloves not every yeare, but every third yeare...is a greate growth' ('Discription of the Iland of Amboyna' in *The First Letter Book*, p. 74). 'Every third yeare is farre more fruitfull then either of the former two, and is called the great monson' (*Voyage of John Saris*, Hakl. Soc. ed., p. 59).

of cloves, and every yeare by degrees brought the price lower, untill they had brought them to 50 rialls per bahar, which was the price they nowe paye, which was a greate losse to the countrye people; soe if wee would have cloves wee must give 95 rialls, as they gave at first, and after by degrees to bringe the price downe as they had; att which price they would sell us the small quantitye they had. Whereunto they replyed that I was resolvd not to give more then 70 rialls, which if itt pleased them to accept, they should send mee word this night, for that in the morninge I was determyned to sett saile. In the eveninge came one of the Arancayes aboard and desired to prove our waightes to see howe they agreed with the Hollanders; which as soone as they had proved, they send [sent] me word that I should have that small quantitie they had at my price of 70 rialls, seeinge I would give noe more.

Aprill 6. The next morninge I sent ashore the beame and skale where they had appointed, at the old towne, out of sight of the Hollenders; where Benjamin Fary and the juribassa stayed till night to weigh them, and at night I sent the boate for them. Soe that from the 6 to the 9th wee contynued sendinge aboard cloves by night, which were weighed at an Arancayes house called Gumalla Tecous, which was the cheifest man of the ould towne and greatlie respected amongst the countrye people, in soe much that if hee had butt lifte up his hand against the Dutch they would soone have bene made an end of. In the interim of this buysines I went to the Arancaies house to visitt him, giveinge him hartie thankes for the kinde usage of our people, and carried him a small present; where at my comeinge hee told mee that the Hollanders had threatned them to build a castle in their countrie, to which he awnswered that if their owne goods, as cloves, were cause to bringe them into slavery, they would soone cutt downe their trees, or sett fire att them, that the

Hollanders should have little proffitt by their castle; that hee and the countrie people could live in the mountaynes better then they should doe in their castell; and that the Dutch should not keepe them in soe much subjection as not to enterteyne their antient freinds, whoe were subjects to a greate kinge and had offred them greate kindnes; and that they would sell their owne goods to those that would give most for them; with many other speeches to the same effect.

Beinge in this conference with the Arancaye, there was newes brought that all the Hollanders were come from Cambello and had taken a proa to come thither by water. The Arancaye awnswered the messenger that if they come in freindshipp they should be welcome; if otherwise, he would soone cutt of their heads. But belike the Dutch were otherwise counselled, for they came not thither. Soe aboute noone I went aboard, where presentlie came the Governor to mee with many complements; and amongst the rest told me that there was an iland over against Cambello, called Manippa[1], a very fruitfull place and a good porte, where there weare yearlie growinge aboute 40 bahars of cloves, where the Hollanders had noe factory; which if wee would goe thither and take a house, that wee should not wante store of cloves brought from Hitto, Lugho, and Cambello, and other places. Moreover he said that if nowe wee would goe thether with our shipp to see the place, he would write his letter in our behalfe, the iland beeinge under his jurisdiccion. I awnswerd that happilie before our departure wee would see the place, if he would give us his letter; with many other complements. After a present given him, hee departed. Nowe the Hollanders perceiveinge (notwithstandinge their threatnings) that wee had bought some cloves, they sent to

[1] Manipa, an island to the west of Ceram.

Ambonia castell to cause two shipps to come to Hitto in sight of us to scare us, and withall sent abourd our shipp three cheife marchants with a letter to mee in Dutch; butt I would take noe notice of itt, beinge in a language that I could not understand, and they would not enterprette it to mee. Soe I told them that they should sett downe their buysines in Portugues, French, Italian or English[1] and I would awnsweare them; with this they retorned. The commander of the Dutch, as I understoode, was very much vext that wee had bought these small quantities of cloves, threatninge the Arancaye Tecoos that hee should loose his head; soe that perceiveinge the shipps to bee neere, and their threatnings, made him somethinge abate his former resolution, not suffringe any more cloves to bee weighed in his house. Soe I sent for our people aboard with the beame and skale, and brought this night aboute 20 bahars aboard and came all awaie; the Arancaye tellinge me that the next daie there was a greate counsell to bee held with the Hollenders and Arancayes.

Aprill 10. In the morninge, while the Hollenders and the Arancayes weare in councell aboute us, I sent aland to the newe towne to waye a parcell of cloves; where the Arancaye Tecous had appointed to meete me to advise me of the councell held per the Hollanders; where I had not staied longe ere he came sweeteinge in a greate chafe, sayinge that they had againe threatned to have his head, and that the rest of the Arancayes beganne to take their heades out of the coller, which had formerlie animated him to helpe us and nowe laide all on his necke; wherefore he came from the counsell in a rage, tellinge the Hollanders that if they sought to have his head for enterteyneinge us, he [they?] must likewise seeke all the Arancayes heades

[1] Cokayne knew Italian and Portuguese, and Jourdain was conversant with the latter language, and probably with French also.

that weare present, because all of them were of councell aboute us and all consented to what hee had done; soe that they would not all loose their heades for sellinge their owne goods. Soe hee concluded, sayinge: If you will have any good in this countrye, you must not come with one small shipp; for, said he, the comon people knowe not the difference betweene your kinges, butt looke to the present forces; soe they perceive that the Dutch are stronger then you, therefore they goe from their words for feare of two ships thatt are att Hitto; and, said hee, if you had butt one shipp more they would not care a poynte for the Hollenders. Farther said he: If you retourne the next yeare with two or three shipps, which is the yeare of the greate monson of cloves, the Hollanders shall not have one pound, for I will ordayne (said he) the matter in such order that the countrye shall paie them what they owe, and then they cannott force us to give them our cloves; whereas nowe there are manye poore men that have taken rotten cloath of them at greate rates for their necessitie, with promise to sell them all their cloves; which is the contract which the Dutch soe much talketh of. This, said hee, is the matter betweene the Dutch and us.

Aprill 11. The next daie the Governor retourned againe aboard aboute eleven at night and told mee all thatt had passed with the Hollanders in councell; that their cheifest anger was against the Arancaye Tecoos, for consentinge us to weigh cloves in his house. But, said hee, the Arancaye cared not for there threatnings; sayinge farther, if the Dutch tooke not the better heede the Arancaye will shortlie have all their heades, for that he is honnored amongst the countrye people as kinge, and all stand in feare of him; which was the cause that the Dutch were soe eager against him. Alsoe he told me that the comander and the cheife factor were to departe the next daie for Hitto.

Aprill 12. And the next morninge, beeing the 12th, [came] Cottellas with three other of their principall marchannts which the comander had left (he beinge gone this night for Hitto) to bringe this letter aboard translated into Portugues. Theffect was to notifie mee to departe the countrye; otherwise whatsoever hapned unto mee by their forces they protested not to be culpable of; with any [many ?] other circumstances as by the letter may appeare. To which I awnswered that whatt I had done must bee awnswered, butt not to them; therefore I, puttinge the letter into my pockett, told them that silence was the awnswere that they should deliver to there comander, which was a lesson learned from himselfe; and for the rest I referred the matter untill wee mett betwixt Dover and Calice; with which awnswere they departed.

When wee perceived that the Arancaye Tecoos stoode in feare, and thatt wee had already bought and receyved the most parte of the cloves that were to bee had, wee weighed from thence and rid within a cove farther to the eastward aboute a mile, within pistoll shott of, four fathome water, which is neere the common waye that all the people passeth from out of the countrye; soe that wee weare enforced [enformed ?] that if wee would goe thether many poore people would bringe us cloves which nowe weare afraide because wee rid soe neere the Hollanders house; as alsoe this pound or cove is as good as a bad harbor, and neere water and wood, which was one of the cheifest causes that wee removed. Here wee had brought us by night some small parcells of cloves, but not many. But heare the people weare more bold to conferre with us, beinge out of sight of the Hollanders. And in the meane time that wee were fillinge our water and cuttinge of wood, there came two Arancaies of Cambello, sayinge if wee would goe thether with our shipp wee should have aboute 40 bahars of cloves; to whome I made promise to bee there, God willinge, within ten dayes at farthest, they likewise promisinge to keepe their cloves soe longe for us. And the reason whie I sett soe longe time was, because I determined to goe for Hitto and Mamello to challenge the Captaine of Hittoes promise made mee to send me cloves, and had not sent one pound. In this cove or pound I stayed till the 20th of Aprill, woodinge and wateringe, and bought some cloves; in which time passed many accidents betweene the Hollanders and us; but in fine,

Aprill 20. Wee sett saile in the morninge with little winde of the shore, which carried us aboute a league of, towards Hitto, and then it fell calme. And lyinge becalmed, the Arancaye Tecoos with his proa, with other Arancayes, came aboard with many complements from the Governor and other Arancaies; doubtinge very much that I went awaye discontented, for which they seemed to bee sorrye, excusinge themselves, sayinge that they had done as much as they durst doe, and more then they knowe well howe to awnswere; sayinge that the Hollanders would make them paye well for itt after our departure; desiringe us to come the next yeare with more force; then they would pay the Hollanders what they owed them, and there would remayne cloves enoughe to lade two such shipps as ours was, all which we should have if wee brought two shipps to countenance the matter. But, said they, when the Hollanders are paid their debts, which wilbee this next yeare, if then they will urge us to sell our cloves to them, they vowed to cutt downe the trees and live in the mountaines; they should have small profitt by ther factorie; that they would noe longer remayne in such slavery, butt would bee free to sell their goods to him that would give most for them; with many other speeches[1]. The winde nowe beeinge

[1] According to Coen, Jourdain assured Tikos that the English would return the following year to buy their cloves (Tiele's *Bouwstoffen*, i. 48).

come at S.E. a pretty gale, they departed, and wee stoode towards Hitto. Butt in the eveninge the winde fallinge calme all night, the corrent had almost sett us out of the straicts before the morninge; soe that with much adoe wee seased the shore of Ambonia, where wee anchored two leagues from Lugho in 50 fathome water; where wee rid all this daye, and tooke in some wood and water. And the next daie, seeinge wee weare out of hope to gett Mamello, by reason of a stronge corrent which setteth out of the straictes, I sent the boate to Hitto, in the which went Nicholas Bangham to talke with the Captaine concerninge his promise; whoe awnswered that he could not doe itt except he should loose his countrye, for that the Hollanders had sett greate penalties on his head if he suffred butt one pound of cloves to bee sould unto us; cravinge pardon untill the next yeare, that then they would paye the Hollanders their debts; then it was free for them to sell there cloves to whome they would; promisinge if our shipps came the next yeare, which was the greate monson, he would not faile to sell a good quantetie to us; with many other kinde wordes. They tooke ther leaves of them and went aboard a Holland shipp, which was one of the three which laye att Hitto, and was newelie come from Japan[1]; wherefore *Aprill 23.* I caused him to goe aboard to buye some bread and fresh porke, they beeinge laden therewith to furnishe their castells; but they neither for love nor money would not spare any. Butt in the shipp there was an English sailer, which had secreetlie brought a letter from Mr. Adams directed to Augustine Spaldinge[2], in which letter there was

[1] The *Leeuw met Pylen*, on board of which Hendrik Brouwer, the Dutch chief at Hirado, had just returned from Japan.

[2] This was the letter of Jan. 12, 1613, sent in duplicate by William Adams to Augustin Spalding at Bantam, which is now in the India Office (*O. C.* 96). It has been printed in Rundall's *Memorials of Japon* (p. 40) and also in *Letters Received* (i. 208). In it Adams

a draught by him drawne of the countrye of Japan; which with much adoe hee gate of him for two rialls of eight which he gave him. And in the eveninge he retourned to the shipp; and the 24 [23rd ?], aboute two in the afternoone, wee sett saile, havinge broken our cable in weyinge of our anchour, lyinge amongst rockes, soe wee lost our ankor.

[*Aprill* 24.] And the 24th wee anchored in Cambello Roade aboute noone in 30 fathome water, good ground. This is a very good roade. You may ride a pretty birth of the shore in 10 and 15 fathome, where three juncks ridd within us. In this towne of Cambello and Lasede[1], which is annother towne by the seaside within a mile of itt, I bought aboute 15 bahars of cloves, which was all that was remayneinge out of the Hollenders hands. Lasede doth yeald more cloves then Cambello, and the people thereof were willinge that wee should leave there a factorye; which I determyned to have done if I could have had the Arancaies of Cambellos consent, butt he was soe fearfull of the Dutch that he durst not consent unto itt; besides the Arancaye of Lughoe came overland unto us and wild us not to trust to the people of Lasede and Cambello, sayinge that they were poore men and weake, that whatsoever they promised us they would not bee ~~able to~~ performe, because they weare of little force; rather, said he, lett it rest till the next yeare; then you may settle a factorie at Lugho and annother at Cambello; for if these at Lugho consent, Cambello will not refuse, because they are as one. In this roade I stayed aboute these fewe daies [cloves ?] and conferringe with the countrie people nine daies; in which time the Dutch factour came divers times aboard, and I went likewise ashore to their house, which standeth very

---

mentions that he encloses a 'pattron of Japan.' The sailor who carried the letter was named Thomas Hill (see endorsement).

[1] Lassidi or Lissidi is described by Valentyn as lying $1\frac{1}{2}$ (Dutch) miles north of Kambelo.

pleasantlie, and a very prettye howse, butt built with timber and strawe. In the time of our beeinge in this roade the Dutch Generall[1] landed in a boate which came from Manippa, where he had lefte his shipp, and came from Tornattee, and by reason of the stronge corrent which setteth to the northward she was not able to gett any farther, butt was forced to ankour and send their boate.

Of the Country of Ambonia, Cambello, Lugho and Lasede.

This countrye of Ambonia is butt a small iland, where the Hollanders have a very stronge castell; butt the most parte of the people are gone from the place where the castell standeth, and dwell on the topps of hills amongst the woods. Hitto and Mamello are two of the cheefest villages within the straicts, neere which townes are the most parte of the cloves growinge. The Dutch have a factory onelie at Hitto, and annother at the castle. The iland is subject to the Kinge of Turnattee; whome the Hollanders doe protecte, or rather keepe as a prisonner, for the Kinge doth nothinge butt what the Hollanders please; soe that I understand that if he could cunninglie gett from them, he would have noe more of their proteccion, because it is little better then slavery. Alsoe Cambello, Lugho and Lasede, with other townes, doe belonge to the same Kinge of Turnattee, with many other ilandes there aboutes; butt these three places doe yeild store of cloves, as many or more then Ambonia; and the Dutch have twoe factories, vizt. at Cambello and Lugho. This iland is parte of the iland of Seran, and is the westermost, where these townes are at the entringe of the Straightes of Hitto. At this end of the iland there are cloves as aforesaid. Att noe other parte thereof are any, for it is a very greate iland, which trendeth almost as farre as the ilands of Banda. Lugho

[1] Pieter Both (see p. 247).

lyeth aboute three leagues within the Straightes, over against Hitto; and Cambello and Lasede lye without the Straicts on the wester side. It is by sea from Cambello to Lugho aboute ten leagues, butt by land not above two leagues; and Hitto from Lugho is aboute four leagues. The people of those places are generallye weery of the Hollanders keepinge them in slaverye; soe that they would willinglie bee freed of itt if they knewe howe. At the entringe of these Straicts there are three small ilands[1], half a mile one from annother, lyinge neere Ambonia side. There goes a great corrent which sett[s] upon them, if you are becalmed; butt there is noe danger, because there it is steepe too and when you come neere them you may anker. The corrent will not drive directlie upon them, butt close by them; soe that if a man doe not knowe them, it will putt him in greate feare, doubtinge of rocks; but there is noe danger, as aforesaid.

Maye 3. Havinge finished our buysines at Cambello, we sett saile for Macassar. But by the waye wee were minded to stopp att Bouton[2], to see whatt might bee done aboute the sale of our goods, as alsoe to speake with Mr. Welden[3], an Englishman lefte there by Captaine David Middleton, whoe could enforme us att large of all the countries adjasente. Soe the 8th of Maye

Maye 8.

wee fell with the land of Bouton in the morninge; and havinge a stiffe gale at S.S.E. wee shott faire into a

---

[1] The Three Brothers.

[2] Buton, a large island at the south-eastern corner of Celebes.

[3] Richard Welden, of whom see a note on p. 308 of *Letters Received*, vol. iii. Saris, on his way to Japan, found him voyaging to Banda in the service of the King of Buton (*Voyage of John Saris*, p. 15). Purchas says 'Master Welding had served him in his warres, and gotten victories for him and honour for himselfe and his nation' (*Pilgrimage*, ed. 1626, p. 608).

David Middleton visited Buton in April, 1608, and again in January, 1610.

baye. Wee could not double the pointe of Sampullana[1], which is the wester pointe of the iland where wee touched outward bound, where there is very good watringe within a baye, where there is a good roade in 12 fathome water. Here wee laye voltinge to and againe to double this pointe; but the winde beeinge scante and the corrent against us, wee were putt leeward; soe that the 10th in the morninge wee weare in a deepe baye, as wee supposed, and to the norward of us wee sawe twoe ilands[2]. This which seemed to bee a baye was the entringe of the Straicts of Bouton to the northward; butt I could not perswade our maister nor pilott thereunto, they affirmeinge it to bee the mayne land of Bouton, because they could not perceive any goinge thorough, because the land of the Sellibis lyeth right in the gutt of the Straicts, soe that itt seemeth to bee all a firme land[3]. I contended with them that it was by our latitude the Straicts of Bouton and noe other, for that the other land which wee sawe to the norward was farther north by 12 leagues then the Straicts of Bouton was laied in; but by noe meanes they would not be perswaded, sayinge that they would not take upon them to carrye in the shipp to cast her awaie, butt if I would command them to goe in there the danger thereof should lye on my necke; which I would not take upon mee, in reguard that there was a pilott appointed, who had bene there not above ten monnethes since, and made himselfe certayne that the Straicts were farther to the norward. Soe wee stoode alonge to the norther parte of the land which was to the norward of us, sendinge our boate before us soundinge;

---

[1] Probably Siumpu Island, which, according to the Admiralty Pilot, when seen from the westward cannot be distinguished from the south part of Buton until close-to.

[2] Possibly Kabaena and Muna.

[3] From this it seems that Jourdain regarded the channel between Muna (which he evidently took to be a portion of Buton) and Kabaena as forming part of the Straits of Buton.

and in the eveninge, aboute sonne settinge, wee anchored within the pointe of a land, half a mile of the shore, in 35 fathome water; and aboute a league to the eastward of us wee sawe a bigge towne on the topp of a very high mountaine, and att night wee sawe many fishers on the shore with lightes, but none came neere us.

Maye 11. The next daie wee sent the boate farther to the westward, to seeke for a better place to anchour in, because wee doubted that our anchour laye in fowle ground. Soe aboute ten in the morninge our boate returned and brought us word that a league to the westward there was a faire baye and good ground to anchour in, and a river of water hard by. Soe aboute noone wee weyed, and stoode into the baye and anchored in seven fathome water, a very good roade for the easterlie monson. Nowe our pilott came cryinge to mee and said that wee were past the Straicts of Bouton, and that which hee made to bee a baye was the Straicts. Then said I unto him: Are you nowe soe skilfull of the place, and yesterdaye, when wee passed by itt, when I shewed you sundrye reasons that itt was the Straicts, you tooke pepper in the nose[1] because I would seeme to knowe itt better then you that had passed itt two or three times: and nowe howe are you certaine that it was the Straightes? I knowe it, said hee, because when I passed the Straicts with Captaine Middleton, I remember as soone as he was passed the Straicts they sawe a small iland to the larboard side of them, which is (said hee) that iland which wee see to the northward of us[2]; and that the land where wee weare nowe anchored was parte of the Sellibis[3]. Howe (said I) can this be parte of the Sellibes, if wee perceive it to bee an

[1] A proverbial phrase for taking offence.

[2] Apparently Kadatua, but that could not have been northward of their position at this time.

[3] Celebes.

iland? To which he could not awnswere. Whereupon I made him bringe his draught, that hee had made by roate, as children reade their lesson. I demanded whie he had not drawne the iland as well as the rest. He awnswered that he had forgotten itt, for that he made not the draught as he passed by itt, but afterwards, when hee was to come in this voyage, he drewe itt by memorye to shewe Sir Henrie Middleton. You are (said I) a fitt pilott to cast a shipp awaie, and wee wise men to venture our lives with such an unskilfull fellowe, whoe had wrongd himselfe and the Honourable Companie, endangeringe both shipp, goods and many mens lives, which would be required at his handes. Butt, said I, what course is nowe to bee taken, whether it bee possible to beate it upp towards the Straicts, or goe to the norward of the Selebes? He tould me that it was impossible to beate itt upp against winde and tyde, which will runne all this monson against us, this beeinge nowe in the begininge of the monson. Soe I lett it rest untill I knowe farther of the place where wee were anchored, and to that purpose I sent the boate, *Maye* 12. aboute four in the morninge, well manned, towards the towne with our juribassa to enquire of the place where wee weare, and of the Straicts of Bouton. And aboute noone our boate retourned, havinge had speech with three caracores which laye at the place or porte where they usuallye land, whoe had in them above 100 men, beinge men of warre, they havinge warrs with some other of the ilands. These people told our men that this iland was called Laboney[1], belonginge to the Kings of

[1] 'Balonye' and 'Babony' later. Jourdain probably used the second of these spellings, the others being errors of his copyist. It seems to be the present island of Kabaena.

There are many difficulties in the account which follows, but the track laid down on the map shows what appears to be on the whole the most probable course. The channels and islands are only imperfectly known, and detailed maps are not available.

Tornattee and Botton. Those carracores were on the backeside of the Selebes, a people called [*blank*]. They alsoe told them that wee were to leeward of the Straicts, butt that there was annother waye to gett to Bouton, butt itt would be hard gettinge upp, because the windc hanged in our teeth, and the waye dangerous. Soe att their retourne I tould John Derby, our pilott, thatt twice since wee came from Cambello he had lost his head, once aboute the Straicts of Bottone and nowe aboute this iland to be the Selebes. He knewe not what to saie to itt, but streatched [scratched ?] his head like to a bad pilott, he haveinge waged [wagered ?] his head twice aboute these two places before mentioned.

Maye 13. The next daie, beeing the 13, there came two caracores more by us, bound for the towne, butt would not come to speake with us; soe wee sent our boate to them, and when they were out of shott of our shipp, they staied to speake with them, and affirmed what the former told us. Soe that these five caracores were all of the Selebis men of warre, soe that wee were fearfull to send our boate any more amongst them; but with the consent of the maister and pilott with the rest, wee determined to see if wee could beate it upp to windewards as farre as the Straights of Botoune, which was not above 12 leagues; if not, that wee should be able to anker againe in the same place. The next morninge wee sett saile, and voltinge too and againe wee perceived thatt wee were driven to leeward; soe that makinge towards the place from whence wee sett saile,

Maye 15. wee were not able to fetch itt by four miles, butt wee anchored in annother baye to leeward, in as good a place as the first, where weare little cottages which the men of warre had made when they passed that way. Here was alsoe a good river of fresh water, butt good anchoringe.

Maye 16. Seeinge that there was little hope to gett the Straicts of Bouton to windeward, I sent the boate to leeward, wherein went the maister, Cornelius Billinge, to search if there were any passage that waye, betweene the Selebes and the iland of Balonye. And the next daie he retourned and brought newes that there was noe passage that way neere the iland of Babony, for that the sholes laye of att least a league into the sea; butt that neere the Selebes on the lee shore there might bee a passage, which would bee very dangerous to putt thorough upon a lee shore; yett did not venter to see whether ther weare any passage or nott; soe thatt his jorney was to little purpose. The maister beeinge heare [heavie?] with a discoradged minde, seeinge noe remedye but to staye the westerlie monson, fell very sicke.

Maye 18. In all this time there came noe people unto us; onelie nowe and then wee should see some proas afishinge, butt would not come neere us. Soe I sent of our boate with a white flagge to speake with one of them. They spake with them, and made as though they would have come aboard; butt beeinge gotten a little ahead the boate, they made towards the shoare; soe that our boate makinge after them, they fledd and lefte the proa by the shore, which our men brought aboard; wherein our pilott, John Darby, desired with three more to venter to the towne to have caracores from the Kinge to tooe us as farre as the Straicts, as alsoe to knowe the certainetie if there were any passage that waye or nott. Soe itt was agreed upon that the next daie he, the juribassa, and one Englishman more and one blacke should the next daie goe finde out Botoune and retourne, and carry a present to the Kinge of Bouton, with a letter to Mr. Welden, whoe was there resident.

Maye 19. The next daie, beeinge the 19th, aboute two in the morninge the proa with our pilott departed for Bouton, with two Englishmen more and one blacke. And the 28th dicto, our anker beinge fowle, wee wayed with much adoe, and haveinge a slatch of a faire winde wee went to our first roade, because it was better ground; for if wee should have lost our anker wee should have bene in bad case, because wee had butt one more besides our shifte ancour, which all our men were not able to waye. Beeinge anchored in the first roade, wee purposed to staie till the retourne of our pilott from Bottone, and the maister grewe worse and worse every daie, not knowinge whatt course to take to gett out. Therefore hee sent for to speake with mee, tellinge me that any course that I would ordeyne that hee would followe, and would not weigh anchour without my expresse order, because if any thinge otherwise then well should happen (as God forbid) it should lye on my necke. Whereunto I awnswered that hee could bringe in the shipp contrarie to my will, and nowe would laye all onn my necke to carry her out; butt beeinge sicke I would not urge him farther, butt heare wee rid stayinge for our men from Botoune. Beinge nowe 14 (*sic*) daies since they departed, wee concluded to sett saile with the first winde of the shoare, and to stand towards the headland, to seeke a passage that waye, haveinge noe hope to gett windward. Soe this daye in the morning wee sett saile and stoode towards itt, butt wee well perceived it to bee the maine of Selebis. Therefore wee tacked aboute and stoode towardes the souther parte of Babony Iland, because wee might perceive as it weare a passage betweene the Celebes and Babony, although Robert Simonds, the maisters mate, was of opinion that the Straicts were farther to leeward, and was falslie graduated on the platts. Butt when wee approached neere wee might perceyve a suncke iland of two leagues of the northeast pointe of Babony, that wee could not directly discerne whether there were a passage that waye or not; and the night comeinge on wee would not venture to passe any farther untill the morninge to have the whole daye before us. Soe wee stoode too and againe and kept upp with a stiffe gale all night.

June 1. This daie in the morninge, our maister beeinge very ill, his mate would not take upon him the charge to carry the shipp that waye, butt would rather retourne and anchour at the roade where wee weare before. I alledged unto him and the rest of the companie that it was noe way for us to retourne thether, for that any winde that would doe us good wee should not be able to gett forth; and againe, if wee rid in that place there was noe hope of gettinge out untill the next monson, which would be September next, we havinge butt three monnethes victualls in the shipp. As alsoe that monson which would carry us from that place would serve to bringe us noe farther then Boutonne, soe thatt wee should not bee able to gett thorough the Straicts of Deslem till this time twelve monnethes, for that the westerly monson would not serve to carry us to Bantam; and seeinge it was soe, and the little hope which was to bee expected to gett any victualls of these heathens, havinge had already 25 daies experyence and cannot speake with any of the countrye people, therefore my opinion was that it was better to seeke some remedy at first, while our men stand in health and have victualls, then in the end to be forced therunto for wannte of foode.

With these perswations they all agreed to prove our fortune to seeke a passage thatt waye. Soe presentlie wee stoode with a slacke saile to the pointe of the sholes which wee had seene the night before; and when wee came neere wee sent our boate before to sound first on the shoales and to make a signe of the depth, and then to goe alonge by the edge of the sholes soundinge and make us a signe. Soe when we came with the pointe of the shoales wee might discerne a stake which was sett for a marke to passe without itt, and annother stake aboute a mile from thatt, sett both upon the very edge of the shoales, soe that our boate found within halfe pistoll shott of the edge of the sholes 17 fathome, and within a cables length noe ground. Soe itt pleased God that aboute noone wee were past the pointe; and beeinge past itt was as smooth as in a river. And standinge alonge the shore till three in the afternoone wee anchored in 20 fathome water, good ground; where att our men much rejoysed; and our sillye maisters mate would seeme nowe to take charge, which before hee refused.

June 4. The next daie, my selfe not beeinge well, I sent Nicholas Bangham and the maister his mate in the boate to sound alonge the shoare towards annother pointe which was aboute two leagues ahead of us, S.S.W. [S.S.E.?] of us; and aboute ten they retourned, sayinge that they found from 10 to 20 fathome all alonge the shore to the pointe, and beyond it faire sand. The next morninge wee weyed aboute noone and stoode towards the pointe; butt itt fell calme, soe that before wee could gett the pointe we anchored four times because of the currant against us. And aboute four in the afternoone wee anchored hard by the pointe; at which time wee had sight of five caracores comeinge towards the pointe from the southward, wherein came John Darby, our pilott, and juribassa, tellinge us that the Kinge of Bouton had kindlie enterteyned them and sent his owne brother and his sonne in lawe with these caracores to tooe us up. And in the eveninge the two cheife men with a Spaniard renegado came aboard and brought their message from the Kinge of Boutonne, with a letter left by Mr. Welden with the Kinge to any English that should come, hee beinge gone for Banda and Ambonia to trade amongst the Hollanders[1]. Theffect of the message and letter was that the Kinge was desirous to trade with the English, and that the Kinge had sent these caracores to doe me any service that laye in them, and to waite on us till wee came to Botonne, with many other complementes: which beeinge done, I gave to each Arancaye a small present, and they departed to their caracores, appointinge to come att any time that wee shott of a muskett, to tooe our shipp if the winde were calme; for otherwise it was impossible, for when the winde blewe it was right in our teethe.

June 6. This daie in the morninge the caracores came and towed us aboute a league; and then the winde begane to blowe, and wee anchored. Soe did wee daylie either daie or night, for the space of 18 daies that the caracores stayed with us, in which time they towed us aboute 12 leagues, to the wester[2] parte of Babony, where the winde was right against us, but wee had a good place to ankor in, behinde a pointe neere the shore; soe that wee had not above five leagues over to the iland of Boutone[3], and with the winde E.S.E. wee should be able to cease itt. But wee feared that when wee had sett saile, that wee should with the current bee sett over upon the Selebes side, which is very dangerous for sholes, for wee made profe two or three times and were alwaies driven to leewardes that wee could not fetch the place where wee were, and yet in danger of many sholes which lie here under water not seene. Wee passed over one or two where wee had not above 12 foote water, and weare faine to anker in the mayne sea, soe that wee lost our anchour, the winde blowinge hard att S.S.E. and S.E. &

---

1 See note on p. 274.

2 Easter?

3 Muna is probably meant (see note on p. 275).

by South; soe that wee were forced to plie too and againe till the morninge, and with carryinge of a presse saile to keepe up we sprunge the head of our mayne mast; soe that if it had not beene towards daie wee had bene in greate danger. But the morninge appearinge wee went to ancour in our old roade, where the carracores laye waytinge to see whether wee could gett over. But they haveinge spent all their victualls and did live nowe by wild rootes, they concluded that seeinge they could not doe us any more good to staye by us, they would repaire home, and to bringe us refreshinge if in the meane tyme wee gott nott over. And in this time Mr. Billinge, our master, died. And the caracores sett saile for Botton the 23 daie aboute two in the afternoone; by whome I sent our juribassa with a present to the Kinge, to provide us victualls and bringe it us if wee came not to Botonne by the 10th of the next monneth. In this time wee haveinge fitted our maste and all things els, watchinge for a slatch of winde at E. or E.S.E. to carrye us over to Boutonne; and within three daies after it pleased God to send us a pretty gale at E.S.E., beinge the 26 in the morninge, and wee sett saile, and itt contynued six houres little winde, and with much adoe wee seazed Botonne, where wee ankored in 10 fathome water hard aboard the shore, the sea beeinge as a river invironed round with ilands, for after we had shutt in the mouth of the Straicts wee were landlocked. The place that wee seazed was aboute eight leagues within the mouth of the Straicts, where wee landed and stayed till the tyde came; and then by night wee stoode alonge by the shoare by our leade in 14 and 15 fathome hard the shore.

June 27. And the 27 dicto wee ankored at a small towne called Coroney[1], where wee had hoggs, goats and

[1] Valentyn mentions Coroni as a town on the Buton side of the Straits, three or four Dutch miles from the North Cape.

hens brought aboard with other refreshinge. The Kings sonne in lawe was signior of this towne, whoe sent us the hogges. From this place wee departed, takinge advantage of every tide; and the 30th our pilott of little skill would needs double the pointe of a reach on the other shore, [and] brought our shipp upon a corall banke; butt havinge a stiffe gale she broke thorough, and passed without any hurte, God be thanked, beeinge att nine att night. And beinge past this shole, the winde comeinge large, wee ankored on the other side of Bottonne; and the next daie wee passed annother towne called Lambello[1], where the Kinges brother is signiour; butt wee passed forward, haveinge winde and tyde with us. At night wee anchored within pistoll shott of the shore, haveinge passed this daie, being the first of Julie, many shoales and small ilandes, beinge a large channell neere Lambello. But nowe wee come to the norwest of the Straicts, which is not above a cables length broade, and att many places lesse, and noe ground to anker, the land seeinge [beinge?] very high on both sides; at the mouth whereof wee anchored neare a small iland to staie for the tyde. And aboute ten at night, the force of the tyde beinge come, our anchour came home; soe thatt our shipp did drive thorough the narrowe straightes after 1½ a league an hower, for before midnight wee were passed and weare neare Boutoune, where, as soone as wee found ground, wee anchored in 27 fathome. The Kinge haveing understandinge that wee weare come soe neere, not thinkinge wee had past the narrowe gutt, sent us a pilott to bringe us thoroughe, for Mr. Welden, beinge nowe come from Banda, wrote a letter in the Kinges name that wee should not putt thorough without the pilott,

June 30.

Julie 1.

[1] There is a mountain called Lambolo in about the position indicated, but the town seems to have disappeared.

for that there weare many dangers. But it came too late, for wee weare by Gods providence safelie passed in a very darke night, seeinge nothinge butt the high cliffs on both sides[1], towinge with our boate to keepe the shipps head from thwartinge.

Julie 3. And the next daie wee ankored before the towne of Botoune, aboute ten in the morninge; where presentlie the Kinge sent his biggest carracore, called the English caracore[2], with his brother and many other of his cheifest Arancayes to bid us in the Kinges name welcome to his towne, desiringe mee, when I pleased, to come aland; I should be hartilie welcome. Soe I promised that the next morninge I would, God willinge, see the Kinge; with which awnswere they retournd, and presentlie the Kinge sent a present of fresh victualls, as goats and other refreshinge.

Julie 4. And the next daie the Kings brother with dyvers Arancayes came to the waters side, stayeinge my landinge to conducte mee to the Kinge; which I perceiveinge, made the more hast. And att my landinge they brought me to the towne where the Kinge laye, which is aboute a mile from the waters side on the topp of a hill; where I stayed not longe before the Kinge came forth with a good guard before him, with their swords and targetts[3] and head peeces marchinge with a drom before them, the Kinge havinge carryed before him a manner of a crowne, many of his Arancayes followinge him, and Mr. Welden came neere to him to grace him before mee.

---

1 Cp. Clayborne's notes in *Purchas*, i. 455: 'Hee that goeth through [this strait] must take his tyde with him to drive him through, for (lightly) there is never any wind there, the land is so high over the masts on both sides.'

2 Probably the one described by David Middleton (*Purchas*, i. 226), manned by 400 soldiers, besides 100 rowers, and armed with six brasse guns.

3 Shields.

Where after many complements he tooke me by the hand and led mee to the towne howse, where hee had a carpett spred ; where wee conferred aboute our comeinge to his countrye, shewinge himselfe to bee very joyfull that wee were come into his country, sayinge that of longe time hee had desired the freindshipp of the English and nowe hee had his desire to see an English shipp, entreatinge mee to leave some of our people with a factory in his countrye, sayinge that he would build us a faire howse upon his owne charge. Butt I perceiveinge that the leaveinge of a factorie would bee onelie a charge to the Worshipfull Companie, not havinge any trade thatt would countervaile the charge, I excused the matter for this time, promisinge that the next monsone we would, God willinge, be better fitted to leave a factorye ; for at present wee were bound to Macassar, where wee weare to leave a factorye, and we had not men sufficient to leave in both places. Besides, wee were to goe for Benjarmassen and Saccadana, which if wee lefte here a factorye wee were not able to accomplish ; prayinge him to excuse us for this time, butt if itt pleased him to seeke to drawe some trade to his countrye of cloves, mace, sanders wood[1] and such like against the next yeare, there should be a factory lefte as hee desired. Then hee desired to leave two or three men in the country, that he might bee certaine that hee should heare from us againe ; otherwise he much doubted ; sayinge that such victualls as the countrie did afford should cost them nothinge. I thanked him very kindlie, and I would thinke upon itt ; and with this hee arose and carried mee to Mr. Weldens house, wher I gave him a small present. Then hee lefte us and departed to his owne howse, from whence hee sent us store of victualls such as the countrye afforded, as henns, fish, rice and ounes[2],

[1] Sandal wood.

[2] A mistake for 'ombis' (see p. 291).

which is a roote as good or better then turnups, which is their comon bread that they eate, and is better then rice, for our men would rather eate it then rice. And after dinner he retourned to Mr. Weldons howse, where he kindlie tooke his leave of mee, willinge Mr. Welden to bringe us to see his howse before wee went abourd. Soe after I had veiwed his howse and his storehowse where his ordinance laye, which is some 14 small peeces, some brasse, some iron, I repayred towards the waters side, accompanied with the Kings brother and many Arancayes; where I found a great present of ombis and henns which the Kinge had sent. Alsoe I sawe an Italian which the Kinge had enterteyned, whoe had taken upon him to cure the Kinges eldest sonne, whoe had of longe time bene distracted of his witts; to whome I said thatt itt was dangerous to take upon him such a cure, which if he channced to dye under your hand itt will be hard for you to escape with your life. To which he awnswered that he hoped within two daies to see him well, for that this night he was to give him a medicine which would cure him; otherwise, said hee, I would goe with you to the waters side. I bid him looke well to his patient, for that it stoode him more upon then to goe with mee; and soe he departed.

Julie 5. And in the morninge I sent the boate to bee trymmed; and some of our men went upp to see Mr. Welden, where they found the Italian cutt in peeces, for that hee had given the Kinges sonne a potion of opium with wine, that he slept his last; and in the morninge the Italian was hewen in peeces by the Kinges sonnes[1]; and our people beeinge present asked leave to burye him, which was grannted; and this daie in the

[1] Purchas relates this incident briefly in his *Pilgrimage* (ed. 1626, p. 608), on the authority of Martin Pring. It is not, however, mentioned in the published journals of the latter.

eveninge Mr. Welden came aboard with a message from the Kinge; that was that he could not visitt me with some present because his eldest sonne was poysonned by an Italian, that had taken upon him to cure him of his disease and had pawned life for life; and therefore his sonnes had slaine him. Wherefore he was very sorrye that itt should soe happen in my time of beeinge there, in reguard that hee was a Christian; but knowinge that he was none of our nation, he hoped that it was noe offence to mee, for that if hee had not granted his sonnes to have slaine him, he should by them have bene in danger of his owne life for soe little esteeminge of his eldest sonnes life; and they made the more haste in executinge of him, because he was brought thether by the Hollanders, with whome the Kinge att present was at varyance aboute hanginge of a negro, beeinge a Moore[1]. The cause was this, as the Kinge told mee: that this negro had served the Hollanders as a Christian, and after att Banda fled with some 12 Hollanders to the Bandoneses and turned all Moores; soe there was order given by the Generall, wheresoever they mett any of these men they should presentlie hange them. This blackmore by channce came to Boutonne and served the Kinge, butt kept himselfe from the Hollanders sight, the Kinge not knowinge of whatt had formerlie passed. Butt not longe after, the Kinge of Makassar sent an embassadour to the Kinge of Bottonne, and the Kinge in person was to enterteyne him, and entreated the Hollanders that they would honner him soe much as to send those soldiars that they had with their musketts to give a volley of shotte; which they grannted. And this negro beinge with the Kinge, some of the Hollanders knewe him, and in presence of the

[1] The King himself was a Muhammadan. Pieter Both describes him as a man of sixty, very good-natured and sensible, and as well versed in ceremony as any European.

Kinge tooke him prisonner. The Kinge entreated that they would forbeare at that time, and if the negro did owe them ought they should at their owne contents have justice. But the more the Kinge entreated the more earnest they were to carrye him awaye to putt him presentlie to death; whereunto the Kinge said that if they would needs execute him, that they should not doe itt upon his land, but entreated them to carry him aboard there shipp that was in the roade; which they would nott grannte, but before the Kinges face would presentlie doe justice. Then the Kinge desired that they would lett it rest till the next daie, and not doe it before him at the time of his mirthe. Neither of these would they grannte, butt presentlye sett up a gibbett and hanged him before the Kinges face; whereatt the Kinge with all the Arancaies tooke such distaste against them that none of them durst putt their noses out of their forts; for soone after the captaine of the Hollanders, goinge to the towne, was like to be slaine, if his horse legges had nott bene better then his. And this was parte of the cause they soe suddenlie executed the Italian, because he came thether with the Hollanders. Butt shortlie after came the Dutch Generall to Boutoune, to whome the Kinge made complainte of the ill carryadge of the Dutch captaine[1]; and the Generall haveinge had formerlye some thinge against him when he was captaine of the Castle of Bachan, with other matters aboute openinge one of his kinsmans chests which died at Botoune[2], and taken out a chaine of gould and kept it to himselfe, he presentlie tooke the captaine and hanged him upon the same gibbett by the negro, which was yett

[1] See the account given by the Governor-General in his letters to the Directors, printed by Tiele in his *Bouwstoffen*, i. 34, 36. The captain who was hanged was Hendrick van Ray, who had been left behind by Scotte to build forts for the Dutch.

[2] Jacob van der Meyden, the chief of the Dutch factory.

standinge; which did in some sorte satisfie the Kinge of Botoune. Butt the hanginge of the Dutch captaine was soone after my departure, and not while I was there. For after the death of the Kings sonne I could not come any more to talke with him, because they all mourned for him; butt dyvers presents he sent mee daylie of fresh victualls. Soe that I sent him word by Mr. Welden that I was to departe, if he would comand any service.

Julie 8. Soe the 8th of Julie, in the afternoone, I sett saile from Boutoune, with the winde E.S.E., which carried us cleare from the iland before night.

Of the Countrye of Boutoune.

The Hollanders have here in Boutoune two little fortes, where they keepe aboute 30 souldiars, and have in them both aboute five peeces of ordinance. But I knowe not to whatt end they keepe their forts in this place, for it yeildeth nothinge of itt selfe that is worth the speakinge of[1]; onely, as I could understand by the Dutch captaine, thatt they had greate hopes to make indico on itt, the countrye beeinge apt for itt, and some small quantitie growne upon itt, butt I could see none of itt. The greatest parte of their foode is upon fishe and rootes called ombis[2], which they eate in lieu of rice and bread, and is good either rost or boyled, and is very good foode; our men would rather eate them then rice. This roote doth somethinge resemble a pottato roote. The iland of itt selfe is very pleasannt; and many other ilands joyneinge neere itt, where they have warrs. And this is all their trade, to take slaves and sell them, for these of Boutoune

---

[1] The Dutch garrison was withdrawn before long, partly on this ground and partly because of the difficulty of feeding them.

[2] *Umbi* is Malay for a root. The yam (Malay *ubi* or *uwi*) seems to be here indicated.

are thought to bee the best warriars, both by sea and land, that are in all the countrye neere aboute; and the[y] stand in greate feare of the caracores, wherein the Kinge of Boutoune is stronge.

Of our tedious passadge from Ambonia (sic) to Makassar.

Julie 11. The 11th of Julie, aboute six in the afternoone, wee anchored in the roade of Macassar, within a mile of the towne, where wee found an English juncke, which John Parsons, one of the Seventh Voyage in the Globe, had bought to carrye him to Pottana[1]. There came presentlie of unto us Thomas Britt[2], his companion, whoe enfourmed us of the estate of the countrye.

Julie 12. And the next morninge the Kinge sent mee word that he would come aboard; butt because the messenger sawe that I was goinge aland, he came not, butt three or four Portugalls came aboard us. Butt I perceyveinge that the Kinge came not, I made haste aland with the rest of the factours, where I found the Kinge stayinge my comeinge in one of his houses neere the waters side; where he kindlie enterteyned mee. But there weare soe many Portugalls present that I deferred my conferrence untill some other daie, alledginge that I came at present onelie to visitt him and bringe him a small present, which hee kindlie accepted. And soe I went to the English house, where I dined; and in the eveninge I retourned aboard our shipp.

Julie 13. And the next morninge the Kinge sent three of his kinsmen and the Sabendour aboard our shipp, tellinge me that the Kinge of Tellowe[3], his unckle, was

---

1 Patani, on the eastern side of the Malay Peninsula. Floris had despatched him from thence to Macassar in Oct., 1612.

2 Brett.

3 Tallo, a district to the east of Macassar.

come to the towne, desiringe mee to come aland to speake with him. This man was the Kinges protectour in his minoritie; and therefore the Kinge doth much honnour him, and will doe nothinge without his councell.

Att my comeinge aland I found the Kinge and his unckle both together, with many other Arancayes; of whome I demanded leave to settle a factorie to trade with them, desiringe alsoe a convenyent place to make a howse to laye our goods in; which very willinglie they grannted, and the Kinge himselfe appointed the next daie to come to our ould howse, and there to give us 50 fathome square of ground to build a howse in att our pleasure; but that wee were to observe the customes of the countrye, as the Hollanders and other Christians did; the which I agreed unto. And as I departed, the Kinge, speakinge some Portugues, requested me to remember his unckle with some thinge in the morninge when I retourned.

Julie 14. And the next morninge I retourned aland, and carryed a present to the Kinges unckle. And the Kinge went in person, accordinge to promise, to appointe and measure out our ground, and caused the people which dwelt on the ground to remove farther of, because wee should have none neare for feare of fire. Soe the same daye there were above 20 houses taken downe and carryed awaye, except two or three of the best I bought for our present use; as alsoe some of the cokernutt trees which poore people had planted. The Kinge caused me to give them half a riall a peece. There were in this plott of ground aboute 60 cokernutt trees and many other of divers sorts, which were lefte standinge, very pleasant, and two or three wells of very good water within the yard. There was butt a lane or streete betwixt the Dutch house and ours; butt our plott of ground stoode more convenyent. Presentlie I caused banboos or canes to bee bought and began to hedge in our cirquite, because of landinge our goods;

which beeing done and our howse prepared as convenyently as wee could in soe shorte a time, I beganne to land such goods as I thought would vent in the countrye or the Mullaccas. Soe that in this buysines aboute setlinge of our howse and people I spent 22 daies, untill the third of August, leavinge cheife factour in this place George Cockaine, with Benjamyn Fary[1] to second him, with two or three attendannts.

Of the Countrye of Macassar.

This towne of Macassar is the cheife place upon the Selebis, which lieth in 5 degrees south lattitude[2]. It is a very pleasant and fruitfull countrye, and the kindest people in all the Indias to strangers; and would bee a very profitable place for vent of Choramandell and Guzaratt comodities if the Portugall from Malacca did not furnish them; butt, as itt is, if trade bee contynued in the Mulluccos, it is very necessarie for to furnish our shipps outwards bound with rice and Jore[3] gold in quoine; whereof there is greate store of both and is a good marchandize in the Mulluccas. The countrye of itt selfe doth yeild nothinge but rice; onelie the trade which they have from other places, as the Mulluccas, Banda, and Jore, from whence there is yearlie brought store of cloves, mace, nutmeggs, and sanders wood, which the[y] barter for rice and gould; which commodities they have in former times sould to the Portugalls in trucke of their cloathinge of Choromandell and Guzaratt, which yearlye they use to bringe from Malucca[4] in greate quantitye, for the countrye is greate and

---

[1] Purser of the *Darling* (see p. 244). He was afterwards employed at Patani, Macassar and in Siam, where he died in Sept. 1616. A list of documents handed over by Farie to Jourdain on August 1, 1613, will be found in *Letters Received*, i. 272.

[2] More exactly, 5° 9′ S.

[3] Johor, in the Malay Peninsula.

[4] Malacca.

populous, and this towne doth serve all the rest of the iland.

The Kinge is very affable and true harted towards Christians, very severe in justice towards his owne nation. Yf any offend and hath deserved death, he is brought before him, and with a truncke the Kinge will shute him with a little poysonned arrowe[1]. If he will have him live halfe an houre, till hee come to his howse, he will shute him in the arme or legge, butt if hee will have him dye presentlie he will shute him in the breast neere the harte, and then he falleth downe presentlie before him. Others are presentlie crised[2] without any farther tryall of the cause. The Kinge and manie of his people are very expert with a peece, either muskett or other. Many bricke howses. The towne walled with bricke.

August 3. This daye in the morninge aboute three wee sett saile from Macassar with a little gale of the land, accompanyed with the little juncke belonginge to the Seventh Voyage of the Clove[3], whoe before my arryvall at Makassar weare determyned to stopp at Saccadana and Benjermassem, and to that purpose had provided a pilott, as they thought sufficient, to carry them to those places; wherefore I putt in three of our men into the juncke,

---

[1] The *sumpitan*, or small arrow blown through a tube, was the chief missile in use before the introduction of firearms. The arrows were often poisoned, and the old travellers tell terrible stories of their deadliness. Herbert, for instance, in his account of Celebes, says: 'The men use long canes or truncks (cald Sempitans), out of which they can (and use it) blow a little pricking quill, which if it draw the lest drop of blood from any part of the body, it makes him (though the strongest man living) die immediately. Some venoms operate in an houre; others in a moment, the veynes and body (by the virulencie of that poyson) corrupting and rotting presently' (ed. 1638, p. 329). On the other hand Crawfurd (*Descr. Dict.*, 442) states that the most powerful of these vegetable poisons, even when fresh, would not kill a dog under an hour, and that probably few human beings have lost their lives by such means.

[2] Killed with a creese (*krīs*).

[3] An error for 'Globe' (see p. 292).

because I would have as many English as blacks. And the marchant, John Parsons, beeinge somethinge distracted, and taken divers times with a kinde of fallinge sicknes, he beeinge desirous I tooke him into our shipp, because our surgeon should looke to him, untill it pleased God to send us to Sacadana.

Att our settinge saile wee stoode awaye W. and W. & by S., to avoide the shoales of the ilands which lieth W.N.W. from Macassar, beinge seaven in nomber[1], and aboute three and four leagues of, with many sholes and broken grownd aboute them. Wee steered betwixt an iland which lieth to the southward, called Tenakecke[2], and these seven ilands, yet were wee faine to beare upp for one, and alofe for annother, the juncke goinge before us soundinge; notwithstandinge wee passed in 2½ and 3 fathome water on the pointe of some of the sholes. Thus wee contynued till three in the afternoone, bearinge roome for avoydeinge the shoales, and aluffe for annother; and then wee steered with two ilands that are some 12 leagues from Macassar, where wee anchored in 7 fathome water, good sandy ground. These ilands are called Lambaye, two leagues distant the one from the other, S.E. and N.W.[3] There is noe saileinge by night neer Macassar; for when wee came to anker wee might perceive many other shoaldes round aboute us.

Aug. 4. In the morninge aboute six wee sett saile, and steered away N.W. and N.W. & by W. to avoide a shoale which laye betweene the twoe ilandes; and then wee stoode W.S.W. to avoyde annother shole which wee sawe; and passinge neere itt wee found four and five fathome. Beeinge past this shoale, havinge noe ground in 20 fathome, wee steered west till three in the afternoone,

[1] The southern portion of the Spermonde Archipelago.

[2] Tanah Keke.

[3] Apparently Dewakan and Laars Islands.

att which time wee had sight of a very dangerous shoale called the Revatta, which are three rocks like shipps, with shole water three or four leagues round aboute them, beinge W.N.W. of us. These sholes lye from the other twoe ilands from whenc[e] wee came, 14 leagues West and East; and to avoide these sholes wee steered away S.W. and S.W. & by W. And aboute sonne settinge wee had sight of annother iland, W. & by S. of us. Then wee steered awaie West till midnight. Then wee sawe annother iland right ahead some four leagues from the other; soe that I conclude that the wester of these two ilands lies aboute 8 leagues from the taile of the shoales called the Revatta.

Aug. 5. Then our pilott in the juncke steered away N.W. and N.N.W., with a fresh gale at S.E. and E.S.E. Butt wee bare little saile, to lett the juncke keepe ahead us, bearinge a light all night, and wee keepinge our leade goinge every glase. These two ilands which wee passed are called Lusalnua (?). Then the pilott steered awaye W.N.W., thinkinge to see annother iland called Lusaseira; butt haveinge halled too and againe northerly a course could nott see itt.

Aug. 6. But the next morninge we had sight of many high ilands which our pilott knewe nott, because he had missed Lusaseira; soe that nowe he was out of his course, he knewe not where he was. Yet wee steered away W.S.W.; soundinge found 20 fathome, safte grownd. These ilands our pilott John Darbye tooke to bee ilands neere to the coaste of Borneo; butt keepinge our course as formerlye, in the afternoone wee had sight of three ilands more, aboute six leagues to the southward of us. Butt wee could not weather the southermost of them, which bare of us S.S.W.; therefore wee ankored in 15 fathome water, doubtinge whether there weare a passage betweene the iland or nott. and therefore would have day before us.

Aug. 7. In the morninge wee weighed and sett saile; but our consort stayed still att anker untill ten in the morninge, and wee doubtinge some pretended matter amongst them to leave us, wee tacked aboute towards them; and then they sett saile and came up to us, sayinge that they had broken their ruther and they stayed to mend itt before they sett saile. Then wee steered S.W. & by S. and W.S.W., to weather an iland that was to leeward of us; butt haveinge a stiffe gale at S.S.E., the juncke could not beare saile to weather itt, and bare to leeward of all them ilands. Butt wee stoode our course at S.W. & by W. till wee had weathered the ilandes, and then wee steered awaie N.W. to finde againe our consorte; att which time we had sight of many ilands to the southward of us. And in the eveninge wee talked with our consorte, and agreed to steere away N.W. all night. Butt aboute ten a clocke wee sounded and had but 12½ fathome; supposinge to bee neere some iland, wee laye ahull till the morninge.

Aug. 8. Then wee sett saile and steered awaye N.W. And aboute six wee had but 10 fathome water, and presentlye wee had sight of lowe land, not above four leagues of, trendinge W. and by S. And wee stoode alonge the shore, and had from 8 to 10 fathome till noone; and then comeinge neerer the shore wee had but 6 and 7 fathome. This afternoone wee had much winde, that our consort was not able to beare saile to stand upon a tacke, butt was faine to beare roome towards the shore. Soe wee bare roome to speake with them; butt wee durst not come neere, because shee would not steere, haveinge much winde wee feared of bourdinge of them. Then the night comeinge on, wee tooke in our sailes and laye atrye, and the juncke bare towards the shoare before the sea; which wee perceiveinge, aboute eight att night wee sett our forecourse, and stoode awaye South and S.S.W. all night, because wee were neere the mayne land of Borneo. Soe thatt this night wee lost our consorte.

Aug. 9. And this morninge, haveinge lost our consorts companie, wee stood our course W. till ten in the forenoone, in 10 and 12 fathome water; and then wee steered N.W. towards the land, butt could not see the mayne. Then wee steered North to make the land before night, till wee came in 5 and 4½ fathome, butt could see noe land. Therefore we anchored, with a stiffe gale at E.S.E., in a sandye hard ground.

Aug. 10. This daie in the morninge we had much winde at S.E., thatt with much paine wee weyed our anchor and steered away West to gett into deeper water; and before noone wee had 10 and 12 fathome. Then wee stoode againe to make the land att N.N.W.; and aboute three in the afternoone wee had againe sight of land, right ahead us aboute five leagues of; and standinge neere it to see if our pilott, John Darbye, knewe itt, in the eveninge wee perceived a deepe baye, the land bearinge of us S.W. & by W. Butt our pilott knewe not wher hee was. Wee had nowe 6½ fathome, the sea as thicke as pudle; and beeinge neere night wee came to anchor a league of the shore. Butt the ground beeing very softe our anchor would not hold, havinge a greate corrent settinge into the baye; therefore were faine to shue annother anchour[1] and lett it fall; where wee rid all night with two anchours ahead.

Aug. 11. And this daie aboute five in the morninge wee sett saile, and stoode upon a tacke to the offinge S.S.W., to double the pointe of the land. Wee had 13 fathome water till eight; then suddenlie wee fell into 5 and 4 fathome, some four leagues of the land, butt as wee stoode to the

---

[1] This was done by covering the palms with broad triangular pieces of thick plank, the purpose being to give a greater resisting surface and thus secure a better grip.

offinge wee had againe 10 and 12 fathom oze ground hard by. Discerninge the land upon the decke, I perceiveinge our maister to bee unwillinge to putt any neerer the land, he tellinge me that the whole company would nott consent to putt any more soe neere soe dangerous a coast; whereupon I called all of them to knowe if itt weare soe; which they all denied, sayinge that the maister had made itt of himselfe because he was not willinge to adventure any further, and that they were willinge to doe whatt I would command them. Whereupon I called our pilott, and asked him whatt hee thought of the matter. He awnswered that, God willinge, within two daies wee should finde Sacadana, hee thinkinge that the baye where wee were at anchour was the baye of Benjermassem. Soe itt was concluded to stand with a shorte saile all night, and in the morninge to beare to the land to make it certaine.

Aug. 12. This daie in the morninge aboute six wee steered towardes the land at N.W. till noone; and when wee came within four leagues of the land, wee had from seven to five fathome. Then wee steered W. & by S. and W.S.W., the wester land that wee could perceive bearinge W.N.W. of us; and when we had brought the pointe of the land north of us, wee sounded and had from eight to ten fathome; our pilott affirminge that it was not the pointe that goeth into the Baye of Sacadana, sayinge that he knewe that it laye W. and N. from that pointe eight leagues. Butt I bid him looke well on his reckoninge and he should finde that wee had runne the full length; thatt if itt were the pointe of Sacadana, if wee once past it there were noe beatinge up againe to itt. He affirmed that before night wee should see annother pointe, which was the pointe of Sacadana. I would have had him to stand some thinge neerer the shore to take better notice of itt, butt he thought himselfe sure. Soe that wee stoode awaye west till sonne settinge with a stiffe gale, in which time wee runne at least ten leagues, butt we could see noe more land to the westwards; which when he perceived he confessed him selfe to bee in an errour; notwithstandinge he would not confesse that the head land that wee had passed was the cape goinge into the Baye of Sacadana; for that, said he, there are secreete markes which I noted that I could not see. Whereto I replied that he could not well discerne any markes except he had gone neerer the shore. But to conclude, he knewe that wee weare past the pointe, and that it was nowe in vaine to beate up against wi[n]de and tide, and our time which was by Sir Henry Middleton limitted was neere expired, and by a generall voyce there was noe hope of gettinge Sacadana in longe time, the maister, pilott, and marriners all unwillinge to beate it upp; which unwillingnes of them, and unskilnes of the pilott, and our time shorte which wee had to staie, all which considered, with a generall consent wee stoode our course towardes Bantam. Then wee brought our tacks aboard and stoode S.S.W. and S.W. & by S.; which was our course till wee fell with the coast of Java, which was the 15th of August. Aboute noone wee had sight of the highe land neere Jappara, aboute 50 leagues to the eastwards of Bantam. Soe wee kept our course alonge the shore, in 15 and 20 fathome, and when itt fell calme wee anchored. Soe that the 18th, aboute two in the afternoone, wee anchored in the roade of Bantam. And this daie wee mett with a fisher boate whoe tould us that our Generall, Sir Henrie Middleton, was dead[1].

Aug. 18. I arryved at Bantam from the Mullucas or Ambonia in the Darlinge, not knoweinge any thinge of the layinge up of the Trades Encrease; onelie wee had an incklinge by a fisher boate of the death of the English

---

[1] According to Floris (*Marine Records*, xiii.) Middleton died on May 24, 1613, 'mooste of hartesore.'

Generall. But approachinge neere to the Roade, wee might discerne the Trade to ride neere the shore, which seemed much for soe greate a shipp; butt cominge to anker within call of them, in 14 foote water, wee might easilie perceive that shee was aground[1]. Wee hailed them, butt could have noe awnsweare; neither could wee perceive any man sterringe hir ordinance (the most parte

[1] On Aug. 25, 1613, Capt. Best at Tiku heard from a Chinese junk which had been at Bantam 'the death of Sir Henry Middleton, with the losse of most of the men of the *Trades Increase*, and maine mast which brake with forcing her downe to carine her, and that now she was gone from Pulo Panjan to Bantam; that three hundred Chineses dyed in working on her' (*Purchas*, i. 465). About a month earlier Floris (*vide supra*) was informed that the ship 'lyeth a grounde att Bantam withoute maste, with 33 men, the greateste parte being sicke. The shipp is doubbled on the one syde, butt not on the other. In the sayde shippe are deceased some 200 Englishe men and more Chinesians.' John Milward, on reaching Bantam in February, 1615, learned that 'the *Trades-increase* beeing brought on ground on Pulo Penjohn, all her men died in the careening of her; and afterwards it stood them in 500 ryalls of eight a day to hire Javans, of whom 500 died in the worke before they could sheath one side; so that they could hire no more men, and therefore were inforced to leave her imperfect, where shee was sunke in the sea, and after set on fire by the Javans. The Chineses also reported that the Devill appeared on Pulo Penjohn Iland, signifying his offence that the Chineses would undertake such a businesse on his ground and give him nothing (for they were the workemen); whereupon one of the chiefe Chinese carpenters came to Sir Henry Middleton and reported it, desiring to have a buffolo for sacrifice; who denyed, yea, forbad him when hee would have done it at his owne charge, esteeming the want thereof cause of their evills' (*Purchas*, i. 526). As regards her ultimate fate Peyton tells us (*ibid.*, 533) that she 'was fired twice by the Javans and by our people quenched; but the third time fired in so many places at once that industry could not save her.' This appears to have happened in October or November, 1614, for Jourdain and his colleagues at Bantam, writing on January 2, 1615, give the date as 'aboute 2 monethes past.' They go on to say: 'Shee was fired by night sodenly from stemme to starne, that none could come neere to quench it; which wee supose was done of purpose by the Javas, because formarly shee hade bene sett on fire twice and by Godes healpe wee quenched it againe; which nowe was onpossible to doe, because shee was (as wee supose) laid all fore and aft with this country pitch; otherwise shee could not have so sodenly taken fire; which wee suspect was done by the better sort of Javas by the instigation of a renegado Spaniard which is turned Moore, putting them in the head that in tyme shee might serve in lieu of a castell. She was burnt in one night close to the watter; and what was remayning of her, itt is sould for 1050 rials, as per account maye appeare' (*O. C.* 226).

thereof mounted). I saluted them with three peeces, but noe awnswere, nor signe of English coulours, neither from the shipp nor from the towne. And whereas I had the boate halled up to have gone presentlie aland, I caused them to forbeare untill I sawe further from the shipp or shore, causinge all our ordinance to be fitted and all thinges in readines, doubtinge thatt the James[1] (after the death of Sir Henrie Middleton), knowinge of the greate store of wealth thatt was in her, had betrayed their men and taken the shipp, and had secreetlie sett men aboard her to betraye us. And the rather I suspected this treason because I could nott see any signe from the shore from our English men; and the Hollanders flagge abroade hoysed and strooke twice, which I supposed to be a signe made us of some evill pretended by the Javas. Whereupon I shott annother peece for a boate, with determinacion nott to goe aland untill I had certaine notice from thence. But within a shorte space I perceived a proa cominge of the shore; wherein came Edward Langley[2], Christopher Luther[3], Nathaniel Corthorpe[4], and Thomas Harwood[5], all of them like ghostes or men fraighted. I demanded for the Generall and the rest of our freindes in particuler; soe that I could not name any man of noate but was dead, to the number of 140 persons; and the rest which were remayneinge, as well aland and aboard the Trade, weare all sicke, these four persons beinge the strongest of them, whoe were scarce able to goe on their leggs; to whome I awnswered that it seemed they weare

[1] A misreading for 'Javas.'

[2] Factor in the Sixth Voyage. He died at Bantam not long after Jourdain's arrival.

[3] As will be seen later, he accompanied Jourdain in the voyage for Masulipatam. Not long after he sailed for England, but died at the Cape on the way.

[4] The future defender of Pulo Run.

[5] See p. 239.

very weake that they would or could not vouchsafe to shewe noe signe from the land nor shipp. But Luther whispered me in the yeare and told me that they did[1] greatelie care for my comeinge aland, and that they weare not determined to receive mee as principall marchannt, notwithstandinge Sir Henrie Middletons order. Whereunto I replyed little, butt made haste aland, well perceiveinge that their sicknes was not the onelie cause that they shewed noe coulours. And comeinge aland, George Ball[2] and Richard Wesbie[3] mett me and desired mee to goe into their house, which in courtesie (their howse beinge in the waye) I did, not knowinge of any civill warrs which was betwixt the two houses. But this was displeasinge unto the upper house, whereby they intended a cause to picke a quarrell; butt heare I staied not longe but went to there upper house, desiringe Mr. Ball and the rest of the marchannts to accompanie me thether, nott makinge them acquainted of any doubt of receyveinge mee as cheife factour; but boldlie comeinge in, I might soone discerne their pretence[4] by my cold enterteynement. Robert Larkin[5], not able hardlie to stand on his leggs, was there cheife, and in that place presented him selfe; which I well perceiveinge, demanded him for Sir Henries will and whatt order he had lefte for the disposinge of the Worshipfull

---

[1] 'Did not' is evidently meant.

[2] He had succeeded to the charge of the Bantam factory of the Eighth Voyage on the death of Camden. When at the end of March, 1617, George Berkeley (Jourdain's successor) died, the post of chief of the united factories fell to Ball, who held it until relieved by Jourdain in November, 1618. In 1621 he was recalled on account of his private trading, and an action entered against him in the Star Chamber for 70,000*l.* The case appears to have been still proceeding at the time of his death, which was about the beginning of 1625.

[3] Richard Westby was also a merchant of the Eighth Voyage. In the autumn of 1615 he established an English factory at Jambi, on the eastern side of Sumatra. There he remained for three years, and was then murdered by the Dutch (*O. C.* 720, and *Purchas*, i. 676).

[4] Intention. [5] See p. 243.

Companies affaires. Whereunto he awnswered thatt Sir Henry made noe will; butt for the buysines, he had lefte it whollie to his disposinge, and that he had a writinge (which he knewe not where it was) which tended to that purpose. Whereunto I replyed that if there [were?] any such signed by him, if itt pleased him to shewe itt me, it would satisfie mee. Hee awnswered that if I would staie to supper he would seeke itt out and shewe it mee. I tould him upon that condition I would staie till night, entreatinge him to seeke for it by that tyme, and in the meane tyme I would walke to see the towne.

In the eveninge I returned with George Ball and the rest of the factours of the other house, entreatinge them to staie with mee to heare whatt passed; which they weare loth to doe, in reguard that there was greate enmytie betwixt them ever since the death of Sir Henry. Butt att supper Robert Larkin came not, but sent his deputye John Williams[1], of whome I demanded for the writinge; whoe peremptorilie awnswered, vizt. What hast thou to doe to demand any writinge of us, whoe are the Companies factours, and thou a newter? That Sir Henry had wrongd them and the Companie in placeinge mee and puttinge out those to whome it fell by lott or right, and that they were to call accompt from mee of what was in my hands, and that I had nothinge to doe with them; with manie other fowle wordes, which I could not well brooke, butt gave them the like awnswere; insomuch that growinge into greate wordes, Larkin, haveinge lost his paine and sicknes, came runninge forth like a madman, askinge for the bilboes, threatninge that if I would not begone out of his house (as he tearmed itt) he would sett mee into them. Whereat I laughed to see the world soe much altered;

[1] A merchant of the Sixth Voyage. In the autumn of 1613 he was despatched in a junk to take charge of the factory at Sukadana, but died on the way.

but to avoide farther inconveniences I departed and went aboard the shipp to pawse better on the matter, with determination to retourne againe the next daye to see if I could finde them in a better humour.

Aug. 19. The next morninge, accompanied with the rest of the marchannts of the lower house belonginge to the Eighth Voyage, I retourned to the howse, requiringe Robert Larkin and the rest quietlie to delyver up the keyes of the warehouses and mony with account unto mee, accordinge to Sir Henry Middletons order. But they, beeinge armed with guns, halberts and swordes, came out against me as in defiannce, sayinge that they knewe mee not for cheife factour, neither should I have any thinge to doe in thatt buysines; John Williams runninge att mee with his naked sword that I was faine to putt the pointe thereof backe with my hand; which if he had bene stronge, he might have slaine mee. Butt I perceiveinge whereto this matter might growe, and that itt would be a greate scandall to our nation to fall together by the eares, I entreated them that patientlie wee might conferre of the buysines, and that they would laye aside their armes; which after they were pacified, I desired once againe to see Sir Henries writinge for my owne discharge with the Worshipfull Companie att home; that if itt weare his deede, I had noe more to saye in the matter; and if they would not shewe itt mee, that they would give mee a discharge under their hands that they had by force putt mee of from the place of cheife factour. If neyther of these they would consent unto, I craved witnes of the standers by to signe to a writeinge which I had drawne to thatt effect. As for the first, he shewed a writeinge framed by his owne hand to the admittinge of Robert Larkin to be cheife, but not signed by Sir Henrie, butt had taken two witnesses of the raskally sorte to signe itt, sayinge that Sir Henry had affirmed itt by sayinge: Lett itt bee soe, not an hower before hee died. But they did not stand much upon this writinge, because they knewe it to bee falce, as the same witnesses affirmed afterwards, sayinge that it was framed before Sir Henrie died, butt hee would not signe itt; therefore they entreated these two parties to sett their hands to itt after Sir Henrie was dead, and had made a scratch for Sir Henries name. Therefore Larkin would not suffer mee as much as looke on itt, sayinge that it was sufficient he had itt to shewe. Neither would they give mee any writeinge that they putt mee from the place per force. Whereupon I entreated George Ball, Richard Wesbye, William Shepperd[1], Cassarian David[2], John Beaman[3], Nicholas Bangham and John Parsons to bee witnes of what hath in trueth passed in this matter; all whose firmes[4] I have to a writeinge to the tenour aforesaid; which beeinge done I departed for this time.

Within two daies after they sent for mee, desiringe to speake with mee. I awnswered thatt, seeinge they had thruste mee out of the Worshipfull Companies house, I would not retourne thether; butt if there were any occasions which concerned the Companies buysines, I would come to conferre with them att any other house. Soe they appointed to meet mee at a Chinaes howse; where

[1] Apparently he had come out in the Ninth Voyage. Later he got into trouble with the Company for private trading.

[2] A factor of the Eighth Voyage. He was afterwards sent to Sambas in Borneo, and thence proceeded to Sukadana and Banjarmassin. In the spring of 1618 he was despatched with two ships to relieve the English garrison at Pulo Run, but was attacked by the Dutch and forced to surrender.

[3] This seems to be the John Beamon, Beamond, or Beaumont mentioned by Saris as being at Bantam in November, 1612. Later on we find him at Achin and Tiku, and then chief of the English factory at Luhu. He was one of those seized and tortured by the Dutch at Amboyna, but was pardoned after being sentenced to death, and got safely back to England.

[4] Signatures.

they beganne to seeme very sorrowfull of what passed, desiringe mee to come to the house, protestinge greate kindnes. But to the matter, they desired to knowe the best course whether[1] to send the Darlinge, seeinge they had soe much goods and mony lyinge by them. I awnswered that Sir Henrie had determyned to send her at her retourne from Ambonia to Massapotan[2], which I thought was the best course, seeinge shee had alreadye some cloves aboard, which was a principall comoditie for that place; besides they had much purselane[3] lyinge by them and other comodities which would make up a good cargason; all which they lyked very well. And the next daie they beganne to trym upp their China comodities, as purselane and silks, to send in her, with greate protestacions of love and freindshipp; for they cared not whether, nor what they gave mee, soe I would not staie in Bantam to trouble them; and I, as much desirous to be rid of their companie, made as much hast as might bee to fitt our shipp to receive such goods as they would laye into her. Soe that by the 19th of September wee had all things in the shipp except our water, which wee could not fitt our selves well, because the most parte of our caske was rotten, and never a cooper left to tryme itt; soe wee tooke the best of whatt was aboard, as likewise ashore, havinge one which had little skill to trymme itt; but howsoever wee must make a shifte with such as wee had. Soe that we had all things aboard by the 20th of September att night, our cargason beinge in all to the value of 2000 rialls of eight, in China comodities, cloves and monnye.

---

[1] Whither.

[2] Masulipatam, on the Coromandel Coast, where an English factory had been established by the merchants of the *Globe* (Seventh Voyage) two years before.

[3] Porcelain. Bantam was then the great centre for the purchase of Chinese products.

Of our voyage from Bantam to Massapotan.

Sept. 20. Att night we sett saile from Bantam towards Massapotan. And beinge without the Straicts, wee found the winde to hange betweene the N.N.W. and the N.W., soe that wee could not gett alongst the shore of Sumatra; havinge beate too and againe aboute ten daies, and could not gett two degrees to the northward; soe that wee determined to gett of to the southward to seeke a winde to carye us alonge. Butt consideringe the badnes of our caske, I caused the maister to make search whatt water wee had lefte before wee putt of from the land to sea; for that if wee once putt of, there was noe hope of water any where untill wee came to Massapotan. The maister havinge dilligently searched and sounded the caske, found most parte of our water leaked out, soe that there was not remayneinge in the shipp above five butts of water; wherefore wee determined to beate itt upp a little longer to gett Tecoo or Pryaman or Endrapura[1], to gett water before wee putt of. Soe thatt by the 22th of October wee came into Tecoo Roade, havinge butt two hoggesheads of water lefte; yett wee had gone to hard allowance, because our caske did leake out more then wee spent.

Oct. 22. Nowe cominge neere to the ilandes of Tecoo, we might discerne two shipps in the Roade; butt night cominge on, wee could nott gett the Roade, but weare faine to anchour a league to the offinge. And aboute ten att night there came of a boate sent from the Dragon by Generall Best, whoe was come from Achin, with the Dragon and Hosiander[2]. Soe the nexte morninge I went

[1] Indrapura, on the west coast of Sumatra, in 2° S.

[2] '*Oct.* 22. This day the *Darlinge* came into the Roade of Teccoe unto us, bounde for the Coaste of Carrmendell, her captaine Mr. John Jourden, her merchants Christopher Luther, Nicholas Bangam, the master Thomas Herode; with whome when I had conferred, I called a counsell, and upon divers consideracions changed the purpose of her voyage and concluded her retourne agayne for Bantam' (Capt. Best's journal in *I. O. Marine Records*, no. xv.).

in with the shipp within the ilands, where the other shipps were att anchour; where I understoode thatt since our comeinge from Bantam the Hosiander had bene there to understand the state of the country, and was retournd the same daie wee anchored to the offinge, they haveinge gott itt up hard aboard the shore of Sumatra in 12 daies, and wee beatinge itt up a whole monneth. Amongst other conference with the Generall, hee tould me thatt hee much wondred thatt wee would proceede to Massapotan att such a time of the yeare; that there was no doings on thatt coast these five monnethes, alledginge thatt he knewe itt for certayne by a Dutch shipp which he mett upon the coaste of Seilan[1], whoe tould them thatt they were putt of from thence by fowle weather, haveinge lost most parte of their anchours on the Coaste of Choramandell, and weare in greate danger. Therefore hee thought itt good that wee should retourne to Bantam in his companie, and there to take some other course concerninge the Worshipfull Companies affaires, which was there, as he understood, ill manadged. Whereunto I awnswered that, for the buysines att Bantam, I knewe very well that it was not as well managed as itt ought to bee; but if itt were onelye aboute that buysines, itt might very well be done without us. And as for the time of the yeare for the Coaste of Choramandell, I told him that the Hollanders had reported falslie unto him, doubtinge that hee had bene bound thether to have hindred them of their trade; for that I knewe itt to bee the principall time of the yeare for that place, and that the Dutch themselves did usuallie depart from Bantam at that time, as likewise the Globe and the James went neere aboute the same time; besides, I had sufficient notice from Guzaratts that were att Bantam, that nowe this next monneth was the cheifest time. All these

[1] Ceylon.

reasons allegd would not suffice, for that our cloves did sticke in his stomocke to have them for his mony upon accompt of his voyage. Therefore he called a counsell the next daie, where it was concluded by his reasons before allegd thatt wee should retourne for Bantam, there to settle the Worshipfull Companies buysines in order, and then after to proceed either in that voyage or some other. To this I awnswerd thatt I could not stand against a whole courte; butt withall desired that my reasons for the time of the yeare might bee sett downe in writeinge, as alsoe the conclusion of the courte, and that I might have itt under their handes for my discharge; whereunto they all agreed and the courte ended. Butt the next daie goinge aland with the Generall, I brought him a mallim[1] or maister of a Guzaratts shipp, whoe affirmed before him thatt within one monneth would bee the cheefest time for Massapotan, hee beeinge latelie come from thence, and laye att Tecoo aboute the sale of his comodities which he brought from thence. All this could not satisfie the Generall, the cloves smellinge soe sweete that wee must retourne for Bantam in his companie; and seeinge noe remedy, I was content; and the rather because of setlinge the buysines there in better forme. The Generall lendinge us his coopers to mend our caske; which being ended we sett saile[2] from Tecoo, leaveing the Hosiander there tradinge with the countrye people for pepper. And the 11th of November wee anchored in Bantam Roade with the Dragon and the Darlinge.

---

[1] Arabic *mu'allim*, a pilot or sailing-master. See the quotations given in *Hobson-Jobson*, s.v. 'Malum.'

[2] October 30 (Best's journal). Best notes that during the eleven weeks he spent at Tiku he bought from 115 to 120 tons of pepper and buried twenty-five men, the bulk of whom had contracted disease at Pasaman. He consequently advised that no further attempt should be made to trade at the latter place.

Of my reestablishinge in Bantam by a Generall Court.

After our arryvall att Bantam, beinge the 11th of November as is aforesaid, the Generall forthwith determyned to lade his shipp with the pepper and other comodities that was provided for the Trades Encrease, sendinge for all the English factours aboard his shipp, beeinge Sundaie the 13th[1], advisinge them thereof, as alsoe that hee determyned the next daye (God willinge) to bee aland to conferre with them in a generall courte of marchannts aboute all necessarie buysines that did concerne the Worshipfull Companies affaires; willinge all of them to thinke of all needfull buysines concerninge the same; which speech beinge done they departed; willinge mee to goe aland with them to provide all necessaries for the ladinge of pepper the next daie, and to conferre with the rest of the factours of all needfull matters against his comeinge aland.

Nov. 14. Soe the next daie in the morninge, haveinge begun to send pepper aboard before the breese came, which was till ten of the clocke before noone, the Generall willinge all the marchannts to come together, hee propounded that he understoode of some disorders and controversie that there was betwixt the factors of the Sixth and Eighth Voyages, as alsoe of the other Voyages formerlie, which was of the remaynder lefte by Mr. Joanes deceased[2], and other matters which was better knowne to them then hee could repeate, alledginge the greate disgrace it was to our nation and the Honorable Companie our employars to have soe many houses in one place, seperated both in qualitie and freindshipp, beeinge all as itt weare for one Companie; which was a greate scandall to our nation. Whereunto all replyed that it was very

[1] Best says the 12th.

[2] See note on p. 241.

necessarie that it should be (by his good discreetion) sett in order, sayinge that they were all ashamed that itt should bee soe; desiringe him to ordayne it in better manner; and that it was fittinge there should bee butt one head in the countrye; butt for accompts, every man might keepe them aparte for their particuler Voyages, as itt was ordayned by the Worshipfull Companie, untill farther order from them. All which liked the Generall very well; sayinge that hee was very glad that they weare all soe conformable to good orders. And for the better confirmation thereof hee desired to have all our sayings sett downe in writeinge, signed by us all, that he might shewe it (God sendinge him well into England) to the Honourable Companie, and thatt he had not done any thinge without a generall consent; which writeinge beeinge made and signed by us all, itt was delivered to him. Whereupon hee demanded of them whoe they would have amongst us all to be their heade; to which they generallie awnswered that there was no fitter man then my selfe to remaine there to direct the buysines. Whereunto I excused my selfe, sayinge that I was bound in a voyage of importannce, which was likewise in the Companies buysines, and thatt my yeares in servinge the Worshipfull Companye was neere att an end, and my selfe begininge to growe ould, that my determination (by Gods permittance) was to end this voyage and soe to repaire to my countrie. To the which the Generall replyed, sayinge that he marvelled much that I would seeme to refuse thatt which I had sett my hand unto, to have a cheife factour chosen, beinge the first man thatt had signed, and nowe I would bee the first that should breake itt, being chosen by a generall consent, and none willinge that any other should have the place butt my selfe; some of them affirmeinge thatt if I did not accept thereof they would not staie under any other which was present. By which perswations of the Generall and them all, I was content (although against my will) to take the place untill some other of better understandinge were ordayned by the Worshipfull Companie. Soe that Robert Larkin was ordayned to proceede in the voyage for Mussapotan in the Darlinge, the Generall takeinge out the most parte of the cloves to carry for England, payinge in ready money both for them, the pepper and other comodities belonginge to the Sixth Voyage.

After my reestablishinge in Bantam by Generall Best and the departure of the Dragon, which was the 16th of December, 1613, there aryved the Expedition, wherein was Captaine Newport[1]. The time of the yeare beeinge almost past, I made the more haste to lade her with pepper; soe thatt within 20 dayes after her arryvall she was ready to sett saile[2]. Att which time[3] arryved the Clove from Japan, unexpected by the marchants of the Eighth Voyage which laye att Bantam, beeinge George Ball, Richard Wesby, Cassarian David. Butt when Captaine Sayris perceived that his ladinge was not provided, he much stormed att his marchannts; butt they excused themselves, sayinge that hee gave noe order to provide pepper; they thinkinge thatt he would have spent the monson att the Malaccas aboute buyinge of cloves, because they had hard him saye

---

[1] This was the Twelfth Voyage, under Christopher Newport. An account of it, written by Walter Peyton, will be found in *Purchas* (i. 488).

[2] 'The seventeenth [December] wee brought our ship to an anchor in Bantam Road; where wee presently went ashoare to provide her lading. On the nine and twentieth we made an end of lading our whole complement. The second of January we set saile from Bantam for England...Also this day, as we were going out by Pulo Pan Jan, we mett with Generall Saris in the *Cloave*, come from Japan; for whose letters, and the delivery of foure chests, the captaine cast anchor againe...We set saile once againe for England on the fourth of this present' (Peyton, *ut supra*). By the *Expedition* Jourdain sent a long letter to the Company, but unfortunately it is no longer extant.

[3] January 3, 1614; see *The Voyage of John Saris to Japan*, p. 193.

that the Clove should never goe home laden with pepper; soe that there was nott any pepper ready for his ladinge, nor money to buye itt. Therefore I was faine to helpe them in their neede; although Captaine Saris thought itt to be my duty soe to doe, butt beeinge then of severall Voyages I was att first in some doubt to laye out any money for them; butt consideringe that although itt were for severall Voyages, and the necessitie of the tyme, and the little use thatt I had then for money, I was contente to buye some good quantitye of pepper for them. Soe thatt aboute the end of January she was laden. Butt att the first arryvall of Captaine Saris hee seemed to bee very much moved because I was placed cheife by Captaine Best[1]; and principallye because I had nott come aboard before I knewe whatt shipp itt was, she beinge becalmed three leagues of the Roade of Bantam; therefore I sente George Balle in a proa, and to send me word whatt shee was. Soe thatt Captaine Saris tooke such excepcions att itt that when I came aboard he would scarse vouchsafe to looke on mee, threatninge to carrye mee home. To whome I awnswered that I was not there with my will, butt was more willinge to bee att libertie and goe home then to staie there, if his aucthoritie did extend soe farre as to undoe that which was established by annother Generall. Whereatt he was very angrie, askinge whether I would looke into his aucthoritie. Yea, said I, I am bound to see itt for myne owne discharge. Then after his coller was past he began to bee more milder, and embraced mee, biddinge mee welcome. Soe we contynued ever after greate *amici*[2].

---

[1] He afterwards approved the arrangement and agreed to the concentration of all the merchants in one house, for which the King of Bantam had given a site and promised to erect the building for a present of 1500 rials; see Saris's journal and *Letters Received*, ii. 15.

[2] Saris sailed about the 10th of February, 1614. By him Jourdain sent a letter to the Company, which is printed in *Letters Received*

In February there came to Bantam four China juncks with silks, druggs and divers other comodities. The Dutch made a shewe as if they would have had a consorteshipp with us aboute the buyinge of their comodities betwixt us; butt when they perceived our willingnes to joyne with them, they cunninglye went aboute to buye all from us whiles wee weare treatinge aboute the matter; and in the end broke of from us, each to doe his best[1].

Every yeare aboute the end of February there came to Bantam three, four, five and six juncks from China bringinge divers sorts of comodities as is before mentioned. These juncks remayne in Bantam till the end of Maye or June; then they departe, most parte loden with pepper, beinge shipps aboute 300 tonns or more, which doe carry aboute six, seven, and eight thousand sacks of Bantam pepper, besides divers other comodities, as sanders wood, and much money, which they make of cashas[2] or lead money which they bringe out of China, and carrie rialls of eight out of the countrye for them; soe that, notwithstandinge soe much money as is brought to Bantam yearlie by us and the Dutch, which wee paye for pepper, there is greate scarcitie of money, by reason that the China junckes carrie itt yearlie for China; which the Kinge doth suffer because the China marchannts doe bribe him, which hee is content to take although itt be the overthrowe of his commons.

(ii. 14). In this he lamented that it had proved impossible to send a ship to the Moluccas that monsoon, 'for that they [the natives] did depend much uppon the English this yeare, which nowe they wilbe frustrate of ther hopes...if any shipp had gone this yeare theather ther had bene noe doubt of her lading, and would have kept them in hop[e]s untill better oppurtunytye.' Jourdain, it may be noted, had no control over the various ships, their movements being settled by the respective Generals.

[1] Compare the account given on p. 323; also that in Jourdain's letter to the Company dated January 2, 1615 (*Letters Received*, ii. 276).

[2] On the Chinese coins known as *cash* see *Hobson-Jobson*, s.v., and *The Journal of John Saris*, p. 213.

This Pengran Protectour is uncle to the younge Kinge and doth keepe the Kinge in such awe thatt he is almost afraid to aske money of him for his expence, although hee bee nowe of yeares to governe himselfe, beeinge of 22 yeares of age and hath four wives, besides concubines, and six children by his wives; and the Pengran is soe sparinge thatt he sendeth him 10 rialls of eight att a time, tellinge him that all is for his good and for him, entreatinge him to bee content with a mean expence, and he shall finde the more in his coffers. Thus the Kinge with patience perforce passeth his tyme[1]. This Pangran is very subtile and wise in his owne opinion, takinge noe counsell but of those which must saie and doe as he will; soe that the cheifest Arancayes in the countrye dare not move him of any thinge that is distastfull to him; and therefore hee keepeth neere him two or three China slaves, alias China torne coats, beinge become Mahomatans. These, I say, are his cheife councell and doe direct all his buysines under him. He is very fickle of his word; noe trust to his promise, except itt bee for his profitt; a good justicer where hee may gett any thinge by itt. If any man speake to him aboute anie matter that he doth nott like, he will make noe awnswere, butt begin some other matter to putt you out of itt; and if you urge him to awnswere, he wilbee very angrie and departe from you.

Wee have bene troubled manie times with fire; some yeares, three or four times in a monneth. The houses beeinge of strawe, when itt taketh on fire runneth soe suddenlie from howse to house thatt, if itt bee not prevented by pullinge downe the houses before, itt will within one hower burne the whole parishe or China quarter. Wee

---

[1] Compare what has already been said about the King and the *Pangeran* (Prince) on p. 244. Saris speaks of the latter as 'the Governour Pangran Chamarra, who is as Protector to the King, ruling all, the King being as nobody, though of yeares sufficient' (*Purchas*, i. 353).

have had the upper parte of our warehowses divers tymes burnt and the fire gott within the warehowses, butt by dilligence, after the force of the fire is past, wee have putt itt out without any greate losse, God be thanked. Many times the Javas setts the towne on fire on purpose because they may steale, knowinge itt to be good fishinge in troubled water; and the comon sorte of Javas are very cunninge theeves. Butt nowe there is nott soe greate feare of fire as there was, because there are many howses made with timber and covered with slate, which wee call their fire free houses, because they are not soe apte to take fire as the other[1].

Many other thinges have passed in Bantam in the tyme of my beeinge there, as well concerninge the settinge on fire of the Trades Encrease as alsoe betwixt the Dutch and us, which in breife hereafter followeth.

A true Relation of The Hollanders abuses offerred to our nation in the East Indias since the yeare 1612 [1613], *in the tyme of my beeinge in Bantam and the Mullucaes, vizt.*—

In Anno 1612 [1613], in the monneth of January, they made a fayned shewe of league and freindshipp with Sir Henry Middleton concerninge the buyinge of China comodities, makinge a shewe of agreement to joyne together, thereby to buye all the best sortes of the goods att reasonable rates. and underhand went aboute to gett yt all into their owne handes. Which Sir Henry Middleton

[1] Cf. Edmund Scot's account of the troubles of the English in 1603–05 owing to the frequent fires (*Purchas*, i. 167, 168, 170, 177). A dangerous outbreak in January, 1614, is mentioned in Saris's *Journal* (p. 195); and Jourdain, referring to the same incident, says (*O. C.* 128): 'Wee have bene in great daunger three tymes within ten dayes, the towne beeing burnt; yet (God be thanked) wee have not received any harme, ownly some smale charge in covering the godongs [warehouses] with strawe.'

perceyveinge, sent directlye to knowe their myndes whether they should conclude aboute the fayned agreement; whereunto they replyed that every one was to doe their best for their employers; they haveinge (in this time of parley) gotten the cheifest and best parte into their handes; which afterwardes Sir Henrie Middleton could not gett any butt att highe rates, which was the rayseinge of China comodities that yeare.

In April 1613, my selfe beinge sent by Sir Henry Middleton in the Darlinge for Ambonia[1], cominge to the towne of Hitto, I was well enterteyned by the countrye people. The Hollanders havinge there a factorye, went subtillye aboute to prevent our buyinge of cloves, perswadinge mee not to buye any of the countrye people for raizinge the price, assuringe mee that by their meanes I should buye them better cheape. Butt I, not trustinge their faire wordes, wrought with the people of the countrye to buye their cloves and to settle there a factory accordinge to my comission; which they faithfullye promised mee, notwithstandinge the Hollanders had threatned them to burne their towne and secreetlie went aboute to gett all the cloves which were in the towne of Hitto into there handes, and those that would nott willinglie delyver them, they brake open their doores and tooke them perforce, sayinge that the English should not trade with them: seeinge they had defended them from their enemyes the Portugalls, they should nott sell their comodities to any butt them. Whereupon the Governor of Hitto, havinge formerlye promised us a parcell of cloves, came aboard with many of his Arancayes, entreatinge us to departe, for that the Hollanders had threatned to bringe thither their shipps and to burne their towne and take them prisonners and build their a castle, if they in any sorte gave us enterteyne-

[1] See above, p. 247.

ment; affirminge that if wee would goe over to the other syde, to a place called Lugho, that then they would secreetlie send us whatt cloves they could; urginge us very earnestlie to bee gone, for if wee stayed any longer the Hollanders had sworne to build a castle and keepe them in such slavery as that they should never after bee able to doe us any freindshipp; assuringe us that the next yeare they would provide a parcell of cloves for us, in dispight of the Dutch. All this while the Dutch gave us faire wordes and hope of many cloves, and dealinge thus underhand with the countrye people; which I, seeinge noe hope of any good to be done, and to give the people content, I sett sayle for Lugho, which is aboute three leagues oppositt from Hitto.

Item, I was noe sooner come to Lugho butt five of the cheife comanders of the Hollanders were come in a proa after mee. Butt before their commynge I had bene aland with the Governour, whoe had promised us all kindnes and all the cloves that were in the countrye. Butt as soone as the Hollanders had spoken with him and threatned them as they had done att Hitto, the Governours mynde was soone altered; which I perceyveinge went againe aland to conferre with him, whoe advised mee of the Hollanders threatninges and of their forces, sayinge that our force was nothinge to defend them from the Dutch whome they soe much feared; notwithstandinge he would secreetlie cause those which had any cloves to bringe them aboard our shipp by night; butt to grannte us a factorye he could nott without their good will, which hee knewe they would never grannte. And because wee should see their willingnes to trade with us, hee would send for all the Arancayes or cheife men in the countrye, and they would with one voyce, before the Hollanders faces, avouch that they were the cause, by their threatnings and forces, that wee weare not enterteyned in their countrye, they beeinge all willinge to trade with us as well as with them; which the next daye was effected before them in a publique audience, where the Hollanders denied to come at the first callinge, butt when the Governor and Arancayes sent them word the second time that if they came not to awnsweare they would forthwith grannte us trade with them and leave to build a house to our contentes, they presently appeared. Whereupon the Sabendour, by order from the Governor and Arancayes, made a speech unto them. Theffect vizt. These English men are come to trade with us as freinds, and wee all in generall are content to trade with them as wee doe with all other nations, and to that purpose wee have given them our word to buye and sell with them to our best advantage; butt since your comminge from Ambonia you have charged us not to deale with them on paine of emprisonment, threatninge to burne our towne and build castells in our countrye; and wee knowinge your forces to bee such as they nor wee can resiste, wee doe att present, notwithstandinge our willingnes, deny to give them enterteynement except you will leave yt to our owne discretion, which all in generall are willinge to yeild them quiett trade and freindlie enterteynement. Which words beeinge ended, they all held up their handes, makinge a lowde shoute three times, sayinge: Wee are all willinge to enterteyne the English. Which beeinge ended the Governor said unto mee: You see nowe the willingnes of us to enterteyne you; there wants nothinge butt the Hollanders to saye they will nott molest [us?] for itt; which you in your owne language may demand of them. Which after a little pawsinge I said: Sir President[1], att our laste conference I remember you told mee that you wondred very much that wee would presume to come to a place

[1] By a slip Jourdain here gives Coen a title to which he had not yet attained (see note on p. 323).

which did belonge to you, to trade with a nation that was not willinge to receive us. Whereupon I made this motion to the Governor to knowe the trueth. He haveinge honestlie discharged himselfe in this generall audience, layinge all on your threatnings and forces; which nowe, if itt bee nott as they saye, you maye awnswere them. Whereunto hee replyed nott a word unto them nor us, but satte mute. Soe seeinge I could gett nothinge from them, and after I had given the countrye people thankes for their good will, I departed. And att my departure the people gave againe three showtes, sayinge: Wee desire to trade with our freinds the English.

The same night the Sabendor and other of the Arancayes came aboard, tellinge us that the Hollanders had tould them thatt our countrye could not afford any shippinge for their defence, and that our Kinge was poore and could nott sett forth above six shipps, and such small pinnaces as ours, with many other words of infamye; and thatt they would send for their shipps att Amboynia, thatt if wee went nott awaye the sooner they would either take us or sinke us. Notwithstandinge all these words, they would sell us all the cloves in the countrye, willinge us to send our beame aland to prove with theirs, haveinge agreed with them at 70 rialls per baharre. Soe the next daie I sent the beame and marchannts a mile without the towne, where they had appointed to bringe the cloves; which the Hollanders perceyveinge contynued their threatninges to the countrye people, as likewise to us, sendinge a notifycation requyringe mee to departe, as by the same maye appeare; to which I made noe awnsweare, butt went forward in buyinge whatt I could gett; which in the meane tyme, to put the countrye people and us in feare, they caused two shipps and a pinnace to come to Hitto, threatninge every day to come over to us if wee would not begone. Butt when they perceived thatt wee made little reckoninge of them, they pacientlie stayed there and came not over to us; which made the country people see thatt itt was butt their braggs. And havinge gotten as many cloves as were there to bee had, wee went for Cambello, where likewise they sent their embassadours to prevent us, as they had done att Hitto and Lugho. Notwithstandinge wee had as many cloves as were yett unsould; and soe wee departed and lefte the Hollanders.

Anno 1613 [1614]. The Dutch Generall, Peter Butt[1], havinge made complainte as findinge himselfe agreeved thatt the prizes of China comodities weare soe much raysed that there were noe proffitt to bee made by them, alledging itt to bee our owne faults thatt wee did not agree together and buye the China comodities betwixt us, and make one buyer for the whole, intreatinge mee that I would joyne with their President[2] att the comminge of the China juncks; which I was content to doe, and att their arryvall I sent George Ball to talk with the Dutch President to feele him concerninge what was propounded by their Generall Peter Butt; which att the first motion the said President seemed to bee content to joyne with us and make one buyer for the whole, and take onely such comodities as were fittinge for our countrye and leave the trash upon their handes, which would encouradge them ever after to bringe thatt which was good and not such deceiptfull wares as they did usually bringe. Whereupon it was agreed thatt wee should meete in the afternoone att the Dutch house to drawe writinges betwixt us, as well concerninge China comodities as also to conferre aboute the buyinge of pepper. In which conference the Dutch President beganne to digresse from his former speech, alledginge thatt they were att greate charge with their

[1] See note on p. 247. For the incident itself see above, p. 316.

[2] Coen was made President of Bantam in October, 1613.

soldiars and castells, and that there was noe reason but that they should (in consideracion thereof) have the choise of comodities, seeinge their stocke was greater then ours; alledginge farther that they were to buye the trashe comodities as well as the good, to furnishe the Mulluccaes. To which I replyed that for their castells and souldiars wee had nothinge to doe in itt, onely the matter was to conclude aboute the buyinge of China comodities, to bee equallye divided betwixt us, wee haveinge money to paye for itt as well as themselves and marchants to employe in the buysines as well as they; demandinge further of them what quantitye of the trashe comodities they would buye. To which he awnswered that aboute 6000 riails would serve their turne. To which I awnswered that I would take the one halfe, thatt soe small a matter should nott bee the cause of breakinge our pretended[1] agreement; to the which hee would nott agree, for feare leste wee would send those comodities to the Mulluccaes. Upon which his conclusion was thatt except hee might (in consideracion of their greate charge) have the one-fourth parte of all the Lankin[2] silke to himselfe and after devide the rest equally, he would doe nothinge. Whereunto I awnswered that I wondred much att his proposicion, seeinge that formerlye he made noe question thereof, and that I thought my selfe disparadged to come to their howse to mocke mee in that manner; shewinge that our money was as good rialls as theirs, ourselves nothinge inferiour to them in the knowledge of the countrye manner of buyinge and sellinge; soe that if this were all that he would doe, that each must shifte for himselfe. And soe without many wordes els wee departed. And presently they laied out to gett all into their hands, both good and badd; which I perceiveinge, and haveinge much money lyinge deade,

[1] Intended. [2] Nanking.

I presentlie concluded to buye 50,000 rialls of all kindes of silkes, all the Lankin silke included therein; which was the cause thatt I bought soe much thatt yeare, because [when?] the Chineses sawe the Hollanders to crosse us, they would not sell one without annother. And this yeare the Hollanders bought noe Lankin silke, onely some trashe comodities fittinge for the Molluccaes, and thatt att greate rates; whereatt they tooke very greate discontent, notwithstandinge itt was their owne faults; and seekinge to crosse us some other waye, sent for all the China marchannts of the towne of Bantam and offerred to trust them with a parcell of Choromandell comodities to the valewe of 40,000 rialls of eight, vizt.

The Hollanders, knowinge that wee had store of Choromandell comodities, which came in the James, forthwith sent for all the China marchannts, invitinge them to buye their comodities, to bee paid in newe pepper att eight monneths; thereby to binde all the marchannts of the countrye to them, because they should sell their pepper to noe other. And the better to animate them to take their comodities, they sold better cheape then formerlie itt had bene sold att leaste 50 pro cento; thinkinge thereby not onely to binde all the marchannts to deliver them pepper att the time of the yeare, but alsoe to hinder us in the sale of our comodityes, beinge of the same nature, therby to prevent or discouradge us any more to trade in the like, seeing that there is little or noe gaine thereby if wee sould at those prises and upon trust to those that there is greate doubt of payment. Soe thatt I conclude that they esteemed nott any losse soe as they might prevent our buyinge of pepper and discouradge us from the hopefull trade of Massopotan[1]; which by these wyles

[1] 'Thiere is owinge to the Hollenders above 80,000 rials, and they cannot recover one penney this yeare; which is due to them for cloath which they delivered the last yeare to bee paid in pepper, and sould

they have brought all the people of the Molluccaes subject nott to sell any cloves butt to them, alledging that first they must paye their debts before they will permitt them to sell to any other; and this they maynetaine by their force of shippinge, and have sought by all meanes to bringe the like subjection att Bantam; which they will bringe to passe if itt bee not in tyme prevented.

Anno 1615 there was sent twoe shipps for Amboyna, vizt. the Concord and the Thomasin; where meetinge with the Dutch, they sought by all meanes to debarre them of trade, as formerlye they had done[1]. Notwithstandinge our people were very well receyved [at] Cambello and Lugho, where they had a house given them to leave a factory. And att Cambello the castle was given us for a house, the better to live free from the Hollanders. Which when the Hollanders had newes thereof, they repayred thether with their shipps, threatninge the people of the countrye in such wise that they caused our marchannts to gett them out of the countrye and delyver them to the Hollanders; where comminge aboard there shipp the Generall of the Dutch caused them to bee laid in irons, and kept them there with bread and water untill they came to Cambello, where findinge the Concord they delivered them. And when they perceyved our coullours to bee sett on the castell, they never lefte shuteinge with their ordinance untill they had throwne itt downe, which

itt att such a lowe rate only to crose us in the sale of our Cormandel cloath. Knowinge that wee had store of the *James* goodes and the *Globes*, they presently gave out goodes to whome would buye. That which formerly worth 10 rials per corge they sould for 5 rials and 4 rials; and I thincke they will neaver be paid for the most parte. This they did in pollozie, thinckinge that, wee seinge shuch smale profitt by that sorte of goodes, wee would venture that way noe more; which some of them hath not lett to speake that they will beate us out of that trade and make us wearye of itt' (Jourdain to the Company. Dec. 1615: *O. C.* 330).

[1] For this incident consult the papers in *Letters Received*, iii., particularly the preface, p. xxxi.

was againe sett up three or four tymes, they alwaies contynueinge shuteinge att itt untill that our men which were in itt, aboute four in number, were inforced to leave itt; and the countrye people, the best parte of them, for feare of the Dutch ranne into the mountaynes, where they contynued a longe time in enmytie with the Hollanders. And if any of our marchannts went to conferre with any of the countrye, they had alwayes some of the Dutch to dogge them, and would (*sic*) to listen and heare whatt was spoken; and demandinge them the reason, they awnswered that they must doe itt, beinge soe comanded by their Generall. Our people, seeinge themselves to bee too weake for them, durst not withstand these inormyties, knowinge that the Dutch did itt onely to picke a quarrell. As alsoe wheresoever our shipps went they sent their shipps after to watch them because they should not conferre with the countrye people.

Alsoe the same yeare haveinge sent a small pinnace[1] for Banda, our pinnace was halled aland. The maister, John Alexander[2], beeing aboard, the Hollanders came by force and tooke him out of his barke, and carryed him into the mountaynes to shewe them where the Bandoneses weare, carryinge him with his hands bound, with four Japuneses after him with their swords drawne, thatt if hee offerred to goe awaye they should cutt of his head. Thus they carried him into the woods, where the Bandoneses mett with them and slewe many of the Dutch, and would not meddle nor shute att the maister. Butt the Hollanders, perceiveinge themselves in danger, retourned with some losse of men; and by the way did

[1] The *Speedwell*, which accompanied the *Concord*.

[2] A master's mate on the *Hosiander*, but promoted in January, 1615, to be master of the *Speedwell* (*Letters Received*, ii. 285). For his ill-treatment by the Dutch see *ibid.*, iii. 288, 293, and Peyton's journal (*Purchas*, i. 533, and *Brit. Mus. Addl. MSS.* 19276).

buffett the maister, and when they came to the waters side they threwe him into their boate bound hand and foote, treadinge on him in their boats hold, havinge taken from him his cloathes from his backe and other things which hee had aboute him. And beinge brought aboard before the Dutch Generall[1], he made complainte of his hard usage and of his things taken from him; whereunto the Generall replyed sayinge: Itt is well thatt thou haste escaped with thie lyfe. And this was all the recompence thatt he could have, the Generall revilinge him in most outragious manner.

The yeare followinge, anno 1616, the Dutch peremptorilie sent a message to our house att Bantam, requiringe us not to presume to send any shipp for Amboyna, Banda or the Molluccoes; and because wee should the better understand their minds they sent itt in writeinge, as by the same may appeare, requiringe us as aforesaid not to send any shipp to any the said places; which if wee did they protested to prevent our trade, if all their forces would doe itt; and if any slaughter of men happened thereupon, they protested likewise nott to bee culpable thereof. To which was awnswered as by the same writeings may appeare.

And at the cominge of our four shipps to Banda, viz. the Clove, Defence, Thomas and Concord, they presentlye came with a fleete of eleven saile; which the Bandaneses perceyveinge, delivered the castell and countrye by a generall consent of all the cheife of the iland to Richard Hunt[2], alias Potnoll, Your Worships factor there residente, for the use of the English nation, with articles by them

[1] Gerard Reynst, Governor-General, 1614–15.

[2] Nothing is known of Hunt previous to the voyage here mentioned, except that he came out with David Middleton in the *Expedition*, and presumably accompanied him to the Bandas. Peyton calls him 'Richard Pottman' (*Brit. Mus. Addl. MSS.* 19276, p. 78).

drawne for their liberties. And our colours being spread on the castell walls, the Dutch with all their forces came against itt, and shott downe the colours three or four times; and the Hollanders haveinge made greate promises to the people of Lantour, which were within the castle to ayde the Bandaneses, caused them to rebell; which the Bandaneses perceiveinge went forth of the castell and fled; in whose companie went alsoe the said Hunt, for feare of his life, the Hollanders haveinge sworne to hange him, and did offer greate somes of money for his personn. Butt the said Hunte, with helpe of the Bandaneses, gott a proa and came to Macassar, and from thence to Bantam, bringinge with him the earth of the countrye, sticks and stones, delivered him in signe of possession of the countrye[1]. Hee had not bene longe at Bantam butt the Hollanders sought to picke a quarrell with him, my selfe beeinge at Jacatra, in manner followinge. Richard Hunte passinge in a very narrowe streete, mette with two of the Dutch marchannts, which came abrest towards him and would nott give him way to passe by. Soe Hunte put one of them aside to make waye; whereupon the[y] fell to blowes. The Dutch beeinge neere their backe dore, called for there slaves, whoe presentlie came, to the number of 20 persons, and fell upon him and beate him very sore, and halled him through the durte by the haire of the head to there owne howse, and sett him in the boults at their gate in the hott sunne, without hatt, because the countrye people should take notice of what they durst doe unto us. Our people would have fetcht him from thence perforce; butt John Gurney, beeinge left cheife in my absence[2], would nott suffer them, but sent by faire meanes to them to

[1] On all this see *Letters Received*, vol. iv. introduction, p. xvii., and the documents there mentioned.

[2] This fixes the date as July, 1616 (see *Letters Received*, iv. 146). Jourdain had gone across to Jakatra to negotiate with the chief.

delyver him into our owne custodye. Butt they would nott deliver him, butt lett him stand there all the daie in veiwe of all the countrye people to our greate disgrace; which our marchannts perceiveinge, sent a messenger to Jacatra advisinge mee of whatt had passed; and I presentlye embarqued myselfe and came to Bantam, where I found Hunte emprisonned, butt not att the gate as before, but was kept in irons within their house.

This injurye beinge thus publiquely done unto us, I thought good not to send to entreate them for his lybertie, as the Hollanders expected, butt gave order to take the best of their marchannts and use him in the same manner in open veiwe of the countrye; which they perceiveinge, kept house, and complayned to the Kinge. Whereupon the Kinge sent mee word that I should be advised not to fight or make any sturringe in his countrye; that if I would have any thinge of the Hollanders wee should trye itt att sea. Whereupon I went to him and told him the whole circumstance of the matter; which when hee heard, he awnswered that hee nor none of his should meddle neither with thone nor thother of us; willinge mee to doe as I sawe cause, soe farre forth as I meddled nott with any of the countrye. They Dutch perceiveinge that I had bene with the Kinge, the next daie sent home the said Hunte, with a peremptory sayinge thatt notwithstandinge the abuses by the said Hunte they had sent him home, not doubtinge butt thatt I would punnishe him accordinge to his deserts; which if they thought I would not perfourme, they would punnishe him themselves. To which I awnswered vizt. thatt I would not receyve him upon those tearmes, butt that hee should retourne with them againe, and what punnishment they durst laye upon him the like I would doe to the best of their marchannts; butt if hee [they ?] were willinge to give us satisfaccion for the injurie done, not onelie to him butt in generall to our nation, they should send me their cape marchant, that was the cause of all these broyles, thatt I might laye him in irons in publique manner to the veiwe of the countrie people, as they had done to ours; and when wee had once made equall the injury done, then I would examine the cause, and if he were found in the faulte he should be punnished accordinglie; and the like I expected from them. With this awnswere they retorned, butt the Presedent would not receive him any more into there house, butt thrust him out of dores. But I would not receyve him into the house untill I had better satisfaccion from them, butt secreetly caused him to goe to Jacatra, there to abide untill farther order. Soe thatt before wee could have any convenyent oportunitye to take any of their marchannts (because they went alwaies guarded with many Jappons, and we unwillinge to make any revolte in the towne) Captaine Keelinge came into the Roade[1], whoe was informed of the cause; whoe was willinge to wincke at itt, and soe the matter rested; which soe much imboldned the Flemyngs that shortlie after meetinge with some of our saylers in a racke house, there was some words betwixt them, and a Dutch souldiar drewe his sword upon two of our men; and they runninge awaye, because they had noe weopons, the souldiars followinge after them with their swords drawne mett with two more of our Englishmen, whoe in peaceable manner perswaded the Flemings to be quiett; butt they without reguard fell upon them, and cutt three of our men in such manner as thatt all men had thought they had beene slayne, butt were soe sore wounded that they will never bee their owne men againe. The next daie wee sent twoe of our marchannts to complaine of the injurie done us, butt could have noe satisfaccion; rather the cheife actour, whoe was a lieftenant, came daylie before our dore,

[1] Keeling arrived at Bantam in the latter part of September, 1616.

walkinge in braveinge manner, the more to agravate our greifes.

These wrongs beinge offerred unto us in open veiwe of the countrie people, without any satisfaccion, doth in parte make them believe all to be true what the Dutch doth reporte in secreete unto them. As first, to the Kinge of Jambee[1], vizt. The Dutch understandinge thatt wee pretended to send a shipp for Jambee, to settle there a factorie, they to encounter us in the action dispatched a pinnace into the Straicts of Malacca, where their Generall was with two shipps. And they, knowinge that the Kinge of Jore[2] had married the Kinge of Jambees daughter, procured his letter to the Kinge of Jambee, wherein he wrote by the instigation of the Dutch that hee understood that the English had pretended to settle a factorie in his countrye; which hee intreated not to grannte, because the English were a poore and base nation, deflowrers of woemen, greate theeves and drunckards; therefore hee entreated him not to give us any enterteynement in his countrye. Which letter beeinge brought by a Dutchman called Prince[3] in a proa, rowinge alonge the shore against the monson to make the more hast, he arryved at Jambee shortlie after the shipp the Attendante. And having delyvered the Kinge of Jores letter to the Kinge of Jambee, the Kinge sent for Richard Wesby and tould him that he could not grannte him to build any house, butt that he might hire a house, tellinge him whatt the Dutch had reported to the Kinge of Jore; and therefore he would first see whether wee weare people of that disposition or nott, before he would give leave to builde; which after hee had seene our behaviour and informed himselfe of the Portugalls there tradinge, he presentlie granted us to builde, although the Flemings

---

[1] Jambi, on the eastern side of Sumatra. [2] Johor.

[3] Cornelius Prince (*Letters Received*, iii. 200).

contynually wrought against itt; all which appeareth by Richard Wesbyes letter, and confirmed by Prince and annother Dutch marchant that delivered the letter to the Kinge of Jambee, and confessed it unto mee at Bantam[1].

These are the abuses which to my knowledge hath bene done by the Dutch after my comeinge to Bantam with Sir Henrye Middleton, Anno 1612 [1613], which doth tend whollie to the cuttinge us of our trade in the East Indies. Their grounds in breife are these, vizt. Inprimis, in seekinge by subtiltye to hold us underhand with faire words to beate the bushe, while they would cunninglie carrye awaie the birde, if they were not prevented; as may appeare by their dealinges att Amboyna and Bantam formerly allegd.

Secondly, when they see that their cunninge dealinge underhand will not serve their purpose, they thinke to discouradge us and eate us out of trade by sellinge cheape; supposinge thereby that wee will in tyme bee weary of a trade where there is little proffitt; and wee giveinge itt over, the trade of Coramandell shall remayne whollie to themselves.

Thirdlie, they trust in all countryes where they deale, byndinge the countrye people to sell them all their comodities, as in the Molluccaes; and doe daily practise the like att Bantam, thinkinge by this meanes to gett all the pepper into there hands.

Fourthlie, they seeke by secreete and open injuries to drawe the peoples hartes from us; as by defameinge us secreetly and abusinge us openlye in veiwe of the world; which wee in bearinge soe much with their insolencye makes us to be thought a weake nation, not able to right

[1] See *Letters Received*, iii. 160, 199, 202, 324, etc. This establishment of an English factory at Jambi by Richard Westby took place in October, 1615.

ourselves, much lesse to protect annother nation; as they to many kinges have reported.

Dec. 12, 1616. This daie, beinge the 12th of December, I came aboard the Clove[1] to fitt my cabbin and muster our companie; where I remayned till the 14th dicto, and finished my accompts.

Dec. 14. I retourned aland and tooke my leave of the Kinge, whoe presented mee with a cowe and ten sacks of pepper, which I lefte in Mr. George Barkleys[2] hands, and the same daye retourned aboard.

Dec. 15. Mr. Barkley came aboard with the marchannts and some of the countrye people, and dined, and retourned aland at eveninge.

Dec. 16. In the morninge aboute six of the clocke wee sett saile from Bantam Roade, and anckored betwixt Pulla Pengan and Palembam Pointe[3], where wee tooke in woode.

Dec. 17. Mr. Ball with other marchanntes came off to us and brought their letters, with Mr. Barkleys to the Honourable Companie. And soe wee tooke

Dec. 18. our leaves of them; and after dinner they departed, and wee sett saile and wente of.

Dec. 19. We have[inge?] gott upp as farr as Little Bassy[4], an iland which doth make the Straicts before you enter into Bantam, some eight leagues from thence, wee weare taken with a W.S.W. winde soe feirce thatt wee were faine to putt roome againe for Palembam Pointe;

---

[1] The *Clove*, after her return to England from the voyage to Japan, had been fitted out again and arrived at Bantam at the end of 1615. Thence she was sent with three other ships to the Bandas and Moluccas under Samuel Castleton, and on her return was careened and got ready for the voyage home.

[2] His successor as Agent.

[3] See note on p. 239.

[4] Pulo Sebesi, in the Straits of Sunda, between Verlaten and Sebuku Islands.

where wee roode with contrary winds and stormy weather till the 22 dicto, takinge in of wood and water, which wee found nere the pointe. In this time wee were putt backe twice and lost an anchor.

Dec. 23. Wee sett saile once againe, and gott out on the coaste of Sumatra, where wee ankored in 28 fathome, to stopp a tyde which came very feirclie against us.

Dec. 24. In the morninge wee sett saile and gott some five leagues ahead alonge the coast of Sumatra, butt could nott finde any place to anker in; and the tide beeinge comeinge against us, fearinge to be putt againe to leeward, wee bare roome for Pulla Bassy and there ankored betwixt Sumatra and the iland in 35 fathome in fowle ground; havinge lost one anchor neere the same place formerly, and nowe wee onlie galled our cable, beeinge reasonable faire weather.

Dec. 25. Wee sett saile with the winde at N.W. and N.N.W., and gott of neere the Salte Hills[1]; butt beeinge becalmed and the current against us, wee anchored in 50 fathome, with twoe cables on an end, because wee would not putt backe againe, havinge much adoe to weigh our ankour.

Dec. 26. In the morninge with much paines wee wayed anchour with the tide, and stoode of att West, the winde beeinge att N.N.W., little winde. And aboute eight of the clocke itt fell calme, butt the current helpinge us, settinge to the offinge. And in the afternoone the winde came att W.S.W., and wee stoode of N.W. and N.W. & by W.; soe that this daye at night wee had the Salt Hill east of us some four leagues.

Dec. 27. It was calme untill noone, and then wee had an easie gale att S. and S. & by E. Wee stoode our course

---

[1] See note on p. 239.

S.W. & by W. In the eveninge wee had much rayne, and the wynde varyable, and calmes.

. . . .

Jan. 4 [1617]. ...This daye aboute five of the clocke in the eveninge wee had sight of Keelinge Iland[1], some six leagues N.N.W. of, the middle parte of the souther parte att N.W. and by N., risinge in four partes like ilands, a lowe land, plaine, with fewe trees, as itt seemed....

. . . .

Jan. 16. ...Att noone per observacion 22 d. 45 m.; and att sonne settinge varriation [*blank*]. This daye our maister, Richard Dale[2], fell by the eares with the carpenter, for upholdinge his boye to stricke the boatson. The matter beinge examined, I caused the boye to have 12 whips att the capston, and the carpenter in the bilbowes eight howers....

. . . .

Jan. 24. ...Att noone lattitude 28 d. 22 m. These twoe dayes I finde the shipp gone farther to the southward then per judgment I can allowe her, that I thinke some corrent setteth to the southward. This daie aboute nine in the morninge Mr. Bewly, being crased in his wittes, lept overboard, and wee goinge before the winde could nott save him, havinge a stiffe gale, and was drowned before wee could have out our boate....

. . . .

---

[1] 'This day wee see Keelings eoyland, that boore N.N.W. som 5 leages oft' (Bardon's journal). 'The 4 of this month wee fell with Keelings Iland, which lyeth 190 leages from the Salt Ilands, in the latitude of 12 degrees and 12 minutes south, and hath varyation 7 degrees and 10 mynutes to the westward' (Monden's journal).

The Cocos or Keeling Islands lie about 600 miles S.W. by W. of Java Head, almost in the track of vessels making for the Cape of Good Hope. They were formally annexed by England in 1857, and are now under the government of the Straits Settlements. It is generally accepted that they were discovered in October or November, 1609, by Capt. William Keeling on his homeward voyage from Bantam; but I can find no actual account of the discovery.

[2] He had been first coxswain and then mate of the *Clove* in her voyage to Japan (see Saris's journal).

Jan. 29. Very much winde att S.S.E. Course West, havinge sayled these 24 howers 40 leagues att W. & by S.; havinge butt our two courses abroad these 24 howers, and the yards very lowe. This daie wee had a much overgrowne sea. Att noone, darke weather; noe observacion, but by estimation 30 d. 50 m. Aboute four in the afternoone the winde at S.W.; much winde, thatt were faine to lye a trye with a gouse wing[1] of the mayne course, with much winde all night. This is the fourth daye that wee have not seene the sonne.

. . . .

Feb. 19. Winde E.S.E. and S.E. & by E.; little winde this 24 howers; alwaies a greate sea out of the W.S.W. Att noone per observacion 34 d. 34 m., havinge made these 24 howers 15 leagues W.N.W. ½ Westerly. Here wee finde the current to leave us. Att noone wee stand awaye W. and by N., with a little gale at East, untill four in the afternoone; att which time wee had sight of land[2] bearinge of us the westermost parte N.W. & by W. and the easter parte N. & by W., reasonable highe land risinge in hummocks, with one highe mountaine att the easter parte and three hummocks att the wester, one bigger [then?] the other[s?], ragged land; by judgment 12 leagues of. Then wee stoode awaye W.S.W. with a stiffe gale. At night varriation 5 d. 50 m.

Feb. 20. In the morninge a stiffe gale at N.E. & by E. and E.N.E.; and from forenoone wee stoode awaye W.N.W. to see the land. Att noone itt fell calme, thatt wee sawe not the land. Per observacion att noone 35 d. 11 m., and wee steered still W.N.W. untill the morninge, havinge sayled these 24 howers and made a W. & by S. ½ Southerly

---

[1] '*Goosewings of a sail*, the clues or lower corners of a ship's mainsail or fore-sail, when the middle part is furled or tied up to the yard' (Falconer's *Dict. Marine*).

[2] The African mainland.

35 leagues, besides allowance for the current which setteth with us; which upon sight of Cape Dagullas will shewe, for thatt by my reckoninge I am 50 leagues to the eastward of itt and lyeth west northerly. It contynued calme all night, thatt this daie wee sawe noe land. Att sonsettinge varriation 3 d. 20 m.

Feb. 21. Little winde in the morninge att S.S.W. Course W.N.W. and N.W. and by W. to make the land, butt itt fell calme till two in the afternoone. Per observacion 34 d. 53 m. Att which time wee sounded and had ground in 48 fathome, fayre browne sand; butt wee could see noe land, beinge very hazie, untill three in the afternoone, W.N.W. of us, lowe land. Wee have sailed these 24 howers 14 leagues, W. and by N. ½ Northerly. Att eveninge itt fell calme. In this tyme wee sounded att [and?] had 48, 47, 45 and 40 fathome, faire broune sand. Varriation att night 3 d. Otherwise by our soundinge wee should take this land to bee Cape de Gullas, beinge butt lowe land.

Feb. 22. Beinge calme this last night untill six in the morninge, att which time the wynde came up in a shower at E.S.E. and East, wee sawe the land very plaine, beeinge aboute seven leagues of, lowe land with trees, lyinge N.W. and by N. of us, and the northermost parte lowe land lyinge of us N. and by E. with high land over itt. The westermost land laye W.N.W., rizinge with two hummocks, one bigger then the other, and wee steered awaye W.S.W. This land seemed to bee Cape de Gullas by the risinge of the land and by our soundinge; butt by our reckoninge and varriation wee were shorte 30 leagues of itt. Att noone darke weather; noe observation, butt by judgment 34 d. 50 m.; havinge sayled these 24 howers 16 leagues West Northerly. Att two in the afternoone wee sawe land of us lyinge W. and S., which wee take to be Cape da Gullas. Then wee steered S.W. and by W. and W.S.W. In the eveninge wee made an other head land lyinge W.N.W. of us, havinge brought Cape Dagullas N.W. Northerly. Wee affirme this land to bee the Cape Dagullas, risinge like the former, and this other land riseth like a gurnetts head, nott much unlike Portland. Noate that you have 30 leagues to the westward of Cape Dagullas from 40 to 60 fathome, and after you passe itt to the eastward noe ground in 70 fathome.

Feb. 23. Much winde att East and E. and by N. And att four in the morninge wee stoode in N. and N. and by W. for the Cape Bona Esperansa; which wee sawe in the morninge aboute 15 leagues N.N.W. of us, and wee stoode with our twoe courses and bonnetts. Much winde. Varriation in the morninge 40 m. Att noone wee weare thwarte Cape Falso, some five leagues of. By observacion att noone 34 d. 27 m., havinge sailed these 24 howers 30 leagues West S. West Westerlye and 15 leagues N.N.W.; haveinge had noe ground after eight at night, beinge to the westward of Cape Dagullas. In the eveninge lesse winde, and wee passed Cape Esperansa, faire by the Baye of Saldanha, that wee might discerne the Table and the Sugar Loafe; and then, beinge night and the winde scantinge upon us, wee laye too and againe all night, with little winde.

Feb. 24. Faire weather and calme untill two in the afternoone, and then in a fogge the winde came att W.S.W. and S.W., butt soe darke wee could not see the ships length; soe that wee were forced to tacke aboute and lye too and againe all night, the fogge still contynued. Att which time wee tackt aboute wee were within two leagues of the pointe turninge into the baye, and within two leagues of Penguin Iland, bearinge N.E. and by N. of us, and the pointe N.E. and by East.

Feb. 25. All the day much fogge, that wee could nott see the ships length, much lesse the land, untill two in the afternoone. Then itt cleared up, and wee stood in E. with the winde att S. and by East and S.S.E., a pretty gale, the pointe bearinge of us E.N.E., and some five leagues of us. Wee steered into the roade of Saldania in the night, beeinge faire by itt in the eveninge; soe wee went in by our leade and ankored in the baye aboute ten of the clocke. And this eveninge before sonne sett, wee had sight of two shipps to the westward of us, neere Penguin Iland, and they stoode into the baye with us; butt the winde scantinge upon them, could nott fetch itt in this night.

Feb. 26. Aboute ten in the morninge came in the two shipps which we sawe overnight, and anchored by us, the one beinge 160 tons, the other of 110 tonnes, the one belonginge to Sir Robert Ritch, wherein was Captaine Samuell Newce, and in the smaller shipp was Captaine Thomas Joanes, belonginge to [*blank*] Etalian. These shipps had a lycense onelye from my Lord Admyrall to goe for the coaste of Guinney, as I understood by Captaine Newce; butt beinge att sea came to the Cape Bona Esperansa to looke for China juncks or for Dieu or Chaule shipps outward or homeward to the Red Sea. Butt I finde them selves to be weared of their voyage, beeinge drawne this waye against there wills by the maryners and Thomas Joanes and Cellyns the chirurgeon. The bigger of the shipps is called the Francis and the other the Lion[1].

The same daye I went aland to seeke refreshinge, and wee had some leane calves which wee bought and brought aboard. And on the stones aland[2] wee sawe thatt the Amsterdam and the Greate Selan arryved att Saldania the 20th of Februarye, which is the 10th dicto per our stile,

---

[1] For this interloping expedition and its fate see *The Voyage of Sir Thomas Roe*, 420 *n*.

[2] See note on p. 13.

and departed hence the 4th of March, which is the 22th of February; wherein was cheife comander George Spelbergem bound home, and are to touch att St Helena[1]. He had as much refreshinge as he desired. Alsoe wee perceived that Captaine Keelinge withe the Dragon and Expedition departed from Saldania the first of February, havinge stayed 29 daies refreshinge them[2]. In the tyme of our beeinge in this roade wee could nott gett any refreshinge after the first daie, although the people came downe with greate store of cattle and sheepe and many people armed, contrarye to their former uses. The next daie after our arrivall they brought downe above 5000 head of cattle, which made me to doubt some plott of treason, with aboute 1000 armed men; but wee weare armed to prevent the worst; butt of these cattle they would not sell any unlesse wee would goe with our people to Cories house, which is an Indian which was carried for England in the Hectour per Captaine Towerson[3]. Soe wee agreed, if itt were nott farre, to goe with some 60 armed men thether to see the reason; he tellinge us that his enymies would not suffer them to sell us cattle, and if wee would goe to his house thatt they would all flye; then wee should have whatt wee would. Butt when wee were come to the toppe of the hill, some four miles from the tents, wee sawe in the valley aboute 10,000 head of cattle, and by judgment aboute 5,000 people, which fled nott for feare of us. Soe Corye goinge with us, would have had us to goe downe into the valley to them and take the cattle; which I would nott consent unto to endanger our selves amongst soe many beasts. Wee beinge already

[1] This is the great circumnavigatory voyage (1614–17) of Joris van Spilberghen.

[2] He had left Bantam October 10, 1616.

[3] For the curious story of this 'Saldanian' and his experiences in England see *Letters Received*, iii. 295.

weary of our journey retourned to our tents, and Corye in our companie, wee promisinge him to goe to our shippe to fetch more men and come againe the next daie; butt when hee perceived thatt wee pretended noe more to goe in that exploite he departed from us, and never came neere us more, nor any other of them, thinkinge (as wee judge) that wee perceived their treason to drawe us amongst their cattle and the multitude of people, and wee beinge weary and dead for wante of water, there beeinge none, and amongst pushes [bushes?], hills and stony ground, they might easelie have cutt us of; which certaynelie was their plott, which was the reason that they drove awaye all the cattle from thence the next daie; for had those people bene enymies to Corye and the rest which brought their cattle to our tents, they would not have retourned thither with their cattle soe neere to their enymies forces (they standinge in feare of them, as they made shewe to us), butt would have kept their cattle further of from them, as they have done in former tyme. That dogge Corye is the cause of all this rogerye, for that hee understandinge our manner hath made them soe bould thatt they doe nott greatlie care for a peece, whereas in former time one peece would have made a multitude of them to flye; and whereas before they were accustomed to eate rawe stinkinge meate, they are now content to eate the best and boyle itt themselves in potts which they carry with them for that purpose. Soe that here after within fewe yeares there will be noe victualls to be had butt att deare rates; for in my time wee have had a cowe for half a yard of an old yron hoope[1], which nowe they esteeme nott, nor scarce copper, butt will have shineing brasse, which att present they care nott for, because at first they tooke itt to bee gould, and nowe findinge otherwise they

[1] See p. 14.

esteeme itt nott; which sheweth thatt not farre within the countrye there are people that sheweth them the difference; and doubtlesse these people are come downe amongst them, hearinge of soe many shipps as comes this waye. Soe thatt I conclude that if there were a castell made in this place itt would be brought in time to civilitie, and bee a good refuge for all shippinge that travell the East Indias, beinge a fruitfull and healthfull countrye.

The time of our abidinge heare was 18 daies, in which time wee had much winde at E.S.E., that we could nott land to take in our water in four daies together; and after the winde came att N.N.W. and blewe hard; soe thatt wee had nott above four daies faire weather.

Our Course from Saldania to St. Helena.

March 15. Aboute eight of the clocke att night wee sett saile with the winde of the shore, and went betwixt Penguin Iland and the mayne, the winde shortninge upon us. And wee steered all night (beinge past the iland) West and West & by North.

March 16. Winde S.S.W., a good gale; and we steered away W.N.W. Att noone the Table of Saldania bare S.E. of us aboute 12 leagues. Att four in the afternoone wee lost sight of the land, with a still [stiff?] gale att S.S.E. Att noone per judgment lattitude 33 d. 12 m.

. . . .

March 31 [30?]. Winde from the E.S.E. to the E. Faire weather, with a prettye gale. Att noone per observacion 16 d. 14 m., havinge sayled these 24 howers 36 leagues N.W. Att which time wee steered awaye West; and at two in the afternoone wee had sight of St. Helena some 14 leagues off, bearinge W.N.W. the northermost parte, and the souther parte W. & by N. And att four in the afternoone wee laye too and againe untill four in the morninge. Varriation att night 6 degrees 35 m.

March 31. Att four in the morninge, the winde betwixt the S.E. and E.S.E., wee stoode in with the lande, and att eleven or twelve wee ancored att the Chappell Baye[1]. And after dinner wee landed; where wee found a letter from Captaine Keelinge, wherein he wrote of his arrivall and departure, which was the 24th of Februarie, havinge taken good store of hoggs, goats and fishe; giveinge us to understand by his letter that he anchored not at the Chappell butt att the fifth warpe[2] to the westward of the Chappell, which wampt (*sic*) leadeth to the orenge trees. Soe that this daie aboute four in the afternoone wee wayinge, anchored at the same wampt in 32½ fathome, a mile of the shore. It is aboute two miles from the Chappell, and the 5th swampt accomptinge the Chappell for one; where there is better water then att the Chappell, and store of rocke fishe, thatt if a man have small hookes, one man may take upon every rocke as much in a daie as will serve 20 men to eate; and itt is neerer the orenge trees and the goats. For the hoggs, there are very fewe lefte[3]. Captaine

---

[1] The bay in which Jamestown is now situated. The old name is derived from the little chapel dedicated to St Helena built by the Portuguese there. Herbert (ed. 1638, p. 353) gives a view of the island showing the chapel, the 'Chappell valley,' and the 'Lemon valley.' See also the descriptions in Linschoten (Hakl. Soc.'s edn., ii. 254) and Pyrard de Laval (ii. 296).

[2] An error for 'swamp' (see the extract from Monden). What is really meant is a valley with a rivulet running down it into the sea.

[3] 'The 31 [March] wee went into the Rode and anchored in 23 fadome half a mile of the shore against the Chapell. But before you come to the Chappell you shall have a sharpe hill, which is some two miles short of the Chapple. But the best watering place is some three miles to the southwestward of the Chappell; and it is neerer to the lemon trees by at least four miles or better, and better filling of water, and the water far better. And for the better finding of the river, it is the fourth valley or swampe from the Chappell, not reckoning the Chappell valley for one. You shall ride in 28 or 30 fadome half a mile of the shore. Yf you would find the lemon trees,

Keelinge and the two Holland shipps, whoe departed six dayes before our arrivall, had taken all the hogges; soe that in five dayes that wee stayed wee could kill butt one hogge and four goates. Soe thatt findinge itt not to bee worth our labours, wee filled our water and washed our lynnen, and departed the 5th of Aprill; and lefte a letter with Captaine Keelinges and the Dutch shipps, beinge two greate ships of 1000 tonns apeece with 150 persons in each named the Amsterdam and the Greate Selan. And the goates are soe wild that there is greate crafte in catchinge of them, for they presentlie seeinge of people take the rocks, that none can come att them; butt if there were in a shipp a bastard grayhound or some mastife, there might bee many goats taken, for there is store upon the iland. As for lymons, wee had none butt very small, not worth anythinge. Butt within the land, this iland is a very firtill soile and pleasant place and wholesome aire, and very necessarie for shipps homeward bound.

Our Course from St. Helena to England, vizt.

Aprill 5. In the morninge aboute seven or eight wee sett sayle from St. Helena, and att noone it bare S.E. of us, aboute five leagues of. Winde E.N.E. Faire weather.

. . . .

---

keepe the river and sound four miles upp. The trees doe growe in the same river that the shipp doth ride against, and so the river wilbe the best pilott to bring you to the lemon trees. Heere wee stayed some five daies, but had little refreshing, for the lymons were not ripe and the goates to swift a foote for us. Ther ar but fewe hogs ther, and some fishe wee tooke with hookes' (Monden's journal). '[The] 31 daye, being Monday, wee came to a nanker in the second valy affter you be about the poynt wheare the crose did stand. The Chapell stands in this valy. In the afternone wee wayed anker and came to a anker in 32 fadom watter, and heare wee filled our watter; and wee went some three milles in this valy and found some lemones. It is verie smove [smooth?] whear wee gethred our lemones. Wee killed some small quantitie of hogs and gootes and some store of fish' (Bardon's journal).

The valley off which they anchored is still called 'Lemon Valley.'

Maye 14. Winde E.N.E. and E. and by N. Faire weather. This morninge aboute eight of the clocke we had sight of two sailes to the windeward of us, standinge with our foorefoote[1]. Wee sawe that one of them gott upon us. Wee stroke our topsailes and stayed for her; butt when they were come within shott of us, they shott of three peeces and would come noe neere, butt bore up to her consorte. By their flagge and makinge of their shipp they seemed to bee a Spaniard, as wee suppose bound for the West India[2]. Soe they stoode alonge their course and wee ours. At noone by observacion 19 d. 58 m., havinge made these 24 howers 31 leagues N. & by W. ¼ W.

Maye 15. Winde N.E. and N.E. and by E. Faire weather. This daie wee passed the zenith. And att noone per judgment 21 d. 16 m., having sailed these 24 howers 26½ leagues N.N.W. ¼ N.

. . . .

June 1. ...Att noone by judgment 36 d. 28 m., havinge made these 24 howers 42 leagues N.E. Easterly. This daie wee were att the end of the weeds in the sea[3], havinge contynued with us very thicke from the 23 dicto.

. . . .

June 5. ...Att noone per observacion 38 d. 28 m., havinge sailed these 24 howers 22 leagues N.E. ¾ N. This daie aboute three in the afternoone came up to us a small

---

[1] For an explanation of this expression see the quotation from Manwayring in the *Oxford Eng. Dict.*, s.v.

[2] Bardon says that one was about eighty tons burden, the other between two and three hundred.

[3] They were of course just emerging from the Sargasso Sea, the northern limit of which is in about 35°.

'The 17 of this month wee saw many weedes driving by the ships side, and great store of theis small things which ar called carvilles' [the paper nautilus or argonaut]. 'The 18 and 19th daies...wee sawe great store of the said weedes, being in the latitude of 24 degrees wher wee saw the thickest of them. The weedes drives in streames, as if it weare a streame leache, and it lyeth north east and south west. The weedes ar full of small berries about the bignes of a peppercorne when the huske is of' (Monden's journal).

French man of warre, and spake with us and came under our starne[1]. The winde beinge a stiffe gale, wee knewe nott well whatt he said.

June 6. Aboute five in the morninge wee had sight of Flowers and Corne [Corve?][2], the southermost bearinge E.N.E. of us. The winde att W.N.W. and after came att W.S.W. a faire gale, butt much sea out of the N.W. Wee lost sight of our consorte, who promised to speake with us in the morninge, butt he lingred staying for his pillage. Att noone per observacion lattitude 39 d. 48 m., havinge sayled these 24 howers 34 leagues N.E. & by N. Att noone the norther parte of Corne [Corve?] was E. of us, some six leagues of; soe thatt I make the iland to lye in 39 d. 48 m. Butt by my reckoninge some northerly corent hath sett us 20 leagues to the eastward, for att noone by my reckoninge wee should have bene 26 leagues west of itt.

. . . .

June 16. In the morninge, winde S.S.E. Aboute seven in the morninge we sawe a sayle to leeward, and wee spake with them[3]. They told us that the Lizard was 35 leagues betweene the N.E. and N.E. & E. of us, and Siley[4] some 12 leagues north....

June 17. Wind W. and W. & by N., a stiffe gale. In the morninge wee had sight of the Lizard. Then wee steered E.N.E. and N.E. & by E. This daie wee spake with a fisher boate, whoe told us thatt we were shorte of the Start eight leagues. Att ten in the forenoone, havinge had

---

[1] 'At four of the clocke wee met with a French man of warre some 18 leages southwest from Flowers, one of some 60 tonnes, with four gonnes in her. She spake with us and gave us a peice of ordinance, and wee gave him an other, and so parted' (Monden's journal).

[2] Flores and Corvo, the two westernmost islands of the Azores.

[3] 'It was Mr. Gardner of Wappinge' (Bardon's journal).

[4] Scilly.

a stiffe gale, our shipp was shott farther ahead then wee expected. Att night wee weare aboute 12 leagues shorte of Portland.

June 18. Att night wee weare shorte of Faire Lee[1] aboute six leagues, beinge past Bechee before night.

June 19. In the morninge aboute seven wee were as high as the Nestes[2], where the winde tooke us shorte, cominge up att the E.S.E. and S.E. & by E.[3]

[1] Possibly Fairlight, near Hastings.

[2] The Ness, *i.e.*, Dungeness.

[3] At this point Jourdain's journal ceases. His two shipmates, however, continue their entries a little longer. '[June 19.] We came to an anker in Dover Road at four of the clocke in the afternone' (Bardon's journal). 'The 19 at twelve wee anchored in Dover Roade, the wind being at E.S.E.; at which time wee sent two of our marchants ashore at Dover. The tide being done, wee sett saile for the Downes; and the 20 in the forenoone wee anchored in the Downes' (Monden's journal).

The specimen of Jourdain's signature here given has been photographed from a letter of his to the East India Company preserved at the India Office (*O.C.* 348).

APPENDIX A.

WILLIAM REVETT'S ACCOUNT OF THE SEYCHELLES[1].

(*India Office Records: Marine Journals*, no. vii.)

January 19 [1609]. About ten of the clocke wee had syght of an iland to leeward. Wee observed, and were in 4 degrees 48 mynnutes, when the lande boore E. About two of the clocke wee raysed other ilandes, beinge all of them high landes. Wee steered away with our sheate a lyttell veered betweene the E.N.E. and the E. & by N.

January 20. In the morninge and all the day wee spent about these ilandes, sendinge our skyf ashoare to sownde, and brought with hir from one of the small ilandes seven great lande turtles, wherof they sayd were great store. Wee had many showldings, beinge, as wee take it, broken lande, but wee were come in lesse then 20 fathomes. This day wee fownde noe place fyttinge to come to an ancor; wherfore wee spent the day and night keepinge our selves to wyndward to beare up the next day, having the wynde all this while north-westerlie. In standinge of these ilandes some five leagues by supposition, wee had but 30 fathomes water, and within one league wee had 25 fathomes; which makes us thinke these ilandes have bene all one fyrme lande.

January 21. This day in the morninge about nine of the clocke wee came to ancor under one of the ilandes in some 13 fathomes walter, havinge the eastermost part of the iland, beinge a stonny rocke, bearinge next hande E.N.E. on our starboard syde, and another small ilande which boore next hande S.E. & by E.;

---

[1] See note on p. 47.

having ilandes and rockes in a mannour rownde about us to the noumber of 25 or 30, which made the part wee ryd in a very good roade, not rydinge above a musket shott of the shoare. Here wee ryd to walter, wood and refreshe our selves untill the primo February; dewringe which tyme noe occurrent happened worthy the relatinge. Only wee fownde heere good store of cocos, some fresh fyshe (wherof most part were skates), lande turtles of so huge a bidgnes which men will thinke incredible; of which our company had small lust to eate of, beinge such huge defourmed creatures and footed with five clawes lyke a beare. Wee kylled also many doves with poles of wood, which was a sygne of the small frequentation of this place; yet for those which are forced and stand in neede of walter and such things as afforenamed it is an excellent place and comfortabell, in regard of the securety and good wateringe place wee fownd there, facill to bee fetched aboard; as also heere groweth such goodly shipp tymber as the lyke or better cannot bee seene, both for hayght, strayghtnes and bidgnes. Thus much I thought good to wryte touchinge these ilandes.

APPENDIX B.

WILLIAM REVETT'S NARRATIVE OF EVENTS AT ADEN, HIS VOYAGE TO MOCHA, ETC.[1]

(*India Office Records: Marine Journals*, no. vii.)

From the day dycto [April 10, 1609] to the 8th of May many occurrents happened, as the comminge in of many shippes from Moya[2] and other places; the intreadges[3] of our Jennerall, and his comminge aboard; myne owne goinge ashoare; with other matters I referre mee to others that I perswade myselfe will wryte therof. Only thus much of the citty[4]. It is a garryson, and consystes

---

[1] See note on p. 69.

[2] Mocha.

[3] Intrigues.

[4] Aden.

more in souldiers then in marchannts, though frequented by some fewe marchannts in some fashion from India to furnishe the place itselfe and other places adjoyninge therto with the commodetyes that India affoardes, which noe doubt they make great bennefytt therby. It standeth in a valley, and hath upon the northe syde, upon a lyttell ilande or rocke[1] cut out of the mayne, a fayer castell, to see too invynceabell to bee taken but by famyne. This castell commanndes the poarte and holle cittye, which for antycketye is famous, but now for wannt of repayringe is very much ruinated, and fewe good houses standinge therin, a thinge lammentabell to see the ruines of fayer houses in that sorte to bee raced downe to be grownde. Yet have they a great care, for the beautefyenge their citty, to keepe the walles next unto the sea syde in repparation; which makes the citty shewe owtwardly very fayer. For cittuation and other instructions I referre to former authours, and more espetially to Hugan Linscoten, a Duchman and travillour, who wrytes therof at large[2].

May 8. After some conference had with the Governour some two dayes before by the Jennerall, my sellf, and others, conserninge two shipps laden with indico which were passed by for Mocha, it was agreed that my selfe, W. R., and Phillipp Glascocke should goe for that place, hopinge therby to attayne to our ladinge, and to establish a factory there and so to retourne for Ingland; for the which end I undertooke the journey, and this day tooke boate from Aden, some two myles of the citty. About eleven of the clocke, with the wynde next hande at E.N.E., wee steered away. When wee were cleere of the southermost poynte of the road of Aden, betweene the S.W. and the S.W. & by S., the land trendinge away S.S.W., with showldes lyeng on the other syde of the poynt wher our shipp ryd some two leagues of the shoare; the which showldes when wee had passed, wee steered away W.S.W., but before next hande at S.W. About three of the clocke wee steered away W. and W. & by N. Northerly, all that day and night with a freshe galle.

May 9. In the morninge wee had syght of Babarmandell, which is a necke of a lande that lyeth into the sea some league or more from the mayne, and sheweth farre of as it were an iland, but

---

[1] See p. 76.

[2] See bk. i. p. 14 of the English translation of 1598.

is a baye. At this place begynneth the entrannce into the Read Sea, having the Coast of Abex[1] on the larboard syde and the mayne of Arabia on the starboard, some eight leagues dystannce the one from the other. Wee steered now away betweene the W.N.W. and the N.W. & by W. Here lay at the mouthe on the Abex shoare some two or three small ilandes. Babarmandell is a necke of a lande which ryseth lyke mountaynes here and there, as though there were passages through, and that an iland some league and haulfe into the sea; but when you come nye it, you may perceive it joyneth to the mayne. Into the entrannce of the Read Sea ther lyeth on the starboard syde of us, not above one myle and haulf dystannce, a small ilande[2], which maketh the mouth of the Read Sea. Heere in former tymes, as I was informed, went a chayne from the mayne to the ilande, so that shipps could not enter without leave. Yet on the west syde of the ilande there is a passadge for shippinge, but very danngerous for that it is full of rockes. We steered in our course N. & by W. and betweene the N. & by W. and the N.N.W., the wynde at E.N.E. At the entrannce the sea cockells in such sorte that you would thinke it were showldes, but is nothinge but a currant that setteth in and out of the strayght. About eleven of the clocke wee entred, the landes bearinge next hande E. and W. This is a place of some 20 or 30 cottages of Arrabbs, with a house of white stone where a proffett is intoumbed, who in his lyfe tyme was in great esteemation, as also synce his death resorted too by pylgrymmes for devotion sake[3]; but I will let him sleepe with God or the Divell, not knowing whose servannt hee is, and goe onwardes with the Lordes helpe on my way. Here wee cam to ankor about twelve of the clocke, and stayed here, for the master of our barkes pleasure, untill mydnight, and then weyed with a fresh gale of wynde next hande at E.N.E., our course northewesterly, and all night betweene the N.N.W. and the Northe.

May 10. About nine of the clocke wee lannded at the citty of Mocha, where wee fownde many shippes rydinge, some of

---

[1] See note on p. 106. [2] Perim.

[3] Lord Valentia (*Travels*, ii. 15) mentions that at Ras Bab-el-Mandeb 'on the beach is the tomb of a Mussulmaun saint, which, though a heap of ruins, is much visited.'

Dabull, some of Dieu, some of Chaull, of Surratt, Cocheen and Ormus, which places in jenerall traffycke heather. Here are also two gallees of the Grand Seignours, but are of noe force to hurt us, although [they] keepe the Indean shippes in great awe and feare. At our lanndinge wee were had before the Governour and Capten of the Gallees, from which Capten our Jenerall had letters before our goinge up (by a servannt of his, a Napolitan, which cam downe from Mocha to bee our druggaman[1]) to the ende wee should goe thither with our shipp, for that hee advertysde that that place was the skalle, where all sortes of peopell cam to buye; which letters wee could hardlye buyld upon, for that hee was a Napollitane borne and turned Turke, not makinge any conscience of his soules healthe; which made us make accompte hee would make lesse of our boddyes and goodes, beinge now as hee was aultered both from name and nature, could not but bee autered in condishion, which was to wronge that hee was by unsatiabell meanes to mayntayne that which hee is. Wee were boath of [the] Governour and him kyndly treated, with propositions of manny matters, to which I gave annswer to content them. Wee were not long with them before wee were dysmyssed, and had free lybberty to take a house wher wee would; the which wee were not longe adoinge, for that there was in the citty an insynnewatinge wycked Jewe[2], who, as they are by byrthe borne to bee runnagates, so it was his fortune to bee heere ressydent and in some esteemation, though a talkative, lyenge and covetous fellowe; yet our fortunes, because hee spake the Chrystean tongue and offyshious withall, to bee harboured in a house of his tyll wee could fynde a place more convenient. Where now beinge setled, wee omytted noe tyme for inquesition of that wee came about; and, in such mannour as wee would not bee suspected (because strangers, and never any of our nation in the sorte heere before), betweene this day and the 18th wee infourmed our selves of many mattours, both touchinge that wee went for, as also for fewtewrer tymes, which may prove bennefytiall for our countrey and commonwealth. Heere wee were also infourmed for a certaine of Capten Haukins his beeing with the Hector at a place called Surratt, where hee was kyndly entertayned and had beene with

---

[1] See p. 65.

[2] Possibly the one mentioned on pp. 99, 108.

the Kyng, who had grannted him to establish a factory in Surratt, to which end hee had sent away his shipp for Bantam but remayned him selfe with three more there, where hee had sowld divers goods, espetially of the iron brought out with him, which wee saw apparant to bee trew, for that it was transported to this place to bee sowld by a marchannte of great accompte of the citty of Surratt, and hee where Capten Haukins, as hee sayd, was lodged in his howse, to the great content both of him and them[1]; and the newes not a lyttell joyfull to us, to heare it moare palpably verreyfyed which wee had some light of before. With this newes and others wee had gathered Phillipp Glascock, with letters from me to our Jennerall, and the chowse[2] which the Governour of Aden sent up with us, went downe in the same barke wee came up in, my self remayninge here for a further order. The which tyme of my stey heere alone I imployed in infourminge my selfe of the state of the countrey and trade, with other matters fyttinge to bee knowen, beinge kyndly used by all sortes of men, and sundry tymes invyted to the Governours and Capten[s].

June 9. This day I had syght of our shipp, with the pynnas wee had lost company with at our comminge from Cap Bon Esperance. And about three of the clocke in the afternoone tooke boate with the Admyrall of the Sea[3] to goe aboard our shipp to sallute and entertayne our Jennerall; who bad mee welcome, and after conference went ashoare, accompayned agayne with my selfe and others; who at his comminge ashoare was entertaynd in such sorte as was fittinge for his person and place....

Thus untill the 24th July wee spent in Mocha, in which tyme many occurrents happened, as the returne of Mr. Jurden and Mr. Glascocke from the Bashaw; the repayringe our pynnas, which was had heere agrownd; the death of Mr. Glascocke, which was on the 21 or 22th presente[4], as I heard (beinge ashoare); with the resort of marchannts, to say, Turkes, Moares,

---

[1] Cp. p. 109. [2] See note on p. 69.

[3] 'This night came a boat aboord of us from the towne, with a Turke in her....This man, as I afterward understood, is called Lord of the Sea, for that his office is to go aboord all ships that come thither and to see lighters sent aboord to discharge the ships, and to search that they steale no custome; for which office hee hath diverse duties, which is his onely maintenance' (Middleton in *Purchas*, i. 250).

[4] Cp. p. 103.

Armeneans and others, which cam from Constatinopell, Alleppo, Damascus and Trippolie and other parts unto Swes and Zidda with the carravan, and brought with them clothe, kersyes, tynne, currell and all sorts of sylke stuffes, but pryncipally reddy monnyes; which they invest in this citty to marchannts which commeth from Ethiopia and all parts of India. The citty is sittuated in a playne, and consystes in some 6,000 houses, the three parts wherof are of canes covered of straw. The reason is it rayneth very lyttell there. It hath the walter from wells some myle out of the citty, and brought in by poore pepell upon asses, by which meanes they gett their livinge. It hath neither walles, castell nor fort, nor garde of souldiers. But the cheife manntenannce of it is the trade of marchannts, which with the easterly monsones commeth out of India with the wyndes betweene the east and the northeast, and there stayeth all the sayd monsoone, which continneweth some seven monnethes; the which tyme they have to sell their marchandize unto the marchannts afforesayd which commeth by barke from Swes and Zidda, to transporte their monnyes and goods with west and southwest wyndes which contenneweth five monnethes in the yeare; at the latter ende of which wyndes the India shippes depart, which is about the fyne of Agust, our stille, and with that wynde is carryed for India; and the small barks and shippinge with the fyrst of the east and northeast wynds goeth for Swes and Zidda; which is an infallabell rule amongst them for their trades. Now by reason of troubles in Zidda and other places in those parts, this citty is the skalle and serveth the marchannts of Constantinopell, Alleppo, Trippolie, Damasco and Grand Cairo of turbandes, callicoes of all sortes, pyntadoes and divers other coullored stuffes, as allso white of great vallew, with all sortes of spyce, cotton wolle and in fyne indico, which goeth by this passadge into most parts of the worlde. They bringe also and serveth this place out of India much iron, which they reape great bennefytt by and are shewer of ther sales dewringe the easterly and most part of the westerly monsoone, which they stay for salles, reservinge a tyme by computation for their retourne. And thus muche for the trade.

They make noe meanes to fortefy for that the peopell sayeth they have two proffetts, which remayneth in the citty and have each of them their muscito, which is a church or howse of devotion. These proffetts by watch night and day, as they say, doe guard the citty. The one of them is called Shaomer Shadli[1] and the other Shechla Amoode[2]. Shaomer Shadli was the fyrst inventour for drynking of coffe, and therfore had in esteemation; the other for some superstious matters had in honnour. And with this will leave the Turke and Moore to their inclynations, omytting further to wryte of this place; only in a word will touche the peaceablenes of this peopell, which are very affabell, and degennerate from them in Turky, for that a man may passe heere quyetly all seasons, both day and night, without molestation, goodes lyenge continnually upon the key without pylferinge or purloyninge; the which makes mee hope here wilbee good done in fewterer tymes for the bennefytt of our countrey and commonwealthe.

APPENDIX C.

CAPTAIN SHARPEIGH'S ACCOUNT OF EVENTS AT ADEN AND MOCHA, OF THE SHIPWRECK, AND OF HIS SUBSEQUENT JOURNEY TO AGRA[3].

(*India Office Records: Marine Journals*, no. vii.)

...Aboute the 8th of Maye [April, 1609] wee came to Aden, where in words and wryttinge from the Aga of the citty I had what I desiored for the landinge my goods; but afterwarde he played

---

[1] Shaikh Alī bin Omar Shādilī, the founder and patron saint of Mocha (which is often called Bandar Alī in consequence), is reputed to have been the first to introduce into Arabia the drinking of coffee. See the account in Niebuhr (*Voyage*, i. 349). Another version is that the practice was originated by a certain Kādī of Aden, who had made acquaintance with it on the Abyssinian coast (La Roque's *Voyage to Arabia Felix*, Eng. transln., 1732, p. 308). Playfair (*Yemen*, p. 20) gives both stories. Shaikh Alī is buried inside the walls of Mocha, in a large and well-built tomb having nine clustered domes.

[2] Shaikh Muhammad bin Sa'īd Al-Āmūdī, a native of Doan in Hadramūt, took up his abode in Mocha for the purpose of studying theology and was much venerated by the inhabitants for his learning and sanctity. A festival is still held annually at his tomb, which lies outside the walls, near the Jabbanah, and has a large dome over it. One of the gates of Mocha is named Al-Āmūdī in honour of the saint. (Information from Mr. Hamūd bin Hasan.)

[3] See note under the description of Revett's journal given in the List of Authorities. The first part of the letter is occupied with an account of the voyage, which is omitted as it contains no fresh details of importance.

the Turke with me, for he keptt mee in the towne, not sufferinge mee to goe aboorde; yett ussed mee with greatt kindnes. Within 15 dayes the Basha, whos abidinge is 10 dayes jornie into the countrie, having receaved the Kings letter, sentt a commandement for my good ussage, and what favore the Aga could doe mee in sale of my goods or otherwise he should doe for mee to the uttermoste of his powre; and what cloathe I had he desiored to have it for monny, as muche as any other would give, and the Aga to paye mee ready monie. Spendinge a moneth there, and findinge the Agas pretence to exacte of mee more for custome then wee wer agreed upon, by a slight I gotte aboorde. But wheras by agreementt under wryttinge that I should paye but five per cento of what goods I sould or bought, and for those landed and not sould to relade them without any charge, hee forced mee to paye not only for my goods ashoare (which was not muche besid the cloath) but alsoe for those aboorde; of which his deallinge falce with mee I tooke certifficate from the Cadie[1], whoe I did knowe in Constantinople. Beinge aborde, within a daye after I understoode that att Mocha there was greatt store of indycoe, and noe merchantts to buy it, as alsoe sale for my iron to my likinge; wherupon with a consentt I sentt William Rivett and Philip Glascocke to see what was to be done and pressently to returne or sende mee advice; which within few days he did, by wryttinge and by Philip Glascocke. Upon his advice I pressenttly resolved to goe thither with the ship and pines, which then in greatt misserie came to us. The Agae understandinge soe muche would not suffer mee to lade my goods, but demmanded cloathe of goulde and cloathe of silver for the Basha. Upon my denyall to have none in my shipe, hee sentt mee worde he would sende my merchantts to ansswer it to the Basha; as alsoe the monie which he owed mee for the Bashas account, the Basha to dealle with mee for the custom, which I had alowed in account before the Cadie (whoe gave mee certificate alsoe of that). I was very wyllinge to lett them goe, in hope to have had partt of the monie backe which I was forced by his minesters to pay more then by agreementt I should paye; and for the monie due I made noe doubte but to have it sentt mee. My goods the Aga sentte

[1] See note on p. 92.

aboorde, but John Jordein and Phillip Glascocke he would not permitte to see mee.

The day they tooke their jornie for to goe to the Bashae wee sett sayle for Mocha; and after 12 dayes wee arrived in the Roade, wher wee founde manie ships, wherof 16 wer of greatt burthens and of the Indies. The Agae and Captain of the Gallis receaved mee with greatt curttessie, and assured of sales, for what I would sell, to my contentt. But I founde itt otherwise; for iron beinge one cheefe comoditie which sels well there, was then basely soulde, for one of Surratte brin[g]inge thirty tonns of Captain Haukins iron thither cloyed the place for the instante; and for indico I founde it att 60 and 70 d[ollars][1] per churle[2]. In the time of our staye (in hope of sales and exspecttinge our mens retorne from the Basha) wee trimed our pines, without any disturbe of the countrie people. After some 30 dayes our men came from the Basha, brin[g]inge a forcible command for my good ussage, and what goods I should land, sell, or otherwise not to pay any dutties whatsoever; but for monis, not any he would parte from, the Agae havinge bribbed the Bashas Caya and sayinge all was for custome; and for any wryttings, ether of the Aga or Cadie, the Basha would not reade; and for buying and sellinge for that time I should have free liberttie, but to leave men there he woulde not agree too without the Great Turke his commands. Ther I coulde sell nothinge but a few swoordblades. The captain of a Surratt ship advissed mee of Captain Hawkins enterteinmentt, and how comodities wer soulde and bought att Surratt, and offered mee his service in any thinge hee was able to doe for me in that place. I intreatted for a pillott only (other pleassure there hee could doe mee little); which he promissed mee, and that I beinge ready should send my skife ashoare and he should come aboorde mee; which when the time came he faylled mee, of which Grove was very glade, scorninge any pillott.

From thence wee sett sayle in July; and after some 15 dayes wee with fowld weather came to Socotra, wher the pines, by the masters niclygence, was put to leeward of the islande with very muche winde, but good for to carie her to Surratt. There wee stayed, in takinge in watter and some provitione, some 14 dayes;

---

[1] Rials (strictly speaking, pieces of eight rials). [2] See note on p. 69.

and then with a fayre winde sett sayle for Surratt. Of the Governore of the island I bought some 13 kinttars of allius Socotrina[1] att 20 d[ollars] per kintare[2], and a little sanguie dragonie[3], and coste after 18 d[ollars][4] the kintare. Between Mocha and the portt wher wee did our bussines att Socotora wee lost two ancors and brake other two, thone in the shanke thother one of the flooks offe; soe that wee had leafte but one ancore sounde, and one with one flooke. After six days sayle we fell into whitt watter, and sounded and founde 18 fadome saufte grounde. Keepinge the leade, wee ran in att leaste 30 leauges and never had lesse then 15 fadom till wee wer hard aboord the shoare to the sowthward of Diue some 30 leauges. Abowte a poyntt wee founde a fayre baye and good sholdinge; heare wee came to an ancore in seven fadome, very good grounde, aboute a leauge from the shoare. There wee stayed four dayes, in which time we tooke in some provitione, which the countrie people sould us very wyllingly; but for a pillott to carie us to Surratt wee could gette non, nor any light from them. Only a Banian, beinge of Surratt, desiored passag in the ship, which I permitted. Settinge sayle from thence, we shaped our coorse for Surratt by what the master had learned from the cheefe pillott of the great shipe of Surratt which we leafte in Moca, as alsoe by a plott or draught of the Bay of Cambay given hime per the sayde pillott; which made hime to boulde, and before night we came into five fathom watter and lesse. Then we tacked about, fearinge a further dangiore, standing of two glasses. And cominge into deep watter, as 15 fathom, we tacked aboute, the master sayinge we must over there. Keeping the lead still goeinge, wee came into 10, 9, 8, and att the sudein into 5. The master still resolved to goe over well without dangiore; but att the instant came into 4½ fathom, and upon some knobe the shipe strocke astearne; and though noe greatt blowe, yett caried away her ruder; which much dismayed us. And beinge aflotte, and in good ground and watter sufitient to rid, we came to an ancore, wher wee rode that night and the nixte

---

[1] The aloes of Socotra were considered to be the best.

[2] Arabic *kintār*. Peyton says the 'kintall' 'contayned by our beame one hundred, three pounds and a halfe.' In the text Jourdain (p. 112) counts it as a hundredweight.

[3] Sanguis Draconis, or Dragon's Blood, a resinous exudation from certain trees, used for staining marble and for similar purposes.

[4] Jourdain says 30 (see p. 112).

daye verie quettly and well, att lowe watter noe lesse then $4\frac{1}{2}$ fathom. There we determined to ride to makc provitione to stire the ship. But it pleassed God in the eveninge the ancore gave waye, insoemuch that the ship againe stroke; which caussed us muche to marvell, in regarde shee rode soe well before. The sea goeinge somewhat hye, shee strickinge with greatt force and often, shee begane to be within two howres exstream leake, soe that all hope to save her was tacken awaye. Then we applied our indeavors to save our lives by our boats. The lesser the night before was att the ships stearne splitt, which caused our carpentters muche troble in this exstreametie to fitt her to carie part of the distressed companie ashoare. About midnight, they having in some sortt fitted her, and the ships hould full of watter, we leaft her, being in the two boatts 78 soules, which looded the boatts that wee could save nothinge out of the ship, noe man thinking to gett to the land. Yett it pleassed God to give us fayre weather and a good winde, that the nixt day we fell with the land, thinking it to be the bar of Surratt. But it fell out to be the bar of Gadavie; and coming in within the bar we founde a goodly river and manie boatts. Hear we understoode that the pinnas came into that river, and the Porttingalls having intellygence of her being there came with their frigotts and caried her away; but had noe other thing save stones for their purchasse[1]; our men having notice of their coming gott ashoare with what was worthe any thing, and the ordinance heaved overboorde. Some 40 miells up this river[2] is the towne of Gadavie, wher we landed and wer curttesly enterteined by the Governor; and the nixt day sentt us away, fearing the Porttingalls to come and take us from hime. After two dayes travell we cam to Surratt, wher we founde Will Finche, and three other Inglishmen with hime. Our enterteinment there was suche that the officers of the towne would not sufer us to come into their towne, but confined us to a villag three miles in the countrie, wher we lay about 14 dayes; after which time we sett forward for this place, leaving some of our men in the town, which by stealth gott in, the master being one, and his mattes, with others. After 18 dayes we cam to a cittie called Baramportt[3], wher the nixt day after our arrivall I fell

[1] Prize. Finch (see p. 131 *n.*) says that the Portuguese fished up the two guns which had been thrown overboard.

[2] Jourdain's estimate (in *O.C.* 12)—'12 mylles or more within the rivar'—is much nearer the mark.

[3] Burhānpur.

sicke of a burning feavore, and for almost 50 dayes not able to goe forth of my chamber. In this time divers of the companie leafte me, som returning for Surratt; others tooke their way for this place, leaving mee some 15 men. Being recovered, and furnished with an honorable passe from Caun Canna[1], the Kings Jenerall in these parts, I sett forward for this cittie. But suche was my hard hap that the second day after my departure my cabbenett, with His Majesties letters and all that ever I had in monie, was by our men (Moors of the countrie) stolne away att suche a sudein as it was very strange, myselfe every night sleeping upon it and in the day time not out of my sight; yett suche was my evill forttune that in the morning it was by them tacken away out of my coach, our owne companie rounde aboute it. That being loste, I returned backe with three men for Baramportt to lamentt to the Jenerall, hoping by his means to recover att lest the letters; but with all the inquirie and searche he could make, nothing could be founde, which muche greved hime; and the favore he could doe me was to wrytt to the Kinge of my greatt losse by sea and the losse of the Kings letters, which himselfe was an eiewitnes that I had suche letters. With this attestation I am come to this place, wher the King att presentt is not, but within these 20 dayes wylbe heare; untill when I know not how he wyll take the losse of the letters. Heare I finde Captain Hawkins in verie greatt favore with the Kinge and noblls, insoemuche as besides the ample priveledges grantted for free trade, the Kinge hathe bestowed the pay of 400 horsse upon hime, which wyll prove a greatt matter per anno; and the Kinge hathe promissed within a yeare to increase it to 1000 horsse, which God grantt. For all bussines in these partts I refer to his relation...[2].

---

[1] The Khān-khānān, Mīrzā Abdurrahīm, of whom see a notice in *The Embassy of Sir Thomas Roe*, 90 *n*.

[2] Sharpeigh goes on to discuss the possibility of trade in the Red Sea. Permission must be obtained from Constantinople, and then one factor might be stationed at Mocha, and another at San'a with the Pasha. Broadcloth, kerseys, satins, damasks, iron, tin and swordblades would prove profitable commodities, and Indian piecegoods, etc., could be procured in exchange. Advice is next given as to the proper season for the voyage and the course to be followed. As regards Surat, a profitable trade is certain, but the ships must come provided with pinnaces to carry goods up the river 'in despitte of the Porttingalls, whoe ordinarily in the somer lye att the Bar with 40 or 50 frigatts, that noe boatte can goe in or out without their license.' Sharpeigh goes on to beg the Company to suspend judgment of him until his return. He gives the names of several who have died, and laments the disorders of his crew.

APPENDIX D.

WILLIAM FINCH'S DESCRIPTION OF MĀNDŪ AND GWALIOR[1].

(*Purchas His Pilgrimes*, i. 425, 426.)

The eight [March, 1610], 5 c[os] to Mandow, 3 c[os] whereof is up a steepe stonie mountaine, having way but for a coach at most. This ridge of mountaines extendeth north-east and south-west. On the top at the edge of the mountaine standeth the gate[2] or entrance of the citie, over which is built a faire fort and house of pleasure, the walls extending all along the mountaines side for many coses. On the left hand at the entrance, some two or three miles distant, on the toppe of a picked[3] mountaine, standeth a strong fort[4], and in other places dispersed some ten or twelve more. For 2 c[os] or better within this gate the city is ruined all, save only tombes and meskites, which remayne in great numbers to this day, with some tottered walls of great houses. The olde city is from gate to gate 4 c[os] long north and south, but east and west ten or twelve coses[5]; and yet to the eastward of all lyeth good pasture ground for many courses [coses]. Aloft on this mountaine are some sixteene faire tankes here and there dispersed about the citie. That which is now standing is very faire, but small in comparison of the former, with divers goodly buildings, all of firme stone, and faire high gates, that I suppose the like not to be in all Christendome. At the entrance on the south, within the gate of the city now inhabited, as you passe along on the left hand stands a goodly meskite[6], and over against it a faire palace[7], wherein are interred the bodies of

[1] See note on p. 147.

[2] The Tārāpur or southern gate. Finch approached the city from the south.

[3] Peaked.

[4] The citadel (on the hill known as Songarh) on the extreme west of the city.

[5] See note on p. 148.

[6] The Jāma Masjid, or Great Mosque, built by Hoshang Shāh.

[7] This is the building (near the Jāma Masjid) in which the tombs of the Khaljī kings have recently been discovered (see *Report of the Archæological Survey* for 1902–03, p. 19).

foure kings, with exceeding rich tombes. By the side thereof standeth a high turret[1] of one hundred and seventie steps high, built round with galleries and windowes to every roome, all exceeding for goodly ports[2], arches, pillars; the walls also all interlayed with a greene stone much beautifying. On the north side, where I came forth, lyeth a piece[3] of a foot and an halfe bore in the mouth, but the breech was in the ground. The gate[4] is very strong, with a steepe descent; and without this sixe other, all very strong, with great walled places for courts of guard betweene gate and gate. On this side is also a small port, but the way thereto is exceeding steepe. All alongst on the side also runneth the wall, with flankers ever here and there among; and yet is the hill so steepe of itselfe that it is not almost possible for a man to climbe up on all foure to any part of it. So that to mans judgement it is altogether invincible; and yet was taken, partly by force, partly by treason, by Hamawne[5], this mans grandfather, forcing Seic [Seir] Sha Selim, whose ancestors had conquered it from the Indians some foure hundred yeeres agoe. This Sha Selim was a very powerfull King of Dely, and once forced Hamawne to flye into Persia for ayde; from whence returning with Persian forces, he put him againe to the worst; who yet held out against him all his life time, as also a long time of Ecabars raigne, flying from one mountaine to another. Without the wals of the city on this side the suburbs entred [extend?] 4 c[os] long; but all ruinate, save certaine tombes, meskits and goodly seraies, no man remayning in them[7].

The first of name that took it was Can John[6], a Potan, who built the turret, and lyeth buried in the palace adjoyning, with three of his successors. This citie was built by an Indian some thousand yeeres agoe.

---

[1] The Tower of Victory, erected by Sultān Mahmūd I. in 1443 to commemorate his defeat of Rānā Kumbha of Chitor. The stump of it has lately been found close to the building mentioned in the preceding note.

[2] Gates or porches. [3] Cannon. [4] The Delhi Gate.

[5] The Mogul Emperor Humāyūn took Māndū in 1534 from Bahādur Shāh of Gujarāt, who had captured it in 1526 from the last of the Khaljī kings. When the successful revolt of Sher Shāh forced Humāyūn to seek refuge in Persia, Māndū passed with the rest of the kingdom under the rule of the rebel; but the latter had no personal connexion with the city. Finch's history is very muddled; among other things he seems to have mixed up Sher Shāh and his son Salīm Shāh.

[6] Khān Jahān, father of Sultān Mahmūd I. Finch has confused the two.

[7] Sir James Campbell, in the essay referred to on p. 147, mentions the description of Māndū given by Sir Thomas Herbert in his *Travels*, and suggests

...The thirty one [March, 1610] to Gualere[1], 6 c[os], a pleasant citie with a castle. On the east side is on the top of a steep piked hill a ruinous building where divers great men have been interred. On the west side is the castle, which is a steep craggy cliffe of 6 c[os] compasse at least (divers say eleven), all inclosed with a strong wall. At the going up to the castle adjoyning to the citie is a faire court, enclosed with high walls and shut in with strong gates, where keeps a strong guard, not permitting any to enter without publike order. From hence to the top leads a stone narrow cawsey, walled on both sides; in the way are three gates to be passed, all exceeding strong, with courts of guard to each. At the top of all, at the entrance of the last gate, standeth a mightie elephant of stone very curiously wrought[2]. This gate is also exceeding stately to behold, with a goodly house adjoyning, whose wals are all set with greene and blue stone, with divers gilded turrets on the top[3]. This is the Governours lodging; where is place to keepe nobles that offend. He[4] is said to have three such noble-prisons or castles; this, and Rantimore[5], 40 c[os], to which are sent such nobles as he intends to put to death, which commonly is some two moneths after their arrivall, the Governour then bringing them to the top of the wall, and giving them a dish of milke[6], which having drunke, he is cast downe thence on the rockes; the third is Rotas[7], a castle in the kingdome of Bengala, whither are sent those nobles which are condemned to perpetuall imprisonment, from whence very few returne againe. On the top of this mountaine of Gualere is very good ground, with three or foure faire tankes and many other faire buildings. On the towne side are many houses cut out of the maine rocke, for habitation and sale of goods. On the northwest side at the foot of the hill is a spacious meadow,

---

that, as Herbert himself did not visit the city, he probably obtained the details from his cousin, the Thomas Herbert who was there with Sir Thomas Roe. This conjecture is ingenious, but unnecessary; for there can be little doubt that Herbert simply took his account from Finch's, which was of course available to him in the pages of Purchas.

[1] See p. 152.

[2] The Hāthīyā Pol, or Elephant Gate.

[3] The well-known palace of Mān Sing. The emperor Babar mentions its cupolas covered with domes of gilt copper.

[4] The Mogul Emperor.

[5] Ranthambhor, in Jaipur State.

[6] More correctly, a stupefying decoction of the milky juice of the poppy.

[7] Rohtāsgarh, in Shāhābād district, Bengal.

inclosed with a stone wall, within which are divers gardens and places of pleasure, fit also to keepe horses in time of warre. This castle was the gate or frontier of the kingdome of Dely bordering on Mandow, and is neere a mile of ascent.

APPENDIX E.

COEN'S NARRATIVE OF THE VISIT OF THE *DARLING* TO AMBOYNA AND CERAM[1].

(From a Letter to the Dutch Company, dated Bantam, January 1, 1614, printed in Tiele's *Bouwstoffen voor de Geschiedenis der Nederlanders in den Maleischen Archipel*, Part i. p. 42.)

On the first of April last [1613] an English vessel named the *Darling*, of from 50 to 60 tons burden and commanded by a certain Mr. Jan Jardyn, arrived and anchored before Hytto.

This gave us no small amount of trouble. Jardyn immediately pressed for permission to buy cloves in Hitto, and also for the provision of a house in order that he might leave some persons on shore; to which end he made some presents. He further declared himself willing to give ten rials of eight in the bahar more than we did, even if it cost him a hundred rials of eight the bahar; while if they should refuse to trade with him, he threatened to treat them as enemies, as will appear from the three attestations annexed, in addition to which Your Excellencies will receive from the [Governor] General one given by the Orangkays of Hytto themselves.

These proceedings having been reported to the Castle by Steven Couteels, then resident at Hytto, I was despatched with certain other persons to forestall the Englishman, that he might

[1] See p. 247. All dates are of course New Style, *i.e.*, ten days in advance of English reckoning.

The editor has to thank Dr. W. R. Bisschop and Mr. Donald Ferguson for assistance in making this translation.

get no footing on land. Visiting in turn Hytto, Luha, Combello and Lucydy, I caused all the Orangkays to be summoned and reminded them in earnest manner of the engagements they had made and the obligations they were under, urging them to fulfil their promises. In so doing I used all the civility and all the persuasions in my power, explaining the matter fully to them; but at the same time I warned them to consider the consequences which might follow if they took a contrary course and granted the English permission to trade and to leave a factory. At each place the Orangkayas answered that they would in no way violate their contract, but would stand by us and grant the English neither commerce nor factory; 'provided,' added those of Loeho, 'that you are likewise mindful of us and keep the contract on your side.'

Those of Hitto, although the Captain of Hitto had received many presents from the Englishman[1], fulfilled their promise and refused Jardyn's overtures, telling him that they were unable to trade with him as they were under contract with the Hollanders; whereupon the said captain was very angry and used threatening language to them. Quitting this place, he reached Luha a day before us, and made the same overtures and employed the same menaces as at Hitto. Here the said Jardyn gave us much trouble, and I had many disputes with him; for he is a clever fellow and left no means untried which would in any way serve his designs, which were to establish a factory and start trade. We on our side did everything in our power to frustrate his endeavours, for it would have been all up with us there had he succeeded. However, in spite of all his efforts, his demands were totally rejected, principally through Kimmela Sabadyn[2], who as the representative of the King of Ternate is held in great respect, and was very well disposed towards us. Jardyn could not even obtain permission to erect a hut for the purpose (as he said) of drying some of his goods which had been wetted. Nevertheless, after we had departed from Luha to Combelle and Lucydi in order to forestall him at those places also, presuming that the people of Luha would keep their promises, a certain Orangkay named Ticos, who is a very arro-

---

[1] In *O.C.* 240 Jourdain says that he gave to the Captain of Hitto over 200 rials in presents.

[2] See note on p. 258.

gant man and for some time had been one of our partisans, set up a pair of scales in his quarters and with other persons sold to the English a quantity of cloves. On our return thither, great complaint was made to us concerning his action; whereupon we demanded justice, declared the contract violated and tacitly threatened them that they should feel our power (we having then ready at the Castle[1] no inconsiderable force). In the end, as the townspeople took the responsibility on their own shoulders and excused the Orangkay, it was agreed after much dispute that they should pay a fine of 500 rials of eight and should pledge themselves to have no further dealings with the English; that any individual trading with that nation should be punished with death, and that, should the community offend again in like manner, we should be at liberty to destroy their town and build a fort there. On these conditions we declared ourselves ready to grant them commerce and to make a new contract with a fixed price for cloves throughout the district, provided that all the Orangkays should come to the Castle to agree upon the price with the Governor and Council. This we determined upon, not because we imagined that the contract would be the better observed on account of the price being raised, but in order to gain time and stave off worse evils. Had we refused to give more than 50 rials of eight the bahar, the natives would have been at liberty under the contract to obtain an increased price if they could; and should they make an agreement with this Englishman and settle a price with him in consequence of our refusal, we feared that the Worshipful Mayors[2] would lose all chance of procuring cloves from Amboyna.

Hitherto the Englishman had failed to effect any arrangement; but he was still indefatigable in his efforts, even offering to pay the fine which had been imposed upon the natives on his account. Having carefully considered the proceedings of the aforesaid Jardyn, we came to the conclusion that we were justified in regarding his attitude as hostile and in taking forcible measures to prevent further action on his part. We therefore sent him a summons in writing to desist from his unreasonable proceedings or he would be compelled to do so by force. Nevertheless, we judged it best to take no active measures, but to reserve the

[1] Amboyna Castle. [2] Of the Dutch Company.

matter for Your Worships' decision, or await a better opportunity to sell [him cloves] at a higher price; for we well knew that he must of necessity depart very shortly, and moreover that the natives had few or no cloves left which they could sell to him.

In this document we mentioned by name several persons who had dealt with Jan Jardyn, although in a general assembly of the Orangkays of Loeha the said Jardyn had been told that the Orangkays were under contract with the Hollanders and could not trade with the English: that therefore no commerce could be entered into with the latter except with the consent of the Hollanders or by the permission of the King of Tarnate. This they must themselves avow if called upon and forced to declare the truth.

After this the said Jardyn set sail from Luho to Combello, where he procured a small parcel of cloves.

APPENDIX F.

THE FIGHT AT PATANI AND DEATH OF JOURDAIN.

SWORN DECLARATION OF THOMAS HACKWELL, MASTER OF THE *Sampson*, 25 January, 1622. (*Purchas His Pilgrimes*, i. 693.)

To the first of the said articles he saith and deposeth by charge of his oath that in the road of Patany in the East India, upon the seventeenth day of July, 1619, last past, the *Samson* (whereof this examinant was master) and the *Hound*, belonging to the English Company, were forceably assaulted by three ships of the Hollanders, viz. the *Angell*, the *Morning Starre* and the *Burgarboate*, whereof Hendricke Johnson was commander, and after five glasses fight (two houres and a halfe) eleven of the said ship the *Samson* her men beeing slaine outright, five dismembred, and about thirtie otherwise wounded, Captaine Jordane, being then in the said ship the *Samson* and commander of her, caused a flagge of truce to be hung out, and sent this examinant in the *Samsons* boate aboord the Flemmings to treate with them for a peace; and at the hanging out of the said flagge of truce, and when this examinant left the said Captaine Jordane to goe aboord the Flemmings, he was well; but above halfe an houre after the said flagge of truce was so hung out and this examinant was in parlee with the Flemmings about the said peace, Captaine Jordane, not expecting any violence from the Flemmings during the said parlee, shewed himselfe aboord the *Samson* before the maine mast upon the gratings, where the Flemmings espying him, most treacherously and cruelly shot at him with a musket, and shot him into the bodie neere the heart, of which wound hee dyed within halfe an houre after. And this he saith by charge of his oath.

JOURNAL OF ARNOLD BROWNE, [MASTER'S MATE?] OF THE *Sampson*. (*Ibid.*, ii. 1850.)

June 5, 1619, our ships got into the rode of Patania. Wee were in great danger of driving on a shoald. The President [Jourdain] went to the Queene with a great present. On the 16 [July] wee had sight of foure [three?] Dutch ships, and fitted our selves to fight. No perswasion could move the President to set saile, but hee abode at an anchor till the Dutch ships anchored by us. The next morning, without speaking any word, they shot, and wee answered, but in short time wee had but few left which could do us any pleasure. The weather was now calme and we could not set saile, as before wee might have done; whereupon the President was willing to come to a parlie. I was shot in two places, and perswaded him to fight it out; but when I was gone downe hee sent the master aboord the *Angell* (one of the Dutch ships) to parly about yeelding, and order was presently given to shoot no more; at which time I was spoiled with powder by a shot from the admirall, our master detained, and the President slaine with a shot thorow the bodie, after the ship was yeelded, as I understand. For the master went aboord to give up the ship, with condition that the company should depart with their goods; which they promised, but, after possession taken, heathenlike they broke it. For mine owne part, before I understood of any thing the ship was full of Hollanders; we having at that time eleven men slaine and thirtie three hurt, foure of which were dismembred.

George Muschamp at Jakatra to Nathaniel Courthope, March 9, 1620. (*Ibid.*, i. 678.)

...After all hope was past of comming to you I was appointed chiefe for Siam, and went with the President for Patania, where we fell in the hands of our enemies, and in the defence of our ships and goods performed what we were able. But the elements fought against us; for, contrary to the common course, we had neither wind nor tyde to thwart the ship to bring our ordnance to beare, and they breathed [berthed?] themselves to our great disadvantage; which wee might have helped overnight, if the President had not stood too much upon points of honour in the sight of the countrey people; which in his owne person he endevoured to maintaine, with as much resolution as ever did any commander; and most part of us seconded with our best endevours as long as were able, untill many of us were killed and hurt. Then the President sounded a parley; and in talking with Henrike Johnson received his deaths wound with a musket, and they presently surprized cur ships, made pillage of all we had, but gave most part of us our libertie by reason of our wounds; where I continued foure monethes in miserable torture with the losse of my right legge (shot off with a canon) for want of medicines to apply to it....

George Muschamp at Jakatra to the East India Company, May 3, 1620. (*India Office Records: O.C.*, no. 863.)

...[Just as we were] ready uppon the 16th July to sett saill, and the shipps likewise, we discovered three saill of Flemings; which altered our Presidents purpose and he resolved to remaine three dayes longer in the road, to avoyde the censure of the country people; whereby they birthed themselves to our great disadvantage, one in our bow, the other in our quarter, and the third faire by the *Hound*. The master and all of us that were neare unto him alledged the inconveniences and earnestly importuned we might sett saill; which he would not heare, repliing that it should never be reported that he would runn away from a Fleming. Withall he did animate the shipps companye in the defence of our countryes honnor, with the shipp and goods. Whereuppon all things was prepaired with a good resolution; and the next morning with day they began. We had not [more] then five peeces that would beare with them; they brought six demy cannon of brass to play uppon the half deck, which kild and hurt most of us that were there; so that in the continuance of five glasses there was kild in the *Sampson* 7 English, 5 blacks and about 30 hurt; which moved the President to a parle, and talking with Henrick Jonson, there commander, received his deathes wound with a muskett under the hart. The *Hound* had 2 men kild and 16 miserably burnt with poulder; some affirmeth willingly done by one Domingo, a Portugal, who was the cheif actor in the burning of the *Black Lion*, whereof he made his vants to the Dutch at Patania; which caused the President to give order to keep him in irons. but Mr. Gur[don], having fewe men, released him in the fight; and it is reported confessed uppon his death that he did gather 18 cartrages of powlder together and fired them with a lintstock, wherein he suffered for his villanye, and a great manye poore men with him, the greatest part whereof died....

MARMADUKE STEVINTON AT JAKATRA TO GEORGE BALL AT MASULIPATAM, July 12, 1620. (*Ibid.*, no. 879.)

...The next daie [Friday, July 16] betimes wee espied three great shipps, and made all hast to gett everie man aboord; and came myselfe by two of the clocke in the afternoone, when after speech with our President I departed with Mr. Gourden, our master, whom I repute and esteeme as valiant a proper fellow as ever putt foot in a shipp, notwithstandinge his misfortune the next day; when (in breife) the President nott possiblie perswadable to sett saile and fight, butt scorninge to boudge an anchor in the face of the towne, after wee hadd suffered them all night to birth themselves with their great brasse peeces treble mannd, in the morninge they begann with us, ridinge att pistol shott. When in fine, after five glasses fight, our noble minded President was slayne in parley with Henrie Johnsen their comaunder (whoe hadd binne formerlie in the *Blacke Lion*), to our generall greife and my particuler irrecoverable losse. In the *Sampson* Mr. Boulten, merchant, kild, with ten of the other companie, Mr. Muschampes right legg shott and after dismembred, with some 30 more wounded. In the *Hownd* amongst our 34 men, wee weare nott idle. Haulfe an hower after the *Sampson* was taken wee bore out our flagg untill our shipp fire[d] (as itt was said by our men either through the willfullnes or neglegence of Domingoe the Portingall, butt the truth was never knowne); 16 of our men burnt, whereof some imediatlie dead and most of the rest shortlie after; some likewise killed; soe that their remayne[d] 8 or 9 able men to doe service; my selfe twise slightlie hurt, butt to noe effect. When they after oppressed us with their forces; which wee seeinge yielded by force, with promise nott to loose anie thinge, though they intendinge nothinge lesse. Soe thatt the 17 July, 1619, was my fatall losse both of estate, accounts, frends and everie thinge which might produce any hope of good....

THOMAS BROCKEDON AND AUGUSTINE SPALDING AT JAKATRA TO GEORGE BALL AT MASULIPATAM, July 12, 1620. (*Ibid.*, no. 880.)

...The last and worst newes is the loss of the *Sampson* and *Hound* and the death of Capt. Jurdaine, surprized by Henrick Jonson, commaunder of three ships, who went to revenge the loss of the *Lion*; which he could not have done if the President would have given way to weigh ankor and fought under saile before they birthed themselves; which was the loss of himself and manye others. Howsoever, his resolution pretended the creditt of our nation in the presence of the country people and deserves a favorable censure....

THE DUTCH GOVERNOR-GENERAL AND HIS COUNCIL TO THE DUTCH EAST INDIA COMPANY, dated Jakatra, January 22, 1620 (N.S.). (Translated from De Jonge's *Opkomst van het Nederlandsch Gezag in Oost-Indie*, iv. 195.)

...We have previously informed Your Worships that we had sent the ships *Engel*, *Bergerboot* and *Morgensterre* to Patana with a good stock for trading there, and with express charge (in accordance with the resolution adopted in consequence of the English designs), if they could attack the English with advantage, to make prize of their ships and goods. These vessels, on reaching Patana July 26 [N. S.], found in the roads the English ships *Sampson* and *Hound*, with 137 men and 45 guns, and having in the evening moored close to them, the next morning at dawn made a vigorous attack. The fight was maintained with great resolution on both sides for three glasses, and then the English surrendered, praying vehemently for quarter. They had 39 men killed, including Capt. Jean Jardyn, their President (who is held to be responsible for all these calamities), and about 50 wounded. On our side ten were slain and a few wounded....

THE DUTCH EAST INDIA COMPANY TO THE ENGLISH EAST INDIA COMPANY, July —, 1620. (*India Office Records: Java*, ii. pt. 1[1].)

...Three of our shippes being arryved at Petania the 26 of July 1619 [N. S.] found there two of your shipps, the *Sampson* and the *Hound*, with whom (prosecuting former hostilitie) they encountred the space of one hower and a halfe, yours defending themselves well. And after the death of 39 men (amongst others Mr. John Jordans) they yielded to ours, and your men were sett on shore in the cittie of Petania in the factory you have there. Our people have taken notice of all that they have found in the said shipps, so that the restitution may be made in conformitie of the articles of treatie....

THE SAME TO THE SAME, September 11, 1620[2]. (*Ibid.*[3])

...Having heretofore understood the reservacion you have had concerning your President Jordane, we have caused the whole story thereof to be related to Mr. Robert Barley[4], who seemeth to busy himselfe in your affaires in these parts, and do not doubt but he hath by his letters made a true report of yt; by which you may have understood that as our shipps before Bantam [Patani] were fallen fowle together, and after fyght yt was found good to come to a parley, that your President and

---

[1] A contemporary translation from the French.

[2] In answer to the English Company's reply to the former, expressing amazement and indignation at the news, 'so much the more because we are infourmed by other letters and reports that our said President receyved his mortall wound by a shott as he stood in parley with your commaunder, Hendrick Jansson, after a flagg of truce was hanged out.'

[3] A contemporary translation from the Dutch.

[4] Robert Barlow, the English Company's intelligencer at Amsterdam.

our commaunder being come above the hatches and begining to conferr together, some of our other shippes, which were not, nor could be, advertised of the foresaid parley by reason of the shortnes of the tyme, coming uppon them still in warlike manner, yt happened that out of the shipp called the *Morning Starre* divers shott, as well of musketts as of cannon, were discharged (among which a great iron bullett went through our owne commaunders shipp), and in ignorance of what before had passed betwixt the chiefs of both the fleetes a musket shott was also discharged which hitt your President in the belly, so as he dyed of it, without any speciall ayme at his person, but the mischeife might as well have befallen our commaunder as your President....

Declaration of Cassarian David, Bartholomew Churchman and George Pettys. (*Purchas His Pilgrimes*, i. 696.)

...Upon the newes of the taking of our two ships called the *Samson* and the *Hound* in Patania Road, Hendricke Janson, the commander of three ships, viz. the *Angell*, the *Morning Starre* and the *Burger-boat*, sent a letter by the upper steresman of the *Starre* (who had but one arme) to their Generall John Peter Sacone [Jan Pieterszoon Coen], then at Jacatra, of the taking of our two ships. He, the said Sacone, then said: 'You have now, Hendricke Janson, given me good satisfaction, in that Captaine Jordayne is dead'; and at his returne thither gratified him with fourteene hundred gilders in a chaine of gold, putting it himselfe about his necke; not leaving any one unrewarded that had beene at the taking of our two ships, and one hundred pieces of eight to him that shot him, notwithstanding our flag of truce was hung out. Wee affirme also that the said Generall John Peter Sacone, upon the newes brought him by a ship called the *Hart* from the Coast of Carmandele of the death of Sir Thomas Dale, then said: 'Dale is dead, and Jordaynes blood I have; if I had George Cockins [Cokayne's] life to I were then satisfied'....

BIBLIOGRAPHY, WITH BRITISH MUSEUM PRESS-MARKS.

Abū al Fadhl Ibn Mubārak, *Al Hindī.* The Āīn-i-Akbarī by Abul Fazl 'Allāmī. Translated from the original Persian by H. Blochmann. (Bibliotheca Indica. N. S. vol. 61.) 2 pt. *Asiatic Society of Bengal: Calcutta,* 1873. 8°. [14002. aa.]

Annesley, George Arthur, *Earl of Mountmorres.* Voyages and Travels to India, Ceylon, the Red Sea, Abyssinia...1802—1806. 4 vols. *William Miller; F. C. and J. Rivington: London,* 1809—11. 4°.
[10058. l. 13—16. L. P. 215. d. 1—3. 455. f. 12—14. G. 2276—8.]

Badger, George Percy. *See* Barthéma, Lodovico.

Ball, Valentine. *See* Tavernier, Jean Baptiste.

Barnes, Ernest, *Captain, I.S.C.* Dhar and Mandu. Illustrated. (Journal of the Bombay Branch of the Royal Asiatic Society, vol. xxi. pp. 339—391.) *The Society: Bombay,* 1903. 8°. [Ac. 8827.]

Barthéma, Lodovico. Itinerario...nello Egypto, nella Surria, nella Arabia Deserta. ff. 100. *S. guillereti de Loreno & H. de Nani: Roma,* 1510. 4°. [G. 6770.]

—— The Travels of Ludovico di Varthema in Egypt, Syria, Arabia Deserta and Arabia Felix, in Persia, India, and Ethiopia, A.D. 1503 to 1508. Translated from the original Italian edition of 1510, with a preface, by John Winter Jones, Esq., F.S.A., and edited, with notes and an introduction, by George Percy Badger, late Government Chaplain in the Presidency of Bombay. pp. cxxi. 321. 1 map. (Series I. vol. 32.) *Hakluyt Society: London,* 1863. 8°. [Ac. 6172/30.]

Bell, Harry Charles Purvis. *See* Pyrard, François.

Bermudas. The Historye of the Bermudaes or Summer Islands. [Attributed to Capt. Nathaniel Butler.] Edited from a MS. (750) in the Sloane Collection, British Museum, by General Sir J. Henry Lefroy, R.A. pp. xii. 327. 1 map, 3 illus. Glossary. (Series I. vol. 65.) *Hakluyt Society: London,* 1882. 8°. [Ac. 6172/57.]

Bethune, Charles Ramsay Drinkwater. *See* Hawkins, *Sir* Richard.

Birdwood, *Sir* George Christopher Molesworth, *K.C.I.E.* *See* East Indies; East India Company. 1893.

Blochmann, H. *See* Abū al Fadhl Ibn Mubārak.

Bombay. Gazetteer of the Bombay Presidency, prepared under the orders of Government. [Edited by Sir James MacNabb Campbell.] 26 vols. *Government Central Press: Bombay,* 1877—1896. 8°. [10055. g, h.]

Both, Pieter. Reyse naer Oost Indien. *See* East Indies. *Dutch East India Company.* Begin ende Voortgangh, *etc.* 1646. obl. fol.

Bowrey, Thomas. A Geographical account of Countries round the Bay of Bengal, 1669 to 1679.... Edited by Lt.-Col. Sir Richard Carnac Temple, Bart. [Bibliography, pp. 327—332. 19 illustrations & 1 chart.] pp. lvi. 387. (Series II. vol. 12.) *Hakluyt Society: London,* 1905. 8°. [Ac. 6172/87.]

Broek, Pieter van den. Wonderlijcke Historische ende Journaelsche aenteijckeningh van 't ghene P. v. d. Broek op sijne Reysen van Cabo Verde, Angola, Guinea, Oost-Indien...ontmoet zijn, *etc.* pp. 112. *Joost Hartgerts: Amstelredam,* 1648. 4°. [566. f. 24.]

Burnell, Arthur Coke. *See* Linschoten, Jan Huyghen van. *See also* Yule, *Sir* Henry, *K.C.S.I.*

Burney, William. *See* Falconer, William, *Poet.*

Butler, Nathaniel. *See* Bermudas.

Campbell, *Sir* James MacNabb. *See also* Bombay.

Campbell, *Sir* James MacNabb. Mándu. (Journal of the Bombay Branch of the Royal Asiatic Society. vol. xix. pp. 154—201.) *The Society: Bombay,* 1896. 8°. [Ac. 8827.]

Clayborne, Thomas. Second Voyage into the East Indies. *See* Purchas, Samuel, *the Elder.*

Cocks, Richard. Diary of Richard Cocks, Cape-Merchant in the English Factory in Japan, 1615—1622. With Correspondence. (Add. MSS. 31,300—1, British Museum). Edited by Edward Maunde Thompson. 2 vols. (Series I. vols. 66, 67.) *Hakluyt Society: London,* 1883. 8°. [Ac. 6172/58.]

—— Japanese edition. With additional notes by N. Murakami. 2 vols. *The Sankōsha: Tōkyō,* 1899. 8°. [10058. dd. 23.]

Compans, Henri Ternaux-. *See* Ternaux-Compans.

Corney, Bolton. *See* Middleton, *Sir* Henry.

Coverte, Robert. A True and almost incredible Report of an Englishman (Robert Coverte) that (being cast away in the good ship called the Assention in Cambaya) travelled by land throw many unknowne Kingdomes and great Cities. With a particular description, *etc.* B. L. pp. 68. *W. Hall for T. Archer and R. Redmer: London,* 1612. 4°. [c. 32. d. 7. 299. b. 29. G. 6917.]

Crooke, William. *See* Yule, *Sir* Henry.

Cunningham, *Sir* Alexander, *K.C.I.E.* *See* India. *Archaeological Survey.*

Danvers, Frederick Charles. *See* East Indies. *East India Company.* 1896.

Dasent, John Roche. *See* England. *Privy Council.*

Davies, John, *of Kidwelly. See* Mandelslo, Johann Albrecht von.

Downton, Nicholas. Extracts of the Journall of Captain Nicholas Downton. *See* Purchas, Samuel, *the Elder.*

Dowson, John. *See* Elliot, *Sir* Henry Miers.

Du Bartas, Guillaume de Saluste. *See* Saluste Du Bartas.

Dunn, Samuel. *See* Herbert, William.

East-Indian Voyage. *See* Middleton, *Sir* Henry.

East Indies. Calendar of State Papers. Colonial Series. (Vols. 2—4.) East Indies, China and Japan. 1513—1616, 1617—1621, 1622—1624.... Edited by W. Noel Sainsbury. 3 vols. *Longmans, Green and Co.: London*, 1862—78. 8°. [2078. d. 9507. a. 5.]

—— *East India Company.* The Register of Letters, *etc.*, of the Governour and Company of Merchants of London trading into the East Indies, 1600—1619. Edited by Sir G. Birdwood... assisted by W. Foster. pp. lxxxiv. 530. *B. Quaritch: London*, 1893. 8°. [9057. c. 8.]

—— *East India Company.* Letters Received by the East India Company from its servants in the East, 1602—17. Transcribed from the Original Correspondence Series of the India Office Records. 6 vols. Edited by F. C. Danvers, and Wm. Foster. *Sampson Low and Co.: London*, 1896, *etc.* 8°. [8023. dd.]

—— *Dutch East India Company.* Begin ende Voortgangh van de Vereenighde Nederlandtsche Geoctroyeerde Oost-Indische Compagnie. Vervatende de voornaemste Reysen, by de Inwoonderen der selver Provintien derwaerts gedaen. [Edited by Isaak Commelin.] 4 vols. [with maps and illustrations]. [*Amsterdam*,] 1646. *obl.* fol. [566. f. 16—19.]

—— *Dutch East India Company.* A Collection of Voyages undertaken by the Dutch East-India Company for the Improvement of Trade and Navigation.... Translated into English, and illustrated with several charts. pp. 336. *W. Freeman: London*, 1703. 8°. [979. f. 9. 1045. g. 8. 1045. h. 5. G. 15781.]

Elliot, *Sir* Henry Miers. The History of India, as told by its own historians.... Edited from the posthumous papers of... Sir Henry Miers Elliot by Professor John Dowson. 8 vols. *Trübner and Co.: London*, 1867—77. 8°. [2386. c.]

England. *Historical Manuscripts Commission.* Tenth Report of the Royal Commission on Historical Manuscripts. (The Manuscripts of George Wingfield Digby, Esq., of Sherborne Castle, co. Dorset.) Part I. pp. 520—617. (C. 4548. C. 4576. I. II.) *Eyre and Spottiswoode: London*, 1885—87. fol. [Cat. Desk I. 10. (1—6). N.R.]

—— *Historical Manuscripts Commission.* Twelfth Report. Appendix. Part IV. (V., 14th Report, Appendix. Part I.) The Manuscripts of His Grace the Duke of Rutland, G.C.B., preserved at Belvoir Castle. (C. 5614. C. 5889. II. C. 7476.) 3 vols. *H. M. Stationery Office: London*, 1888—94. 8°. [Cat. Desk I. 7. N. R.]

England. *Historical Manuscripts Commission.* Report on the Manuscripts of the Duke of Buccleuch and Queensberry, K.G., K.T., preserved at Montagu House, Whitehall. (C. 9244. Cd. 930. 1.) 2 vols. *H. M. Stationery Office: London*, 1899—1903. 8°. [Cat. Desk 1. (28). N. R.]

—— *Privy Council.* Acts of the Privy Council of England. New Series.... 1542—1599, *etc.* Edited by J. R. Dasent. vols. 1—29, *etc.* *H. M. Stationery Office: London*, 1890—1905, *etc.* 8°. [2078. f. 9. 9507. a. 1.]

Falconer, William, *Poet.* An Universal Dictionary of the Marine... Modernized and much enlarged by W. Burney, LL.D. 2 pt. *T. Cadell and W. Davies: London*, 1830. 4°. [2112. f. 1769. 8807. f. 5.]

Finch, William, *Merchant.* Observations of William Finch...taken out of his large Journall. *See* Purchas, Samuel, *the Elder.*

Foster, William. *See also* East Indies. *East India Company.*

—— The Embassy of Sir Thomas Roe to the Court of the Great Mogul, 1615—1619. Edited from contemporary records by William Foster, B.A., of the India Office. 2 vols. 1 portrait, 2 maps, and 6 illustrations. (Series II. vols. 1, 2.) *Hakluyt Society: London*, 1899. 8°. [Ac. 6172/78.]

Fryer, John, *M.D.* A New Account of East India and Persia, in eight letters: being nine years Travels begun 1672 and finished 1681.... With maps. pp. xiii. 427. xxiv. *R. R. for R. Chiswell: London*, 1698. fol. [567. i. 20. 983. h. 10. 213. c. 15. G. 2852.]

Gama, Vasco da. A Journal of the First Voyage of Vasco da Gama, 1497—1499. Translated and edited with notes, an introduction, and appendices, by E. G. Ravenstein. pp. xxxvi. 250. 23 illus. and 8 maps. (Series I. vol. 99.) *Hakluyt Society: London*, 1898. 8°. [Ac. 6172/77.]

Gray, Albert, *K.C.* *See* Pyrard, François.

Grey, Edward, *B.C.S.* *See* Valle, Pietro della.

Hamilton, Alexander, *Captain.* A New Account of the East Indies, being the observations and remarks of Capt. Alexander Hamilton, who spent his time there from the year 1688 to 1723. 2 vol. *J. Mosman: Edinburgh*, 1727. 8°. [793. e. 16, 17, and G. 15021–2.]

Harris, Walter Burton. A Journey through the Yemen, and some general remarks upon that country.... Illustrated. pp. xii. 385. *W. Blackwood and Sons: London and Edinburgh*, 1893. 8°. [10076. eee. 25.]

Hawkins, *Sir* Richard, *Knight.* The Observations of Sir Richard Hawkins, Knt., in his Voyage into the South Sea in 1593. Reprinted from the edition of 1622. Edited by Charles Ramsay Drinkwater Bethune, Captain, R.N. pp. xvi. 246. (Series I. vol. 1.) *Hakluyt Society: London*, 1847. 8°. [Ac. 6172/1.]

—— The Hawkins' Voyages during the reigns of Henry VIII., Queen Elizabeth, and James I. The Observations of Sir Richard Hawkins, Knt., in his Voyage into the South Sea in 1593, with the

Voyages of his grandfather William, his father Sir John, and his cousin, William Hawkins. Second edition. Edited, with an introduction, by Clements R. Markham, C.B., F.R.S. pp. lii. 453. 6 illustrations. (Series I. vol. 57.) *Hakluyt Society: London*, 1878. 8°. [Ac. 6172/51.]

Herbert, *Sir* Thomas, *Bart.* A Relation of some yeares travaile, begunne Anno 1626, into Afrique and the greater Asia, especially the territories of the Persian Monarchie, and some parts of the orientall Indies...of their religion, language, habit...and other matters.... Together with the proceedings and death of the three late Ambassadours; Sir D[odmore C[otton], Sir Robert Shirley and the Persian Nogdi-Beg.... By T. H. Esquier. pp. 225. *Wm. Stansby and Jacob Bloome: London*, 1634. fol. [571. k. 26. 1638. 984. f. 28. 984. f. 4.]

Herbert, William. A New Directory for the East Indies. Containing I. The first Discoveries made in the East-Indies by European Voyagers and Travellers. II. The Origin, construction, and application of Nautical and Hydrographical Charts. III. The Natural Causes...of the...Trade-Winds, Monsoons, and Currents throughout the East-India Oceans and Seas. IV. A Description of the Sea-Coasts, *etc.* V. Directions for Navigating, &c. The whole being a work originally begun upon the plan of the Oriental Neptune, augmented and improved by Mr. Willm. Herbert, Mr. Willm. Nichelson, and Others; and now methodised, corrected, and further enlarged by Samuel Dunn, Teacher of the Mathematical Sciences, London. Fifth edition. pp. xxxvi. 554. *Printed for Henry Gregory: London*, 1780. 4°. [571. k. 27.]

Historical Manuscripts Commission. *See* England.

Hunter, *Sir* William Wilson, *K.C.S.I.* The Imperial Gazetteer of India. Second edition. 14 vols. *Trübner and Co.: London*, 1885–87. 8°. [2059. b. 759. cc. 1.]

India. *Archaeological Survey.* Archaeological Reports. [Edited by Sir Alexander Cunningham.] 23 vols. and General Index. *Government Central Press: Simla*, 1871—87. 8°. [2354. g.]

—— New Imperial Series. vol. 1, *etc.* *Calcutta*, 1874, *etc.* 4°. and fol. [1710. b.]

India Office. List of Marine Records of the late East India Company preserved in the Record Department of the India Office. [With an introduction by F. C. Danvers.] pp. xxi. 160. *India Office: London*, 1896. fol. [8805. g. 40. 11900. k. 31.]

Jones, John Winter. *See* Barthéma, Lodovico.

Jones, Thomas. A Briefe Narration of the fourth Voyage to the East-Indies. *See* Purchas, Samuel, *the Elder.*

Jonge, Johan Karel Jakob de, De Opkomst van het Nederlandsch Gezag in Oost-Indië. Deel 1, *etc.* *'s Gravenhage*, 1862, *etc.* 8°. [9056. gg.]

Jordanus [Catalani], *Bishop of Columbum.* Mirabilia Descripta. The Wonders of the East, by Friar Jordanus, of the Order of Preachers and Bishop of Columbum in India the Greater, *circa* 1330. Translated from the Latin original, as published at Paris in 1839, in the "Recueil de Voyages et de Mémoires," of the

Society of Geography, with the addition of a commentary, by Colonel Henry Yule, C.B., F.R.G.S., late of the Royal Engineers (Bengal). pp. xvii. 68. (Series I. vol. 31.) *Hakluyt Society: London*, 1863. 8°. [Ac. 6172/29.]

Kay, Henry Cassels. *See* 'Umārah Ibn 'Alī, al-Ḥakamī.

Lancaster, *Sir* James, *the Navigator.* The Voyages of Sir James Lancaster, Kt., to the East Indies. With abstracts of Journals of Voyages to the East Indies, during the seventeenth century, preserved in the India Office. And the Voyage of Captain John Knight, 1606, to seek the North-West Passage. Edited by Clements R. Markham, C.B., F.R.S. pp. xxii. 314. (Series I. vol. 56.) *Hakluyt Society: London*, 1877. 8°. [Ac 6172/49.]

La Roque (Jean de). Voyage de l'Arabie Heureuse...fait par les François pour la première fois...1708, 1709 & 1710. Avec la relation...d'un Voyage fait du port de Moka à la Cour du Roy d'Yemen...1711, 1712, & 1713, *etc.* pp. 403. *André Cailleau: Paris*, 1716. 12°.
[1047. b. 16. *Amsterdam*, 1716. 978. e. 9. 280. g. 33. G. 15615.]

—— A Voyage to Arabia the Happy, *etc.* pp. xii. 312. *G. Strahan: London*, 1726. 12°. [978. e. 10.]

—— A Voyage to Arabia Fælix...To which is added, An account of the Captivity of Sir Henry Middleton at Mokha by the Turks, in 1612. pp. xvi. 372. *James Hodges: London*, 1742. 8°. [280. g. 27.]

Lefroy, *Sir* John Henry, *General. See* Bermudas.

—— Memorials of the discovery and early settlement of the Bermudas or Somers Islands, 1515—1685. Compiled from the Colonial Records and other original sources by Major-General J. H. Lefroy, R.A. 2 vols. *Longmans, Green and Co.: London*, 1877—79. 8°. [9551. k. 9.]

Linschoten, Jan Huyghen van. John Huyghen Van Linschoten his discours of Voyages into ye Easte & West Indies. Devided into foure Bookes. Translated out of Dutch into English by W. P. [i.e. William Phillip]. B. L. pp. 462. Maps, and illustrations. *J. Wolfe: London*, 1598. fol.
[983. g. 13. 212. d. 9. G. 7008.]

—— The Voyage of John Huyghen van Linschoten to the East Indies. From the old English translation [by Wm. Phillip] of 1598. The First Book. Containing his Description of the East. In two volumes. Edited, the First Volume by the late Arthur Coke Burnell, Ph.D., C.I.E., of the Madras Civil Service; the Second Volume by Mr. Pieter Anton Tiele, of Utrecht. 2 vols. 1 portrait. (Series I. vols. 70, 71.) *Hakluyt Society; London*, 1885. 8°. [Ac. 6172/59.]

Major, Richard Henry, *F.S.A.* India in the Fifteenth Century. Being a Collection of Narratives of Voyages [of Abd-er-Razzak, Nicolò Conti, Athanasius Nikitin, and Hieronimo di Santo Stefano] to India in the Century preceding the Portuguese Discovery of the Cape of Good Hope, from Latin, Persian, Russian, and Italian sources. Now first translated into English. Edited, with an introduction, by R. H. Major, Esq., F.S.A. pp. xc. 49. 39. 32. 10. (Series I. vol. 22.) *Hakluyt Society: London*, 1857. 8°. [Ac. 6172/20.]

Mandelslo, Johann Albrecht von. The Voyages and Travels of J. A. de Mandelslo...into the East Indies. Begun in...1638 and finish'd in 1640. Containing a particular description of the Great Mogul's Empire, the kingdoms of Deccan,...Zeilon, Coromandel, Pegu...Japan...China.... Rendered into English by John Davies of Kidwelly. pp. 287. (In Adam Olearius' "Voyages, *etc.*") *Thomas Dring and John Starkey: London*, 1662. fol.
[983. f. 1. 1669. 2nd edn. C. 67. g. 7.]

Manwayring, *Sir* Henry. The Seaman's Dictionary. (Fit to be imprinted for the Good of the Republicke. John Booker, Septemb. 20. 1644.) pp. 118. *Printed by G. M. for John Bellamy: London*, 1644. 4°. [E. 9. (11). 1670. 533. f. 40.]

Markham, *Sir* Clements Robert, *K.C.B.* *See* Hawkins, *Sir* Richard. *See also* Lancaster, *Sir* James.

Methold, William. Relations of the Kingdome of Golchonda and other neighbouring nations within the Gulfe of Bengala...and the English Trade in those parts. *See* Purchas, Samuel, *the Elder.*

Middleton, David. The Voyage of M. David Middleton to Java and Banda [in 1609]. *See* Purchas, Samuel, *the Elder.*

Middleton, *Sir* Henry. The Last East-Indian Voyage. Containing much variety of the State of the severall kingdomes where they have traded: with the Letters of three severall Kings to the Kings Majestie of England, begun by one of the Voyage [i.e. Sir Henry Middleton], since continued out of the faithfull observations of them that are come home. pp. 74. *Printed by T. P. for Walter Burre: London*, 1606. 4°. [C. 32. f. 36. G. 6497.]

—— [Another edition.] The Voyage of Sir Henry Middleton to Bantam and the Maluco Islands. Being the Second Voyage set forth by the Governor and Company of Merchants of London trading into the East Indies. From the rare edition of 1606. Annotated and edited by Bolton Corney, M.R.S.L. pp. xi. 83. 52. viii. 3 maps, 3 illustrations. (Series I. vol. 19.) *Hakluyt Society: London*, 1856. 8°. [Ac. 6172/17.]

—— The Sixth Voyage sent forth [in 1610] by the East-Indian Company...written by Sir Henry Middleton. *See* Purchas, Samuel, *the Elder.*

Mourier, Ferdinand Louis. *See* Niebuhr, Carsten.

Murakami, N. *See* Cocks, Richard.

Murray, James Augustus Henry. A New English Dictionary on historical principles. Founded mainly on the materials collected by the Philological Society. Edited by Dr James A. H. Murray, *etc.* *Clarendon Press: Oxford*, 1884, *etc.* fol.
[Cat. Desk 1. 12982. l.]

Niebuhr, Carsten. Beschreibung von Arabien. *Nicolaus Möller: Kopenhagen*, 1772. 4°. [981. e. 10.]

—— Description de l'Arabie d'après les observations et recherches faites dans le pays même. [Translated from the German by F. L. Mourier.] *Nicolas Möller: Copenhague*, 1773. 4°.
[10075. h. 1. 981. f. 13. 1774. 685. h. 13. (2). 148. h. 11. G. 2818.]

—— C. Niebuhr's Reisebeschreibung nach Arabien und anderen umliegenden Ländern. 3 Bde. *Kopenhagen, Hamburg*, 1774—1837. 4°. [981. f. 10—12.]

Niebuhr, Carsten. Voyage en Arabie...traduit de l'Allemand [by F. L. Mourier]. 2 tom. *S. J. Baalde: Amsterdam,* 1776—80. 4°. [981. f. 14, 15. 682. g. 10. G. 2816, 7.]

Nikitin, Athanasius, *of Twer.* *See* Major, Richard Henry, *F.S.A.*

'Omārah. *See* 'Umārah Ibn 'Alī.

Oxford English Dictionary. *See* Murray, James A. H.

Oxford, Register of the University of. Edited by Andrew Clark, M.A. 1887. [2121 d.]

Payton, Walter. A Journall of all principall matters passed in the twelfth Voyage to the East-Indies.... The captaine whereof was M. C. Newport, being set out anno 1612. Second Voyage of Captain W. Peyton in January 1614. *See* Purchas, Samuel, *the Elder.*

Peyton, Walter. *See* Payton.

Phillip, William. *See* Linschoten, Jan Huyghen van.

Playfair, *Sir* Robert Lambert, *K.C.M.G.* History of Arabia Felix or Yemen from the commencement of the Christian era to the present time; including an account of the British settlement of Aden. pp. xii. 193. (Selections from the Records of the Bombay Government. N. S. no. 49.) *Printed for Government: Byculla,* 1859. 8°. [I. S. Ser. 350.]

Pring, James Hurly. Captaine Martin Pring, the last of the Elizabethan seamen. Giving a notice of his Voyages, *etc.* pp. 34. *W. H. Luke: Plymouth,* 1888. 8°. [10604. f. 14. (8). 10816. cc. 20.]

Pring, Martin. Briefe Notes of two Voyages of Master Martin Pring into the East Indies. The Second Voyage of Captaine Pring into the East Indies. *See* Purchas, Samuel, *the Elder.*

Purchas, Samuel, *the Elder.* Purchas His Pilgrimes. In five Bookes. 4 pts. *H. Fetherstone: London,* 1625. fol. [984. h. 4—7. 213. d. 2—5. 679. h. 11—14. G. 6838—41. Mr Grenville's copy comprises the very rare cancelled p. 65 in Part 1., which contains a variation of the Map of the World, by H. Hondius.]

—— Purchas his Pilgrimage.... The fourth edition much enlarged with additions...and three whole treatises annexed, one of Russia... by Sr Jerome Horsey; the second, of the Gulfe of Bengala, by Master William Methold; the third, of the Saracenicall Empire, translated out of Arabike by Thomas Erpenius. pp. 1047. *W. Stansby for H. Fetherstone: London,* 1626. fol. *Forming the fifth volume of the "Pilgrimes."* [679. h. 15. 984. h. 8. 213. d. 1. G. 6842.]

—— Hakluytus Posthumus, or, Purchas His Pilgrimes. [With a general Index.] 20 vols. *James MacLehose and Sons: Glasgow,* 1905—06. 8°. [010026. k.]

Pyrard, François, *de Laval.* The Voyage of François Pyrard, of Laval, to the East Indies, the Maldives, the Moluccas and Brazil. Translated into English from the Third French Edition of 1619, and edited, with notes, by Albert Gray, formerly of the Ceylon Civil Service, assisted by Harry Charles Purvis Bell, of the Ceylon Civil Service. 3 vols. 18 illustrations, and 3 maps. (Series I. vols. 76, 77, 80.) *Hakluyt Society: London,* 1887—90. 8°. [Ac. 6172/63.]

Ravenstein, Ernest George. *See* Gama, Vasco da.

Roe, *Sir* Thomas. *See* Foster, William.

Sainsbury, William Noel. *See* East Indies. 1862.

Saluste Du Bartas, Guillaume de. Bartas his Devine Weekes and Workes translated...by Joshua Sylvester. 2 pt. *H. Lownes: London*, 1605—06. 4°. [11475. e. 27. G. 11295.]

Saris, John, *Captain*. *See* Satow, *Sir* Ernest Mason.

Satow, *Sir* Ernest Mason, *K.C.M.G.* The Voyage of Captain John Saris to Japan, 1613. Edited from contemporary records by Sir Ernest M. Satow, K.C.M.G. Map and 5 illustrations. pp. lxxxvii. 242. (Series II. vol. 5.) *Hakluyt Society: London*, 1900. 8°. [Ac. 6175/81.]

Scott, Edmund, *Traveller*. An Exact Discourse of the Subtilties, Fashi-shions [*sic*], Pollicies, Religion, and Ceremonies of the East Indians, as well Chyneses as Javans, there abyding and dweling. Together with the manner of trading with those people, aswell by us English as by the Hollanders: as also what hath happened to the English Nation at Bantan in the East Indies, since the 2. of February 1602 untill the 6. of October 1605. Whereunto is added a briefe Description of Java Major. Written by Edmund Scott, resident there, and in other places neere adjoyng, the space of three yeeres and a halfe. pp. 101. *Printed by W. W. for Walter Burre: London*, 1606. 4°. [582. e. 3. (4). G. 6947.]

—— [Another edition.] A Discourse of Java, &c. *See* Purchas, Samuel, *the Elder*.

Sharpey, Alexander. Fourth Voyage to the East Indies. *See* Purchas, Samuel, *the Elder*.

Smith, John, *Governor of Virginia*. An Accidence or, The Path-way to Experience, Necessary for all Young Sea-men. pp. 42. *Jonas Man and Benjamin Fisher: London*, 1626. 4°. [533. d. 3. (1). 533. f. 21. (1).]

—— [Another edition.] The Seaman's Grammar. B. L. *Andrew Kemb: London*, 1653 [1652]. 4°. [E. 679. (9). 1691. 51. c. 8. 1692. C. 31. e. 40.]

Surat Gazetteer. *See* Bombay Gazetteer, vol. 2.

Sylvester, Joshua. *See* Saluste Du Bartas, Guillaume de.

Tavernier, Jean Baptiste. Les Six Voyages de Jean Baptiste Tavernier, Ecuyer, Baron d'Aubonne, en Turquie, en Perse et aux Indes. 2 tom. *Gervais Clouzier et Claude Barbin: Paris*, 1676. 4°. [567. g. 14, 15.]

—— Collections of Travels through Turkey into Persia and the East Indies.... Being the Travels of Monsieur Tavernier, Bernier and other great men. [Translated by John Phillips and Edmund Everard.] Adorned with many Copper-plates. 2 vols. *Moses Pitt: London*, 1684. fol. [567. i. 19.]

—— Travels in India.... Translated from the original French edition of 1676, with a biographical sketch...by V. Ball. 2 vol. *Macmillan and Co.: London*, 1889. 8°. [2356. c. 20. 1676. 567. g. 14, 15.]

Temple, *Sir* Richard Carnac, *Bart.* *See* Bowrey, Thomas.

Ternaux-Compans, Henri. Bibliothèque Asiatique et Africaine, ou, Catalogue des ouvrages relatifs à l'Asie et à l'Afrique, qui ont paru depuis la découverte de l'imprimerie jusqu'en 1700. pp. vi. 347. *Arthus Bertrand: Paris,* 1841. 8°.
[G. 6979. 011900. ee. 32. 619. d. 31.]

Terry, Edward, *Chaplain to Sir Thomas Roe.* A Voyage to East India. Wherein some things are taken notice of in our passage thither, but many more in our abode there, within that rich and most spacious empire of the Great Mogul. pp. 545. (Portrait of the Author.) *By T. W. for J. Martin and J. Allestrye: London,* 1655. 8°. [149. a. 25. E. 1614. G. 6504. 1777. 979. h. 22.]

Thompson, *Sir* Edward Maunde, *K.C.B.* *See* Cocks, Richard.

Tiele, Pieter Anton. *See* Linschoten, Jan Huyghen van.

—— Bouwstoffen voor de Geschiedenis der Nederlanders in den Maleischen Archipel. [This is the special title of the "Tweede reeks" of Jonge: Opkomst van het Nederlandsch Gezag in Oost-Indië.]

'Umārah Ibn 'Alī, al-Ḥakamī. Yaman, its early mediaeval history. By Najm Ad-din 'Omārah Al-Hakami.... The original texts with translation and notes by Henry Cassels Kay. pp. xx. 358. 152. *E. Arnold: London,* 1892. 8°. [14555. a. 21.]

Valentia, George Arthur, *Viscount.* *See* Annesley, G. A., *Earl of Mountmorres.*

Valentijn, François. Oud en Nieuw Oost-Indien...in vyf deelen. 8 vols. *Joannes van Braam: Dordrecht; Gerard onder de Linden: Amsterdam,* 1724—26. fol.
[10028. i. 455. g. 3. G. 7027—31.]

Valle, Pietro della. The Travels of Pietro della Valle in India. From the old English translation of 1664, by G. Havers. In two volumes. Edited, with a life of the author, an introduction and notes, by Edward Grey, late Bengal Civil Service. 2 vols. 2 maps and 2 illustrations. (Series I. vols. 84, 85.) *Hakluyt Society: London,* 1892. 8°.
[Ac. 6172/67. 1665. 567. i. 17. 983. f. 10. 212. d. 1.]

Varthema, Ludovico di. *See* Barthéma, Lodovico.

Yule, *Sir* Henry, *K.C.S.I., C.B.* *See also* Jordanus [Catalani].

—— and Burnell, Arthur Coke. Hobson-Jobson. Being a Glossary of Anglo-Indian Colloquial Words and Phrases, and of kindred terms. Second edition. By W. Crooke. pp. xlviii. 870. *John Murray: London,* 1903. 8°. [2274. e. 7.]

Zwemer, Samuel M., *Rev.* Arabia. The Cradle of Islam. pp. 434. *Oliphant Anderson and Ferrier: Edinburgh,* 1900. 8°.
[10076. cc. 8.]

INDEX.

[*The letter* n. *indicates that the reference is to a footnote.*]